D0934875

ROBESPIERRE

WITHDRAWN

WITHDRAWN

ROBESPIERRE
A REVOLUTIONARY LIFE

PETER McPHEE

Batavia Public Library
Batavia, Illinois

YALE UNIVERSITY PRESS
NEW HAVEN AND LONDON

Published with assistance from the Annie Burr Lewis Fund.

Copyright © 2012 Peter McPhee

All rights reserved. This book may not be reproduced in whole or in part, in any form (beyond that copying permitted by Sections 107 and 108 of the U.S. Copyright Law and except by reviewers for the public press) without written permission from the publishers.

For information about this and other Yale University Press publications, please contact:
U.S. Office: sales.press@yale.edu   www.yalebooks.com
Europe Office: sales@yaleup.co.uk   www.yalebooks.co.uk

Set in Arno Pro by IDSUK (DataConnection) Ltd
Printed in Great Britain by TJ International Ltd, Padstow, Cornwall

Library of Congress Cataloging-in-Publication Data

McPhee, Peter, 1948–
    Robespierre : a revolutionary life / Peter McPhee.
      P. cm.
    Includes bibliographical references.
    ISBN 978–0–300–11811–7 (cloth : alk. paper)
    1. Robespierre, Maximilien, 1758–1794. 2. Revolutionaries—France—Biography.
3. Statesmen—France—Biography. 4. France—History—Revolution, 1789–1799.
5. France—History—Reign of Terror, 1793–1794. 6. France—Politics and
government—1789–1799.   I. Title.
    DC146.R6M38 2012
    944.04092–dc23
    [B]
                                                                      2011027640

A catalogue record for this book is available from the British Library.

10 9 8 7 6 5 4 3 2 1

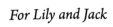

For Lily and Jack

Charlotte Robespierre, 1830

'It is for history to recognize one day whether Maximilien Robespierre was really guilty of all the revolutionary excesses of which he was accused by his colleagues after his death.'[1]

Marc Bloch, 1941

'Can we be so sure of ourselves and our times as we distinguish between the just and the damned among our forebears? . . . Robespierristes, anti-Robespierristes, we beg for mercy: for pity's sake, just tell us who was Robespierre.'[2]

Contents

Illustrations

Acknowledgements

I have been intrigued by Maximilien Robespierre ever since, as a student, I pondered how it could be that someone who articulated the highest principles of 1789 could come to be seen as the personification of 'the reign of Terror' in 1793–94. Was this a tragic case of the dangers of ideological and personal rigidity, as powerful literary dramatizations taught me, or rather an extreme example of how great leaders may be vilified by those they have served and saved? Or something quite different?

All historians accumulate debts to those who have posed and answered the questions that interest them. In Robespierre's case, these are legion, since many hundreds of historians have been drawn to write about 'the Incorruptible'. More direct debts are owed to those who have assisted my own attempt to tell his story. Juliet Flesch undertook a range of research activities with patience, acuity and remarkable expertise. Colleagues and friends have been most generous and insightful in their reading of the entire manuscript, in particular, Marisa Linton (Kingston University), Elizabeth Macknight (University of Aberdeen), Deborah Mayersen (University of Queensland), John Merriman (Yale University), my sister Hilary McPhee and my son Kit McPhee. Charlotte Allen has wondered with me throughout the project how tantalizing scraps of evidence about an individual's personality and physique might explain the adulation and loathing he attracted. Heather McCallum, Rachael Lonsdale, Candida Brazil and Tami Halliday have offered encouragement and wisdom for Yale University Press; copy-editing was effected expertly by Richard Mason.

Others have offered specific assistance or advice: Isobel Brooks, Howard Brown, Peter Campbell, Vincent Cantié, Helen Davies, Glyn Davis, Sophie Freeman, Jeff Horn, Bill Murray, Marcus Robson, Tim Tackett, Lindsay Tanner, Geoffrey Wall and Amanda Whiting.

I benefited from access to the fine collection of material in the Baillieu Library of the University of Melbourne, much of it acquired through the Pitt Bequest established by a former teacher of the French Revolution, Kathleen Fitzpatrick. The service provided by the staff of the Archives Nationales in Paris and of departmental and other repositories has underlined my good fortune in being the historian of a country of great archival guardianship. Unfortunately, a recent acquisition by the Archives Nationales, of Robespierre's first drafts of some speeches, occurred too late, in May 2011, to be accessible for this biography.

***

I am writing these lines in Collioure, on the Mediterranean border with Spain, and almost as far from Robespierre's native Arras as it is possible to be in mainland France. Had Robespierre ever come to the little port, the labourers, fishers and winegrowers would have found his French incomprehensible. Their Catalan would have baffled him. And yet the destinies of the Arras lawyer and the Catalans of Collioure were to become inextricably linked by war and death in 1792–94, and the Colliourencs never forgot him. The French Revolution was a rural and provincial upheaval as much as a Parisian one, and its character and pulse were the result of challenges and responses in villages and towns across the nation. That is why my understanding of Maximilien Robespierre begins at a particular place and time in a provincial town.

Abbreviations

AHR	*American Historical Review*
AHRF	*Annales historiques de la Révolution française*
	(Note: the *AHRF* changed from volumes to individual issue numbers from 1977.)
Annales	*Annales. Histoire, Sciences Sociales*
ARBR	Amis de Robespierre pour le Bicentenaire de la Révolution
FH	*French History*
FHS	*French Historical Studies*
JMH	*Journal of Modern History*
MLN	*Modern Language Notes*
P&P	*Past and Present*

INTRODUCTION

'Clay in the hands of writers'

Maximilien Robespierre's best friend was Antoine-Joseph Buissart, like him a lawyer but more than twenty years his senior. Early in November 1789 Robespierre sent his third long letter of that momentous year to Buissart in their home town of Arras, reporting on the developments in Versailles and Paris, where Robespierre was a member of the revolutionary National Assembly. He admitted that Buissart had every right to be annoyed with the infrequent correspondence from 'the greatest of your friends'. But the revolutionary upheaval had been all-absorbing, and deeply satisfying. The achievements of the people's representatives had been extraordinary. So much still seemed uncertain, however, including the length of time it would take to complete the task of regenerating the nation: 'please give, I beg you, my affectionate respects to Madame Buissart; her company and yours will be mainly responsible for making my time in Arras pleasant when I come back, just as it provoked my sharpest regrets when I left that town. *But I think I will be here for a few months yet.*'[1]

Indeed he was. It was not for another two years that Robespierre had the chance to return to Arras and the pleasure of the company of Buissart and his wife Charlotte. Robespierre was by then a figure of national renown, wildly popular with most Parisians and commonly dubbed 'the Incorruptible'. The 'few months' that he predicted to Buissart in 1789 had turned into momentous years of change affecting every aspect of public life in the nation: from the ancient feudal system to the courts and the Catholic Church. The labours of the National Assembly largely done in 1791, Robespierre had successfully proposed that its members be ineligible for its successor, the Legislative Assembly. Once again, Robespierre could think about life after revolution. During a holiday back in Arras and the province of Artois in October and November 1791, he went to the nearby little town of Béthune for three days. The official reception was chilly—Robespierre was seen as something of a troublemaker due to the uncompromising radicalism of his pronouncements—but the popular welcome was enthusiastic. Robespierre wrote afterwards to a friend, perhaps Buissart again, that, *'if I come back to Artois, Béthune would be the place where I'd live with most pleasure'*. He raised the idea of finding an appointment as judge on a local court.[2]

Robespierre may have yearned for a quiet life in his province, but he never had the chance. Less than three years later he was dead, reviled as thoroughly as he had once been idolized. In October 1791, of course, he had no idea that his life would lead to such a fate. Like his 'Jacobin' contemporaries, he was seeking to make sense of the chaos of a world in revolutionary upheaval and to use his talents to create stability and certainty for a new order. Historians know where his life would lead by July 1794; he could only imagine the future.

Biography's great challenge is how to write of the past as if it was the present rather than simply reading history backwards. Since we usually know the broad outlines of an individual's life, it is tempting—and perhaps unavoidable—for us to construct such a life as if its stages were neatly arranged stepping-stones rather than encounters with circumstances beyond one's control and with choices whose consequences were unknowable. For no other individual in history is this challenge sharper than for Maximilien Robespierre, for as soon as he died at the age of thirty-six, people rushed to vilify him as much as he had been lionized while alive, and projected onto him actions and motives based on rumour or their own guilt. His entire life was read backwards and presented as an inexorable trajectory leading to tyranny and the guillotine.

Was Robespierre the first modern dictator, inhuman and fanatical, an obsessive who used his political power to try to impose his rigid ideal of a land of Spartan 'virtue'? Or was he a principled, self-abnegating visionary, the great revolutionary martyr who succeeded in leading the French Revolution and the Republic to safety in the face of overwhelming military odds? Were the controls on individual liberties and the mass arrests and executions of 'the Terror' of the Year II (1793–94) the necessary price to pay to save the Revolution? Or was this year a time of horror, of unnecessary death, incarceration and privation?[3] Robespierre has always been a polarizing figure, but the negative image is far stronger. French opinion polls at the time of the bicentenary of the Revolution in 1989 revealed that he was the figure who aroused the most negative feelings, and he was well behind even Louis XVI and Marie-Antoinette in positive responses.[4]

Despite the comparatively limited loss of life during the one year 1793–94 in which Robespierre was a member of the government, preposterous parallels have been drawn with Mao, Pol Pot, and even Stalin and Hitler. For Eli Sagan, he was a paranoid psychopath, a vicious narcissist, 'one of the great exterminators of innocent people'. Studying him, he writes, was a journey into 'the heart of darkness'.[5] Hilary Mantel, author of a major novel set during the Terror, has described Robespierre as a 'bundle of contradictions', in his inconsistent attitudes to war, capital punishment, 'the people', and government institutions. 'He had a militant faith, not in a Christian god, but in a good revolutionary god who had made men equal.' He reminds Mantel of 'the conviction of [Islamic] militants, their rage for purity, their willingness to die'; for others, he resembles President Ahmedinejad of Iran.[6] He has been likened to both Tony Blair and George Bush and to their enemy, Wikileaks founder Julian Assange.[7] For the radical critic Slavoj Žižek, Robespierre's iron resolve is used to condemn capitalism. To him, the complacency implicit in the title of Ruth Scurr's recent biography of Robespierre, *Fatal Purity*, highlights the failings of Western leadership faced with urgent crises.[8]

On the French left today, Robespierre is still often seen as a reminder of what has been forgotten about militant commitment to social justice, exemplified in the speech in Arras on the eve of the bicentenary of 1789 by Michel Vovelle, the Sorbonne professor charged with organizing the academic side of the commemorations in 1989. The title of Vovelle's speech—'Why Are We Still Robespierrists?'—recalled the title of a 1920 lecture given by Robespierre's greatest admirer, another Sorbonne professor, Albert Mathiez.[9] A common premise of the positive biographies has been that all of Robespierre's actions were proportional and necessary responses to counter-revolution. For the historian Claude Mazauric, former member of the Central Committee of the French Communist Party, Robespierre was the man of peace and principle in 1792, who then 'submitted' to the needs of the revolutionary state in assuming its leadership in the direst of circumstances: 'his place in history is unique'.[10]

The polarity of these images of Robespierre highlights the peculiar nature of biography. The writer is necessarily drawn into a shifting dialogue with someone who cannot respond to the author's questioning or prejudices. This dialogue is intensely personal. In the words of Sylvia Plath's biographer, Janet Malcolm, 'it really isn't for me to say who is good and who is bad, who is noble and who is faintly ridiculous. . . . The distinguished dead are clay in the hands of writers . . .'.[11]

Relatively little is known of the first thirty-one of Robespierre's thirty-six years of life, and few biographers have lingered over such evidence as we do have: it is the five years of Revolution that beckon. We possess eleven solid volumes— some 5,660 pages in all—of his works, but these consist overwhelmingly of his speeches and journalism during the revolutionary years.[12] One of our difficulties in writing about him is that we have little by way of private papers: just a few personal letters and poems written in his twenties. He never reflected publicly on his life and its meaning: he died suddenly and young. The reflections of others, from the lengthy accounts of his sister Charlotte and a master at his secondary school in Paris to the many comments by participants in the Revolution, are all coloured by the circumstances in which they were written.[13] My biography will seek to dissolve some of the barriers between the public and private in Robespierre's life, but will necessarily be constrained by the great gaps in what we know.[14]

Maximilien Robespierre was only thirty-one at the time of the Revolution of 1789. For him and his peers, the shock of remaking a world in chaos was swamped in 1792 by an awesome struggle against counter-revolution and military invasion. But most of the more than one hundred biographies of Robespierre have an oddly unhuman and static quality, as if he was simply the embodiment of a set of revolutionary principles that he sought to realize with increasing rigidity across his five-year political career. Whether portrayed as the personification of Jacobin dictatorship or of democratic purity, 'Robespierre' has been reified into 'ideology incarnate' rather than understood as a young man, as uncertain about the future as he was exhilarated by its possibilities.[15]

Most accounts of Robespierre's life devote no more than a chapter to his youth and formation between 1758 and 1789, as if his first thirty-one years do not really matter. The chaos of the years after 1789 placed him, like all French people, in an unprecedented, unanticipated world of revolution, anxiety and uncertainty, and the role he came to play could not have been predicted in 1789.

Nevertheless, his reactions to the unfolding drama, achievements and horror of 1789–94 were not those of an innocent: he brought to his participation in the Revolution values and beliefs that had developed across three decades of family life, schooling and work.

The language in which Robespierre and his contemporaries expressed their views is startling to us in its appeals to sentiment, virtue and conscience, and has often led biographers to dismiss him as maudlin, self-obsessed and over-emotional.[16] The discourse of these revolutionaries is indeed disconcerting in its emphasis on 'patriotic' emotions and values. Robespierre was no exception, and his speeches were laced with appeals to sincerity, sacrifice and the virtues. Particularly after the establishment of the Republic in September 1792, they were also peppered with references to the figures of ancient Greece and Rome and their conspiracies. These were no mere rhetorical embellishments: like most of the educated middle-class men of the revolutionary assemblies, Robespierre assumed the classical world to be a well of wisdom from which directly relevant lessons must be drawn.

Robespierre's biography is particularly difficult to write for all these reasons. We cannot pretend we do not know that Robespierre ended up as a household name, the embodiment of the Jacobin Revolution. From our perspective, his life seems coherent, every action or reaction part of a logical 'character' we have constructed. Robespierre is a man who was only in a position of power as a member of government for one year. He initiated few specific policies that were accepted. And yet detractors and apologists alike have regarded him as in some sense the embodiment of the Revolution: attitudes to the Revolution and to Robespierre are almost always aligned.

But Robespierre's life cannot be reduced to the years of the French Revolution, and nor can the Revolution be reduced to the political maelstrom of Paris in 1789–94. The young revolutionary was formed by his childhood, schooling and working life, most of it spent in the small provincial centre of a distinctive region in northern France. This is a biography that therefore seeks to be as much about the 'making' of Maximilien Robespierre as about his revolutionary career. Who was this man who arrived in Versailles just a few days before his thirty-first birthday?

CHAPTER 1

A 'serious, grown-up, hardworking' little boy
ARRAS 1758–69

Like other French provincial centres, Arras today is a sprawl of new suburbs and retail shopping complexes fanning out from its quiet old neighbourhoods. Its distinctiveness derives from its special attraction as a tourist centre, especially for those interested in the protracted battles and ingenious defences of the First World War. By contrast, in the eighteenth century the town of twenty thousand people could be walked across in fifteen minutes. The elegant Flemish-style houses that line its famous squares today are faithful copies of the eighteenth-century edifices mostly destroyed in the bloody bombardments of May–July 1915, but in every other way Arras is unrecognizable. Today it is the quiet prefecture of the department of Pas-de-Calais; in the 1750s it was a swirl of activity as the capital of the province of Artois. Despite its compactness, it was then a tapestry of small neighbourhoods with a distinctive social and occupational character: the well-to-do parishes of noble and bourgeois families; the crowded streets of the poor along the polluted arms of the River Scarpe and its tributary the Crinchon; the army 'citadelle'; and a separate 'town' clustered with the edifices of administration, the Church elite and the judiciary.

Several hundred children were born in Arras in 1758. One of them was Maximilien-Marie-Isidore Derobespierre, who would come to be known simply as Maximilien Robespierre. He was born and baptized on 6 May, the son of François Derobespierre, a lawyer, and Jacqueline Carraut, daughter of a brewer.[1] A family drama had played out in the months beforehand, for Jacqueline had been five months pregnant at the time of her marriage on 3 January, and

François' parents had refused to attend the ceremony in the well-to-do parish church of St-Jean-en-Ronville in the south of the old town. This may have been from the shame of such a marriage in a devout town dominated by the Catholic Church, or from vexation at the results of François' improper behaviour. One can only speculate about the conversations that might have taken place in the months between the realization of Jacqueline's pregnancy and the marriage. The parish priest of St-Jean had obliged the families by dispensing with two of the three announcements of marriage banns, and announced the single bann just two days before the wedding. But this was published both at St-Jean and at St-Géry, the other wealthy parish of Arras, and everyone in the Derobespierres' social circles knew of the scandal.[2]

Born in 1732 in Arras, François had received his education from a religious order in Tortefontaine, west of Arras, but at age seventeen renounced his vocation shortly before his final vows and was further educated in law at Douai. He became a lawyer in the Council of Artois, the highest court in the province. One of eight children, he was regarded by some as the difficult member of a reputable and distinguished judicial dynasty. According to a priest who knew the family well, François 'was reputed, in the town of Arras, to be somewhat scatterbrained, and above all, fond of his own opinions'.[3] He came from a long-established and highly respectable family, and his rushed marriage to Jacqueline Carraut would have been deeply embarrassing for his parents. (It was not the first such scandal in the family: François' uncle Robert had fathered an illegitimate child in nearby Carvin several decades earlier.)[4]

The trajectory of the infant Maximilien Robespierre's paternal family over the preceding three centuries has much to tell us about the structures of power and privilege in Artois. Like bourgeois dynasties across the kingdom, they had been adept at making themselves useful to the pillars of society: the Church, the seigneurial nobility and the monarchy itself. The Robespierre family—also known as de Robespierres, DRobespierres or Desrobespierres—were long established in the towns of Artois, for example, at Béthune, Lens and Carvin.[5] The family may have been related to a Bauduin de Rouvespierres, a canon in Cambrai Cathedral in the early fifteenth century, but the lineage may be traced with more certainty back to Robert de Robespierre, a legal officer for the seigneur of Vaudricourt, near Béthune, in the 1460s. It may well have been as a result of holding this office that the family was accorded the right to add the prefix 'de' normally reserved for noble families.[6] Across the following century the Robespierres established themselves as merchants in Lens, eleven miles north of Arras, working as grocers and hoteliers. But from another Robert de Robespierre (1591–1663), the males of the family fathered a long line of men of the law, working as much for the royal and seigneurial system as in private practice.

Robert and his descendants held official legal posts in the small towns of Artois at a time when it was part of the Spanish Netherlands and when the armies of Spain and France swept across the region during the Thirty Years War (1618–48). In 1659 the Treaty of the Pyrenees between France and Spain recognized Artois as French. Despite the uncertainties of frontier life, Robert and his descendants established themselves as royal notaries in Carvin, a small administrative centre of 3,500 people northeast of Lens, before Maximilien de Robespierre moved the twenty-two miles to Arras in 1722 to become a lawyer in the Council of Artois, the pinnacle of success for a man of the law. This was the grandfather of the revolutionary.

Maximilien became solidly embedded in the legal fraternity of the provincial capital, an 'Arrageois', but his legal practice seems to have been of secondary importance to his income from urban and rural property.[7] Like previous genera-tions of Robespierres, he was attracted to a woman from the world of commerce. In 1731 he married Marie Poiteau, an innkeeper's daughter from the wealthy parish of St-Géry. Maximilien and Marie settled in another well-to-do parish, St-Aubert, and had eight children there, one of whom, François, as we have noted, married Jacqueline Carraut in January 1758.

The Carrauts were from a less comfortable and distinguished lineage, even if they were as solidly Artésien as the Robespierres. They first appear in parish records in the little village of Hestrus, then as weavers in Étrun, just four miles west of Arras. They remained tied to the land, even as they established them-selves more firmly in the capital. Maximilien's maternal grandfather Jacques (born in 1701) was a brewer who in 1732 married Marie (born 1693), daughter of a tenant farmer in Lattre-St-Quentin, nine miles west of Arras. Robespierre's cousins on his mother's side were children of an oil-grain merchant in Arras. When Jacqueline married François Derobespierre in 1758, Jacques Carraut was running a small brewery in the Rue Ronville, on the edge of the wealthy parish where his daughter was to marry. Unlike François' father, Jacques was at the wedding.[8]

At the time of their marriage François and Jacqueline were aged twenty-six
and twenty-two respectively. It seems that the Robespierres became reconciled
to their son's behaviour, since François' father agreed to be Maximilien's god-
father a few months later, just as Jacques Carraut's wife Marie agreed to be
the boy's godmother. Despite the inauspicious beginnings to their married life,
and the long delay before their marriage once Jacqueline found she was pregnant, they then had a fecund relationship. After Maximilien, Jacqueline
gave birth in quick succession to Charlotte (1760), Henriette (1761) and
Augustin (1763). The children were baptized in different parishes, suggesting
that François struggled to settle with his young family, even though he had
enough legal cases to establish a successful practice: thirty-four in 1763 and
thirty-two in 1764.[9]

In the year after Augustin's birth, 1764, tragedy struck hard at the young
family. A fifth child died during childbirth on 7 July; Jacqueline, aged twenty-
nine, died of complications nine days later, on the 16th, and was buried in
St-Aubert in the presence of an officer from the army garrison and her brother.[10]
Her death devastated the young family.

For whatever reason, François did not attend his wife's funeral. In December
of that year he took a position at Oisy-le-Verger fifteen miles east of Arras as
the legal officer of a vast feudal estate. After this position ended in July 1765 he
reappeared sporadically in Arras. It is unlikely that he saw his four surviving
children during these visits, or that he was in a position to provide for them. In
November 1765 François was back in Arras debating with his peers whether the
corporation of lawyers should offer condolences to Louis XV on the illness of
the dauphin. François reappeared in March 1766 to borrow 700 livres from his
sister Henriette. In October 1768 his mother, widowed since 1762, agreed to
give him his part of her modest estate before he left and headed east to work
across the border in Mannheim. He was again back in Arras in February–May
1772, with fifteen cases to plead; by then, however, Maximilien and Charlotte
were away at schools far from Arras.[11]

The children were dispersed. Maximilien's paternal aunts looked after
Henriette and Charlotte, while Maximilien and Augustin, aged six and one, went
to live with their elderly grandparents and maternal aunts Henriette and Eulalie
at the Carrauts' brewery. So, although born into a long line of lawyers and
officials, Maximilien was now to be brought up in a milieu of manual work, with

the sounds of carts and workers shouting in the local Picard dialect in the Rue Ronville. It was at the age of six, too, that he caught smallpox, leaving him with a slightly pockmarked face.

It is tempting to see in the desperately sad circumstances of Maximilien's childhood the clues to the character of the man he became, and many biographers have warmed to such a temptation. After all, he may have been the offspring of a couple who had only married from social necessity. Then a loved mother had died in childbirth when he was just six, leaving him as the oldest of four children who were split up between the families of relatives. His father, often described as unstable or dissolute, seems never to have seen his children again. Did such a childhood produce a boy who was starved of parental affection and whose position as the eldest of four 'orphans' turned him into a prematurely serious, anxious and hardworking child suspicious of intimacy and resentful of those in happier circumstances? When did he realize that a family heritage of professional success and eminence had also been snatched away by personal tragedy?

Some have seen in the supposed 'traumas' and 'poverty' of his childhood the clue to the man. Most famously, the biography by the French politician and writer Max Gallo has interpreted the collapse of Maximilien's immediate family in 1764 as the clue to his 'pathological sensitivity' and 'terrible need for acceptance': he never recovered from the distress of his father's guilt and his mother's death.[12] Others have seized the chance to project supposed personal traits—none of them attractive—onto the small boy on the basis of these few scraps of evidence about the loss of both parents during his childhood. Laurent Dingli has articulated the view of a traumatized little boy who lost a loved mother (who nevertheless, he claims, took no notice of him because she was preoccupied with having more children) and was then abandoned by a 'lunatic, dissipated' father. For Dingli, this explains why Robespierre would always be particularly sensitive to what he saw as treachery or corruption, and why he would always be obsessed by his fantasy of an ancient world peopled by heroes. The sadness of his childhood sowed the seeds of an incapacity to develop intimate relationships, even of phobias about appearance, cleanliness and physical intimacy.[13]

There is no clear evidence to provide the basis for these conclusions; nor do we know much in general about the bonds of affection that might have existed in a middle-class family in Arras.[14] One could as readily assume that Maximilien had a loving relationship with his mother in the crucial first six years of his life and was subsequently raised by caring relatives who helped him cope with a devastating loss and ensured that the children saw each other regularly. That is certainly the implication of the one account that we have of his child-hood, by his younger sister Charlotte, pieced together before her death in 1834.[15] Her memoirs are riveting, redolent of her deep affection for her brother and written when she was living a modest existence in the shadows of Paris.

Twenty months younger than Maximilien, Charlotte recalled how her brother's eyes would fill with tears whenever they spoke of their mother Jacqueline, 'as good a wife as she was a mother'. Charlotte insisted, however, that her father was a good and decent man, 'honoured and cherished by the whole town'. He was utterly devastated by his wife's death and unable to continue to practise law effectively. The children did not see him again. Charlotte recalled that the death of her mother was deeply distressing for Maximilien and made him a rather serious, obedient child. From a typically 'noisy, boisterous and light-hearted' little boy, he became 'serious, grown-up (raisonnable), hard-working'. He was now more interested in reading and building model chapels than in noisy games: that would accord with the pious surroundings in which his aunts were raising him. Every Sunday the girls were sent to the Rue Ronville to spend time with their brothers, 'days of happiness and joy' when they would look at Maximilien's collections of pictures. Charlotte recalled, too, that he adored his pet pigeons and sparrows and was furious when his sisters neglected one of them, leading to its death.[16]

Maximilien's sisters were living no more than a few minutes away for a small boy running through the town centre towards where he had been born in the wealthier neighbourhood close to the cathedral, courts and administration. What was the urban environment into which the child emerged from infancy?

His immediate physical environment was one of noise, work and movement, for it was dominated by what has been described as the most ambitious church building project of the century. The urban landscape of generations of Arras children before and after him was dominated by the imposing abbey of St-Vaast, but that was not the case for Maximilien, because after the spire of the abbey church collapsed in 1741 the Abbot Armand Gaston de Rohan had resolved to demolish the entire sprawling ensemble and the nearby church of La Madeleine in which Maximilien had been baptized.[17] In its scale and style, this massive project, completed only in 1770, was one of the outstanding examples of neoclassical rebuilding also evident in Paris at the churches of La Madeleine and Ste-Geneviève and in other provincial centres. When Maximilien was a little boy, however, it was just a vast building site.[18]

The town of Arras in which the child Maximilien grew up was, like other centres of similar size—Dijon, Grenoble, Limoges, Poitiers and La Rochelle—a church, government and military centre, with small-scale artisanal industry closely linked to a rural hinterland. This was a provincial capital like many others of the eighteenth century, in which the institutions of the First and Second Estates of the realm—the clergy and nobility—managed the income from their vast rural estates, in all covering about half the region. Despite their right to use the prefix 'de', the Robespierres were not nobles, but they were embedded in the network of power, privilege and wealth of Artésien society through servicing the structures of ecclesiastical and seigneurial power.[19] The lines of social demarcation were too finely drawn for a Robespierre to have been accepted into the Artois nobility. Instead, they had often married people from the trades and small business, a milieu from which they themselves had emerged. François' marriage in 1758 to the daughter of a brewer was unusual only in its timing. The Robespierres were 'cultural intermediaries', a bridge between the privileged elites and respectable commoners.

If the child Maximilien every day had demolition and rebuilding imprinted on his senses, his daily domestic experience, in contrast, was one of ordered, routine calm. Many years later, a priest from Arras who was no friend of Robespierre remembered the two Carraut aunts who cared for Maximilien and Augustin as women 'very well known for their piety'. From his childhood, Maximilien would have been immersed in their religious beliefs and routines in a town where one person in twenty-five was a priest, nun, monk, canon or other religious. His was a thoroughly Catholic childhood in one of the Church's strongholds. It appears that the reformist currents of Jansenism had had little impact on the local clergy, who remained comfortable and conservative.[20]

The 'city of a hundred steeples' dominated its flat hinterland. There were as many as eight hundred members of the First Estate living in Arras, communities linked to St-Vaast, the cathedral, twelve parish churches, eighteen monasteries and convents, a dozen retreat houses, and many hospitals, hospices and small chapels. Arras was a powerhouse of the elite of the Catholic Church. The bishop was among the well-remunerated prelates of the kingdom, with a yearly income of about 40,000 *livres*, fifty times more than most village priests. Typical of the provincial centres of eighteenth-century France, Arras housed a large number of religious orders: it was atypical, however, in the substantial numbers still resident within them. In 1750 there were almost five hundred religious in the eighteen monasteries and convents. The Church employed directly many of the domestic servants of Arras; indirectly, many of the skilled craftsmen, shopkeepers and tradesmen depended on the First Estate as well.[21]

The parish clergy were at the other end of the ecclesiastical hierarchy in terms of social background and influence, but were a powerful and relatively wealthy body nonetheless. The twelve parish churches of Arras were serviced by forty-eight priests and curates. Thoroughly trained and confident in their theology, they were also far better remunerated than the parish clergy of the countryside, who often survived on no more than 750 *livres* annually, like smallholding peasants, despite the demands on their time and attention in one of the most observant dioceses in the kingdom. By contrast, priests in the wealthiest parishes in Arras, St-Géry and St-Jean, had yearly incomes of about 9,000 *livres* by the 1780s.[22] Arras was truly a bastion of the faith.

Just as spectacular as the building site of the massive new abbey was the construction of an entire new quarter on the initiative of the town government, on the marshy fields situated between the army citadel and the medieval ramparts of the town. Former marshland became the smart 'Basse-Ville' of Arras, marked by wide, tree-lined streets and an imposing octagonal public space. At the time of Augustin's birth in 1763 the Robespierres were listed as living on the Rue des Jésuites in the parish of St-Étienne of the developing new quarter. From the age of six, Maximilien just had to go down to the end of the Rue Ronville, where the Carrauts lived, to see what was happening over there.

Maximilien's infant world was one of construction sites on all sides, for Arras was undergoing the large-scale rebuilding of private dwellings as well as of St-Vaast and the new Basse-Ville. The great landowners—mostly from fifty noble families—had begun erecting the elegant townhouses whose restored facades continue to give Arras its distinctive style today. There were over 1,500 building or rebuilding permits issued in the thirty years before Maximilien's birth. Successful middle-class professional and merchant families, as well as nobles and religious institutions, took advantage of a long boom in rural production to construct buildings that exuded eminence and confidence. There were strict controls over the size and facades of houses, requiring them to have two storeys as well as a ground floor and cellar. This was not only in the interests of civic pride, but reflected military imperatives to increase the number of rooms available for billets.

For soldiers were everywhere in this strategic town. After the siege of Arras by the Spanish army in 1654 and the Treaty of the Pyrenees in 1659, a massive army 'citadelle' was constructed in the southeast of the town, as much to intimidate the local population as to ensure that the territorial consequences of the treaty were secure. With its nearby barracks, the garrison could shelter up to five thousand men and one thousand horses; there was civilian stabling for just as many more horses.[23] But many other soldiers had to be billeted in private houses: they were therefore omnipresent in the town. The Robespierres may have known some of the officers, for a witness at Jacqueline's burial was one Antoine-Henry Galhant, lieutenant major of the garrison.

Medieval Arras had had a powerful economic reach across much of Europe; indeed, 'Arras' was then a common generic name for tapestries in English and Italian. By the second half of the eighteenth century the town's economic influence was essentially confined to its region. Important as Arras was as a seat of royal and provincial administration and justice, it was now first and foremost a country town whose key economic functions lay in the commerce of agricultural products. Its textile manufacturing could no longer compete with Lille to the north and Amiens to the south. Most people were reliant on the countryside for their employment or revenues. This was particularly so for the Church, because the bulk of its income came from the produce of its vast estates and rights over those who worked them through rents and seigneurial dues. The Robespierres serviced this system, and depended on it.

As owners of a small brewery, the Carrauts were linked to the second great source of economic power in Arrageois society, the grain trade. On market days the country came to town. Built on the site of the former orchards of the St-Vaast abbey, the two great squares of Arras—together covering about two hectares—housed one of the largest grain markets in eighteenth-century France. The Petit Marché, just a minute away from the Carrauts on Rue Ronville, was dominated by the town hall and its belfry; to its north the huge flat expanse of the Grand Marché was surrounded by hotels and the fine houses of merchants. Many of the 155 houses that lined the squares carried stone carvings of crossed wheatsheaves on their ornate facades above the arcades under which market business was transacted.

Except for the new Basse-Ville, Arras was still contained within its medieval ramparts, and was more crowded than ever, with 20,000 people living in its 2,600 buildings. Old Arras remained a medieval city in its ground plan, with a network of dark and narrow streets surrounding the major axes and the two great central squares. Half the population of Arras were merchants and craftsmen, although their level of affluence varied sharply. Young Maximilien lived close by a tantalizing variety of shops and products. In Précourt's small shop, for example, rice sat side by side with fruit in syrup and worming powders; damaged goods were put on sale, with descriptions such as 'spoiled tea which smells nasty' and 'tea dust'. There were hundreds of households in the clothing and leather industries, and many more in the building trades.

The wage earners in these industries, and those who were unable to work regularly for whatever reason, were the most common groups of all. One in three people could be described as living a hand-to-mouth existence, relying on occasional or low-paid work, charity or crime. The lace industry, mostly under-taken at home, occupied thousands of women in the countryside and the working-class parishes of the town. Day labourers and the poor mostly lived on the opposite side of Arras from Maximilien and his siblings, in the Méaulens neighbourhood and near the Crinchon River, but they were always a presence in the town centre, where eight hundred people worked and lived in cellars accessed via steps down from the two great squares. These were the very poor. Despite the booming building and grain trades, it appears that begging, prostitu-tion, vagrancy and delinquency were part of the fabric of urban life.

As Maximilien walked through these crowded streets on his way to school or church, or ran through them to see Charlotte and Henriette and playmates, he would pass priests and nuns, lawyers and public officials, stonemasons and carpenters, labourers and market women. Soldiers of all ranks were everywhere. Occasionally, a high official, abbess or noble made their way through the throng. Several times a week Arras resounded to the din of shouting farmers and their cattle hauling groaning wagons. On those days the smells of cattle overwhelmed those of horses. Always there were beggars and lots of small children. For

Maximilien, this was the way the world was, one filled with the accents and smells of the countryside and the tones of polite society, the oaths of manual workers and farmers, the noise from the one hundred bars and taverns in Arras, the language of clothes, cleanliness and gesture that he needed to absorb. Words themselves marked off social distinctions between the French—albeit accented—of the well-to-do and the local Picard dialect of farmers and manual workers.

Maximilien sometimes visited the hamlet of Bel-Avesnes near Lattre-St-Quentin nine miles west of Arras, where the Carraut family had kept a farm, but in general his childhood was experienced in an urban bustle of people and animals and the noise of construction sites and markets. His own family was mobile, too, often moving to different parts of the town. The places in which the boy played, watched and listened were undergoing remarkable transformations. Noise, movement and contrasting odours were just the way things were. Maximilien was therefore surrounded by renewal and busyness, demolition and improvement, as well as by the quiet respect his religious aunts showed for devotion and good works. These were the women who helped him adjust to the sad changes in his family life in 1764.

Arras had a long history of provision of schooling and across the eighteenth century primary education came to be regarded as essential. Basic literacy had already reached 63 per cent, and 75 per cent in bourgeois parishes. Maximilien happened to be gifted and studious, and his aunts ensured that he could already read by the time he started attending the College of Arras at the age of eight. They were without the means to employ a private teacher to teach him to write; as the College also offered free instruction in Latin, he was enrolled there in 1766. This was a church school: the teachers were priests from the Society of the Oratory of Jesus, or Oratorians, and the bishop was on the governing council that had administered it since the Jesuits were banned from conducting schools in 1762. The school sought 'to provide the State with virtuous and Christian citizens, and to prepare the homeland's subjects'. To that end the boys studied the elements of history and world geography. The most prestigious prizes were for Latin, but there was an increasing emphasis on French for younger boys 'to construct correct sentences in a language which must still be foreign to them'.[24]

Maximilien was one of about four hundred boys there, half of them boarders from other towns and the countryside, but he soon distinguished himself by his quick mind. He seems to have been a clever, determined child, and perhaps his growing awareness that he might one day be responsible for three younger siblings gave him an added sense of duty. At the age of eleven he was one of a group chosen to participate in a public literary performance, showing their aptitude to comment on Latin texts. More was to come. There were four scholarships to be awarded annually by the abbot of St-Vaast to study at the prestigious College of Louis-le-Grand in Paris, of which the College of Arras was an affiliate. Maximilien was chosen, and his family agreed that the little boy would accept what was a lucrative and important scholarship, a gateway leading far beyond the Artois in which generations of Robespierres had been successful.[25]

The child Maximilien had inhabited a familiar, intimate world dominated by women: his mother, his paternal and maternal aunts, his grandmothers and two sisters. Charlotte had already left Arras for Tournai in 1768, aged eight, to be taught to 'make lace and sew, and anything else judged to be useful'.[26] Now, in October 1769, aged eleven, Maximilien was put on the coach for Paris and the thoroughly masculine world of Louis-le-Grand.

CHAPTER 2

'An extremely strong desire to succeed'
PARIS 1769–81

Maximilien's carriage went south through Bapaume to Amiens, with a connection to Paris via Beauvais. The 120 miles took twenty-four hours, an exhausting trip for a boy whose previous journeys had taken him only as far as the Carraut farm nine miles from Arras.[1] The first sight of a metropolis thirty times the size of his home town, as his carriage approached from the hills to the north, would have been an overwhelming experience for an eleven year old. Then, between St-Denis and its imposing basilica and the walls of the city, there were the 'false towns' (*faubourgs*) to negotiate, where Paris had spilled out beyond its walls into makeshift shelters alongside old villages, the home of impoverished migrants and noxious industries such as tanning and chemicals, lost among the wheatfields and vegetable patches of those who provisioned the metropolis. The windmills of Montmartre signalled the inexhaustible need of a huge city for the flour for its bread.

The same year that Maximilien arrived in Paris, the Genevan philosopher Jean-Jacques Rousseau completed work on his autobiographical *Confessions*. In it he described his own first impressions of Paris as a young man:

> I had imagined a town as beautiful as it was large, with a most imposing aspect including nothing but superb streets, palaces of marble and gold. Coming in from the faubourg Saint-Marceau, I saw only dirty, stinking alleys, ugly black houses, an air of filth and poverty . . . I was so struck at all this at first that all the truly magnificent things I have since seen in Paris could not erase this first impression.[2]

Maximilien entered the city from the north rather than the south, but his initial impressions may have been as disappointing as had been those of the man who was to become his intellectual master. On market days Arras had been a crush of people and animals, a chaos of noise and smells, but nothing could have prepared Maximilien for the clutter of narrow, twisting streets, tall tenement buildings—many of them whitewashed, unlike those of Rousseau's memory—and the occasional grandeur of aristocratic mansions. This was a city of constant movement and noise, of opulence and decay, brilliance and filth. Maximilien entered Paris through the Porte-de-la-Chapelle, crossing close enough to the markets—les Halles—to inhale their well-known stench of rotting fish, and at the end of the Rue St-Denis he would have been appalled by the smell of animal blood near the abattoirs. His carriage crossed the Seine near Notre-Dame Cathedral. The river was alive with boats, barges and people, its bridges cluttered with carts, carriages and animals, even houses and shops. Hundreds of washerwomen slapped their laundry on its banks.

Maximilien's coach wound up the hill known as the Montagne Ste-Geneviève and southwards through the Latin Quarter, Europe's greatest concentration of colleges and their faculties, booksellers and writers. One of the colleges was the College of Louis-le-Grand, just across the Rue St-Jacques from the Sorbonne, part of the University of Paris. The boy may have been welcomed by the Canon de la Roche from Notre-Dame, one of the Robespierre family's distant relatives, who, according to Charlotte, was to be Maximilien's 'protector and mentor'.[3] Like other new boys, Maximilien was immediately tested for academic preparedness by five examiners, then formally admitted; being younger than most boys at his level, he was enrolled in a lower class than the one he had completed in Arras.

Louis-le-Grand was one of the thirty-eight colleges in the Latin Quarter that together made up the Faculty of Arts of the University of Paris.[4] Long recognized as the elite secondary school in the kingdom, Louis-le-Grand had undergone dramatic changes in the years before Robespierre's arrival. The knowledge that the attempted assassination of Louis XV in 1757 was the work of a former College employee, Robert-François Damiens, had accentuated old suspicions about the loyalties of the Jesuits, then in charge of the College. The bankruptcy of its director and the decision of the Jesuits to take the matter before the highest court in the realm, the Parlement of Paris, exposed the College to further damaging attacks and in 1762 the Jesuits were ordered to close it.[5] In 1763 the

College was restructured under the Oratorian order and became formally linked to the Sorbonne. It was now placed under the direct patronage of the king, with a particular mission of providing secondary education for scholarship boys. The Jesuits' expulsion from the kingdom in 1764 also coincided with energetic and prolonged debate about the nature and purpose of education, with Rousseau's *Émile* (1762) being only the most sweeping of many statements. For the next thirty years educationalists argued for a more 'patriotic' education that would have more relevance as a force for social improvement than the teaching of theology and 'dead' languages.

In terms of his classmates, Maximilien was in familiar company. Although a few sons of nobles attended, the great majority were boys like him, sons of lawyers and other professionals or of merchants and manufacturers. There were only a few bright sons of tailors, drapers, grocers, masons and other artisans. Despite the overwhelmingly rural nature of French society, just one scholarship boy in eight was from the countryside, and even then they were sons of wealthy farmers. Clever peasant boys did not go to the College. The students were mostly from the northeast of the kingdom, like Maximilien.[6] One of the charges against the Jesuits had been that they had neglected the scholarship programme. Thanks to more efficient management of endowments, by the time Maximilien arrived virtually all of the five hundred boys were on scholarships. He came to know other clever boys his own age, such as Louis Beffroy de Reigny and François Suleau. There was also the younger Camille Desmoulins (born 1760), the son of an army officer and seigneur from Guise, not so far from Arras, and an older boy, Stanislas Fréron (born 1754), the son of the proprietor of a famous periodical, the *Année littéraire*. Fréron was the nephew of the Abbé Royou, one of the philosophy teachers, and Fréron's youngest brother Claude-Michel enrolled the same day as Maximilien.[7]

At the College, Robespierre would have encountered other boys from Arras, although he did not refer to them or to the College in speeches that he later gave on education. One Arrageois we do know to have been there at the same time was the Abbé Léon-Bonaventure Proyart, fifteen years Maximilien's senior and a 'prefect' and deputy principal at the school. Proyart's family was as solidly embedded in Artois society as was Robespierre's: one of his relatives was a lawyer at the Council of Artois, like Robespierre's grandfather and father. But Proyart's links with local society were primarily through the Church and landholding. He came to loathe Robespierre, and rounded on him after his death in the most vituperative of terms. It may be, however, that some of Proyart's memories of the young scholar contain a grain of truth, since they are not essential to his argument that he was a monster from childhood:

> although he had first to fight against more redoubtable competitors than those he had left in his province, he did so without losing heart, and so stubbornly, that in less than two years, he managed to shine amongst his peers. . . .

> He thought of nothing but his studies, he neglected everything for his studies, his studies were his God. . . .

> He said little, spoke only when people seemed disposed to listen to him, and always in a decisive and confident tone. Although desperate and insatiable for praise, when it was given, he received it with an air of cold modesty. . . .[8]

Despite the lively wider debates about the purpose of education, little had changed in the curriculum with the departure of the Jesuits from the College. The introduction of natural science and some mathematics for older boys was the main innovation. Maximilien was to spend eight years following a carefully structured programme of study. The youngest boys (the Seventh Class, or 'grammarians') studied Latin grammar and some French; boys of fifteen or sixteen years ('rhetoricians' or 'humanists') studied Latin, French and some Greek; the oldest 'philosophers' took moral philosophy and logic. They were introduced to Christian thought through the writings of the seventeenth-century bishops and theological rivals Bossuet and Fénelon, and to ancient history through the great aristocrat Montesquieu's recent *Greatness and Decline of the Romans*. Two further years of logic and moral philosophy were necessary for the award of Master of Arts. The year Robespierre completed his studies, the boys were expected to compose a speech in French in which 'a bishop from the Council of Nicea thanks Constantine for the protection he accords the Church'.[9]

Louis-le-Grand was one of a very small number of colleges in Paris that still took the study of Greek seriously. Aristotle's *Ethics* was a key text, teaching that pride, jealousy, licentiousness and greed were the antitheses of wisdom, justice, temperance and knowledge, and that discipline, humility and piety could lead the weak to a state of virtue. In addition, a recent French translation of Plutarch's

Parallel Lives made the perfect text for expanding interest in the lessons of history. But this was a curriculum dominated by Latin: indeed, that was the language used for the teaching of philosophy. From texts by Horace, Virgil and especially Cicero, and digests of other writers, such as Tacitus, Livy and Sallust, the boys also learnt ancient history and politics, particularly of late republican and Augustan Rome. The classics saturated the curriculum: the boys were immersed in classical Rome and its language to the point where Roman culture was more familiar than recent French history. We cannot be certain that the boys read Cicero's *De Oratore* (*On Oratory*), but certainly they were trained to write speeches using his five-part model of rhetoric: introduction, narration, confirmation, refutation and peroration.[10]

The texts that dominated the curriculum—and which were to be referred to regularly thereafter by Robespierre and his generation—had been written between 80 BC and AD 120, at a time when the greatest days of the Roman Republic were assumed to have been in the past. Its lost virtues were described in the classics as patriotism and love of liberty, austerity and industry, self-sacrifice and courage, integrity and justice—a stark contrast with the vices of luxury, greed, conspiracy and corruption the authors saw around them.[11] One of the texts we know to have been used in the curriculum was Cicero's account of the Catiline conspiracy, when he had acted decisively and uncompromisingly against a plot to seize power in first-century BC Rome by Lucius Sergius Catilina's aristocratic faction. Camille Desmoulins would later recall 'how many times ... did I embrace Cicero, my eyes wet with tears'. The text suited the College, since Cicero's account emphasized the conspirators' immoral behaviour and their use of sex and bribery to achieve their ends:

All foreign affairs are tranquilized. . . . Domestic war alone remains. The only plots against us are within our own walls, the danger is within, the enemy is within. . . .

For on the one side are fighting modesty, on the other wantonness; on the one chastity, on the other uncleanness; on the one honesty, on the other fraud; on the one piety, on the other wickedness; on the one consistency, on the other insanity; on the one honour, on the other baseness; on the one continence, on the other lust; in short, equity, temperance, fortitude, prudence . . .[12]

Cicero's text juxtaposed the vices and virtues, the latter under conspiratorial threat, and such a juxtaposition seems to have become embedded in Maximilien's way of thinking.

The explicit mission of the College was not so much instruction as education in its widest sense: the cultivation of the capacity for logical, disciplined learning, the inculcation of desirable traits of taste and behaviour, and the development of mature young men who would accept moral, religious and civic responsibilities. In Louis XV's terms, the purpose was 'education in morals and discipline'; in the words of the College's own regulations, it was to provide students with 'a solid and Christian education and so become useful to the State and to religion'. Although the high points of the academic year were the examinations and prizes, ultimately the attainment of *vertu* was understood to be the achievement of these wider moral attributes, and facility in Latin was assumed to be the appropriate vehicle for such attainment.

The boys' daily lives were tightly controlled and revolved around religious and academic discipline and routine, codified into a long list of regulations just two months after Maximilien arrived. This was a set of rules that was as much about instilling values of proper personal dealings with others as it was about prescribing the times and places for study and leisure. It began with the expectations of the masters in creating an atmosphere of 'harmony and peace' and leading by their own example of 'love of right conduct, and hard work'. Students were to be inspired to 'sentiments of piety and religion' by the cultivation of the 'honest and sensitive mind' rather than 'severity'. The values embedded in the regulations were harmony and consideration; diligence and piety; restraint and obedience: 'They will tolerate no vulgarity, insults, reproaches, or malicious nicknames. Swearing or other outrageous behaviour, for whatever cause, will be rigorously forbidden and severely punished'.

Boys were expected to display modest and Christian behaviour towards all involved with their education, from the masters to fellow students and domestic staff:

In conversation they will be more eager to listen than to speak. . . .

They will gladly praise others, but without affectation or silliness, and they will never speak advantageously of themselves.

They will speak gently and courteously to the servants. It is expressly forbidden to treat them harshly or with condescension.[13]

The boys rose at 5.30 a.m. to be ready for prayer and devotional reading. They then undertook ninety minutes of study, beginning with the learning and recitation of Scripture, before they had breakfast. Their days were long, closely monitored, and devoted to study and prayer: 'no moment in the classroom, conferences, preparations or other exercises shall be lost in amusement or in wandering about the house or in anything unrelated to these exercises'. By 9.15 p.m. the boys had said their prayers and were in their dormitory beds. Even at mealtimes, apart from saying the *Benedicite* and *Grace*, and the *De Profundis* at supper and dinner, the boys were expected to eat in silence and listen to a reading.[14]

The virtues of piety were reinforced by the Abbé Proyart's account of the life of a young scholar, Décalogne de la Perrie, who had died during Maximilien's first term, aged sixteen. From *The Virtuous Schoolboy, or the Edifying Life of a Schoolboy at the University of Paris*, Maximilien and his schoolmates would have learnt that, after his first communion, Décalogne had resolved that each day:

My first thought will be of God . . .

During times of study, I will only think of work set by my masters. I will not speak to those beside me without permission . . .

During games, I will often lift up my heart to God . . .

I will obey my masters completely. If they punish me, I will never object if punished unreasonably.[15]

We cannot know whether the pious prescriptions in Proyart's homage to Décalogne were absorbed by the boys or became the object of ridicule.

Boys were expected to dress modestly, in clean and decent clothes, and to wash their hands at least once daily. This was a life to be lived in the sight of God and other boys and masters: there were no private spaces, and 'if any boy lets himself form dirty habits all possible means will be used to correct him, to the point of punishment if necessary'. While the boys undressed each evening they listened to a reading from the life of the saint whose feast was the following day. Close friendships were discouraged as a sign of 'tacit contempt' for others:

'connections between students, if they become too close, often give rise to back-biting, calumny, defiance of masters, dissipation, and waste of time'.[16]

Like all institutional rules, these were prescriptive of ideal behaviour and did not necessarily reflect how the boys actually behaved: reading between the lines, it is likely that they were indeed noisy, boisterous and unpleasant at times. Nevertheless, the severity of the sanctions suggests that the College authorities had the necessary power to insist on order. Maximilien had been a child raised by loving female relatives within extended families in the intimate world of a small provincial town; as a boy in his early teens he now needed to live according to the exacting disciplines of a scholastic and masculine world.

The boys were closeted from the outside. They were well fed, and were rarely allowed extra supplies from their families. They were occasionally permitted visitors or to be taken on outings by a 'reliable and known person'; there is no evidence, however, that Maximilien was in a position to enjoy such treats. His family contact, the elderly Canon de La Roche, had died two years after Maximilien arrived in Paris. Instead, he would have joined with his classmates in the group outings that occurred for half-days most weeks, under the watchful eye of masters and other staff. Inner Paris was perceived to be full of temptation and danger, and it is likely that most of the outings were to the countryside through the city walls a short distance south: there the regulations instructed the boys to avoid 'anything that may lead to tumult or complaint, such as chasing after game, entering vineyards, trampling in wheatfields, etc.'[17]

Certainly Maximilien would have returned to Arras for the summer holidays, but his family was now sadly diminished. His father François had left Arras, and France, for good, abandoning his profession to establish a French-language school in Munich, where he died in 1777. Maximilien's Carraut grandparents died in 1775 and 1778. In between, there were other changes in his immediate family. The two aunts who had raised him had married, both aged forty-one: Eulalie in 1776 to the notary and merchant Robert-François Deshorties, Henriette in 1777 to the doctor François du Rut.[18]

Maximilien's sisters were also studying elsewhere: Charlotte (from 1768) and Henriette (from 1773) were enrolled in the Maison des Soeurs Manarre just across the border in Tournai (modern-day Belgium), where they were taught reading, writing, sewing and other domestic skills. Charlotte later recalled periods of great happiness when the children were reunited in Arras for the summer holidays, even though these were punctuated by grief at what seemed an annual ritual of losing a close relative. None was more harrowing than the death of their sister Henriette in 1780, aged just nineteen. This loss, she believed, had 'a much greater impact on Maximilien's character than one would think: it made him sad and melancholy'.[19] He wrote a loving homage to Henriette, a poem kept by Charlotte until her death:

Song addressed to Miss Henriette . . .
Do you want to know, O charming Henriette,
Why love is the greatest of the gods? . . .

Unfolding all the riches of his gifts,
With a thousand charms he graced your pretty face.
He put tenderness in your lovely eyes
And gave you the most eloquent voice.

He endowed you with the smile of the Graces,
In every feature, Goodness he displayed.
Laughter he taught to follow in your traces
And to your footsteps harnessed gaiety.

He arranged your raven tresses
To show the whiteness of your skin.
Taking the belt of Venus from her grasp,
He adorned you with it with his hand divine.[20]

During the summer holidays there were also school friends to see from Arras and Paris. One of the reasons why the Abbé Proyart came to dislike Robespierre so intensely was that he felt slighted that, when he 'came to Arras, at holiday times, Robespierre, the one among all the young men of that town educated at Louis-le-Grand who owed more to him than any disciple owes his master, was the only one to neglect him and saw him only by accident'. Certainly, relations between the two were cool. When Robespierre learned in April 1778 that the Bishop of Arras was in Paris, he wrote a crisp note to Proyart stating that he would like to see the bishop, but 'I have no coat, and lack many things without which I cannot leave the house. I hope that you will be so good as to trouble yourself to tell him in person of my situation, so as to obtain from him what I need in order to appear before him.'[21]

Proyart's animus smacks of wounded pride and may also explain why he resented the influence on Robespierre of another teacher, the Abbé Hérivaux: 'none of his masters contributed so much to the growth of the republican virus fermenting in his soul than his Professor of Rhetoric. An enthusiastic admirer of the heroes of ancient Rome, M. *Hérivaux*, whose students nicknamed him *The Roman*, thought that Robespierre's personality had strong Roman features.' Indeed, Hérivaux chose Robespierre from among the five hundred pupils to deliver compliments to Louis XVI and Marie-Antoinette in 1775 as they crossed Paris after their coronation in Reims. As Proyart recalled it: 'Robespierre it was who was charged with offering these, in the name of his Fellow-students, in a Speech in Verse composed by his Professor. I was present at the time and recall that the King deigned to look down kindly.' In fact, it seems that the royal couple, incommoded by wet weather, stayed in the coach and left the young scholar standing in the rain as soon as he had completed his speech.[22] But Proyart was certainly correct in his recollection of Robespierre's assiduous approach to learning, and about his ability. His name was a common one at prize-giving ceremonies in the College between 1772 and 1776, where he won several second prizes.[23]

The award of the Master of Arts was necessary to enter one of the University's three professional schools of medicine, theology and law. As noted, Maximilien had come from a very long line of lawyers, and his grandfather and father had both practised in the highest provincial court. Whatever the bewilderment or resentment he felt at his father's behaviour after his mother's death in 1764, he was clear in his mind that he too was to be a lawyer. Maximilien was already possessed of a remarkable determination and self-belief. In January 1776—not yet eighteen, and still with several years of College study ahead of him before undertaking law—he wrote courteously to the distinguished lawyer Guy-Jean-Baptiste Target, already describing himself as a law student, and made a minor enquiry perhaps only designed as a pretext to introduce himself.[24]

Later, just as he was about to begin his studies of the law in October 1779, Maximilien wrote to one of the most eminent lawyers in the country, the aristocratic Jean-Baptiste Mercier-Dupaty, President of the Parlement of Bordeaux and famous for his critiques of judicial error.[25] His most famous intervention in public affairs had been his successful, eloquent defence of aristocratic high courts in 1775 as a bulwark against 'royal despotism'. Robespierre excused himself for his direct approach on the basis of his unbounded regard for the judge. To his passion to succeed at the bar, he added:

> I bring at the very least a highly competitive spirit and an extremely strong desire to succeed. But since the counsel of a wise master would be of great assistance in reaching my goal, I am desirous of finding one who would be so kind as to draw up a plan of study for me. . . . If you believe, Sir, that it would be better to do this in person than by letter, I beg you to indicate when I may have the honour of speaking with you.

We do not know whether Mercier-Dupaty responded. But the nature of the request suggests that Maximilien was as astute as he was ambitious, aware no doubt that, with his grandfather and father dead, his professional success would require other mentors and contacts. For these senior lawyers were emerging as leading national figures in a powerful legal culture of reform, profoundly influenced by Montesquieu and Cesare Beccaria, for whom key concerns were degrading physical punishments and the maze of law codes and special prerogatives.[26]

Now twenty, Maximilien had considerably more freedom, since law students left the College buildings to study and were expected to return only once classes were over, even though there were just two lectures each day. They were required to attend Mass daily, and the common excuse that they needed to leave to gain experience in an attorney's office was subject to close documentation. But the College's rules for law students, and the concern expressed about their behaviour by an authority as high as the Parlement of Paris, suggest that many took advantage of their supposed legal apprenticeships to enjoy other aspects of life in Paris.[27]

Maximilien was certainly now able to explore the city. His immediate environs in the Latin Quarter were a tangle of narrow streets, which in the nineteenth century were to be sliced through by the broad swathes of the Boulevards St-Michel and St-Germain and the Rue des Écoles. But Louis-le-Grand and the Sorbonne were just a short walk down the hill to the Île de la Cité and the Palais de Justice, in which were crammed sixteen of the city's thirty-five separate courts. As many as forty thousand Parisians worked in what constituted a judicial city within the metropolis.

In Paris, its population variously estimated at between 550,000 and 650,000, Maximilien was confronted with an urban world both familiar and strikingly different. As in Arras, the building industry boomed, and new houses were being constructed for the wealthy who had left the essentially medieval centre where, above street-level workshops and stores, the various social strata of the population continued to live, distinguished by their level of income, in tenement buildings. There were some large 'manufactories', but Paris remained a city dominated by craft workshops.[28] This was a city of commerce and law, of professional and artisan families, of labourers, beggars and prostitutes. More than seven thousand Parisians—almost one in every hundred—served in the religious community composed of fifty-two parishes, three cathedral chapters and 140 monasteries and convents. But there was also a tavern or café for every two hundred Parisians. Although in some ways Paris resembled Arras on a grand scale, there were contrasts too. The presence of religious in the streets of Arras was four times as common as in Paris. Similarly, there were eight thousand soldiers in the city, but their presence was not nearly as marked as that of the garrison in Arras.

We do not know with which legal office Maximilien undertook his legal apprenticeship. This was likely to have been more formative than the narrow Sorbonne curriculum, which had centred on civil law and canon law, with little attention paid to administrative or criminal law, let alone to theoretical and historical questions.[29] But by the time Maximilien had begun his studies in law in the late 1770s, he was exposed to rich and agitated debates about the nature of secular and ecclesiastical authority. In particular, the consequences of the expulsion of the Jesuits were still being played out between the Archbishop of Paris and his allies, who accused influential Paris 'Jansenists' of being close to Calvinism. Whereas Maximilien had been raised by devout aunts in a town dominated by the clergy and its institutions, he was now coming to maturity in a teeming metropolis where the most basic questions about the sources of certainty concerning legitimate authority were being posed at every level of society. This was a city in which the visible presence of the Church clashed with an evident decline in churchgoing and respect for ecclesiastical hierarchy. The accession of the devout young Louis XVI in 1774 did not change that.[30]

According to the Abbé Proyart, it was during his final year at the College that Robespierre began to read 'evil books'. Proyart recalled that another prefect (the Abbé Yves-Marie Audrein) who 'opened a door suddenly, found him on the commode, reading a very nasty pamphlet. . . . his reading of blasphemous books, begun during his philosophy year and continuing during his studies in law . . .'. What might Robespierre have been reading? The board of Louis-le-Grand had expressed concern at the presence among the boys of Rousseau's *Nouvelle Héloïse* and Rabelais' ribald *Pantagruel*. Or perhaps he had obtained one of the flood of cheap publications circulating clandestinely in the 'Grub Street' of Paris, pamphlets in which the perceived sexual and moral hypocrisy of the high clergy and nobility—reinforced by notorious public scandal—was both mocked and relished.[31] Such publications were 'blasphemous', as Proyart claimed; however, they were not anticlerical or irreligious. Rather, their mix of salaciousness and moralizing expressed a yearning for a clergy of simple, sure morality and dedication, a similar impulse that explains the popularity of Rousseau's moral, emotional tales in *Émile* and *Nouvelle Héloïse*.

This was not all that Maximilien was reading. As a law student, recalled Proyart, Robespierre 'read curious memoirs, followed famous cases, ran to the Palais to hear flashy speeches for the defence and pronounce judgments on the most celebrated lawyers'. Proyart may well have been referring to the proliferation at that time of published trial briefs with print runs of up to twenty thousand. These *causes célèbres* that Parisians devoured were often characterized by their repudiation of a traditional aristocratic world depicted as violent, feudal and immoral, opposed to the values of citizenship, rationality and utility.[32] Through the world of the Paris legal profession and its most scandalous cases, Robespierre was exposed to a vigorous critique of the privileged orders and of the allegedly outmoded claims to social order and function on which they relied. The powerful sense among certain Paris lawyers that they were capable of a leading role in articulating an alternative vision was to mark the young man and his peers.

It may have been at this point, too, that Maximilien met Jean-Jacques Rousseau, or at least saw him. Some years later, he wrote a homage, his *Dedication to the Spirit of Jean-Jacques Rousseau*, in which he claimed that 'I saw you in your last days and this memory is a source of proud joy to me: I looked upon your august features . . .'. Rousseau died in 1778, so Robespierre would only have been in his late teens at the time of this encounter. Whether or not a meeting had actually occurred, Robespierre had had an intellectual encounter with Rousseau, perhaps through *Émile*, the *Social Contract* or the *Nouvelle Héloïse*, which affected him profoundly.[33]

Ordinarily, two years were required for the bachelor's degree in law, and a further two years for the *license*. This could be accelerated: Robespierre began his law course in October 1779 and was able to complete it in rapid time, just eighteen months. He took out his *license* in May 1781 and was enrolled on the register, as an *avocat* or barrister, in the Parlement of Paris the following August.[34] Despite Proyart's personal disappointment in him, Robespierre had not been one of the troublesome law students whose behaviour so bothered the Parlement, and when he graduated the College authorities were so pleased with his conduct as well as his aptitude that they took an unusual step. When he left the College in July 1781 his academic excellence was recognized by the award of a special prize of 600 *livres*—effectively a year's living allowance—'in view of the report of M. the Principal on the outstanding abilities of Sieur de Robespierre, a scholarship student of Arras College, who is about to conclude his studies, and on his good conduct for twelve years and his success in his classes, as shown both in University prizes and in examinations in philosophy and law'.[35]

The College of Louis-le-Grand had been Maximilien's home for twelve years. In later life he spoke very rarely of his childhood and youth, but admitted in 1791 that his education by Oratorians—whether in Arras or Paris—aroused 'memories which will always be dear to me'.[36] He had been like most of the other boys at the College: a clever, diligent young man from a provincial and bourgeois background. He had had a less fortunate childhood than most; nevertheless, his innate ability and determination had resulted in an outstanding record of academic achievement and behaviour. He had absorbed a rich knowledge of the classics in particular and had developed the self-discipline necessary to succeed in a rigorous, competitive environment. He had a law degree from the Sorbonne, a swathe of prizes, and the personal assurance that could come only from succeeding in the largest city in the realm. In his final years of study he had entered the culture of the legal profession in Paris at a particularly agitated and exciting time. Now he was returning to Arras and to Charlotte, who had just completed her own schooling in Tournai. They were very much on their own, a brother aged twenty-three and a sister of twenty-one.

CHAPTER 3

'Such a talented man'
ARRAS 1781–84

Maximilien returned to his home town in 1781 after an absence of twelve years, a qualified lawyer educated at the best secondary school and university in the country. As a small boy he had experienced Arras by absorbing meanings from his extended family and his schoolmasters and fellow pupils. Now he was returning to his home town as a man, altogether more attuned to structures of power and with the confidence of the boy from the provinces who had made good in mainland Europe's largest city. Here was a clever, ambitious young man coming home to his beloved sister with a wealth of knowledge but a modest wealth of means.

He had spent his childhood in a provincial city dominated by the institutions of the Catholic Church. His Paris education had been made possible by the capacity of that Church to provide a scholarship to a bright boy whose personal misfortunes—his mother's death, his father's flight—must have been only partly softened by support from dutiful wider families. Robespierre's academic successes and dedication were to benefit his younger brother Augustin, then studying at the College of Douai, for Maximilien convinced the new Abbot of St-Vaast, Cardinal Édouard de Rohan, to transfer the scholarship he had had at Louis-le-Grand directly to Augustin, who was now seventeen. So Augustin spent the years 1781–88 at Louis-le-Grand, and therefore the two brothers would continue to see very little of each other after 1769, apart from summer holidays.[1]

Maximilien's family circumstances were now very different. Not only was his absent father dead, but so were most of his close relatives. The judicial establishment in Arras knew that they were welcoming home a talented young colleague, but his financial resources were meagre and he and Charlotte would be reliant on his capacity to attract clients, mainly through the good graces of established lawyers: he was bereft of the personal networks common among professional families. There was little likelihood that circumstances might ever again take him outside the small, pious and traditional town in which he been a child, one in which he would always be riding the coat-tails of privilege, wealth and power, and where his colleagues and acquaintances all knew of his family's troubled past.

Robespierre's homecoming was no doubt a source of happiness to his diminished family, but he arrived in the middle of a protracted family dispute over the sale of his grandfather's brewery. It had been sold to a relative for about 8,000 *livres*, but only half came to the three surviving children; moreover, his paternal aunt and uncle were still paying off the debts of their brother, Maximilien's father, and sought access to the proceeds of the Carraut estate.[2] Presumably because of this unresolved business, Maximilien and Charlotte initially did not live with their aunt and uncle, but instead rented accommodation in the Rue du Saumon, near the parish church of St-Jean where their parents had married and not far from the Carrauts' brewery.

The town had continued to grow in Maximilien's absence, and in the 1780s counted about twenty-two thousand residents, a few more than its rival St-Omer, but only a fraction of the booming textile city of Lille to the north.[3] Despite the energetic attempts by the town council, supported by customs concessions from the monarchy, to attract textile producers and a trade in woollen cloth, the long-term decline of Arras' industry had continued. Nothing seems to have worked, and the cloth industry continued to falter. Some manufacturing growth continued, but the wealth of the town rested increasingly on the commercialization of grain. The eighteenth century had been free of warfare in Artois, but external conflicts such as the Seven Years War and the American War of Independence created important markets for exports, as did demand from the garrison, with thousands of men and horses to provision. The last disastrous harvest had been as long ago as 1740, and the price of wheat had since doubled. The long-term rise in the price of corn benefited the large landholders receiving rents from the farmers around Arras: the nobility, the clergy (particularly the bishop, the cathedral chapter and the abbeys), and well-to-do bourgeois. This affluence continued to drive the construction industry in the Basse-Ville and the refurbishment of well-to-do noble and bourgeois residences within the town walls.

The Arras to which Maximilien returned was not only a major commercial centre; it was also a pious and conservative provincial hub of the structures of privilege, seigneurialism, law and administration linking the villages of Artois with their capital. Provincial capitals like Arras both serviced and depended on the countryside, providing courts, markets and social order in return for tithes, seigneurial dues and rents. Families from the legal profession like the Robespierres were at the fulcrum of this society.

Artois enjoyed a certain level of self-government and control of taxation through its Estates of Artois, which dated to the fourteenth century. The Estates gathered representatives of the three orders: the upper clergy, nobles with the requisite numbers of noble ancestors, and *échevins* (municipal councillors) of the ten largest towns, who were considered also to represent the common people of town and country. The Estates had been at the pinnacle of local power since their restoration in 1661 following the Treaty of the Pyrenees two years earlier.[4] The Intendancy of Artois, the key royal administrative appointment, was located in Lille and was headed by a series of the kingdom's senior administrators, including from 1778 Charles-Alexandre de Calonne, until his appointment in 1783 as Controller-General of Finances for the kingdom. But the Estates, which met annually in Arras, had kept their key privileges and prerogatives, above all those pertaining to the levying of royal taxes. The province was exempt from the salt tax (*gabelle*), a source of rancour elsewhere. In return, the Estates were responsible, through levying taxes on drinks and livestock, for a 'voluntary gift' to the crown of 400,000 *livres*. The Estates had if anything strengthened their hold on local power by the 1780s. In 1782 Calonne was moved to complain that 'the Estates, having deprived my predecessor of the administration of the communal properties of Artois . . . regulate the interests of the interested parties, ratify or annul the deliberations of all the communities . . .'. The issue of the powers of the aristocratic Estates continued to simmer with the Crown.

The high clergy of Arras were closely integrated with the power structures of the Estates of Artois and the town council, or 'magistracy', of Arras. Artois was one of four provinces in the kingdom with a 'Sovereign Council' rather than a Parlement the highest court in the province since the Council's foundation in

1677, but its powers were constrained by the eminence and authority of the Estates. The Bishop of Arras, Hilaire-Louis de Conzié, presided over the Estates in almost theocratic style.[5] He exercised spiritual authority over the four hundred parishes of a diocese that stretched as far as Armentières to the north and Valenciennes to the east. Conzié had an annual revenue of 40,000 *livres*—typical of most bishops—and sufficient diocesan resources to finance simultaneously the completion of the reconstruction of his episcopal palace by 1780, the establishment of the Sisters of Charity, and the commencement of work on a new seminary. He pursued the rebuilding of the Cathedral of Notre Dame, next to St-Vaast, begun in 1774 and far from completion on Robespierre's return in 1781. Like every other section of society in Artois, however, the First Estate was riven by sharp differences in status and wealth at the same time as its corporate privilege set it apart as a body within the state.

Conzié was at the pinnacle of a noble clerical elite that included the heads of the chapter houses, the noble canons at the cathedral and the heads of the abbey and other religious houses. By 1770 the massive convent buildings of St-Vaast had been completed. Édouard de Rohan had been appointed Abbot of St-Vaast in 1778, 'perhaps the most lucrative abbatial prize of all' in France; in the same year he was made a cardinal, and the year before he had succeeded his uncle as Bishop of Strasbourg. In all he accumulated over 800,000 *livres* in ecclesiastical benefices, which were nevertheless insufficient to cover his debts. As Grand Almoner of France from 1777, Rohan had nominal authority over the kingdom's religious policy; his close involvement in Paris and Versailles politics meant that, for his flock in Strasbourg, and much more so in Arras, his tutelage was nominal.[6]

The great noble families drew their wealth from landed property and seigneurial dues in the region around Arras. Only the illustrious 'old' nobility had the right to sit in the Estates of Artois. They made up about 120 of the 500 heads of family in Artois with noble status. Some of them remained resident in their seigneuries and—like Ferdinand Dubois de Fosseux—were closely involved with agricultural improvement and the affairs of their communities. Dubois was the very ideal of the seigneur, attentive to his community and generous to its priest.[7] For others, the exercise of judicial or municipal functions, attendance at the provincial government (the Estates of Artois), participation in the meetings of the Royal Academy of Arras, and other attractions of urban life had led most to abandon residence on their country estates. Their preferred neighbourhood in Arras was the parish of St-Jean-en-Ronville with its numerous private mansions near the Estates and the mansions of the governor and magistracy. The newer nobility, many of them ennobled by having bought venal titles once acceding to official positions within the Council of Artois, were more often urban residents, grating at the social distance the old nobility continued to measure.

In sources of income and lifestyle, the elite of the Arras bourgeoisie—especially the most successful lawyers and merchants—were little different from many of the new nobles they sought to emulate. But as a social group the bourgeoisie was dominated by lawyers in this town of ten major courts, where there were thirty-one judges, ninety-two barristers (*avocats*), about fifty public prosecutors (*procureurs*), and twenty-five notaries servicing a maze of courts. This was Robespierre's world from 1781. Like all highly talented, restless young people who have succeeded against the odds, he had a deep sense of his ability and a certainty that he represented enlightened thought in a suffocating town. The critical question was whether he would have *entrée* into the privileged, hierarchical world of the Arras legal establishment. He had neither quite the family name nor the family fortune to guarantee easy access into the highest echelons of judicial eminence or social status, but would be dependent on those whom it was risky to offend. Here he was fortunate. He might have been snubbed as too Parisian, too clever by half, as devoid of good breeding; instead, some of the most powerful figures in Arras held out their hands, offering rapid and significant appointments and assistance.

On 8 November 1781 he succeeded in his application to be admitted as an advocate in the Council of Artois.[8] Another lawyer, Guillaume Liborel, twenty years his senior, presented Robespierre's credentials to the Council, and then set him up with an initial, straightforward case in January 1782, albeit one involving a disputed will that it was clear they would lose. Other early cases were equally straightforward, but in Robespierre's favour. In May 1782 he acted successfully for nephews who had been disinherited in favour of others because they chose to remain Catholic rather than follow their uncle's embrace of 'reformed religion'.[9]

The Bishop of Arras then appointed Robespierre to fill a fortuitous vacancy as a magistrate in the Episcopal Court on 9 March 1782, a position for which his peers had often needed to wait a decade. The court had judicial authority within

Arras and almost thirty of the surrounding parishes. Through this court he soon found himself taking cases in opposition to Liborel. It was in this court too that he later had to pronounce a death sentence for murder. His sister Charlotte later recalled his agitation on the eve of the sentencing: 'I know that he is guilty,' Maximilien kept repeating, 'I know that he's a scoundrel, but to have a man killed!'[10]

Despite his promising beginnings, the young lawyer soon understood that he could not afford to pay even a modest rent and, with the negotiations over the family will perhaps now resolved, accepted in late 1782 the hospitality offered by his aunt Henriette and her doctor husband François du Rut in the Rue des Teinturiers. This was close to the locus of judicial activity, directly opposite the cathedral building site and the now complete abbey. As Robespierre's income improved, he and Charlotte moved back to the Basse-Ville, to the Rue des Jésuites. Through du Rut, who was the medical officer at Maximilien's old school, he was welcomed back as a successful old boy, and was invited to give end-of-year addresses on historical subjects such as Henri IV or the Salis-Samade regiment then in garrison at Arras.[11]

Maximilien had needed to seek assistance to begin making his way in the hierarchical, face-to-face world of a provincial legal establishment. He felt other needs as well. In the week after he had argued his first, unsuccessful case, he and Charlotte received a gift of canaries from a friend of hers, a Mademoiselle Duhay, to which he responded with some copies of a 'dissertation' (perhaps a copy of his final speech to the court) and a charming letter.[12] How could they not be 'interesting' canaries, coming from her? 'They are very pretty; having been raised by you, we expected them also to be the gentlest and most sociable of all canaries.' But he was puzzled by their frenzied behaviour at his approach to the cage: 'Should not a countenance such as yours have habituated your canaries to the human face?' Maximilien seems to have been attracted to the generous young friend. Her gift had rekindled the love for small birds that he had had as a child, but nothing more serious developed between them.

Robespierre made an immediate impression on others, too. No doubt some found the young man precocious. His former teacher at Louis-le-Grand, the Abbé Proyart, while still in Paris, seems to have followed his career with interest. While the Abbé's memoirs were thoroughly jaundiced, there may have been a grain of truth in his claim that 'Robespierre, like all Presumptuous Youths who have seen the Capital and imitated its vices, had come back from it full of wind.'[13] Others were pleased with the impression he was making. In February 1782 another lawyer, Ansart, wrote from Arras to his friend Étienne Lenglet, a fellow Arrageois law student in Paris, about Robespierre's performance in the case over the disputed will: 'there's nothing new in our town, except that someone called Robespierre, newly arrived from your part of the country, has made his debut here in a famous case. . . . They say (I have not heard him) that in his delivery, his choice of expressions and the clarity of his speech he leaves everyone else far behind . . .'. Lenglet responded that, indeed, 'this M. de Robespierre is as frightening as you say. Moreover, I am much inclined to applaud his superiority and to congratulate my birthplace on having such a talented man.'[14]

Certainly Robespierre was hard-working and dedicated. Charlotte later recalled that he would rise between six and seven, working until eight, when a wig-maker came to shave and powder him. After a light breakfast—a bowl of milk—he would work again until leaving for the courts at ten. He ate and drank sparingly, preferring fruit and coffee. In the evenings he would walk or meet acquaintances before further work. He was, she insisted, naturally good-humoured and enjoyed light-heartedness, even if he preferred to read or reflect rather than join the family for games of cards. He was an intense man, often consumed by his work to the point of absent-mindedness. Once he poured a ladle of soup onto a tablecloth, not noticing that there was no bowl; on another occasion he was mortified that he had undertaken to accompany Charlotte home from an evening function but had forgotten and had walked home alone with her trailing far behind.[15]

By dint of his demanding routine and his evident ability, Robespierre built up a reasonable if modest clientele: he was far from being as successful as the established stars of the Arras courts. In 1782 he appeared before the Council in thirteen cases that were held over twenty-three sitting days; four were settled out of court, and he won seven cases. The following year, he appeared twenty-eight times at the bar of the Council; he won about two-thirds of the cases. In 1784 he appeared for clients in only thirteen cases, but he won ten of them and he lost outright only one.[16] He was a successful barrister, but his earnings were modest indeed: he could not, in so short a time, rival men such as Liborel who had been practising for twenty or thirty years.

Shortly after returning to Arras from Paris, Robespierre met—probably through legal circles—Antoine-Joseph Buissart, another lawyer and a very wealthy landowner. Although more than twenty years his senior, the two became close friends, with Buissart initially playing a mentoring role for his brilliant young colleague. Maximilien also became very fond of Buissart's wife Charlotte, a cousin of the President of the Council, Briois de Beaumez. Robespierre had returned from Paris rich in ideas and expertise, but materially in straitened circumstances. Buissart, on the other hand, had a most extensive library of many hundreds of volumes, including a full 36-volume set of the *Encyclopédie*, collections of documents from the Damiens trial, six books by Cicero and others by Virgil, Horace and Ovid in Latin and French, and many works of history and science.[17]

Buissart was a passionate amateur scientist—nicknamed 'the barometer' by locals—and it was he who gave Robespierre his breakthrough case as a barrister by arranging for him to defend Vissery de Bois-Valé, a lawyer from St-Omer.[18] The massive and intricate lightning conductor that Vissery had erected had alarmed neighbours to the point where they had obtained a court order to have it dismantled. But Vissery refused to be defeated: he appealed to the Council of Artois at Arras and charged Buissart with presenting his defence. Buissart compiled a voluminous report. Drawing on this investigative work done by his friend and mentor, Robespierre was able in 1783 to have the ruling overturned in a context of references to enlightenment triumphing over 'obscurantism'. 'Gentlemen', he pleaded to the Council, 'you must defend Science. The fact that the whole of Europe is watching this case will ensure that your decision will be as well-known as possible. . . . Paris, London, Berlin, Stockholm, Turin, St Petersburg will hear almost as soon as Arras of this mark of your wisdom and enthusiasm for scientific progress'.

The national newspaper *Mercure de France* agreed with him. On 23 June 1783 it carried an account of the 'celebrated trial that has long engaged public attention', perhaps written by Buissart himself: 'M. de Robespierre, a young lawyer of exceptional merit, displayed in this affair, which was the cause of Science and the Arts, an eloquence and sagacity which give one the highest opinion of his learning.'[19] As noted before, while a student in Paris, Robespierre had been prepared to approach directly two of the most famous lawyers in the land, Target and Mercier-Dupaty. Now, his success in the Vissery case emboldened him to approach

Benjamin Franklin himself, noting that it was Franklin's discovery he was defending:[20]

> The desire to assist in uprooting the prejudices which stood against its progress in our province inspired me to have the address I made to the court in this case printed. I dare to hope, Sir, that you will kindly receive a copy of this work ... [I will be] happier still if I can join to this good fortune the honour of earning the approbation of a man the least of whose virtues is of being the most famous man of science in the universe

The parochial fame of men like Foacier de Ruzé, his opponent in the case, Liborel and others had been eclipsed. Robespierre was still only twenty-five years of age.[21]

It was at this time, with the case behind him, that Maximilien—probably with Charlotte—decided to take a trip north to Carvin. In doing so he was visiting his wider family, still numerous and prominent in the small town from which his grandfather had moved in 1722. The journey to Carvin, less than twenty miles from Arras, made a deep impact on Robespierre and he was moved to write an account of it to Charlotte Buissart: 'pleasures are real only if they are shared with friends'.[22] There was nothing unusual in an educated man setting down his wider reflections on a 'voyage', however modest; Robespierre himself quipped that 'I know an author who celebrated a trip of five leagues [about fifteen miles] in both prose and verse.' In his case, however, he kept his reflections for a friend, and they are all the more valuable for that. It is the closest thing we have to a personal reflection from him, albeit mediated by being designed to impress the wife of a prominent lawyer.

Just turned twenty-five, and back in Arras for only eighteen months, Maximilien sought to delight with his brilliance in making allusions to classical authors—even in a round trip of less than fifty miles—and in demonstrating his knowledge of French history. Halfway to Carvin, at Lens, he 'climbed the hill on which the crucifix stands; from there I looked, with a mixture of pity and admiration, over that vast plain where the twenty-year-old Condé won that famous victory over the Spaniards which saved the fatherland'.

Here was a young man bubbling with intellectual energy. He was bubbling with wit as well. He quipped ironically that the voyages of Ulysses and his son

Telemachus were nothing compared to his, and satirized his early departure in a cart: 'the chariot which bore us went through the city gates at the precise moment when that of the Sun rose from the bosom of the Ocean, adorned with a sheet of blazing white, part of which floated on the breath of the zephyrs'. When they arrived in Carvin, 'at the sight of that happy land we all gave a cry of joy like that the Trojans who had escaped Ileum's disaster gave when they discerned the shores of Italy':

> I know of only one similar scene which would compare with it: when Aeneas came ashore with his fleet at Epirus after the capture of Troy . . . Aeneas, who had an excellent heart, Helenus who as the best of the Trojans and Andromache, the tender wife of Hector, shed many tears and heaved many sighs on this occasion. I am prepared to believe that their emotion was no less than ours, but after Helenus, Aeneas and Andromache and us, we must draw the line.

But Robespierre also used his letter to reflect on some of his personal idiosyncracies. He recognized, with some self-deprecation, that ambition and a thin skin were as much part of his character as his capacity for sustained work. The trip had not begun well. The young man, flushed with the excitement of seeing his extended family, had apparently expected other Arrageois to share his sense of occasion. Instead, as he left through the Méaulens gate in the north of Arras early in the morning he passed by stony faces: 'these shopkeepers, stock still in the doorways of their huts, gazed at me fixedly without returning my greeting. I have always had a lot of pride; this sign of contempt cut me to the quick and put me in a seriously bad temper for the rest of the day'. In contrast, he was delighted when his arrival in Carvin—a much smaller town of 3,500 people—caused something of a commotion. His time with his relatives was passed in a glow of warm chatter and feasting. Robespierre plainly had a taste for the pastries of Artois:

> Since we arrived, every moment has been filled with pleasures. Since last Saturday, I have been stuffing myself with tarts. Fate placed my bed in the room where the *patisseries* are kept; this exposes me to the temptation of eating all night long, but I determined that it is good to control one's passions and slept amid these seductive objects. It is true that during the day I made up for this long abstinence.

Maximilien had also dined in Carvin with the local notables, including the Lieutenant of Carvin, 'who shone like Calypso among her nymphs'. He concluded his long letter to Charlotte Buissart with an elaborate and passionate statement of his affection for her:

> We will see each other with the same satisfaction as Ulysses and Telemachus after twenty years' absence. I will forget my bailiffs and lieutenants without difficulty. However seductive a lieutenant may be, Madame, believe me, he cannot compare with you. His face, even when champagne imparts its rosy glow to it, does not display the charm which nature alone gives to yours and the company of all the bailiffs in the world could not console me for the loss of your amiable conversation.

Those who have studied the world of eighteenth-century letters have been struck by the effusiveness of the 'language of endearment' between friends.[23] Robespierre was no exception, and his written expressions of affection, while undoubtedly sincere, were to be marked by such explicit statements of love. This was particularly so for the Buissarts.

Antoine Buissart was also President of the Royal Academy of Arras, the cultural heart of Artois, which comprised a mixture of nobles and clergy from long-established elite families and professional men. Once again, Robespierre enjoyed rapid access through the friendship of those he had impressed on his return, and he had just made his mark in the Vissery case. He was received as one of the thirty members of the Academy on 15 November 1783, nominated by Buissart and Dubois de Fosseux. In the Academy, Robespierre encountered the elite of Arras society and the legal profession, men such as the lawyer Martial Herman, who worked for the royal prosecutor at the Council of Artois; his father was registrar at the Estates and had been a municipal councillor in Arras.[24]

In 1783 the Royal Academy in Arras had taken as its mascot and emblem young eaglets trying their wings at the edge of their nest, and Robespierre was one of three such eaglets in April 1784. The three members-elect each spoke on a particular subject: the lawyer Le Sage spoke against the abuse of talent; Ansart, a doctor (and relative of the lawyer who had reported so warmly on Robespierre's arrival back in Arras), held forth on atmospheric air; while Robespierre 'undertook to prove the origin, the injustice and the disadvantages of the prejudice which causes the infamy of criminals to spill over onto their relatives.[25]

Robespierre had taken the idea of his inaugural speech from the essay-prize topics set by the Royal Society for Sciences and Arts of Metz. He addressed the set questions on the origin of the 'judgement which spreads the shame of the penalties involving the loss of civil rights to all members of the family of a guilty person. Is this judgement more pernicious than useful? And if we decide that it is, how might we avert the disadvantages resulting from it?'[26] His response drew directly on the reflections of Montesquieu on the 'spirit' of monarchical government, on the English philosopher Francis Bacon, and indirectly on Beccaria, demonstrating that he had acquired far more in Paris than the capacity to make classical allusions.

Most importantly, his response revealed Robespierre's core assumption about moral virtue as the foundation stone of healthy societies: 'virtue produces happiness, as the sun produces light, while unhappiness is the result of crime, just as a dirty insect is born in the heart of decay'. His generation of educated middle-class young men had absorbed from Montesquieu, Rousseau and the classics the certainty that a healthy society and its polity were founded on the civic and private virtues. Fundamental to his argument about the origin of the prejudice and the way to erase it was a distinction between forms of government and their underpinning values. 'In despotic states, the law is no more than the will of the prince.' In contrast, referring to Montesquieu, he asserted that

> The essential mainspring of republics is virtue, as the author of *The Spirit of the Laws* has proved, that is to say political virtue which is nothing else but the love of law and country. Their constitutions demand that all peculiar interests, all personal ties, always give way to the general good.... [A citizen] must not spare even the most beloved guilty person when the welfare of the republic demands his punishment.

But this must be a vigilance combined with judicial exactitude: 'we constantly repeat the just maxim that it is better to spare a hundred guilty men than to sacrifice a single innocent one'.

Shortly after making his presentation to the Academy in Arras, Robespierre sent his speech, with a few additions, to the Royal Society of Metz. The prize for the proposed topic was a gold medal valued at 400 *livres*. The Society received twenty-two manuscript dissertations. After examination, it chose one by a barrister at the Paris Parlement, Pierre-Louis Lacretelle, a well-known Metz lawyer. Lacretelle commented generously if condescendingly on Robespierre's entry that 'it is filled with sound opinions and signs of a happy and correct talent'. In the end, the committee was so impressed with Robespierre's entry that he received a special prize of the same value, 400 *livres*, which he used to have it published at his own expense in Paris towards the end of 1784.[27]

Robespierre's speech to the Arras Academy and his success in Metz were a triumph for the young lawyer, but two aspects of his speech would have had his respectable audience on the edge of their seats. First, he went well beyond the legal parameters of the questions posed in the Metz competition to place under scrutiny the very code on which aristocratic society was based. It was something of a commonplace in philosophical and artistic expressions in the 1780s to evoke the perceived civic virtues of the ancient world. But Robespierre had gone further, by probing the foundation of a social order based on birth and its prejudices in monarchies based on 'honour': 'this very custom of making the esteem in which a citizen is held dependent on the antiquity of his lineage, on the fame of his family, the grandeur of his alliances, is already very much related to the prejudice I have spoken about'.[28]

Robespierre had thereby made clear to the most prestigious gathering of the elite of Arras that he regarded the values underpinning their social order as inherently prejudiced and unjust. Second, he singled out a particular example of the prejudice that came from loss of rights to all members of the family of a person guilty of particular crimes: 'I wish the law would impose no stain of any kind on bastards: I wish that it did not appear to punish the sins of their fathers through them by forbidding them civil positions and even church ministry . . .'. He called on those with 'the strength of reason and intelligence' to attack this 'odious prejudice, already greatly weakened by the progress of enlightenment'.

We can only speculate as to whether the barb in Robespierre's reference to noble scorn for commoners—indeed, his very choice of topic for his inaugural speech to the Academy—was an expression of enduring discomfort over the circumstances of his birth. He had not been born out of wedlock, but he must have wondered why his parents had married late in his mother's pregnancy. Did he feel that common knowledge of his father's shame—to be 'descended from a

stigmatized man'—would forever stain him in the eyes of those who mono-
polized power and status in his small provincial town?

Maximilien's intellect and desire for recognition had been sharpened by his
triumphs in the court case over the lightning conductor and in the Arras
Academy, and he decided to enter an essay in the annual prize given by the
Academy of Amiens. Three times it had offered a prize for a eulogy of the local
poet Jean-Baptiste Gresset (1709–77), without feeling able to make the award.
In 1784 it offered a prize for the fourth time, and the sum was to be quadrupled,
to 1,200 *livres*. Robespierre struggled with the essay throughout. He confessed
that, after Gresset's most famous poem, 'the remainder of his career has left little
in the way of literary production for me', instead emphasizing 'his virtue, his
respect for morality, his love of religion'. He took the opportunity to round
on Gresset's fashionable *philosophe* critics: 'writers, more famous for your aloofness than for your talent, you were born to temper the suffering of your fellows,
to cast a few flowers on the pathway of human life and you have sunk to
poisoning it'.[29]

Once again the Amiens judges were strict and refused to award the prize. It
may be that the deliberate enthusiasm of Robespierre's eulogy had been too
obvious, for he had forced himself to praise the Bishop of Amiens, who had been
involved in the case of the Chevalier de la Barre in 1766, who was tortured and
beheaded for sacrilege before his body was burnt on a pyre along with Voltaire's
Philosophical Dictionary. But the essay consolidated his friendship with Dubois
de Fosseux who, on receiving a copy, responded with a long poem in which he
described his young friend as the

> Supporter of the unfortunate, avenger of the innocent,
> You live for virtue, for sweet friendship,
> And you can demand equal measure from my heart.[30]

Robespierre would soon be on more familiar territory in a protracted court case
that was to alienate members of the Church who had paid for his education, and
the established lawyers who might have pushed clients his way.

CHAPTER 4

'Bachelorhood seems to encourage rebelliousness'

ARRAS 1784–89

Robespierre had profound respect for religion and for many of those who practised in its institutions. He had accepted a position on the Episcopal Court in Arras, and in 1784 defended the local Oratorians—his former teachers—against an architect seeking payment for renovations. He also received requests from individual clerics to act in court cases.[1] But he had begun to bother the clerical elite in his home town, and the stars of the Arras bar, like Liborel and François-André Desmazières, were increasingly wary of their young colleague. Liborel had sought to assist Robespierre on his return in 1781 but was to be his key opponent in the long and controversial case of the master shoemaker François-Joseph Deteuf against the Abbey of Anchin from 1783.[2]

Deteuf was accused of having stolen a large sum from a monk who had been employed as the abbey's bursar. In his defence, Deteuf alleged that the monk had accused him both in order to conceal his own thefts and because Deteuf's sister had refused his advances. Robespierre was uncompromising in his defence, displaying what would become a common and controversial strategy of placing a particular episode—in this case accusations against an allegedly debauched monk—in the context of a general attack on an institution. He recognized that 'virtuous' monks are 'valuable to the State, if not in the eyes of frivolous philosophers', but Deteuf 'can hardly provide coarse bread, drenched in his sweat, for his family, while the tranquil inhabitants of the monastery which oppressed him spend their time, in the midst of abundance, in seeking ways to defy his just claim'.

The case dragged on to a successful but rancorous conclusion in 1786, when Robespierre was reprimanded by the Arras bar for 'outrageous remarks concerning the authority of the law and jurisprudence, and insulting to the judges'. The matter was only finally brought to an end by an out-of-court settlement in which Robespierre undertook to withdraw some of his allegations and the abbey offered a considerable material compensation to Deteuf. The sanction did not deter Robespierre and in 1787 he was reprimanded again during another case for 'expressions derogatory to the authority of the Law . . . and insulting to the bench'.[3]

Although Robespierre had only been in the Royal Academy of Arras for one year, when its permanent secretary died in 1785 Robespierre tried to succeed him, but won only one vote of the twelve cast in December, in which ten favoured Dubois de Fosseux. The Academy would reach a national audience under the aegis of its energetic secretary, a nobleman with remarkable standing in the region and who had befriended Robespierre. It is likely that Robespierre maintained close links with his rural relatives through the Carrauts' family farm at Lattre-St-Quentin, and the Carrauts may have had ties to Dubois through his estate at nearby Fosseux; indeed, Dubois gently chided Robespierre that he had missed a session of the Academy in October 1786 because he was 'gambolling about in our district'.[4]

In April 1785 the Academy decided to set for its annual essay competition a question on whether it was desirable to subdivide the large leasehold farms in Artois and, if so, what should be their optimal size. One of those attracted by the topic was a young Picard official of peasant background, François-Noël Babeuf, but his radical essay was received too late to be accepted. Babeuf became one of the most assiduous of the twelve hundred correspondents with whom Dubois exchanged a prodigious twenty-one thousand letters on behalf of the Academy after 1785, from as far away as the merchant Jean-Paul Berge in Collioure on the Spanish border. We do not know whether Robespierre was involved with setting the initial topic that invited Babeuf's egalitarian agrarian proposal; certainly, however, he was well aware of the topic and its essayists. He had also made what would be a lasting impact on Babeuf, for whom 'M. de Robespierre is not interested in making money. He is, and will always remain, the lawyer only of the poor'.[5]

Despite Robespierre's increasing outspokenness in court, his ambitions were not begrudged by his fellow academicians, and in February 1786 he was elected the Academy's director for one year, from April. He was now at the pinnacle of intellectual life in Arras. Traditionally, the new director made a speech, and Robespierre could have recited a series of platitudes about the importance of knowledge and morality. What he resolved to do instead was startling, and recalled his inaugural speech two years earlier when he had fulminated against the legal disadvantages suffered by children born outside wedlock. On 27 April Robespierre spoke 'for seven quarters of an hour' on 'legislation governing the rights and conditions of bastards'. Everyone present knew of his family scandal. He decided to confront the core question of the rights of children conceived outside marriage, with a calm passion, not once referring to himself. His speech was a *tour de force* to which colleagues still referred years later.

Robespierre defined the objective of his speech as 'the protection and happiness of a significant part of humankind'. The speech was memorable not only for a blunt statement that expressed his core belief in the need to address social inequality—'poverty corrupts the People's behaviour and degrades its soul; it predisposes it to crime'—but also because he defined his attitude to marriage and the family as the basis of society:

> Marriage is a fertile source of virtues: it ties the heart to thousands of worthy objects, it accustoms it to the gentle passions, to honest sentiments. It is a rule derived from Nature herself; when one becomes a father, one generally becomes a more honest man. This is especially true for the class of men I'm speaking of. A wife, children are powerful ties which bind a servant to the duties of his estate; they are precious guarantors of fidelity and submission. I do not know why one would prefer to servants of this type, isolated beings in whom the independence of bachelorhood seems to encourage rebelliousness and licence.

It was essential that 'the views of government change with the times and follow the trend of public ideas and customs'. He concluded, more boldly, that children conceived outside marriage should enjoy their father's name and status, and even property rights through inheritance.[6]

Robespierre's former teacher at Louis-le-Grand, the Abbé Proyart, had kept in touch with his clerical peers in his home town and his scathing interpretation of Robespierre's career in the 1780s may reflect accurately the way that senior clergy felt about the difficult young lawyer for whom 'no authority was innocent':[7]

> he never reached the height of his ambition, which was to insinuate himself into the confidence of the Nobles and his Provincial Church hierarchy.

> Despairing of making his services agreeable to the Landed Class, or to anyone with a good Cause or great interests to defend, he devoted himself to every kind of baseness to which the Profession of Lawyer can stoop.

> Thus he wrote against marriage, and in favour of legalizing the political and religious crime of divorce. Thus he built himself up as the Patron of licentiousness, to the point of wanting, in a sense, to authorise polygamy, and to claim that Bastards, even the fruits of adultery, should be included with legitimate Children in the apportionment of the goods of their Progenitors.

Robespierre's presence in the Academy gave him the opportunity to extend his circle of talented acquaintances. Among the men he met in this milieu was a brilliant young army captain in the Arras garrison, Lazare Carnot, already known for his *In Praise of Vauban*, which had received a gold medal at the Academy of Dijon in 1784. Carnot was elected to the Academy of Arras in 1787; he could not know how closely his life would later be tied to Maximilien's.[8] In his capacity as director, Robespierre presided over the Academy's annual public sitting in April 1787 to celebrate the admission of four new honorary members *in absentia*. Among them were two literary women: Marie Le Masson Le Golft of Le Havre and Louise de Kéralio, then living in Paris. The proceedings of the sitting record Robespierre's reply to the speech of thanks from Kéralio, read by the secretary Dubois. Robespierre took the chance to argue that women should be admitted to literary societies on the grounds of the complementarity of their 'nature' with that of men: 'the strength and depth which characterize the genius of Man, the attractiveness and delicacy that distinguish that of Woman . . .'. But he insisted that the academies should be as open to women as to men, not as 'vain adornments of the universe, but to contribute to the glory and the happiness of society'. Robespierre was highly unusual in going beyond conventional gallantries to consider seriously the civic rights of women. His argument delighted Dubois, who circulated it widely, sparking a debate in many academies about women's equal—if complementary—capacities. Robespierre may have regarded Jean-Jacques Rousseau as his intellectual master, but he here parted company with him on the constraints of biology.[9]

One important social and cultural gathering in the town had not included Robespierre in its ranks. In June 1778 a number of young men commencing careers in law, medicine or theology had gathered in a garden at nearby Blangy 'from friendship, through their taste for poetry, roses and wine'. Such was the happy memory of that day that they had resolved to meet each year at the same time. The friendship they promised to celebrate would become the 'Rosati', and its membership a prize for the literati of Arras.[10]

It was not until 1787 that Robespierre became a member. In the speech that Louis Legay, his colleague at the Arras bar, addressed to him on the occasion, he referred to the works of Robespierre since 1782, including the essay that had won an award from the Academy of Metz in defence of children born outside wedlock. The lawyers had been on opposite sides in the Vissery case and Robespierre had strongly opposed Legay's admission to the Academy, and it may be that Robespierre's late invitation to join the Rosati was a calculated admonition. Nevertheless, he was obviously delighted to join and the choice of Legay himself to present his diploma was inspired. Legay welcomed him to share 'the grassy bank on which we become intoxicated, with the cup of Bacchus in our hand, by the voluptuous scents of the rose, born from the blood of Adonis':

> The man whose energetic pen has successfully fought against a prejudice which, in this most enlightened century, links the innocent to the punishment of the guilty; . . . the man whose voice was raised, no less eloquently, against a legislative fault which deprives the unfortunate child whose father and mother inhumanely hide from him out of shame at his birth some of the rights common to all citizens; the man who, from his first steps in a career at the bar has arrested the gaze of his compatriots . . .

Following the usual custom, a diploma in verse was presented to Robespierre, 'who shines in more ways than one', by the Abbé Berthe. He celebrated

Maximilien's facility to deliver 'a sparkling word, a satirical point', while noting that these could be caustic. Berthe was sure that he 'knows how to sing and to drink'; but Robespierre was known to be abstemious, and one of the Rosati's founders, Louis Charamond, then teased him in a poem for drinking water:

Is he a bowl (*aiguière*)?
Is he an aqueduct?

Robespierre was not a gifted singer either. He was immediately chosen to present a poem on 'the Rose' to welcome another new member, another legal rival from the lightning-conductor case, Foacier de Ruzé, 'in which the only faults were the false notes of the singer—M. de Robespierre'. Maximilien celebrated the Rosati by reciting a list of its intellectual forebears: the Greeks and Romans he had studied at Louis-le-Grand, and 'Charlemagne, Charles V, St Louis, Louis XII, Henri IV, Chaulieu, Catinat, Corneille, Fénelon, Vauban, and Condé among the French'. Notably missing from his list of 'men of genius and virtue' were both Jesus and the Christian martyrs and the stars of the Enlightenment.[11]

The Rosati was not a gathering that concerned itself with public affairs; rather it was a place where invitees felt privileged to be among those of like sensibilities who enjoyed literary games, friendship and, above all, fun. In Lazare Carnot's words, 'the Rosati Society is not made up of grave moralists'. It was, nonetheless, a group of self-consciously enlightened men whose networks of ideas and influence pervaded Arras. It was most likely through the Rosati that Robespierre first encountered Joseph Fouché, from January 1788 a science teacher for the Oratorian order at the College of Arras, and who perhaps courted his sister Charlotte.[12] Like Carnot, he would soon be reunited with Maximilien in radically different circumstances.

Robespierre had reached a pinnacle of success in 1787: six years after his celebrated but awkward return to his home town, he was a key figure in the local Academy and the Rosati, and had won a series of major court cases. He had achieved wider recognition as well. He had sent his Paris schoolmate Louis Beffroy de Reigny copies of his publications about Gresset and the lightning conductor, and in 1786 Beffroy commented of Robespierre in his literary review

Les Lunes du cousin Jacques that 'he is not at all surprised by the elegant style and ingenious thoughts'. Beffroy 'remembers perfectly well the role played at the College by his likeable fellow-student; a talent like his cannot be forgotten'.[13] But Maximilien was now twenty-nine, and most of the professional men with whom he associated were married with families. Just as he was celebrating his great triumph in the Deteuf case, and was recognized by his peers in the Academy, he was also longing for love.

Robespierre used the interest a 'kind and famous lady' had taken in a case to write an affectionate if reserved letter to her: 'when one has defended the cause of the unfortunate with the deep and painful feelings the injustice one is compelled to overcome inspires . . . the sweetest, most wonderful [reward] of all is to be able to communicate these feelings to a kind and famous lady whose noble spirit is made to share them'. We do not know whether this was the same woman whose 'spiteful' letter Maximilien responded to six months later in June 1787, but he was obviously hurt and bewildered. He made a declaration of love: 'as for the spiteful things in your letter, I shall respond with a faithful statement of my feelings. The interest I take in people is unlimited, where people like you are concerned. The interest you have inspired in all who appreciate you will die in me only when I am no longer interested in anything, because I know of no-one worthier than you of arousing it.' Three weeks later he wrote again, sending her a copy of a piece of writing, perhaps one of his pleas to the Council.[14] It was a brief and sad letter, a confession from Maximilien of his own unhappiness and a longing to be the source of happiness for someone else: 'the position you are in is absolutely unimportant provided that you are happy. But are you happy? I rather doubt it and the doubt distresses me, because if one is not happy oneself, one would like to take consolation from the happiness of others; one would at least like to see those who most deserve happiness attain it.'

In October 1786 Maximilien wrote a personal letter of support to a woman in Béthune whose case he was fighting, advising her to deal with 'the tricks of the wicked' by retreating into 'your inner self, which is made to console you for the baseness of vile and cruel beings'. This may have been the Mademoiselle Duhay who had given him and Charlotte the canaries in 1782: 'they are very pretty; having been raised by you'. It is likely that she was the recipient of another letter, in June 1788:[15]

It is rare to be able to present a pretty woman with a piece of writing such as the one I am sending you. . . . I beg you to let me know immediately as soon as you find my memoranda boring, so that I can stop writing them as soon as you stop reading them.

Is the puppy you are raising for my sister as pretty as the one you showed me when I came to Béthune? Whatever it is like, it will be received with discrimination and with pleasure. We may even say that however ugly it may be, it will always be pretty. . . . However that may be, my sister asks me to express all that is most affectionate on her behalf, and I am not a man to be less than her when it comes to doing that.

Robespierre wrote other poems, unpublished during his lifetime, one being an attempt at wit in describing the uselessness of handkerchiefs: our forebears 'blew their noses without handkerchiefs and were the happier for it'. Two that were in fact published in 1786–87 were dedicated to Ophélie Mondlen, whom Maximilien had met in Paris. The first was in praise of the 'country man', in which he eulogized the honesty of the simple life of the self-sufficient peasant and his family, troubled 'neither by crime nor terror'. The second was a 'Madrigal':

Believe me, young and lovely Ophélie
Whatever the world says and despite your mirror
Happy in ignorance and beauty,
Keep your modesty always.
Be always wary of the power of your charms.
You will be all the more beloved
If you fear not being so.[16]

Perhaps there were many other love poems and letters: recipients of declarations of love rarely keep them or pass them on if they are unrequited, even if expressed as delicately as were Maximilien's. After 1794, there were other good reasons to dispose of them. We cannot know why his expressions of affection did not result in marriage. Certainly, he was unprepossessing physically. He was short even for the times (perhaps 5 feet 3 inches), slim, with light-brown hair and a pale and slightly pockmarked face. He had poor eyesight and needed spectacles, at times two pairs at once. He also had an uncontrollable facial twitch, affecting his eyes and at times his mouth.[17]

Even if an attractive match as a successful, intelligent lawyer, he may have seemed intimidating. His habit of offering copies of his speeches in court as gifts rather than flowers may not have been endearing. According to one unfriendly observer, Proyart again, 'he even affected a certain austerity in his morals', and this 'distanced him from all dealings with women'.[18] Certainly, however, he had tried repeatedly and tenderly to communicate feelings of affection. Indeed, according to Charlotte, in the years after 1787 he was courting Anaïs Deshorties, his aunt Eulalie's stepdaughter, and it was widely assumed that they would marry.[19]

So the bright and controversial lawyer was both admired and rebuffed. Some found his prolixity and sententiousness irritating. A fellow academician versified:

Robespierre, always the same
Making great strides against prejudice
Always interesting, as he hastens towards his goal
How much shorter it would have seemed without my watch.[20]

Robespierre's predilection for uttering bold pronouncements about wider wrongs in his statements to the courts ensured that legal officers were wary of putting cases his way. In all he had about 110 cases after 1782 and, although overwhelmingly successful, these cases ensured only a modest income.[21] His least successful year was 1785, when he appeared in just twelve cases over fourteen sitting days; 1787 was his busiest year, when he appeared at the bar in twenty-four cases over twenty-five days. In contrast, eight other Arras lawyers had more than fifty cases in 1788. He was without the personal connections to have established a large, lucrative office, but successful enough to maintain a household. In 1787 he and Charlotte moved into a comfortable if modest three-storey house at 9 Rue des Rapporteurs, close to the Council of Artois and just a few steps away from an imposing new theatre 'à l'italienne' constructed in 1785. There they were of sufficient means to have a domestic servant.[22]

By 1787, then, Robespierre was a reasonably successful, at times brilliant, but often troublesome provincial lawyer. He had reached the pinnacle of professional and cultural life in Artois, despite a modest income, but had become increasingly blunt in his critique of the codes of 'honour' underpinning aristocratic society and what he saw as the prejudices and inequities that surrounded him. There was nothing to suggest that Maximilien would not live out his life in this way, entering middle age with Charlotte, caustic about the narrow elite that ruled his province, and saddened that he was not a husband and father instead of one of those 'isolated beings in whom the independence of bachelorhood seems to encourage rebelliousness'.[23] Instead, the kingdom's financial crisis created a situation in which he quickly saw the chance to participate in debates of the highest importance about political power and social justice. His life was to be turned upside down.

In 1787 there had been protracted battles over the power of the aristocratic high courts, or *parlements*, to refuse to register royal decrees. In May 1788, Louis XVI presented to the Parlement of Paris edicts that profoundly altered the organization of the judiciary, effectively taking registration of laws out of the hands of the high courts, and allowing the sovereign to impose new taxes. Like lawyers across the country whose livelihoods and identities were bound up with provincial legal institutions, Robespierre's initial response to the king's reforms was suspicious and negative. The Episcopal Court, on which Robespierre sat, refused to comply 'because the law had not previously been confirmed by the Council'. Like his reform-minded colleagues, Robespierre could not imagine that institutional structures could ever change, and in mid-1788 'ministerial despotism' was the most readily identifiable new threat.[24]

But everything did change with Louis' announcement on 8 August that the Estates-General would convene at Versailles in May 1789, the first such gathering of representatives of the three estates since 1614. France's successful involvement in the war of independence waged by Britain's North American colonies in 1775–83 had partially avenged the humiliations Britain had inflicted in India, Canada and the Caribbean; however, the war had cost France over one billion *livres*, more than twice the usual annual revenue of the state. As the treasury sank into financial crisis after 1783, the costs of servicing this massive debt impelled the monarchy to seek ways of ending the immunity of nobles from taxation. Tensions between the Crown and nobility came to a head in August 1788, with the Parlements insisting that the measures which the king's ministry sought to impose amounted to 'royal despotism'. In such a situation, both sides looked to an Estates-General to provide legitimacy for their claims. They were both mistaken. Instead, the calling of the Estates-General for May 1789 facilitated the expression of tensions at every level of French society, including in Artois.

This was only the immediate reflection of a longer and deeper crisis within French society. The long-term needs of royal state-making that fuelled pressures to remove the nobility's fiscal immunities were paralleled by other challenges to the nobility, in particular from wealthier, larger and more critical professional and commercial classes. Across urban France, a civic culture of 'public opinion' developed in the 1770s and 1780s. A language popularizing concepts of citizen, nation, reason, social contract and 'general will' was being articulated, which clashed with an older aristocratic discourse of orders, customs and corporations. This was certainly the case in Arras, where Robespierre and his peers were self-conscious in their appeals to the language of 'reason'.

The remarkable vigour of debate in the months before May 1789 was facilitated by the suspension of press censorship and the publication of several thousand political pamphlets. This war of words was fuelled by Louis' indecision about the procedures to be followed at Versailles. Would representatives of the three orders meet separately, as at the previous meeting in 1614, or in a single chamber? Louis' decision on 5 December to double the size of the Third Estate representation only served to highlight further this crucial issue of political power, because he remained silent on how voting would occur.

With the calling of the Estates-General, Robespierre would have the opportunity to articulate the grievances smouldering within, and to appeal to the court of public opinion rather than to the courts which served to underpin a system that he had concluded was fundamentally unjust. He seized the occasion with alacrity, directing his oratory and powers of prose against the local privileged elites who sought to dominate the nomination of those who would represent the province at Versailles in May 1789.[25]

A sad coincidence provided Robespierre with the opportunity to set out his grievances and hopes. In September 1788 he heard of the death of Mercier-Dupaty, president of the Parlement of Bordeaux, the eminent author and judicial reformer to whom he had written glowingly when a law student a decade earlier. The Academy of La Rochelle decided to publicize an essay competition in Dupaty's honour. It is almost certain that the author of the eulogy published in

1789, 'M. R., lawyer in *parlement*', was Robespierre. Prominent among Dupaty's concerns—and Robespierre's—had been degrading punishments: Dupaty had most recently been closely involved in controversy over the use of breaking on the wheel in a notorious case in 1783–87. Robespierre's eulogy was striking for his identification with an age that had begun to attack the bounds of cruelty and superstition, and for his idealized role, like Dupaty's, as 'the virtuous citizen who watches over the execution of the law within its walls and keeps order and harmony there':[26]

> He who aspires to the glory of being useful to his fellow citizens, who makes such great and sublime use of his capacities, who dares to say to the powerful of this world, 'You have committed an injustice,' and thus raises himself above other men, must, no doubt, expect to have dangerous enemies: he must believe that hatred and vengefulness will join with envy to bring him down. This has ever been the fate of great men.

But Robespierre went far further than a conventional eulogy of a man of principle setting an example to the legal profession. In attacking 'barbarous prejudices' and 'the outrages to which humanity has been subjected', he returned to his key theme of the vulnerability of the 'poor and unknown, unfortunate victims of our criminal laws'. 'Do you know why there are so many indigents?', he asked:

> It's because you hold all the wealth in your greedy hands. Why are this father, this mother, these children exposed to all the rigours of the weather, without a roof over their heads, suffering all the horrors of hunger? It's because you inhabit sumptuous houses to which your gold attracts everything which can serve your flabbiness and occupy your idleness. It's because your luxury devours the sustenance of a thousand men in a single day.[27]

Robespierre's attack on privilege and idle wealth—and the tenor of Artois' participation in the lead-up to the convening of the Estates-General—was made in the context of a serious harvest crisis that hit most of the kingdom. The level of interest in public affairs also encouraged the foundation of a local newspaper, the *Affiches d'Artois*, the first number of which appeared on 2 December 1788.[28]

Adding to the sense of moment were events across the border. Thousands of defeated Dutch 'patriots' had earlier taken refuge in northern France, dependent on Louis' good graces for shelter and support, yet bitter about the failure of the king and his government to come to their aid during their insurrection against their Prussian rulers in 1787.[29] By March 1788, the refugees had been brought under the authority of the French monarchy and dispersed into refugee depots in nearby St-Omer, Gravelines, Dunkirk and Béthune. Their presence was a constant reminder of the promise and failure of change.

Who would be eligible to choose deputies to attend the Estates-General, and what would be the basis of the constituencies that did so? The only noblemen with seats in the Estates of Artois were those who could prove the requisite generations of nobility and who were the lords of parishes or principal churches. The clergy was represented by the bishops of Arras and St-Omer, the abbots of eighteen monasteries, as well as the heads of the chapterhouses and collegial churches of the diocese; the parish priests had no voice.[30] The Third Estate was represented by the municipal councillors of Arras and the deputies of other major towns, but each deputation had only one to three votes, so that the entire Estate was represented in fact by only about thirty votes, all urban, as against almost forty for the clergy and one hundred for the nobility. Moreover, the Estates had guarded the power of nominating the councillors of the towns: the Third Estate deputies were, hardly surprisingly, those most comfortable within the power structures of the region.

The Estates of Artois met in Arras in December 1788 and insisted that 'the primary source of the People's woes is the vices of its Government'. Robespierre now burned his bridges with the privileged orders of Artois. He was already detested by local notables following the 1788 publication of his *Letter addressed by an advocate of the Council of Artois to his friend, advocate at the Parlement of Douai*, in which he railed against the claims of the Estates to represent the province and which he revisited with the announcement of the calling of the Estates-General. In January 1789, in a brochure entitled *To the Artois Nation, on the necessity of reforming the Estates of Artois*, he denounced those privileged bodies that he claimed were nothing but 'a league of a few citizens who by themselves have seized the power that belongs only to Peoples'. The eighty-three-page brochure was anonymous, but no one was in any doubt about the authorship of the sweeping—and at times inexact—broadside.[31]

To Robespierre the Estates of Artois had become nothing but a self-perpetuating oligarchy where even representatives of the Third Estate were chosen by the privileged orders, and so he called bluntly for representatives to be directly elected. But while returning to the people 'the freedom to choose its own representatives', he saw those representatives as having to speak on the people's behalf: 'the great mass of the people who inhabit our towns and countryside are crushed by poverty, to the extreme where, completely absorbed in the cares of maintaining their survival, they are incapable of reflecting on the causes of their misfortune, of knowing the rights that nature has given them . . .'. Liborel, still smarting from his clashes with Robespierre during the Deteuf case, and also a long-standing municipal officer in Arras, fulminated in response that 'sordid self-interest and base greed is at your heart, and rampant jealousy is leading you to try to drag down to your level talented men and disinterested lawyers who owe their public standing only to their ability and enlightenment'.[32] Like their peers in France's other provinces, the legal fraternity in Arras had had an *esprit de corps* that was based on generational and family ties, and on the sense of elite difference inculcated by immersion through Latin in the world of the ancients.[33] As the exigencies of the kingdom's bankruptcy brought into sharp focus the perquisites of privilege in the 1780s, this solidarity was sundered. Robespierre and his former mentors were rapidly and sharply estranged.

On 24 January 1789 Louis announced the details of the forthcoming meeting of the Estates-General to resolve such problems of electoral process in Artois, as elsewhere. The Estates of Artois now found their traditional powers undermined by the Crown. The 'constitutions' of the provincial Estates were effectively abolished and the members of the Estates lost their positions as representatives.[34] This was a highly charged situation. On 22 February, Robespierre's fellow Rosati, Charamond, wrote to Dubois de Fosseux of 'News from the Bar': 'last Friday there was a dispute between Messrs Le Sage and de Robespierre, the latter having been publicly described by the other as a rascal, a *foutaquin* [likely a variant of *foutriquet*—a pipsqueak], while shoving his fist in his face'. Le Sage, 'taken with drink', made it known that he would refuse to sit on a magistrate's court in future with Robespierre. The Arras judiciary was fracturing, for many lawyers regarded this as 'a public affront to all lawyers who are happy to communicate and plead with Robespierre', and resolved to boycott the court.[35]

Robespierre had a key case to plead before the Council of Artois in early 1789, and made the most of the tense national context to refer to the special role the king was to play 'to lead men to happiness and virtue'.[36] The case concerned an elderly farmer who had been imprisoned under a royal arrest warrant (*lettre de cachet*) in 1774. He was freed in November 1786, but without restitution of property rights. He then turned to Robespierre who, early in 1789, appeared before the Council. Again Robespierre's *mémoire* to the court went further than an attack on the 'horrible system of *lettres de cachet*', under the guise of an appeal to the king in the context of the looming Estates-General in May. No government had achieved God's will that mankind should enjoy happiness and justice; but now Louis XVI was called by Providence to usher in a reign of virtue that would make France God's chosen land. Robespierre's long, emotional speech to the court was above all a plea to Louis in the context of 1789, in which his role would be

to lead men to happiness, through virtue, and to virtue through legislation founded on the immutable principles of universal morality. . . . Cast your eyes beyond this shining circle of courtiers, who hide princes from the sight of men, beyond those magnificent palaces that hide the cottages from them and behold the artisans, the labourers in despair . . . *the People*, so holy and so majestic in the eyes of reason, almost forced, by excessive poverty, into forgetting the dignity of Man and the principles of morality.[37]

On 7 March 1789, Louis XVI announced that all electoral procedures in Artois would be the same as those in the rest of France. Arras, the seat of the Estates, had thus lost an institution emblematic of its role of provincial capital, and Robespierre had been vindicated. But how would the eight Third Estate representatives for Artois be chosen? Robespierre published a second expanded edition of *To the Artois Nation*, probably in April, the basis of a remarkably energetic electoral campaign.[38] At the heart of the debates about power and its representation was the question of how the countryside was to be represented. Not only were the Third Estate representatives of the towns not chosen by their inhabitants but, stated Robespierre, the countryside had no representation at all. One consequence of this was the lack of measures taken by the Estates to remedy the crippling economic situation of subsistence in the province: 'on every side unfortunates water with tears of despair the earth that their sweat fertilized in vain.'[39] Robespierre had articulated two key political principles at the core of his view of the world: the poor are deserving of justice in an unjust world; and there should be democratic representation.

In the spring of 1789, people all over France were also required to formulate proposals for the reform of public life by compiling 'lists of grievances' (*cahiers de doléances*) to present to the king. The drawing up of these *cahiers* in the context of an economic subsistence crisis, political uncertainty and fiscal chaos was a decisive moment in focusing social friction. At least on the surface, the *cahiers* drawn up by all three orders revealed a remarkable level of agreement: they assumed that the meeting of the Estates-General in May would be but the first of a regular cycle; and they saw the need for comprehensive reform to taxation, the judiciary, the Catholic Church and administration. On fundamental matters of social order and political power, however, entrenched divisions were to undermine the possibilities of consensual reform. Rural communities and the nobility were in sharp disagreement about seigneurial dues, and bourgeois across the country challenged the nobility by advocating 'careers open to talent', equality of taxation, and the ending of privilege. Many parish priests agreed with the commons about taxation reform in particular, while insisting on the prerogatives of their own order.

In response to the increasing hostility of Arras' elites, Robespierre presented himself as the defender of the interests of the countryside and of working people in the towns. In March he was invited to meet the Guild of Shoemakers or Lesser Cobblers, who asked him to draft their *cahier*. The shoemakers were one of Arras' thirty-nine guilds and corporations, and its poorest. He used the *cahier* to inveigh against the poverty and daily prejudices from which the poor suffered. In particular, he singled out the 1786 free-trade treaty with England, which had caused the price of leather to rise; as the wages of shoemakers had not risen in proportion, their incomes had collapsed. The shoemakers therefore asked 'the nation' to review the treaty.[40]

Robespierre had long since earned the enmity of the most powerful men in Arras: the bishop (Conzié), high nobles such as the Governor of Artois (the Duke de Guînes, from a prestigious noble family), the President of the Council of Artois (Briois de Beaumez), and prominent lawyers such as Liborel and Desmazières. For several years Beaumez had held weekly gatherings of the town's leading lawyers at his mansion, discussing ways in which the complex customary laws of Artois might be reformed. In March 1788 he had decided to exclude Robespierre, who had complained that the younger lawyers were smarting under the condescension of their superiors.[41] But the political battles of early 1789 also led Robespierre to confront one of the key members of the social and political elite, and an old friend: Ferdinand Dubois de Fosseux, seigneur of Fosseux, municipal councillor of Arras, permanent secretary of the Royal Academy, and an active Rosati. Dubois was uniformly respected and enjoyed wide support across Artois society, being not only closely involved in drafting the *cahier* of the Second Estate but also being asked to draft those of the Third Estate of Arras and of the entire district.

The assemblies of the Third Estate of Arras began in the church of the College of the Oratory, Robespierre's old school, at 7 a.m. on 23 March, when the corporations gathered, including the cobblers whose *cahier* Robespierre had drafted. A gruelling five-week period of electioneering had begun. Robespierre also attended another rowdy meeting, of citizens not in trade corporations, who proceeded to nominate twelve delegates to join the fifty-three from the corporations. Robespierre turned on the municipal councillors of Arras who, he argued, were too compromised by their involvement with the Estates of Artois and were in any case unrepresentative. Nominated by the Estates of Artois, except for two who were chosen by the bishop, the officers constituted an oligarchy that effectively had the capacity to designate its successors. They claimed to represent the community, however, and sought as such to dominate the coming elections to the Estates-General.[42]

The sixty-five delegates were to attend a meeting of the Third Estate in the Town Hall on 26 March with a view to drafting a single *cahier* for the commoners of Arras and to nominate the deputies to the Assembly of the *bailliage*, or district. Here frictions within the commons came to the surface. Some of the councillors—including Robespierre's old friend Dubois—sought to require the delegation to include eight men nominated by the municipal council itself. An angry debate that lasted all day saw them offered two, which Robespierre still considered excessive. The political battles and accusations were bruising. On 27 March the Baron d'Aix reported to Monseigneur the Count de Puységur of the stormy session:

Robespierre having intervened to speak of 'the unhappy people, long oppressed', the Mayor demanded that the speaker's words be expunged: 'M. de Robespierre replied that . . . in order to undertake the most prompt and certain means of giving it its precious and sacred rights, which had been stripped from it, he had not been able to avoid recalling that its fellow citizens had long been unhappy and oppressed.'[43]

Robespierre explicitly criticized his close friend Dubois, whom he felt had no right to speak in a Third Estate meeting.

The councillors in fact resigned on 28 March, but the next day Dubois sought again to exert influence over the drafting of the *cahier* for the Third Estate. By the time the Assembly reached the end of its four-day sitting, it had produced only an amalgam of grievances and advice, some of it contradictory, but needed to proceed to the nomination of the twenty-four deputies from Arras to the district Assembly. Robespierre was the fourteenth elected. On 30 March these 24 were among some 554 deputies who arrived at the church of the College of the Oratory, representing the 245 communities of the district of Arras.[44]

At about the same time as the second edition of *To the Artois Nation* appeared, Robespierre published, again anonymously, *The Enemies of the People Unmasked by an Account of What Happened in the Assemblies of the Third Estate of the City of Arras*.[45] In this he again attacked Dubois, as well as other lawyers who had thrown in their lot with the traditional structures of power. The *Affiches d'Artois* now labelled him 'the ingratiating babbler' (*le babil complimenteur*), and Liborel leapt to the defence of these alleged 'enemies': a gulf had opened that would never be bridged.

On 20 April 1789 more than one thousand representatives of the clergy, the nobility and the Third Estate met in St-Vaast to draft the general *cahiers* and to elect the deputies from Artois to the Estates-General to convene in Versailles on 5 May. Separate meetings of the three orders only confirmed the split that had emerged. The Duc de Guînes commented tartly on the role that Robespierre had played in rebuffing an attempt at reconciliation: 'each Order having retired to its Chamber, the Lieutenant-Governor, who presides over it, suggested to that of the Third that a deputation be sent to the first two Orders as a sign of its sentiments. A lawyer arose and said that no thanks were due to people who had done no more than renounce abuses. This view was adopted by the majority.'[46] Some of the 'old nobility' and the high clergy withdrew in outrage. Bishop Conzié declined to be elected, and was followed by Guînes. Four parish priests were elected as deputies, then four 'liberal' nobles, including a hero of the American War of Independence, Charles de Lameth. The election for the eight Third Estate deputies began on Friday, 24 April, and lasted until the 28th; it was particularly protracted because voting among the twelve hundred electors proceeded by the election of one deputy at a time. Robespierre was elected on the fourth ballot, joining two other lawyers, a merchant and four farmers.

The Abbé Proyart was scathing about Robespierre's electioneering:

We saw him constantly crawling at the feet of the People, [who are] ever credulous, although always duped by their most assiduous Flatterers. He had Village Folk as Kin, whom he had until then disdained and whom he barely knew; he remembered them when he thought they might be of use to him. He sent his Brother [Augustin] to them, charged with assuring them of his tender regard, and with making them, on one hand, imagine the great honour which would reflect on the entire Family if, through their good offices with the Peasants of their Canton, they contrived to have him named deputy to the Estates-General. . . .

While Robespierre the Younger thus went from Village to Village, seeking votes for his Brother, other voluntary Emissaries spread out among the bawdy-houses and bars of the City and Suburbs of Arras, winding people up, extolling Robespierre as a Great Man.[47]

Proyart accused Robespierre of using peasant hatred of conscription to stir up support. In actuality, there was much more on the minds of peasants than the military levies. Perhaps one-third of the rural communities of Artois were in open conflict with their seigneur over matters such as the control and use of disputed 'common lands', the lords' right to plant trees along paths and their monopoly over flour-mills, and the fastidiousness with which some seigneurs were revising registers of feudal dues payable by communities. As elsewhere in France, the calling of the Estates-General, and the king's instruction that rural parishes draw up their lists of grievances and participate in electing representatives, had served to heighten villagers' boldness and perceptions of the justice of their cause.[48]

There were many thousands of provincial professional men who shared Robespierre's critique of the structures of their society, even if few were as trenchant and bold in their articulation of the principles on which a better world might be based. Robespierre was not the first—and certainly not the last— young person who had come to see his home town with different eyes after a lengthy education in the metropolis. He had been torn between the need for acceptance in the town he loved and a growing irritation at its entrenched conservatism. Most important radicals and revolutionaries in modern history have come from provincial towns, like him educated and brilliant enough to understand how the system works and for whom, and yet so marginal to that system that it grated daily.

The Abbé Proyart was convinced that Robespierre would have remained an unpleasant provincial nobody had not Louis XVI provided the political opportunity in May 1789. For Proyart, the Revolution now under way was both unnecessary and regrettable, for it brought to the surface monsters who would otherwise have rotted slowly in a provincial backwater.[49] Robespierre might well have remained a small-town lawyer had other opportunities not presented themselves in 1788, but his life had been far from unremarkable: despite many personal sadnesses, he had had a brilliant education and a volatile, controversial career. Well before Louis announced that he was convening a meeting of the Estates-General, Robespierre had become thoroughly alienated from— and had alienated—those who occupied the highest positions in the complex, aristocratic hierarchies in the Church, judiciary and administration. In his opening speech to the Academy of Arras in April 1784 he had identified the codes of 'honour' of monarchical and noble society as the root cause of prejudice against the unfortunate. In his eulogy of Dupaty in 1788 he went much further, broadening this into an indictment of the poverty endemic in his society.[50]

A combination of his upbringing, his youthful success in Paris, his confidence in his own abilities and the companionship of a devoted, intelligent sister had instilled in Maximilien Robespierre a steely resilience and ambition. The stark confrontation with privileged interests during the winter of 1788–89 confirmed his daily experience as a lawyer across the previous few years. He polarized people: he inspired affection and admiration, but also indignation and even rage. His reputation as 'the people's lawyer' and passionate involvement in the acrimonious local politics of that winter and spring did not endear him to everyone, and his election as a Third Estate deputy was a close-run thing.

Robespierre now had only a few days to reach Versailles, where the opening of the Estates-General was set for 5 May. As he prepared to depart, his legal colleague Fourdrin furnished the *Affiches d'Artois* with a racehorse form-guide to the Artois deputies. Some notes were sycophantic—Charles de Lameth is 'a pure-blood blessed with the best qualities'. Others were witty—the farmer Petit is 'better suited to a cart than a saddle; eats a lot, drinks even more'. But Robespierre's was neither brief nor gentle:

> The Madman, a fearful two-headed nag [*double bidet à crains*], intolerant of bit and whip, as evil-tempered as a mule, dares bite only from behind for fear of the whip. People are astonished that he was chosen, but he is said to be destined to play the part of the laughable ass [*risible peccata*], following the brilliant races run by the likes of Mirabeau, Bergasse, Malouet, etc., whose gait he has been trained to mimic so grotesquely.[51]

Years before, Robespierre had acknowledged in his letter to Charlotte Buissart about his trip to Carvin that he had a thin skin. Fourdrin's personal barbs must have been as painful as they were cruel.

CHAPTER 5

'We are winning'
VERSAILLES 1789

ALMOST eight years had passed since Maximilien had taken the road home from Paris to Arras. Now, on the eve of his thirty-first birthday, he was returning south, to the capital of the realm at Versailles, ten miles west of Paris. The editor of the *Affiches d'Artois*, Barbe-Thérèse Marchand, was to claim later that she had assisted Robespierre move his modest wardrobe to the meeting of the Estates-General:

> a black cloth coat, a satin waistcoat in fairly good condition, a waistcoat of raz de Saint-Maur rather the worse for wear, three pairs of trousers—one of black velvet, one of black cloth, and one of serge. He possessed six shirts, six collars, six handkerchiefs, three pairs of stockings (one pair almost new), one pair of well-worn shoes, and a new pair. His lawyer's gown, carefully folded, was packed into this small trunk. If we add to this list two clothes-brushes, two shoe-brushes, a box containing silk, cotton, wool, and needles (for he did not scorn to sew on his own buttons), and a bag of powder and a puff, we have the young man's entire wardrobe.[1]

Robespierre took pains with his appearance, and never lost his habit of having a barber call each morning to shave him and powder and dress his wig. His clothing was sober, except for a predilection for colourful waistcoats. Those who had known him in Arras agreed that he was ambitious, fastidious and hard-working, but they disagreed about his character. Some found him reclusive and cold, calculating and envious; others who knew him well thought him affectionate and admirable, a lawyer of brilliance and principle. In any case, he was a seasoned and determined public advocate with a personal network and reputation, who was now moving to the centre of power, convinced of the sublime cause espoused by his peers across the kingdom and seasoned by his experiences in Arras.

The gathering of the Third Estate was an exhilarating experience for him. Here were 'the people's representatives' from all over the kingdom, speaking with the accents—and sometimes the languages—of Brittany and the Basque country, Roussillon and Alsace, Paris and the Périgord. But men who struggled to make sense of each other's accents found that they shared a deep affinity about the inequities of their society and its political forms, and a set of ideals on which a new age could be founded.

Robespierre was less affluent than most of his fellow Third Estate deputies, but in other ways was very much of the same milieu. In all, almost half the 646 commoner deputies were lawyers, men whose experience in public speaking, knowledge of affairs of state, and naturally 'oppositional' civic role equipped them with the confidence to claim to represent their fellow commoners. Like him, most of the lawyers and other professional men were from provincial centres, men whose careers had made them known and respected locally.[2]

The gathering of so many Third Estate representatives was unprecedented and, while all found such an occasion momentous, many found it intimidating, especially if they were new to the capital or from the distant south. Robespierre was neither. Paris—if not Versailles—was very familiar to him, unlike to most deputies. Apart from his fellow Artois deputies, there were others in the Estates-General or observing it whom he had met previously. There were old acquaintances from Louis-le-Grand: although Camille Desmoulins was the son of a seigneur from Picardy and Stanislas Fréron was related to a staunchly royalist family, they were both impassioned supporters of the rights of the Third Estate.[3] One of Robespierre's teachers at the college, Jean-Baptiste Dumouchel, was a clerical deputy, far more open to the idea of change than another master, Fréron's uncle the Abbé Royou.

The issue of whether the three Estates would meet separately or together was fundamental. Within two days of the royal reception of the deputies, the atmosphere was electrified when the Third Estate refused to meet separately to verify its credentials or take a roll call. It simply started deliberations in its meeting room. This was a momentous step. Maximilien's close friend in Arras, Antoine Buissart, was hungry for news, and on 24 May Robespierre wrote him a detailed account of his understanding of the events in the first three weeks of the Estates-General.[4] It was an acute and passionate letter, detailing the refusal of the Third Estate to follow the king's request to meet separately:

> The deputies of the commons (for the term Third Estate is proscribed here as a label from its former servitude) believed otherwise [and] resolved that all the powers of all the deputies of all classes had to be established in common by the entire National Assembly, and that if the clergy and nobility persisted in their refusal to join the body of the nation which resided in the commons, the commons would declare themselves to be the National Assembly and act accordingly.

He was delighted with the 'firm patriotism' of the Third Estate deputies from Artois, especially the farmers.

Robespierre was also full of praise for the Rennes deputy Isaac Le Chapelier and Jean-Paul Rabaut de St-Étienne, a Protestant pastor from Nîmes, even though he opposed the latter's motion to approach the two privileged orders in an attempt at mediation. On the other hand, some of those with the highest profiles had disappointed him: Jean-Joseph Mounier, Baron Malouet and even Target, to whom he had written with such respect as a student a decade earlier, and for whom Desmoulins was acting as secretary: Target now simply 'uttered commonplaces with a great deal of emphasis, aligning himself on the side which had already won the greatest number of votes'.[5]

Apart from a few 'rational' nobles, like the Marquis de Lafayette, Robespierre was scathing about the two main groups of aristocrats among the 282 noble deputies: those who had dominated the Parlements, or high courts, and who 'would sacrifice the entire human race' to preserve their power; and the 'great' of the court, 'who possess all the feelings suggested by the pride of aristocrats and the servile obsequiousness of courtesans'. Two-thirds of the 303 First Estate deputies were parish priests, and the minority of archbishops and bishops among the delegates were excoriated by Robespierre for the pressure they were applying to the priests who were naturally predisposed to join the commoners of the former Third Estate. 'They have gone so far as to insinuate that we want to attack the Catholic religion,' he complained.

At Versailles he lived close to the palace at 16 Rue d'Étang (today Rue du Maréchal Foch), with three Artois deputies who were farmers rather than with the other lawyers and property owners. His house was near to both the palace and the café Amaury where the Breton deputies gathered, and he rapidly became identified with and joined the more radical deputies informally known as the Breton Club, including Mirabeau, Jérôme Pétion, the Lameth brothers and the Abbé Sieyès.[6] These were deputies who had all the panache, *savoir faire* and social ease that Robespierre lacked. Many others were far more imposing in speech or physical stature. But what set him apart very early was his remarkable determination.

On 6 June, Robespierre made his first speech of note, attacking the Church hierarchy after the Archbishop of Nîmes had come to the Third Estate to beg it to begin the proceedings of the Estates-General in the interests of doing something for the poor. Robespierre retorted: 'let the bishops renounce a luxury which is an offence to Christian humility; let them sell their coaches and horses, and give that to the poor'. A liberal pastor from Geneva, Étienne Dumont, observing the session, recalled that 'everyone was asking who was the speaker; he was unknown'. He met Robespierre twice: 'he had a sinister look; he didn't look you in the face, he had a constant and irritating twitch in his eyes. . . . He told me that he was as shy as a child, that he trembled every time he approached the podium, and was hardly conscious of his surroundings (*il ne se sentait plus*) when he began to speak.'[7] Étienne Reybaz, like Dumont a close friend of and speech-writer for Mirabeau, ventured that Robespierre 'is too verbose, he doesn't know how to stop; but he has depths of eloquence and acerbity (*aigreur*) which will make him stand out from the crowd'. Although the speech brought him attention, Robespierre resolved in future to avoid speaking without notes. Henceforth he prepared speeches carefully, repeatedly crossing out unsatisfactory sentences. The press was now starting to take notice of him, while spelling his unusual name variously as Robert-pierre, Rabess-Pierre, Robertz-Pierre and Robesse-Pierre.[8]

The commoner deputies had rapidly developed a unity of purpose, insistent on their dignity and responsibility to 'the Nation', and on 17 June proclaimed themselves the National Assembly, capable of acting in the interests of the entire kingdom. Three days later they found their meeting-chamber locked; suspicious and resolute, they adjourned to a nearby indoor tennis court and took an oath never to separate. Maximilien was a keen signatory, the forty-fifth. This was the first revolutionary challenge to absolutism and privilege. The king appeared to capitulate, ordering all deputies to meet in a common assembly, but at the same time his officials invested Paris, ten miles away, with twenty thousand soldiers, mostly foreign mercenaries. Despite his nervous early speeches, Robespierre was one of twenty-four deputies chosen to present an address to the king on 9 July in Versailles, expressing concern about these troop movements.[9] In the end, however, the National Assembly was only saved from probable forced dissolution through violent insurrection by thousands of Parisian working people, angry at an escalation in the price of bread, and certain that the Assembly was under military threat. Robespierre's old school companions Desmoulins and Fréron were among those who encouraged their revolt. Their main target on 14 July was the Bastille fortress in the *faubourg* St-Antoine, known to have supplies of arms and gunpowder; it was also an awesome symbol of the arbitrary authority of the monarchy. About one hundred Parisians died after the governor of the fortress ordered his troops to open fire on the besieging crowd. The capture of the Bastille marked the successful insistence of Parisian working people that this was their cause too, and it sent shock waves both across the kingdom and all of Europe.

A week after the storming of the Bastille, Robespierre sent another long letter to Antoine Buissart, in which he traced the meaning of the uprising with unbounded enthusiasm: 'the present Revolution, my dear friend, has made us witness in a few days the greatest events the history of mankind can reveal'.[10] He was convinced that the aristocratic opponents of change had been determined to use force to crush the National Assembly. That was the meaning of the calling up of troops around Versailles and Paris. He was stunned by the Parisian response: a 'general insurrection, a patriotic army of 300,000 men, made up of citizens of all ranks'. In the aftermath of the fighting, the Marquis de Launay, the governor of the Bastille, and Jacques de Flesselles, the provost or mayor, were killed in bloody retribution. Robespierre accepted this as their 'punishment': 'the first convicted of having ordered the cannon of the Bastille to fire on the deputies of the inhabitants . . . the other of having joined, with the highest members of the court, in the plot against the people'.

Robespierre and the other deputies had been at Versailles during the insurrection. But when Louis XVI decided to travel to Paris on 17 July, shortly after news of the flight of his brother the Count d'Artois, he was flanked by one hundred National Assembly deputies, and Robespierre was among those chosen. Any hesitation he might have felt about the violent retribution suffered by Launay and Flesselles was now cancelled out by the 'imposing and sublime spectacle' of the people of Paris welcoming Louis, who accepted a cockade that married the white of the Bourbon family to the blue and red of Paris, thus symbolizing the unity of king and nation. Robespierre's comment, that 'the image of this great event—the surrender of the crown to the people—was engraved forever on the hearts of all who witnessed it', expressed his increasing firmness about the power of the Assembly over the monarchy.

Robespierre's reactions to the astonishing events of the week before were visceral and enduring. They were predicated on a series of certainties that proved indelible in his mind. In particular, the Third Estate deputies personified the people's will, which it was the Assembly's duty to interpret and implement. The popular revolt of 14 July and the welcome extended to Louis by the city on the 17th were to him the purest expression of the people's will and its unity with the patriotic elements of the National Assembly. In contrast, the 'unpatriotic' elements of the nobility were in league with the court in planning to crush the people's Assembly. In a letter home to the Buissarts, he offered to Charlotte to 'convey your compliments to your dear cousin Briois de Beaumez; he is however not the cousin of good citizens; he has spared no effort to uphold voting by order and to prevent his colleagues from joining the Commons . . . bad citizens must be recognized, for the good of the nation'. The bitter political divisions of the winter of 1788–89 in Arras had persisted. A fellow member of the Rosati, Charamond, reported to Dubois de Fosseux on 26 July that 'a few fans of the freakish Robespierre have delivered a letter from him to his sister. Here it is: "My sister, I can give you the latest word, I am well, we have escaped from the greatest danger, we are winning, I will say no more".'[11]

Sporadic cases of collective killing did not cease with the taking of the Bastille. On 17 July, at St-Germain-en-Laye, a miller was murdered; on the 18th, at Poissy, a farmer was only just rescued after the intervention of deputies despatched by the Assembly.[12] On the 20th the Marquis de Lally-Tollendal, one of the noble deputies for Paris, proposed disseminating a proclamation authorizing municipalities to form militias composed only of those certain to be reliable if confronted with unrest. Robespierre leapt to his feet: 'What has happened in this riot in Paris? General freedom, little blood spilt, a few heads chopped off, of course, but they were the heads of guilty people. . . . It is to this uprising that the Nation owes its liberty.'[13] In the tumult of revolutionary upheaval the questions of who should protect the people against their enemies, and when the people should lay down their arms, were pivotal. Robespierre supported Mirabeau's powerful call for a citizens' militia, but baulked at the exclusion from this 'National Guard' of those too poor to provide their own equipment.

More violence was to come. On 22 July the royal governor of Paris since 1776, Louis Bertier de Sauvigny, was caught as he tried to flee Paris. He and his father-in-law Joseph Foulon, who had replaced Necker in the ministry, were battered to death and decapitated, their heads paraded through Paris in retribution for allegedly conspiring to worsen the long period of hunger through which Parisians had lived in 1788–89. After the death of Foulon, Robespierre wrote to Antoine Buissart simply that 'M. Foulon was hanged yesterday by the people's decree.' Only prompt action to call to account those guilty of conspiring to kill the people on 14 July could forestall such acts, he warned the Assembly: 'Do you want to calm the People? Speak to them in the language of justice and reason. Let them be sure that their enemies will not escape the vengeance of the law, and sentiments of justice will replace those of hatred.'[14]

Robespierre was one of those who understood what the Revolution might entail. It was not that he was flippant about violence: he had a horror of the taking of life. Such was his conviction of the justice of the people's cause against entrenched oppression, however, that he was prepared to accept that some individuals particularly detested for their own violence would be targets of retribution. Only prompt action by the National Assembly to respond to popular grievances could create a new system of government that would render such splenetic action not only unnecessary but illegal.

The Revolution had occurred in a society in which violence was intrinsic to systems of justice and the language of power. The young Picard revolutionary François-Noël Babeuf had quipped in 1789 that the *ancien régime* was at fault for the violence of the revolutionaries: 'our masters, instead of policing us, made us barbaric because they are so themselves'.[15] Indeed, revolutionaries often defined the *ancien régime* as a tyranny of violence in all its forms. Others shared the dismissive attitude imputed to the deputy Antoine Barnave after Foulon's death in July 1789—'What then, is the blood which has just flowed so pure?'[16] But Robespierre did not justify or excuse the violence of 1789 on these grounds. He knew enough classical and English history to understand that revolutionary upheavals were by their nature very violent, and urged the Assembly to put in place the reforms that would make recourse to violence unnecessary.

The bewilderment, fear and anxiety of the deputies as news came in of the unprecedented events in Paris on 14 July had turned to exhilaration as the king accepted a *fait accompli*: the world could indeed be remade by human will.[17] The realization was absorbed at the same time as agitated news of other events— some shocking, some reassuring—poured into the Assembly: sporadic, startling incidents of violent retribution, seizures of power by commoners in towns and villages, acts of civic duty and generosity.

News of the storming of the Bastille had reached a countryside simmering with conflict, hope and fear. Harvest failure in 1788 had been followed by a harsh winter, and widespread hunger as new crops ripened was matched by hopes invested in the Estates-General. Rumours—the 'Great Fear'—swept the countryside that nobles would take revenge in the wake of the Parisian revolution by hiring 'brigands' to destroy crops. Robespierre and the other Artois deputies were rapidly informed of the details of the Great Fear in their region. There the price of grain had tripled between 1787 and June 1789. A current of the Fear spread from Picardy to Artois: the *Affiches d'Artois* reported that during the night of 27 July, a rumour had spread that green wheat was being harvested.[18] Across most of the country, when such acts of revenge by the nobility failed to materialize, armed peasant militias seized foodstuffs or compelled seigneurs or their agents to hand over feudal registers.

The social structure of the kingdom was woven from the fabric of seigneurialism and privilege: what were deputies to make of the seizure and destruction of seigneurial registers of dues payable, or of the refusal to pay seigneurial dues as well as royal taxes and church tithes? On the night of 4 August, nobles mounted the rostrum of the Assembly to respond to the Great Fear by renouncing their privileges and abolishing feudal dues.[19] In the succeeding week, however, they made a distinction between instances of 'personal servitude' (such as the lord's monopolies of ovens and presses), which were abolished outright, and 'property rights' (especially seigneurial dues payable on harvests), for which peasants would have to pay compensation before ceasing payment. This distinction was to fuel ongoing peasant revolt for the next three years.

In the feverish atmosphere of 4 August it was not only individual clergy and nobles who made sacrifices of their own privileges—and those of others. In March the *cahiers* of the three Estates of Artois had been insistent that the privileges guaranteed to the province through the Treaty of the Pyrenees in 1659 (exemption from the salt tax, the right to levy its own taxes, a provincial Estates of Artois) be preserved. Now, in the aftermath of 4 August, all sixteen Artois deputies renounced the 'privileges, liberties and exemptions' of their province.[20] This was a paradigm shift of identity. Four months earlier, on 20 April, the meeting of the Artois nobility had made a remarkably trenchant statement of the distinctiveness of their *pays*: 'the Artois Nation can only be present at the Estates-General as an equal State (*co-État*) given that Artois was not reunited with the kingdom as part of a whole but as a complete entity within a larger totality'. Most of them remained attentive to the need to maintain close ties with their constituents; for Robespierre, however, the transition from defender of the rights of Artois to representative of the French nation was rapid and complete. This could only accentuate the polarities in attitudes towards him in his home town.[21]

Later, on 27 August, the Assembly voted its Declaration of the Rights of Man and of the Citizen. Fundamental to the Declaration was the assertion of the essence of liberalism, that 'liberty consists of the power to do whatever is not injurious to others'. The Declaration guaranteed rights of free speech and association, of religion and opinion. This was to be a nation in which all were to be equal in legal status, and subject to the same public responsibilities: it was an invitation to become citizens of a nation instead of subjects of a king. But, while the Declaration proclaimed the universality of rights and the civic equality of all citizens, it was ambiguous on whether all would have political as well as legal equality, and was silent on how the means to exercise one's talents could be secured by those without the education or property necessary to do so.

Robespierre did not play a prominent role in the debates around the August Decrees and the Declaration of the Rights of Man and of the Citizen, but intervened occasionally to insist on progressive taxation, religious and press freedoms, and on the accountability of those in office.[22] In every case, Robespierre's argument was that the state, through its representative body, had the right to impose obligations, such as taxation, or to limit the untramelled exercise of individual freedoms in the interests of the general good. Others agreed. Despite the optimistic and universal tone of the Declaration, therefore, the guarantee of rights that it stipulated was made entirely conditional on them being exercised within the limits of the law, defined as 'the expression of the general will'. While 'the law has the right only to forbid acts that are harmful to society', the Declaration hence left open to legislators the definition of the limits to the exercise of such freedoms.[23]

In the Assembly, deputies unused to parliamentary procedure thought nothing of talking among themselves or moving about the chamber. Robespierre, whose voice was not sonorous and whose accent was sometimes mocked, was interrupted to the point of having to stand down from the podium on at least one occasion.[24] As early as September, he was being targeted as fertile material for the satirical press as one of the active radicals, along with Mirabeau, Pétion, Barnave and the Abbé Grégoire. The press delighted, for example, in a fabricated 'lovers correspondence' between Robespierre and Suzanne Forber, 'a seamstress from Arras'.[25] But he had plainly decided to make the most of this unprecedented opportunity to make a difference, and no amount of noble condescension or mocking of his accent and discourse would deter him. His mother in the first place, then his aunts and sisters, especially Charlotte, and his teachers in Arras and Paris had equipped the young man with a backbone of steel. He possessed a quite extraordinary will, born of thirty years of standing up to the sniggerers and the sanctimonious, like the good Abbé Proyart.

Robespierre had started to make a reputation and was invited to dine with the Finance Minister Jacques Necker. Years later, a bitter Germaine de Staël, Necker's daughter, recalled that 'I chatted with him several times at my father's house, in 1789, at which time he was known only as a lawyer from Artois, with highly exaggerated democratic principles. His features were low-bred, his complexion pale, his veins of a greenish colour; he would maintain the most absurd propositions with a sangfroid which seemed like conviction.' Others were laudatory. In June, Boniface Mougins de Roquefort, parish priest of Grasse and its Third Estate deputy, wrote to contacts in Artois that Robespierre 'speaks very well. . . . One must do him justice; he has a great deal of enthusiasm and does not deviate from the principles which must lead us to public regeneration.' Similarly, Charles-François Bouche, a Third Estate deputy from Aix, wrote to a friend of Robespierre's 'great, elevated, brave and patriotic spirit . . . I pity his enemies if he has any. He is a man to disappoint them by his good conduct.'[26]

After accepting the Declaration of the Rights of Man and of the Citizen, the Assembly moved quickly to confront the question of the relationship between the Assembly as representative of the sovereign people and the executive powers of the king. The crucial issue was that of royal sanction for the Assembly's decisions. On 11 September a proposal was passed granting the king the right of suspensive veto, with the decision of the Assembly to stand if two successive Assemblies maintained it. Robespierre, who opposed any veto, had planned to deliver a major speech but was pre-empted by the Assembly's decision; he then decided to have his speech printed instead.[27] It was indeed a major statement, for he went well beyond the issue of the suspensive veto to outline his fundamental principles about the nature of popular sovereignty and its expression:

> All men are capable, by their very nature, of governing themselves through their own will; all men united in a political body, that is to say the Nation, therefore have the same right. This common will, or legislative Power, composed of the will of individuals, is inalienable, sovereign and independent in society as a whole, just as it was in each individual man. Laws are simply acts of this general will. Since a great Nation cannot physically exercise legislative power, it entrusts this exercise to its representatives, in whom its power resides.

The world was watching, he exhorted his fellow deputies, and he worried that his fellow citizens lacked the long experience of battles for political liberties of their English neighbours. How could the French shed their 'frivolity' and 'moral weakness' to fulfil their mission of being a model for the whole of Europe? The answer lay in a literal interpretation of the principles incarnated in the Declaration of the Rights of Man and of the Citizen: 'these are principles of justice, of innate rights, which no human law can change.'[28]

Both the August Decrees and the Declaration met with refusal from Louis. The Estates-General had been summoned to offer him advice on the state of his kingdom: did his acceptance of the existence of a 'National Assembly' require him to accept its decisions? Once again the standing of the Assembly seemed in question as rumours swirled through Versailles and Paris, fuelled by anxiety over flour shortages despite the good harvest several months earlier. This time it was the market women of Paris who took the initiative, convinced that the king had to sanction the decrees and return to Paris: in this way they believed that the nobles' conspiracy to starve Paris would be broken.

The arrival of thousands of determined women at Versailles on 5 October was a turning point in Robespierre's career, for he was at the rostrum when a delegation of them spilled into the Assembly, and responded by ordering an inquiry into the provision of food in Paris. The next day Louis acceded to demands that the royal family return to Paris with the women and National Guard. The National Assembly decided to follow. The Revolution seemed secure and complete, but was based on the fiction that the king's recalcitrance was due solely to the malign influence of his court.

The Assembly closed its sessions in Versailles on 15 October and reopened in Paris on the 19th, first in the archbishop's palace, then in the Manège, Louis XV's riding-school on the north side of the Tuileries gardens. Robespierre now took up lodgings on the third floor of a tenement at 30 Rue Saintonge in the Marais, walking the two miles daily to the National Assembly or to the Breton Club. He was now back in the familiar surroundings of the metropolis, and may have taken advantage of the move to Paris to distance himself physically from the farmer deputies from Artois. His brother Augustin had spent several months with him in Versailles; now he returned to Arras.

The Assembly was in an invidious position. On the one hand, most deputies were relieved to be one step removed from the royal court and that the key decrees had received royal sanction; on the other, they were profoundly discomfited by the Assembly's vulnerability to popular pressure from Parisians. On 21 October a baker, Denis François, accused of hoarding part of his stock, was lynched and decapitated on the Place de Grève outside the town hall. After Barnave and Mirabeau had spoken in support of the Paris Commune's request for martial law, Robespierre retorted: 'There are other measures we must take, Gentlemen, if we are to get to the source of the problem. It is a matter of finding out why the people are starving.' Robespierre was unsuccessful in opposing martial law, but urged the Assembly to focus as well on the evident 'conspiracy' against the Revolution, evident in a menacing pastoral letter distributed by the

Bishop of Tréguier and in the alleged hoarding of essential foodstuffs: 'in fact, everywhere it seems that people are determined to stifle in its infancy the freedom of France which we have bought so dear.'[29] As deputies grappled with the enormity of what had transpired—no less than a revolution—and their own responsibility to create a new world, it is unsurprising that they were tempted to explain unwelcome news as evidence of malevolence, even conspiracy, by the opponents of change. Robespierre was among the first to be convinced.

The euphoria of the autumn of 1789 was tempered by an awareness of the magnitude of what remained to be done. The revolutionaries' declaration of the principles of the new regime presupposed that every aspect of public life would be reshaped. The *ancien régime*, as it was now called, had been overthrown, but what was to be put in its place? Over the next two years, the deputies threw themselves into the task of reworking every dimension of public life. The reconstruction of France was based on a belief in the equal status of French citizens whatever their social or geographic origin. In every aspect of public life— administration, the judiciary, taxation, the armed forces, the Church, policing— a system of corporate rights, appointment and hierarchy gave way to one upholding civil equality, accountability and popular sovereignty. The institutional structure of the *ancien régime* had been characterized by extraordinary provincial diversity controlled by a network of royal appointees. Now this was reversed: at every level officials were to be elected, and the institutions in which they worked were everywhere to be uniform. The institutional bedrock would be the forty-one thousand new 'communes', mostly based on the parishes of the *ancien régime*, the base of a nested hierarchy of cantons, districts and eighty-three 'departments' replacing the ancient provinces.[30] The complex set of royal, aristocratic and clerical courts and their regional variants was replaced by a single national system deliberately made more accessible, humane and egalitarian.

The central issue of political legitimacy—how would popular sovereignty be expressed and by whom?—was to distance Robespierre from the majority of his fellow deputies. His view of a healthy society and polity was drawn from his education in the civic virtues of the classical republics, and from his understanding of Rousseau's ideal of direct participation and the need for transparency in all dealings between the people and their representatives. The common people were seen by him as the embodiment of virtue, despite the weight of their poverty and ignorance. Their existence could and should be improved through human action—'the first of all laws is the well-being of the people'—and the role of virtuous individuals who could voice the 'general will', not necessarily the same as majority opinion.[31]

The task of governing a large country had forced Robespierre to break with Rousseau's critique of representative government, but his opposition to any deviation from the principle of full popular sovereignty was based on a Rousseauian desire to align the Assembly with the people's will. In late October the Assembly heard proposals to restrict the vote to 'active' citizens paying direct taxes to the equivalent of wages for three days' labour, thereby excluding one-third of adult men; these actives would choose 'eligibles' from those paying the equivalent of ten days' work in tax and they in turn would choose deputies from the wealthy paying the *marc d'argent* (about fifty-four *livres*) in tax. Robespierre supported the Abbé Grégoire's criticism that this would enable the emergence of a new aristocracy, of the rich, and in any case was in flagrant contradiction to the Declaration: 'the constitution establishes that sovereignty is vested in the people, in every single person. Each individual has the right therefore to participate in the law which governs him and the administration of public life which governs him. Otherwise it is not true that all men have equal rights, that all men are citizens.' Only a handful of deputies was of like mind. But Robespierre's stance was popular with provincial political societies, and those from St-Malo in the north and Perpignan in the south, from opposite ends of the kingdom, wrote to congratulate him.[32]

As debate continued to rage on the right to vote, Robespierre kept insisting on the moral effects that would flow to those now excluded from the 'sacred rights to which they are entitled as men', such as Jews and actors, the latter deemed to be 'untrustworthy'. He did not refer to women. Removal of 'absurd prejudice' against actors would result in theatres becoming 'public schools of good behaviour and patriotism'. Similarly, he supported the Abbé Grégoire's campaign in favour of Jewish equality: 'you have been told things about Jews which have been vastly exaggerated and which often belie history. The vices of the Jews have their roots in the degradation into which you have plunged them. They will be good when they see some benefit in being so . . .'.[33] By the end of 1789 full citizenship had been granted to Protestants and, late in the following January, to the Sephardi Jews of Bordeaux and Avignon. The Ashkenazi Jews of the east had to wait until the end of September 1791 for equal recognition.

In late 1789, in the context of municipal elections to be held early in 1790, Robespierre drafted an address to the people of the northeastern provinces of Flanders, Hainaut, Cambrésis and Artois. He highlighted the development of the Constitution which, although it was unlikely to be totally as he wished, was nevertheless an outcome of the principles of the Declaration of Rights:

1. The aim of society is the happiness of all.
2. All men are born free and with equal rights, and cannot cease to be so.
3. The principle of sovereignty resides in the nation; all power emanates and can emanate only from it.[34]

The fundamental tension for him was that only a virtuous citizenry could enable a true democracy to thrive. The role of the Assembly must be to 'raise our fellow citizens' souls ... to the levels of ideas and feelings required by this great and superb revolution'. Until a body of the people's representatives had succeeded in enacting just laws and creating a fundamentally virtuous society, no government could abolish the people's right to resist oppression: 'the march of revolutions is not subject to the ordinances which govern the peaceful state of an established constitution'. If there was a gulf—as there was bound to be—between people's behaviour and virtuous behaviour, then it was evident that malign forces were to blame, not only for centuries of prejudice and oppression, but now for conspiracy.[35]

Robespierre's persistent recourse to the principles in the Declaration had begun to grate with those anxious for compromise and stability. On 8 October he had proposed that ancient monarchical formulae for registering decrees (such as 'as this is our pleasure') should be replaced by 'Louis, by the grace of God and by the Will of the Nation, King of the French, to all citizens of the French Empire: People, here is the law which your representatives have made, and to which I have affixed the royal seal.' There was uproar, and a deputy retorted to Robespierre's sing-song intonement by shouting 'we want no psalm-singing here!' But he was remarkably determined and resolute. Indeed, this young man elected low on the list of Artois deputies to the Estates-General delivered no fewer than thirty-eight speeches in 1789. Making oneself heard required not just strong lungs but a persistence in insisting on the right to speak amid the clamour.[36]

His thin skin was often pricked. There were scores of new newspapers enjoying complete freedom of the press. One of the royalist newspapers, the *Actes des Apôtres*, published a long, tendentious portrait of Robespierre in November. The article—most likely from the pen of his former classmate François Suleau—mocked his provincial fame, particularly in the case of the lightning conductor, and sniggered at his pronunciation of 'aristocrassique', implying that he was at heart a peasant. It assured its readers that 'if Mirabeau is the flame from Provence, Robespierre is just the candle from Arras', perhaps a clever allusion to the Chapelle de la Ste-Chandelle on the Petit Marché at Arras. Others were more complimentary, the clerical deputy Abbé Poncelin de la Roche-Tilhac from Senlis describing Robespierre as someone who, 'without becoming too heated, says very good things'. Charles de Lameth, who had renounced his mandate as a noble deputy from Artois in June to express his support for the National Assembly, lauded 'the courage and zeal which have always characterized him and with which he defends the interests of society's least fortunate'.[37]

Early in November 1789, Robespierre sent his third long letter of that momentous year to Antoine Buissart.[38] The letter gave Robespierre the chance to reflect on the point the Revolution had reached. He was delighted that church property had been nationalized and that the role of the aristocratic Parlements as the high courts had been ended. 'Feudal aristocracy has been pretty well annihilated; the greatest abuses seem to have disappeared at the wish of the representatives of the Nation.' But he wondered 'will we be free? I think we may still ask this question. . . . The new Constitution appears to me at least to contain some basic defects which prevent good citizens from rejoicing.' Most important was his continuing concern over the proposal by the 'aristocratic party' in the Assembly that even municipal bodies should be elected on a property franchise. While a lawyer in Arras, Robespierre had seen the aristocracy as based on illegitimate claims to the honour of a caste; now he expressed visceral hatred towards it as the primary obstacle to France's regeneration. And there was so much still to do before he could experience the pleasures of the company of his friends in Arras, especially Antoine and Charlotte Buissart: 'I think I will be here for a few months yet.'

CHAPTER 6

'Daring to clean out the Augean stables'
PARIS 1789–91

Early in March 1790, Robespierre wrote again to Antoine Buissart, excusing his silence once more, and referring to the Herculean task of reform: 'you could not imagine the multitude and difficulty of the matters which justify my silence; ... the patriotic deputies to the National Assembly, daring to clean out the Augean stables, are embarked on a project which may be beyond human capacity. ... I take up my pen more to give you a sign of my eternal friendship, of which you can have no doubt, than to enjoy a sustained conversation with you.'[1]

One stall in the Augean stables early in 1790 was full of the unresolved consequences issuing from the peasant revolt of the summer of 1789. The first of these matters, that of forest rights and access to commons, went to the heart of the long-standing struggles between peasants and lords over control of resources. It was acute across the country but had a special dimension in Artois and Flanders. Here a 1669 royal ordinance had stipulated the generous conditions under which seigneurs could exercise their right of *triage* to alienate one-third of forests and commons from community access, but the Council of Artois had exempted them even from these conditions. This 'usurpation' was uppermost in Robespierre's mind and as early as May 1789 he may have drafted a motion to request 'restitution of the communal property invaded by the lords' in the northeast. He returned to it in December in response to the Assembly's attempts to suppress invasions of forests and common lands as rural communities across the country took matters into their own hands.[2]

Such was the resonance of the issue that the debate expanded to include the kingdom in general. It ended with a decree abolishing the right of *triage*, but only seigneurial seizures over the last thirty years were affected. Robespierre objected again: 'these usurpers will continue to enjoy the property they have assumed, and, under the fanciful pretext of not making the law retrospective . . . you are prolonging into the future the destructive deprivation of rights of which [the people] have been stripped and the most hateful memorial of the feudal empire'. Rural communities with long memories were not about to forego demands for restitution outside that time limit. On occasion they simply broke the law: for example, at Noyelles-sous-Lens, just north of Arras, the poorest inhabitants (described by officials as 'those who don't understand French') seized and divided the commons in June 1790.[3]

The second issue was even more divisive. While the August decrees had commenced with the resounding statement that the feudal system had been 'abolished entirely', the decision to treat harvest dues—the most onerous of all—as a type of property for whose loss seigneurs could expect compensation from their communities was even more provocative than the hesitation over commons. On 9 February 1790 the Abbé Grégoire reported to the Assembly on the unrest in Quercy, Rouergue, Périgord and Limousin in the south, and in parts of Brittany, where bands of armed peasants had been attacking *châteaux*. After Jean-Denis Lanjuinais had argued that the reasons for the unrest in Brittany were the unresolved matters in the August decrees, Robespierre intervened in support and was drawn into an exchange with nobles who labelled those involved as 'brigands', not 'the people' to whom Robespierre referred: 'you must not forget that we are living in times when all powers have been abolished, when the people feel suddenly relieved of long-standing oppression. . . . Do not forget that men who are led astray by the memory of their misfortunes are not hard-ened criminals.' On 20 February discussion turned to a law drafted by the Breton deputy Isaac Le Chapelier, which would despatch troops to the regions in ques-tion, with recourse to martial law. Again and unsuccessfully, Robespierre argued that, if 'a few *châteaux* in Brittany have been burned', then it was because their owners were those most hostile to the Revolution. In any case, he added, the Assembly should be well aware of the deliberate attempts being made to incite discontent by circulating the wildest rumours or exaggerations: 'France is certainly divided in two parts: the people and the aristocracy. The latter is dying, but its long drawn-out death-throes are not without convulsions.'[4]

On 20 April the question moved on to hunting rights. Philippe-Antoine Merlin de Douai, for the Committee on Feudalism, insisted that the decrees of 4 August had only granted the right to landowners to kill game on their own lands. Across the country, however, large-scale destruction of game had been occurring regardless of property rights. Robespierre was one of several deputies to call for unlimited freedom to hunt: 'I maintain that hunting is not a right that derives from property. As soon as the land has been cleared, hunting must be free to all citizens without distinction. In any case, wild animals belong to the first inhabitant. I therefore call for unlimited freedom to hunt, as long as measures are taken to preserve crops and public safety.'[5] Not for the first time, a radical suggestion from him caused uproar in the Assembly.

Unlike many of the best-known deputies—for example, Mirabeau, Barère, Camus, Malouet and Sieyès—Robespierre had not frequented the polished world of the salons before 1789, and his oratory was often longwinded or ill-judged. In July 1790 constant interruptions prevented him from finishing his speech when he sought to respond to the American War of Independence hero Paul Jones. Robespierre was never placed on one of the Assembly's thirty working committees—and perhaps did not seek to be—and quickly became known as one of those in the most radical minority, together with three other provincial lawyers, Jérôme Pétion from Chartres, François Buzot from Évreux and Pierre-Louis Prieur from Châlons-sur-Marne. Unlike him, however, they were in the thick of committee work.[6]

Whereas his relations with his Arras constituency were becoming tangled by his outspokenness, Robespierre was increasingly at home in the Society of Friends of the Constitution, in Paris commonly known as the Jacobin Club from its headquarters in a former convent in the Rue St-Honoré. It was here from November 1789 where he made trial runs at speeches later to be delivered in the Assembly. The Society was a gathering of men rather like him who were willing to pay a subscription to discuss affairs of state, more congenial for him than the 'intriguers' of the Assembly or the rough world of café oratory. By August 1790 the Society had 152 provincial affiliates, including Arras, where his brother Augustin was a keen participant.

Elected president of the Jacobin Club for a period from late March 1790, Robespierre had to sustain a national correspondence, writing to newly affiliated branches. He often accompanied such letters of encouragement by enclosing a printed copy of one of his speeches 'devoted to the most sacred rights of man and the first principles of public felicity'.[7] At the same time, he kept up a detailed correspondence, for example, on the status of rural legislation with constituents like Charles Michaud, parish priest of Bomy in Artois, counselling him to be prudent about the ardour with which he expressed himself to those 'whose patriotism is not yet sufficiently developed'. His signature changed after the Assembly abolished hereditary nobility and titles on 19 June 1790. Although his surname 'de Robespierre' was ancient and carried neither noble status nor title, Maximilien decided it was the right moment to cease using the prefix, and a letter of 27 June to the Friends of the Constitution in Arras is the last example we have of its use by him.[8]

Revolutionaries were not only remaking France. From the outset they were conscious of regenerating Europe's great power, one that had suffered a series of humiliations, notably with the loss of Canada in the Seven Years War (1756–63). The shock of realizing that they were recasting the social and political foundations of the most powerful country in Europe was always accompanied by a will to restore French prestige in the international arena. The two were understood to be part of the same regenerative project. From 1790, too, important and often demanding groups of political refugees were clustered in Paris and in towns around Arras: refugees from the failed upheavals in Brabant, Liège and Brussels.[9]

At the core of foreign policy was whether decisions about war and peace, and foreign policy in general, were to remain with the king as head of the executive or to pass to the Assembly. The final compromise secured by Mirabeau in May, that the Assembly would have to act on the basis of proposals put by the king, was a triumph for Robespierre and his close ally Pétion. Robespierre argued trenchantly that France should forever renounce wars of territorial expansion and should never act against the liberty of other peoples, concepts ultimately included in the Constitution of 1791.[10] This did not preclude the annexation of an enclave such as the papal territory in Avignon and the Comtat-Venaissin because of the rights of its people to self-determination. In the end, argued Robespierre, 'a nation is simply a society of men who have united through a common interest under a common government and set of laws'.[11] If they or others across the Rhine should decide to become part of the new France, then it was not a matter for their rulers.

But how could the armed forces be brought into harmony with the revolutionary practices of popular sovereignty and the exercise of individual rights and still be powerful enough to reclaim France's place in the world? It was one thing to accept that the armed forces would have to be exempt from the Revolution's core principle of filling public positions by election, but it rankled with Robespierre that, for example, there were still different types of punishment separating officers from other soldiers. The issue erupted in the summer of 1790, following troop revolts in Nancy, Metz, Béthune and elsewhere. But when the Marquis de Bouillé had thirty-three soldiers from the Châteauvieux regiment at Nancy broken on the wheel or hanged for mutiny and forty-one sentenced to the galleys for life, only Robespierre, Pétion and a few others in the Assembly protested.[12] Social order was paramount for the vast majority.

The Assembly had inherited the monarchy's bankruptcy, and the problem was now aggravated by popular refusal to pay taxes. Several measures were taken to address this crisis. In early November 1789 the vast church lands had been nationalized as *biens nationaux* and, from November 1790, sold at auction, mainly to local bourgeois and the wealthiest peasants. These sales were also used to back the issue of *assignats*, a paper currency dating from the previous December that soon began to decline in real purchasing power. Robespierre supported the sale of *biens nationaux* and the *assignats*, attributing the cause of inflation not to the printing of vast quantities of paper currency but to the machinations of hated 'hoarders' (*accapareurs*) and 'speculators' (*agioteurs*).[13] Fiscal exemptions were finally ended by a new system of taxation, based on the estimated value of property, which was introduced from the beginning of 1791.

Until mid-1790 the Revolution was overwhelmingly popular: comprehensive changes in public life occurred within a context of mass optimism and support. The Festival of Federation, on the first anniversary of the storming of the Bastille, celebrated the unity of the Church, monarchy and Revolution. Two days earlier, however, the Assembly had voted in a reform that was to shatter this unity. The widespread agreement in the *cahiers* on the need for church reform enabled the Assembly to push through the nationalization of church lands, the closing of contemplative orders and the granting of religious liberty to Protestants and Jews. But mounting clerical opposition to these changes ultimately focused on the Civil Constitution of the Clergy voted on 12 July 1790. The Assembly's reforms were to polarize the nation. Many priests were materially advantaged by the new salary scale, and only the upper clergy would have regretted that bishops' stipends were dramatically reduced. Most contentious, however, was the issue of how the clergy were to be appointed in future: in requiring the

election of priests and bishops, the Assembly outraged the Church's assumption
that authority passed from God through his upper clergy.

Robespierre was mainstream in his support for the Civil Constitution, seeing
priests simply as elected officials, but he was also supportive of priests' public
functions, now to be paid for from taxes. His remarks had none of the anticlerical
bitterness of increasing numbers of deputies: although he was scathing
about inequalities within the former First Estate and conventional in his critique
of the cloistered life, he supported increased salaries for parish clergy, whom
he saw as 'magistrates whose duty is to maintain and carry on public worship'.
He wanted priests to wear clerical garb only when officiating.[14] He had no
sympathy whatever for the idea that the Church should be self-governing. When
a clerical deputy from Angers moved that bishops be elected by the synod of the
clergy of their department, not surprisingly, Robespierre spoke against the
motion:

> So you are going to reconstitute the clergy as a political entity, independent
> and exceptional within the State; you are going to breathe new life into this
> entity at the very moment that you have abolished it, in the name of reason and
> liberty. You are proposing to open the first door to the monstrous abuses
> which the political existence of the clergy as a privileged corporation produced.
> Gentlemen, beware.

He was more radical on one matter: he advocated the right of priests to marry.
This earned him an anxious message from Augustin in Arras that he would
further inflame antipathy towards him in devout Artois, while causing a flood of
support from elsewhere, including from many religious.[15]

Satirical newspapers—many now openly anti-revolutionary—singled out
Robespierre more and more. His former classmate François Suleau was a key
contributor to the *Actes des Apôtres* in 1790, and mockingly republished
Robespierre's youthful love poem to Ophélie Mondlen. Allegations from Arras
had followed him, for others noted that he was known by 'public opinion' to be
illegitimate. A clerical deputy for Paris, the Abbé de Montesquiou-Fezensac,
published a lengthy *Address to the Provinces*, in which he denounced the 'revolutionary anarchy' led by 'little Robespierre, known only in Arras for his ingrati-
tude towards the bishop who had had him brought up'. Robespierre was likened

to Don Quixote, except that he was fighting on the wrong side, and condemned as a man 'whose subtle venom has corrupted France ... destroying good sense, taste and truth'.[16]

These attacks took their toll. In May–June he spoke only occasionally at the Jacobin Club, and it may be that the pressures of being a frequent and outspoken defender of the principles he considered intrinsic to the Revolution of 1789 had exhausted him. This might explain why someone who had been intransigent about protecting the rights of free assembly and petition did not speak during the debate on 14 June on the law, proposed by Le Chapelier, sharply restricting the rights of wage earners to bargain collectively.[17]

Pressures of work and worry were taxing him to the point of irritability. In the 7 June 1790 issue of the *Révolutions de France et de Brabant*, its editor, Maximilien's old friend and hero of 1789, Camille Desmoulins, had reported, incorrectly, that Robespierre had criticized Mirabeau's successful motion on peace and war to a crowd of citizens in the Tuileries gardens. Robespierre took exception to the error and asked Desmoulins to insert a formal correction. Desmoulins was astonished that such a minor error should require rectification; more so, he was puzzled by Robespierre's prickly tone: 'you should at least greet an old classmate with a slight inclination of the head. I like you no less for being faithful to your principles even if you are not so to friendship.'[18] But they seem to have made their peace: a few months later Robespierre, with Pétion and Jacques-Pierre Brissot (editor of the *Patriote français*), was witness to the marriage of Camille and Lucile Duplessis. They were married by the former principal at Louis-le-Grand, the Abbé Bérardier. When Robespierre wrote later to Desmoulins in the hope that he would refer to a speech he had delivered on the National Guard, he teased him that 'neither the beautiful eyes nor beautiful virtues of the charming Lucile constitute reasons not to announce my work'—and Desmoulins duly praised it in the next issue of his paper.[19]

Robespierre's rooms at 30 Rue de Saintonge were modest. One reason for this was that he was apparently sending half his salary back to Arras to support Charlotte and Augustin. This was a point made by the playwright Pierre Villiers, who spent seven months in 1790 as his secretary. Villiers also claimed that Robespierre was visited occasionally by a woman of 'modest condition' in her mid-twenties, 'who idolized him, and whom he treated more or less badly. Often he refused to admit her.' Writing more than a decade later, Villiers had his own reasons for exaggerating or fabricating, and the implication of a sexual liaison is very probably nonsense.[20]

Villiers recalled the impressive volume of mail the deputy received each day, especially from women. Certainly Robespierre seems to have been attractive to those women drawn to men who seem both passionate and vulnerable, and in need of happiness. Among the letters that Robespierre kept were several from Marguerite Chalabre. She was a few years older than Maximilien; she alluded to being descended from a marquisate.[21] Whatever the case, she was intensely interested in the politics of the Revolution, and an unalloyed admirer of Robespierre. She was persistent in her praise and invitations, more than once asking 'do me the honour, Sir, to accept a little dinner with patriots'. He seems to have responded, as he had to female admirers in Arras, with a copy of a recent speech or newspaper article.

He had other new friends. In 1790 a young lieutenant colonel of the National Guard of the department of Aisne, Louis-Antoine St-Just, wrote to Robespierre, asking him to consider a petition. The letter was filled with praise, beginning 'you, who uphold our tottering country against the torrent of despotism and intrigue, you whom I know, as I know God, only through his miracles'. Through their correspondence, the two became friends. Like St-Just, Robespierre was profoundly bothered by the 'intrigue' that was thwarting the Revolution's progress. The nation seemed to be divided between 'the people' and their 'aristocrat' enemies, and some of the latter were plainly adept at misleading those long oppressed by ignorance and poverty—and thereby strewing obstacles in the path of regeneration.[22]

Robespierre became well known particularly over his identification of the covert threat posed by aristocrats pretending to be patriots. In January 1790 the Nancy deputy Adrien Duquesnoy, who in October 1789 had used his *Journal de la ville* to describe Robespierre as a 'vile and detestable incendiary', commented of his speech on an incident in the naval garrison at Toulon that, 'as usual, M. de Robespierre spoke of plots, conspiracies, etc.'[23] By mid-1790 it seemed obvious to Robespierre and others that those opposed to the Revolution were organizing to overthrow it and that yet others were vacillating. The unravelling of the unity expressed in the autumn of 1789 led many 'patriots' to question the motives of those increasingly in opposition.[24] Robespierre was not alone, and nor were the Jacobins more prone than others to believe in conspiracies. For their part, royalists blamed 'the left wing, and the monstrous assembly of the principal enemies of the Church and of the Monarchy; Jews, Protestants, Deists'. During 1790 the anti-revolutionary satirical press made Robespierre a favourite target. In all there were forty-four attacks on him in the *Actes des Apôtres*, seventy-five in the *Petit Gautier* and thirty-two in the *Sabots Jacobites*. When in October he was elected President of the Tribunal of the District of Versailles, he was labelled a 'criminal' who 'will hang lots of people'.[25]

The widespread belief in 1789 in an 'aristocratic plot', which allegedly aimed to starve Parisians into inactivity, had underpinned the storming of the Bastille and the events of October, and was echoed each time revolutionaries needed to argue against opposition to their policies and to rationalize violence. There was plenty of evidence. Since fleeing the Revolution in 1789, Louis' younger brother the Count d'Artois had built a court and army in exile across the eastern border in Coblenz. The abandonment of the National Assembly by hundreds of noble and clerical deputies generated well-founded anxiety that they were at work undermining it in the provinces, as did the role of the noble prelates and the Pope in convincing half the clergy to refuse an oath of loyalty to the Constitution.

The nature of court and ministerial politics before 1789 had created a political culture of personal influence, preferment and faction in which access to the king was widely assumed to involve manoeuvring or conspiracy by cabals.[26] The National Assembly sought a rupture with this *ancien régime* political culture through a parliamentary system of constitutional monarchy, with guarantees of individual and civic rights protected and defined by the law. But the belief that 'the king is good but his ministers are wicked' survived the Revolution of 1789 and was intrinsic to the vehemence with which Marie-Antoinette was attacked as having emasculated the king. By mid-1790 there was a revolutionary—and counter-revolutionary—rhetoric of verbal imagery that defined opponents as conspirators, traitors and enemies.[27]

From the outset the ideals of liberty and equality had been compromised by pragmatic considerations of vested interests, a sure sign to Robespierre of the insidious motives of the Revolution's enemies. A similar hesitancy was expressed over whether the principles of 1789 should be extended to the Caribbean colonies. A bitter debate pitted the colonial lobby (the Club Massiac) against the Society of Friends of the Blacks, created in February 1788 by Jacques-Pierre Brissot and others. In a series of debates across the first five months of 1791 the

Colonial Committee, dominated by planter interests, argued that the National Assembly only be permitted to consider colonial matters that came from its Committee, a ploy not only to avoid the issue of slavery but even that of 'free men of colour'. In May, Antoine Barnave insisted that the interests of commerce, the navy and agriculture were more important than the imposition of revolutionary principles in the colonies. In a protracted debate Robespierre supported Grégoire and Lanjuinais against the colonial lobby: 'they tell you that you will lose your colonies unless you strip free citizens of colour of their political rights. … What I ask is that we should not compromise the interests humanity holds most dear, the sacred rights of a significant number of our fellow citizens …'. The next day the debates became more heated as they spilled over into the wider question of slavery. 'Death to the colonies,' shouted Robespierre to strident objections, 'if the colonists want, through threats, to force us to legislate as best suits them.' On 15 May, however, the Assembly adopted Jean-François Reubell's amendment, setting the question of slavery to one side but making equal citizens of 'persons of colour born of a free father and mother'.[28]

In Robespierre's words, the Assembly had given 'constitutional sanction to slavery in the colonies'. He did not at this point advocate immediate abolition of slavery, but rather opposed any decree that might suggest the Revolution condoned it.[29] His impassioned defence of the rights of slaves as well as free persons of colour earned him a barb from a royalist journalist which would become commonplace, that he was not only a 'bloodthirsty innovator' but also the nephew of the would-be regicide of Louis XV, Robert Damiens (from a village near Arras and, like Robespierre, infected by years spent at Louis-le-Grand). A pro-slavery pamphlet repeated the jibe that Robespierre was 'just the candle from Arras', part of an English plot to destroy the colonies and thereby France itself.[30]

In the spring of 1791, as deputies laboured to give substance to the principles of 1789 in France's first Constitution, Robespierre became the chief mouthpiece of opposition to compromise in the interests of stability and order. He broke irrevocably with the 'triumvirate' revolutionary leadership of Adrien Duport, Antoine Barnave and Charles de Lameth, the liberal noble from Artois with whom he had often agreed. On issue after issue—immunity of deputies from prosecution unless the Parliament rescinded it,[31] the privacy of the mail service, trials by jury, freedom of the press, the abolition of capital punishment—he argued trenchantly from first principles. Whatever the damage he saw as being done to the progress of the Revolution—and to his own health—by the vituperation and machinations of the people's enemies, he was adamant that individual rights and freedoms should not be compromised.

Early in February 1791 the Assembly considered key details of the reorganization of criminal justice, such as the nature of jury trials. Robespierre was insistent on the principle of unanimity in such trials—'society demands that condemnation be based on the very highest degree of moral certitude'—and pointed out that proposed measures for the selection of juries again highlighted the injustice of the taxation qualification for voting, 'since citizens are thereby somehow divided into two categories, one of which is destined to be judged and the other to judge'.[32]

Robespierre's pre-revolutionary support for women becoming full members of royal academies never extended to support for their formal political rights. However, he intervened to support a law enforcing equal inheritance between children in April 1791, which was among the most important reforms to family law of the revolutionary period. During the protracted debates, he set out his core principle that 'equality is the source of all that is good; extreme inequality is the source of all evils'. While deputies from Normandy and the south sought to preserve the rights of fathers to control the distribution of family property, others attacked it as a 'vicious social system' threatening both morality and the principle of equality underpinning the new social order. Among them were Pétion and Robespierre. The latter attacked patriarchal power as inimical to relations between fathers and children, which should be based on 'the nature, care, tenderness, and virtue of fathers'. He went as far as to argue that 'after his death, an individual's property should be returned to society's public domain . . . the public interest is equality'. His comments again aroused the rage of the majority.[33]

The Revolution of 1789 had removed all constraints on freedom of the press, unleashing a torrent of brilliant, and often febrile, opinion and reportage. By early 1791 there was mounting concern in the Assembly about the proliferation of obscene and vilifying images, newspapers and plays, causing some to call for municipal authorities to have powers to intervene. Although both men had been favourite targets, Robespierre, with Pétion, was insistent that private action for libel was preferable to restrictions on press freedoms: 'freedom of the press cannot be distinguished from freedom of speech: they are both as sacred as

nature'. Similarly, he insisted that 'nothing must constrain the freedom of theatres. . . . Public opinion is the only arbiter of the general good.' Suggestions that
packets of 'aristocratic' newspapers or correspondence might be opened by
concerned authorities were strongly and successfully opposed by him as a precedent which could one day be used against 'patriots'. Even the royalist press was
forced to admire his integrity. The former philosophy teacher at Louis-le-Grand,
the Abbé Royou, had launched in 1790 the newspaper *Ami du roi*. Despite his
ultraroyalist politics, and having dismissed the former student as an 'obscure
barker from the bar', Royou was warm in his praise in May 1791: 'we must do
justice to M. Robespierre. . . . No secret interest, no party spirit, no individual
consideration has been able to shake or weaken his zeal for a case which seemed
to him to be intimately linked to the public good . . . he puts his principles above
his interests.'[34]

In May 1791 the Assembly moved to consider a report on a draft penal
code presented by Lepeletier de St-Fargeau for the Constitutional and Criminal
Legislation Committees. Lepeletier requested an initial decision on whether the
death penalty should be retained. Robespierre called on his reserves of classical
allegory in an attempt to have it abolished as both unjust and ineffective: 'under
Tiberius, the panegyric of Brutus was a crime which warranted death. Caligula
condemned to death those who had taken their clothes off in front of his statue.
Once tyranny had invented the crime of high treason, fanaticism and ignorance
in their turn invented crimes of outrage against Divine Majesty, which could be
expiated only with blood.'[35] His argument was unsuccessful. The range of capital
offences was drastically reduced, however, and in October 1789 the Assembly
had already accepted a proposal from another opponent of the death penalty,
Joseph Guillotin, that a single, less painful means of execution be used in the
unfortunate event that the death penalty was retained.

By the spring of 1791 the deputies were exhausted, and increasingly concerned
by the struggles for parliamentary supremacy being waged between the Duport–
Barnave–Lameth 'triumvirate' and their allies and, on the other hand, supporters
of Lafayette. When Robespierre argued on 16 May that members of the National
Assembly be ineligible for re-election to the succeeding Legislative Assembly,
almost all the Assembly rushed to support him.[36]

The work of the National Assembly had been vast in scope and energy.
The foundations of a new social order were laid, underpinned by an assumption

of the national unity of a fraternity of citizens. This was a revolutionary transformation of public life.[37] At the same time, the Assembly was walking a tightrope.
On one side, the Assembly was alienating itself from the popular base of the
Revolution by its compromise on feudal dues, its exclusion of 'passive' citizens
from the political process, and its implementation of economic liberalism. On
the other side lay a growing hostility from nobles and the elite of the Church
angered by their loss of status, wealth and privilege, and bolstered in many areas
by a disillusioned parish clergy and their parishioners. Parish priests were
required to take a civic oath in order to continue their functions, and their difficult choice—felt as one between loyalty to the Revolution and loyalty to God
and the Pope—was often influenced by parishioner sentiment. By mid-1791
two Frances had emerged, the pro-reform areas of the southeast, the Paris basin,
and much of the centre, contrasting with the west and southwest, most of the
north and east, and the southern Massif Central.

Robespierre was well aware of the explosive situation in the south, where friction over the anti-seigneurial legislation and religious reform was exacerbated by
long-standing Catholic–Protestant antipathy. Robespierre's assiduous correspondence, his support for the reunion of Avignon and Comtat-Venaissin with
France, and his reputation for consistency, had won him a high level of support
from Jacobins in Marseilles, Aix, Avignon and Toulon in particular, especially
when southern 'patriots' sought him as a new 'protector' after Mirabeau's death
on 2 April. Once again, early in June, he admitted to the Toulonnais that he had
not written earlier because of 'a period of indisposition brought on by an excess
of work, which kept me home for a few days'.[38]

This was another sign that Robespierre's health was suffering from the
volume of work he was handling. Nevertheless, on 11 June 1791 he accepted
the position of public prosecutor in the Criminal Court of the department of
Paris, to which he had been overwhelmingly elected two days earlier without
his knowledge. The right-wing press now accused him of attending the Duke
d'Orléans' orgies, of spending his salary on prostitutes, and more. Adrien
Duport, elected president of the Court, resigned in protest at the election of
Robespierre, eliciting a blistering retort from Camille Desmoulins in the
Révolutions de France et de Brabant: 'you rejected Robespierre, the embodiment
of probity, from your tribunal. . . . You are not unaware of the universal esteem in
which he is held, and the civic awards with which he has been crowned by the

fraternal societies. You have witnessed a hundred times the unanimous applause his speeches and even just his presence have elicited from the Jacobins.'[39]

On 12 June Robespierre sent a brief and touching letter to Antoine Buissart, again referring to his fragility: 'I feel only trepidation at the arduous labours to which this important position will condemn me, at a time when I needed rest after such lengthy turmoil. . . . But I am called to a turbulent destiny. I must follow it, until I have made the last sacrifice I can offer to my homeland.' Robespierre's decision to accept election as public prosecutor meant that he would have to resign an existing position as judge on the Versailles tribunal. He wrote to friends there that he felt impelled to accept the Paris position even though Versailles would have been a 'peaceful retreat' where 'I could occasionally enjoy myself, devote myself to study and to fostering the great verities'. His friends were hurt and on 20 June 1791 Robespierre went to the Jacobin Club in Versailles to explain his decision in person.[40]

That same night, Louis XVI fled Paris, publicly repudiating the direction the Revolution had taken, especially in reforms to the Church. On the evening of the next day, he was recognized near the eastern frontier and arrested in the village of Varennes. The king's attempted flight changed everything, adding incontrovertible evidence to the narrative of conspiracy. From this point onwards revolutionaries were certain that Louis and those around him had conspired to facilitate an enemy invasion. The majority in the Assembly nevertheless contrived to keep Louis on the throne: the alternative seemed chaos.[41]

On 14 July a torrid debate erupted in the Assembly, with Robespierre arguing that 'royal inviolability is an invention' and that Louis should be deposed. It was not a call for a republic: while he could not identify a Cromwell who might emerge to impose a new despotism, he was concerned at powerful factions (referring to the 'triumvirate' of Barnave, Duport and Lameth) 'which are more active and more powerful than is appropriate to a free people'. In his *Révolutions de France et de Brabant*, Desmoulins had reminded Robespierre in 1790 that 'when [in college] we longed for the tribune of Rome and of Athens' and enthused about the possibilities of a republic in the new France. Like most others, however, Robespierre saw the participatory democracy of the ancient city-states as unworkable in a large nation.[42]

The German Charles-Engelberg Oelsner, a member of the Jacobin Club who had been in Paris since 1789, claimed that he had been with Robespierre at

Marguerite Chalabre's house when he responded to a question about his preferred system of government: 'that of Lycurgus'. As a schoolboy Robespierre would have read Plutarch's summary of the small Spartan senate: 'a central weight, like ballast in a ship, which always kept things in a just equilibrium, the twenty-eight always adhering to the kings so far as to resist democracy and, on the other hand, supporting the people against the establishment of absolute monarchy'. Given Robespierre's misgivings about a parliamentary system in which representatives set themselves apart from the people, he may well have been attracted to the idea of a small senate as guides 'if the people decide crookedly'.[43]

Louis was suspended temporarily from his position as king, but the Assembly was determined to quell any popular unrest that might threaten the constitutional monarchy. On 17 July an unarmed demonstration to demand Louis' abdication was organized on the Champ de Mars by the democratic Cordeliers Club, among whose leaders were Georges Danton, Jean-Paul Marat and Desmoulins. A petition was to be signed on the same 'altar of the homeland' on which the Festival of Federation had been celebrated a year earlier. Lafayette, the commander of the National Guard, was ordered to disperse the petitioners; his guardsmen killed perhaps fifty of them. Although the Jacobins had withdrawn support for the petition, Robespierre joined the general outrage at the Jacobin Club on the evening of the killings on the Champ de Mars: 'these people believed they had the right to present a petition to their representatives and their blood was spilled on the altar of the homeland'.[44]

Such was the punitive atmosphere after the killings on the Champ de Mars that Robespierre felt compelled to draft a letter from the Jacobin Club to the Assembly. In it he stressed that the Jacobins' own petition had been withdrawn, and he criticized muddled and 'destructive notions of false republicanism'. In late July he was much less defensive in an *Adresse de Maximilien Robespierre aux Français*, in which he insisted that he had never regarded the Declaration of the Rights of Man and of the Citizen as 'idle theory': 'I have regarded it as a body of judicial axioms at once universal, unchangeable, and imprescriptible, intended to be applied to all mankind.' It was more important than whether France was a republic or a monarchy, as long as 'the majesty of the people in the face of its delegate was not diminished'.[45]

The blame for the killings lay with 'the most dastardly and corrupt of men', 'who regard the slightest restlessness, inseparable from any revolution, as the destruction of society, as the overthrow of the universe'. These were the most prominent of those seeking at all costs to end the Revolution, men such as Barnave and Lafayette. But most of the members of the National Assembly were concerned to consolidate the state of the Revolution as expressed in the new Constitution, and more than 260 of them deserted the Jacobin Club for the Feuillants, similarly named after its meeting place in a former convent. Robespierre was now in a tiny radical minority—no more than about thirty deputies—and isolated from all the Artois members of the Assembly.[46]

After the killings on the Champ de Mars, Robespierre was at the Jacobin Club when some National Guardsmen burst in shouting threats at those they held responsible for the divisions inside France. It was at this meeting that his fellow Jacobin Maurice Duplay offered him protection. Duplay was a joiner and carpenter of some means. He owned three houses, but it was in the residence he rented at 366 Rue St-Honoré, close to both the Assembly and the Jacobin Club, that he suggested Robespierre install himself. Maurice and his wife Françoise were more than twenty years older than Robespierre, and their family included a boy of fourteen, a nephew and three daughters. The eldest daughter, aged twenty, was called Éléonore, her pet name being Cornélie, after Cornelia Africana of ancient Rome. She and Maximilien became close friends. Robespierre had an upstairs bed-sitting-room in the two-storied building overlooking a small court-yard, and seems to have spent almost all his time there when he was not at the Assembly or Jacobin Club. This was a simple room: a small desk, a bed, some straw-seated chairs, a bookcase. One of the neighbours was Marguerite Chalabre.[47]

In the final months of the National Assembly, Robespierre became the key spokesman for the democratic opposition. Although it was he who had moved that Mirabeau should be the first person interred in Ste-Geneviève in April 1791, the tenor of his speeches changed after Mirabeau's death, as if the man's massive presence had been a burden. Robespierre was now bolder and more assured in his position as the spokesman for democracy. He had earned a reputation as the voice of the principles of 1789, waging a ceaseless battle against the compro-misers whom he held responsible for the increasing polarization between those for whom the Revolution had gone too far and the masses of urban and rural people disappointed at the lack of concrete change to their material well-being.

Just as in Arras, his personal demeanour and intractability polarized those who encountered him. The British composer and political commentator William

Augustus Miles wrote home to a friend that he studied Robespierre every night at the Jacobin Club: 'he is cool, measured and resolved. He is *in his heart* a republican. . . . He is a stern man, rigid in his principles, plain, unaffected in his manners, no foppery in his dress, certainly above corruption, despising wealth . . .'. Despite the dismissive asides and laughter of Duport and the Lameths, concluded Miles, 'he is really a character to be contemplated; he is growing every hour into consequence'.[48] Among those who agreed was the royal family portraitist Adélaïde Labille-Guiard, who chose Robespierre as one of fourteen deputies whose portraits she exhibited in the Paris salon. By the time the salon opened in September, the other portraits represented some among Robespierre's Feuillants opponents, as was the artist.[49]

Others had come to despise and fear him. Oelsner wrote towards September 1791 that Robespierre was long-winded, incapable of compromise, and ignorant about France's neighbours, yet with the appeal of a leader of a sect:

He speaks with the enthusiasm of a lover of himself and of the people, and after pouring out his heart thousands upon thousands of times, he falls exhausted on the bosom of his mistress. It is hard to describe the intoxication with which he is received. A wave of his hand is enough to transform public joy to a funeral bell for his adversaries. The People are so convinced of Robespierre's virtue, so predisposed in his favour, that they could watch him picking their neighbour's pocket without believing it.

Like Germaine de Staël, Oelsner interpreted Robespierre's lack of ease in social situations as boorishness: 'I do not know anyone more unbearable, more arrogant, more taciturn or more boring. At Madame de Kéralio's I have seen him hold himself apart for an hour, playing with a big dog.' He was convinced that, should Robespierre follow through his 'bloody projects', his obsession with the evil intentions of his opponents could only end in a 'blood-soaked catastrophe'.[50] Even a fellow Jacobin, Dubois-Crancé, was frightened by his intransigence at about the same time:

. . . he was vain and jealous, but just and virtuous; his greatest detractors could never once accuse him of the slightest deviation. . . . this man, fed on the moral ideas of Rousseau, felt brave enough to imitate his exemplar; he had the same austerity of principles, of customs, the untamed character, the unconciliatory spirit, the proud simplicity, even the moroseness. . . . If the Assembly had been made up of Robespierre alone, France today would perhaps be but a heap of rubble . . . .[51]

Dubois-Crancé also described him as the 'general of the *sans-culottes*'. In 1791 active democrats among the working people of Paris commonly became known by the term, which was both a political label for a militant patriot and a social description signifying men of the people who did not wear the knee-breeches and stockings of the upper classes. By August 1791, Robespierre, Pétion and others had forged a new political alliance between the democrats of the Jacobin Club and these militants. Robespierre cemented the alliance in two major speeches in August, one on the 11th making a final attack on the distinction between 'active' and 'passive' citizens, the other on the 22nd linking civic rights with social justice. In the latter he spoke for the poor:

The coarse clothes which cover my body, the humble roof beneath which I have the right to live in privacy and peace, the modest wages with which I support my wife and children—all this does not amount to an estate, a *château* . . . what is the origin of that excessive inequality which concentrates all the wealth of the country in a few hands? Is it not bad laws, bad government, and the vices of a corrupt society?[52]

On 5 July and 27 August Leopold II of Austria and Frederick William II of Prussia had warned the National Assembly about the safety of Louis XVI and the royal family. It suited the Assembly to heed that warning, but for reasons of internal order. On 14 September, Louis XVI promulgated the Constitution that embodied the Assembly's work since 1789. France was to be a constitutional monarchy in which power was shared between the king, as head of the executive, and a legislative assembly elected by a restrictive property franchise. When, on 30 September, Louis signed a decree to dissolve the Assembly, groups of citizens were waiting for Robespierre, Pétion and the Abbé Grégoire, with cries of 'Long live the deputies without stain! Long live the Incorruptible!', a reference to the nickname Robespierre had enjoyed since May. Students from Louis-le-Grand handed them wreaths of oak-leaves interlaced with tricolour ribbons, saying

'Receive the prize of your civic virtue and incorruptibility'. It was reported that Robespierre leapt from his carriage. 'Citizens,' he cried, 'What are you doing? What humiliating posture are you adopting? Is this my reward for my two years' work for you? Have you already forgotten that you are a free people?' He was then stopped by women, one of whom presented her child. 'At least,' she said, 'You will allow this child to kiss you'. One of the women then made a speech to Robespierre:

> In the midst of corruption, you have remained the unshakeable support of truth; always steadfast, always incorruptible; always following your conscience, you have fought to maintain the purity of a constitution dictated by philosophy for the good of humankind. . . . This people, I say, speaks your name only with high regard; you are its guardian angel, its hope, its consolation.[53]

So an unprepossessing Artois deputy who had only narrowly been elected in 1789, and who had none of the physical attributes of a natural orator, had reached a point of popularity where he was chaired in triumph from the final session of the National Assembly in September 1791. The acclaim for Robespierre came from the profound respect he had won across more than two years as the personification of unequivocal commitment to the principles of 1789, a refusal to compromise with the persons and practices of the *ancien régime*. His resilience in the face of his own nervousness and the frequent ridicule or condescension of others was bolstered by the mounting evidence that not all of his fellow deputies shared his mission but instead contrived to exclude sections of the people from power or manoeuvred for personal advantage.[54]

Other deputies were livid with jealousy at this popularity. One of them, Périsse du Luc from Lyon, fulminated at 'the ludicrousness of the eulogies, adulation and wreaths lavished on the ridiculous trio of Robespierre, Pétion and Grégoire, those mediocre men who haven't done a stroke of work on the Constitution, from whom not a single decree, a single law about anything has issued . . .'.[55] Many found Robespierre's long, digressive speeches dull or even irritating, and interrupted to tell him so. But the distinctive resoluteness that had characterized his style as a lawyer in Arras toughened rather than weakened his insistence. He spoke on. His measured delivery was perfect for the scribes of the scores of newspapers who reported the sessions of the Assembly. There, as at the

Jacobin Club, he evinced a remarkable capacity to confront those with whom he disagreed, to absorb criticism, without appearing to stumble. In all, he was twentieth of the most frequent speakers in the Assembly, with 276 speeches and interventions: Camus made 605 and Mirabeau 439, whereas two-thirds spoke once or twice, if at all. Mirabeau himself was said to have quipped that 'this man will go far: he believes everything he says'. In the end, Robespierre's claim to be expressing the core principles of 1789 became more widely accepted.[56]

After the king's flight, and the departure of many Jacobins to join the Feuillants, Robespierre had been almost alone at the Jacobin Club. Former associates had rounded on him in letters home, Michel Maupetit describing him as atrocious and treacherous and François Bouchette as 'a bad fellow'. Within months, however, leading figures such as Grégoire, Bertrand Barère, Pierre-Louis Prieur, Sieyès, Rabaut St-Étienne and Dubois-Crancé himself had rejoined, and Jacobin numbers had swelled to perhaps eight hundred. At the Club in particular, Robespierre came to be perceived as the Revolution's authentic voice. In 1790 he had used the Assembly as his rostrum, delivering sixty-eight speeches compared with only three at the Club. In 1791, in contrast, as well as delivering no fewer than seventy-seven speeches before the National Assembly was dissolved in September, he made sixty-three to his Jacobin colleagues.[57]

Robespierre was not charismatic, so it is all the more remarkable that he came so quickly to be admired or detested by his peers and the wider public. He did so by a combination of extraordinary resolve and compelling argument. His childhood and schooling had developed in him a great capacity for intense study, combined with a fierce will that compensated for his insecurities. His relentless articulation of the core principles of the Revolution, and his insistence that improving the civic and material dignity of the poor was one of them, won him both loyalty and loathing. This was brought home with a rush when he made his first return to Arras in more than two years.

CHAPTER 7

'Numerous and implacable enemies'
ARRAS 1791

Maximilien was never much of a traveller. While a lawyer in Arras in the 1780s he had limited himself to his memorable short trip through Lens to Carvin, and visits to relatives and clients in the towns and villages near Arras. There is no evidence that he ventured to other provinces or that he ever saw the sea to the west. But the road from Arras to Paris was very familiar to him from his annual trips to and from the College of Louis-le-Grand in the 1770s. Now in October 1791 he was taking the road again, returning home for the first time in thirty months. This trip to Artois was to be a turning point in his life, confronting him with the hard realities of provincial responses to the Revolution and ultimately convincing him of his own future priorities.

From the outset of the Revolution, Robespierre had been caught between his commitment to the general direction that revolutionary reform should take and his role as a deputy of a province with distinctive characteristics and privileges. Although in 1789 the sixteen Artois deputies had all voted to rescind the special privileges of their province, Robespierre, as the most outspoken, was singled out as responsible by those who would consequently lose position, income and tax privileges. Robespierre was stung by allegations from Arras that he was compromising the province's interests, and he responded to an article in the *Affiches d'Artois* in November 1789 that stated he was in favour of the sale of church property, it being 'good neither for religion nor the State'. He complained that the 'partisans of the old abuses' were targeting him 'with a torrent of libels, of calumnies of all kinds, as extraordinary and absurd as they are atrocious'. One of these 'calumnies' was a furious letter to him from a lawyer in Arras in December: 'so, scoundrel, you will no doubt stay in this august National Assembly, where respectable men are embarrassed to be with you. All your legal colleagues swear you will never again set foot in this town, and I warn you that all the people of the countryside will crush you as soon as they find you.'[1]

In late 1789, in the context of municipal elections to be held in early 1790, Robespierre had drafted an *Address to the Belgian People* in response to these recriminations. He used the term 'Belgian' in a cultural rather than geographical sense, since he was addressing the people of Flanders, Hainaut, Cambrésis and Artois. Steeped in classical history as he was, it may also have seemed entirely logical to refer to the northeast of France in the terms of the ancient 'Gallia Belgica', especially with the support for the Revolution across the border in Brabant in the Austrian Netherlands. He stressed the achievements of the Assembly to date, including the body blows it had directed against the seigneurial system: 'you wanted certain seigneurial rights to be suppressed, others softened, others surrendered; the National Assembly exceeded your expectations in this; it suppressed, without any conditions for compensation the most unjust, those most contrary to the rights of humanity.' While the August decrees on feudalism had indeed abolished personal obligations and rights, such as serfdom, unpaid labour and hunting privileges, as he stressed, he was less frank about those seigneurial dues for which rural communities would need to pay heavy compensation.[2]

While in Paris, Robespierre had been kept well informed of the progress of the Revolution in Arras and Artois by his brother Augustin and his old friend Antoine Buissart, and had often expressed his concern about the attenuated change that had occurred in positions of power. Early in November 1789 Robespierre had written to Buissart, admitting that he was bothered by reports that Arras was lacking in revolutionary zeal: 'What are people thinking? What are they saying? What are they doing in Artois? What are you doing yourself? . . . Who are the men in charge of things now? I have just received a letter from a patriot, who laments the obstinacy of the aristocracy . . . '.[3] From the outset power had shifted within the elite of Arras rather than against it. In the municipal elections of early 1790, participation was only about 25 per cent of 'active' citizens. Despite their falling-out in 1789, Robespierre would have been pleased that Dubois de Fosseux was easily elected as the first popularly chosen mayor of

Arras, but less so that the new municipal council was dominated by many of the nobles and merchants who had run the town before 1789.[4]

Much of the energy of the 'patriots' in Artois was consumed by scuffles between Arras and St-Omer over which should be the capital of the new department of Pas-de-Calais, which had been created in January 1790 from the old province of Artois plus some coastal areas from Picardy, such as the region around Calais. Ultimately, Arras would be the centre of the new department, with its 8 districts, 86 cantons and over 900 communes. The compromise was that St-Omer would be its episcopal seat: in Arras there were loud protests against the consequent dissolution of the cathedral chapter and its expenditures. Revolutionary reform destroyed the old Council of Artois: now there would be just a district court. Most of the two hundred judges and lawyers of the complex former judicial apparatus were soon unemployed or scrabbling for work.[5]

The legislation on forests and the status of lands that villages claimed were communal property seized illegally by seigneurs over preceding centuries was particularly relevant to Artois, as Robespierre pointed out in a letter to Buissart the day his motion was passed in the Assembly.[6] But the unsatisfactory conditions imposed on rural communities seeking to reclaim communal lands or to challenge compensation payments for seigneurial dues would only irritate those communities while also alienating former lords.

Robespierre's personal involvement in the rural legislation made him a target for discontent at home, as did his repeated criticism in 1790 of the direct tax qualification necessary for 'active' citizenship. The latter drew him in to an acrimonious battle with the noble deputy Briois de Beaumez. Beaumez had known Robespierre since their days in the Academy of Arras; he was also Charlotte Buissart's cousin. The two men had clashed during the battles over the privileges of the Estates of Artois in the winter of 1788–89, and were to continue to do so in Versailles and Paris. During the debate on male suffrage, Robespierre had ended his speech of 25 January 1790 with a blunt assertion that 'all Frenchmen must be admissible to all public positions without any other distinction than that of virtues and talents'. If the distinction between 'active' and 'passive' citizens based on direct tax contributions was adopted, he had noted, its effect would be particularly inequitable in Artois, a relatively privileged province in fiscal terms, where there were low direct taxes in contrast to heavy indirect taxes. This provided Beaumez with a perfect opportunity. He wrote to his father (like him a former president of the Council of Artois) that the implication of Robespierre's speech was that Artésiens did not pay enough in direct taxes. A former colleague in the Rosati and legal opponent, the judge Foacier de Ruzé, published the accusation in an *Address from an Artésien to his Compatriots* which, according to Robespierre's brother Augustin, had a dramatic impact in Arras and its rural environs in June. He told Maximilien of his fear that 'you will seal with your blood the people's cause', that there were some among his enemies 'unhappy enough to strike you down'.

Robespierre decided to respond with an open *Letter to M. de Beaumez*. The letter was also signed by seven other deputies from Artois: five from the Third Estate and two influential nobles (Charles de Lameth and the Marquis de Croix). Robespierre highlighted the schemes of 'the aristocrats' that 'in hundreds of places have distanced the people from the assemblies' through deliberate misinformation. In another *Address to the Artésien People* he explained the reasons compelling him to defend himself just as he was compelled to defend his constituents. Again he attacked those involved in 'the deadly scheme of strangling freedom at birth, busily angering the People, deceived about its real defenders ... let the bravest of my slanderers come out of the shadows, where they are all hiding ...'.[7] The worst of them was Beaumez, one of those who, 'having enthusiastically defended all the abuses of the *ancien régime* which benefited them, were clever enough to refrain from claiming to remember them, as soon as they appeared to vanish forever'. As for Robespierre, he would not 'compromise with vanity, nor with influence, nor with seduction': it was enough for him 'to have served his fellow citizens, without wanting anything, without hoping for anything from anyone'.

Certainly he could no longer hope for support from Barbe-Thérèse Marchand, the owner and editor of the *Affiches d'Artois* in Arras. She had once been on good terms with Maximilien and Charlotte, assisting him with his campaign in 1789 and probably providing him with financial support as he left for Versailles. Their friendship had rapidly faded across 1789, and by the spring of 1790 she was implacably opposed to the radicalism of the Revolution. In April 1790, Charlotte had had a showdown with her and wrote to her brother:

> We've had a falling-out. I allowed myself to tell her what all good patriots ought
> to think about her newspaper, what you thought about it. I reproached her for

always putting in odious remarks about the people. She got angry. She maintains there are no aristocrats in Arras, that she knows them all to be patriots, that it's only hotheads who find her gazette aristocratic; she told me a heap of nonsense and since then she hasn't been sending us her paper any longer.[8]

There were personal difficulties closer to home. From Arras, Augustin wrote to Maximilien on 19 June 1790, expressing practical concerns: 'if you want to bring peace to our small household as well you must send us money. What you sent has been used to pay Madame Nicolas the rent and there is almost nothing left.... We have just put on mourning for Franklin' (who had died on 17 April).[9] He noted that his brother's open letter to Beaumez had been distributed to all the popular political clubs. What was really concerning Augustin, however, was the continuing rural unrest which, despite the Assembly's decree of 15 March on communal lands, showed no signs of abating. He wrote of one village:

> The peasants are refusing to pay tithes, some because, they say, those who are levying them are not entitled to them. .... A great many of the inhabitants of this community want to divide up the marshland; I know from honest people who have come to consult me that this division would be detrimental and that it is requested only by the muddleheaded. I beg you to bring peace to this municipality ....

The source of these worries was the unresolved issues in the countryside, where the Assembly's attempt to placate the former seigneurial owners of the great estates had forced it to compromise over ownership of common lands and the complete abolition of feudal obligations. In September 1790 Dubois de Fosseux, as president of the Directory of Pas-de-Calais, sent a detailed circular with fifty-nine questions to every commune, seeking information, for example, on the vexed issue of common lands and other legal actions between rural communities and their former lords. The responses—from 772 of the 941 communes—highlighted the extent of tensions. While the monopoly of seigneurs over grain mills had now been removed as a grievance, for example, that of common lands in particular remained, despite the laws of March 1790.[10]

Robespierre's interventions in support of collective rights in the countryside in early 1790 were very much in accord with majority opinion in the villages of

Artois. But Artésien rural society was marked by a distinctive social structure, with tenants of large farms—four of whom had been his close associates as deputies at Versailles—surrounded by a mass of smallholders and labourers. His campaign for universal male suffrage necessarily put Robespierre at odds with the well-to-do 'fermocratie'—perhaps 5 per cent of the rural population—which was quite content with the way in which the restricted suffrage and extensive powers for municipalities reinforced their local control after the initial upheavals of 1789–90. His less frequent direct involvement in rural issues after 1790 may reflect Robespierre's inability to articulate a rural policy that would take account of these different interests, given that he considered the rural masses to be essentially homogeneous.[11]

Despite the continuing unrest in the countryside around Arras, there was still optimism about the future of the Revolution. On 3 June 1790 the National Guards from the neighbouring department of the Somme had joined with those of Pas-de-Calais in a festival on the town's great square, the Grand Marché. The National Guard and troops garrisoned in Arras assembled around an Altar of the Fatherland in the presence of the mayor and the bishop, Louis de Conzié. Dubois de Fosseux gave a rousing speech, exalting the new values of fraternity, peace and 'that happiness which virtue alone may enjoy'. Those present swore an oath, and the Te Deum was sung. Six weeks later, on the first anniversary of the taking of the Bastille, the grandeur of the Festival of Federation in Arras moved even Conzié, already an outspoken critic of the Revolution, to reassure local authorities that 'religion recognizes in you its worthy children'.[12]

But two days before the Festival of Federation, on 12 July 1790, the National Assembly had voted in the Civil Constitution of the Clergy. With the nationalization of church property on 2 November 1789, this decision overturned the temporal and religious organization of a powerful clerical establishment and had a dramatic impact on a profoundly Catholic region. The department was charged with the sale of the church's massive properties, eagerly bought up by wealthy bourgeois and nobles, but making vulnerable all those who had been dependent on the Church for employment or charity.

The application of the Civil Constitution of the Clergy, aligning the organization of dioceses with that of the new departments, had been envisaged in terms of public service. Urban parishes were to be rationalized to one for every six thousand people. The bishop and priests were to be elected by all active citizens from among clerical candidates who had ministered for at least five years in the case of priests and fifteen years in that of bishops. As civil servants paid by the state, they had also to swear an oath of fidelity to that Constitution. Fewer than one-fifth of the parish clergy of Pas-de-Calais took the oath. Many others sought unsuccessfully to take a conditional oath swearing fidelity only in secular matters. Only two parish priests swore the oath in Arras, where the eleven former parishes were replaced by just four. As in other provincial centres across the country, a test of strength began in Arras between 'juring' or 'constitutional' and 'non-juring' or 'refractory' clergy. Such was the shortage of priests that the first 'constitutional' bishop, the former parish priest Pierre-Joseph Porion—Conzié now having emigrated—moved to accelerate men as young as nineteen into the ministry.[13]

The division between juring and non-juring clergy sharply aggravated conflicts about the Revolution in general, already laid bare by the public rift between Robespierre and Beaumez. The two were still arguing about the suffrage issue in the National Assembly in August 1791. As we have noted, relations between Robespierre and his home province had soured, reflected in a request he made to the district of Arras early in 1791 to be removed from the list of taxpayers for his former residence, 'having definitively left the place where he lived'. But the campaign of Robespierre and his fellow deputies had some success. The Society of the Friends of the Constitution, the affiliate of the Paris Jacobin Club, was at first moderate and hesitant in its politics, but became in 1791 a local force relaying to Arras through Robespierre's network of allies (his brother Augustin, Martial Herman and Antoine Buissart in particular) the priorities and concerns of the Jacobin Club. By mid-1791 the Society numbered about three hundred members, and took over as its quarters the former church of St-Étienne. As Robespierre began to think of his first trip home since 1789, he was more optimistic: public spirit had improved since the Society began to contest 'the aristocratic influence of *the former "respectable" people* of all classes'.[14]

Robespierre may have delayed his departure for Arras to be present at the convening of the new Legislative Assembly of 745 deputies in Paris on 1 October. Among the deputies, all new to Parliament, was Lazare Carnot, well-known to Robespierre from their time together in the Academy and the Rosati. Arras itself had elected a young and conservative lawyer, Sixte Deusy, much admired by Mme Marchand: Augustin had been defeated in the elections, but was now public prosecutor for Arras and on the departmental administration.[15]

So Robespierre left Paris with mixed emotions, no doubt eager to see family and friends after thirty months, yet well aware of the political and personal divisions that would confront him. Preparations for his trip were made by Augustin, Charlotte, the Buissarts, Armand Guffroy, justice of the peace for the district of Arras, and Joseph Lebon, the constitutional priest of the village of Neuville-Vitasse, who would soon become friendly with Maximilien.[16] Charlotte and a group of ten others travelled to Bapaume, thirteen miles south of Arras, to welcome him and participate in a banquet in his honour. Robespierre arrived at Bapaume on 14 October, at a moment of tension. A regiment of the Parisian National Guard, some of them veterans of 14 July 1789, had found themselves there without provisions, in filthy lodgings, and responded by an auto-da-fé of royal and noble coats of arms. On the 15th more Guardsmen from Seine-et-Oise arrived before Robespierre set off for Arras, with the group of his supporters swelling to up to two hundred along the way.

Once he arrived in Arras, Robespierre sent a detailed account of his return home to his 'dear friend' Maurice Duplay, urging him to 'convey my great affection to Madame Duplay, your young ladies and my little friend', their son Jacques.[17] He had come 'safely into port' in Bapaume, and was moved when the National Guards, 'together with the patriots of Bapaume, presented me with a civic wreath with expressions of the most fraternal affection'. But the municipal and district officers had snubbed him. In Arras, too, 'the people received me with manifestations of an affection I cannot describe, and of which I cannot think without emotion; they had forgotten nothing to demonstrate it to me; a multitude of citizens had come from the city to meet me.' But here, too, his enemies among the 'aristocrats'—dismissed as 'Feuillants'—were conspicuously absent, despite taking the precaution of lighting their windows to show support as the crowd surged through the streets.

Forty years later Charlotte could still recall the pleasure she felt at being able to embrace her brother after more than two years, and the eruption of celebration in Arras when he insisted on alighting from the coach to walk through the streets. But Robespierre soon became aware of the level of resentment and opposition from the town's old elites, supported by many of those who had been dependent on them. The local newspaper, the *Affiches d'Artois*, was dismissive of

Robespierre's return, snorting that among those who had accompanied Augustin and Charlotte to Bapaume were a former usher at the municipal theatre and two laundrywomen. On 18 October it reported that 'M. de Robespierre has arrived at last', perhaps reinserting the 'de' to prick at Maximilien's democratic skin: 'we would not have noticed his entry into the town had he not been accompanied by thirty officers from the Parisian Army garrisoned at Bapaume, who had received him with acclaim and had extended their respects so far as to conduct him to Arras'. The public welcome in his home town developed into a demonstration the next day outside Mme Marchand's home, demanding that she show more respect towards Robespierre. She retorted: 'I asked them for permission to laugh from time to time; so many people are crying!'[18]

Robespierre did not linger in Arras. The enthusiasm with which he was welcomed by many was tempered by the distress of others within the judicial and clerical milieux he knew so well.[19] Within a week he travelled twenty miles north to the town of Béthune for three days (23–25 October), passing through the village of Aix, where his carriage was decorated with flowers and oak branches: a peasant woman was heard to shout 'We have no laurel trees, but oak lasts longer.' In Béthune the official response was again chilly—no member of the municipality or other public official received him—but the popular reception was even more enthusiastic than at Arras. The executive of the Society of Friends of the Constitution made a record of the visit of 'the man who had long held a place in our hearts', under their motto 'Liberty or Death'.[20] 'The honour of presenting him with the civic wreath was envied by the ladies: the men deferred to them. His modesty forbade his allowing it to be placed on his head; he held it to his heart.' As when he was besieged at the close of the National Assembly the previous month, Robespierre was plainly discomfited by personal adulation, urging those present to proceed with the Society's deliberations. 'M. Bouthillier of the Golden Lion had the joy of putting him up. How well he deserved it, this worthy citizen, who, begging for the honour of lodging him, said: *Had I only one bed and were I asked for it on behalf of the King or Robespierre, the gallant Deputy would take precedence!*'[21]

Rather than spending a lot of time in Arras itself, Robespierre preferred to travel to see friends in the countryside and to reflect and rest, perhaps at the Carraut farm at Bel-Avesnes nine miles west of the town. He and Augustin dined with the priest Joseph Lebon in the latter's village of Neuville-Vitasse.[22] While

Robespierre may simply have wished to distance himself from the dispiriting divisions in his home town, another reason for this may have been personal. In her memoirs, Charlotte later recalled that Maximilien and Anaïs Deshorties, his aunt Eulalie's stepdaughter, had been in love and courting for several years before his departure for Paris in 1789. According to Charlotte, he was devastated to return to Arras in 1791 and find the love of his life married to another lawyer, his former friend Leduc. In fact, Anaïs only married him ten months later, in August 1792, but Maximilien may have found her presence in Arras uncomfortable.[23]

It may have been during this time of rest that Robespierre penned a remarkable reflection, the *Dedication to the Spirit of Jean-Jacques Rousseau*.[24] The publication of the second volume of Rousseau's *Confessions* in 1788 had had a profound impact on Robespierre, who announced that 'I want to follow in his venerated path.' In his *Dedication* he contemplated his own place in history as he praised

the most eloquent and virtuous of men: today, more than ever, we need eloquence and virtue. Divine man, you taught me to know myself: from an early age, you made me appreciate the dignity of nature and reflect on the great principles of social order. The old edifice has crumbled; the portico of a new edifice has been raised on the rubble and thanks to you, I have added my stone to it. . . .

The recompense of the virtuous man is the consciousness of having wanted the good of one's fellow man. . . . Like you I want to buy these goods through a life of work, even at the price of premature death.

[I am] called to play a role in the midst of the greatest events ever to shake the world, watching the death-throes of despotism and the awakening of true sovereignty; soon to see explode on all sides the gathering storms of which no human mind can foresee all the results. . . .[25]

Robespierre claimed—improbably—that he had seen Rousseau before his death, and had seen on his face the marks of 'the black sorrows to which the injustice of men had condemned you'. He may have been particularly attracted to the 'divine' Rousseau because he too had lost his mother (after childbirth) and his father had deserted him when young. As with many others, however,

Robespierre fully identified above all with Rousseau's concern about the necessity of 'virtue' in the creation of a healthy body politic. Rousseau's premise, that
'the people' are inherently good, however corrupted by poverty and the self-
serving behaviour of powerful elites, had become the core principle in
Robespierre's understanding of popular sovereignty. He had come to believe that
he, too, was 'a virtuous man', called to devote his life to creating a state of virtue
to serve the people.[26]

Whether Robespierre had penned this reflection on his 'perilous career' while
in the Artois countryside, or earlier during the travails of the National Assembly,
he was being forced to confront the divisions and challenges that the Revolution
faced, and what this might mean for him. His sympathy for the rural poor had
made him vulnerable to charges that he was in favour of radical egalitarianism.
One of his admirers was François-Noël Babeuf, who had written to the Academy
in Arras in 1787, when Robespierre was a prominent member. Babeuf, whose
early revolutionary project concerned the full abolition of seigneurial dues and
land redistribution to the propertyless (the 'agrarian law'), saw in Robespierre a
natural ally. 'Scrutinize Robespierre,' he wrote to a friend in September 1791,
'and you will find him an agrarian in the final analysis'. In fact, Robespierre was
not an 'agrarian' in the sense of forced land redistribution, but following his
remarks about changing the laws of inheritance made back in April many like
Babeuf believed he was.[27]

Even more concerning for Robespierre was the danger represented by the
needless alienation of non-juring clergy. To his great annoyance, an extract from
a blunt letter he wrote to an unknown acquaintance in Paris on 4 November was
given to the press and published in the widely read *Courrier des 83 départements*
and *Annales patriotiques*.[28] In it he criticized the ineptitude over the implementation of Church reform: 'wherever an aristocratic priest finds a proselytizer, he
makes a new enemy of the Revolution; since the ignoramuses he misleads are
incapable of discerning between the *religious* and the *national* interest . . .'. As a
result of his visit to Arras, Robespierre had been confronted with the impact of
Church reform on the old ecclesiastical centre. The closing of religious orders,
the transfer of the bishopric to St-Omer, and the reduction in parish churches
had all caused unemployment and resentment.

He was made sharply aware of the way in which non-jurors were openly
turning their congregations against the Revolution and enacting their own

festivals. Despite his public sympathy for religious belief, in private Robespierre was sarcastic about the hold of 'fanaticism' on the faithful of the countryside, telling Duplay:

A miracle has just occurred here . . . a non-juring priest was saying Mass in the chapel which contains the Holy relic; genteel pious women were listening. In the middle of the Mass a man throws two crutches he had brought, spreads his arms, walks; he shows the scar on his leg, produces papers which prove that he had been grievously wounded; the man's wife arrives at this miracle; she asks for her husband; they tell her he is walking without crutches; she swoons; she regains her senses praising God and proclaiming a miracle. . . . I do not propose to remain for long in this holy land; I am not worthy of it.[29]

Robespierre's trips to other towns in the region disconcerted him because of the absence of military preparedness and the large number of well-to-do openly discussing their plans to emigrate. 'On our way,' he wrote to Duplay of his trip home to Arras, 'we found the inns filled with emigrants. The innkeepers told us that they were astonished by the numbers they had been accommodating for some time.' He expressed to Duplay his anxieties about the threat this posed in a provincial capital so close to the frontier, particularly in the context of the king's attempted flight in June 1791 and the menacing Declaration of Pillnitz (27 August) signed by the Holy Roman Emperor, Leopold II of Austria, and Frederick William II of Prussia. Indeed, emigration had gathered pace in Pas-de-Calais ever since the flight and capture of the king in June, because all assumed this was a sign that war was imminent. In the town of Montreuil to the west, where there were normally sixty-three resident noble families, only six remained by the autumn, and even they were talking of leaving the country.[30]

Robespierre's return home to Arras and its countryside had been a chastening and instructive experience, for all the joy and support with which his family and political supporters had showered him. He had experienced at first hand what many reports from the provinces had indicated to the Assembly: smouldering discontent among many people about the practical consequences of reforms to the Church; deep frustration in rural communities about the attenuated nature of the supposed end of seigneurialism; division among supporters of the

Revolution as well as outright opposition to revolutionary change from opponents; and mounting anxiety about the likelihood of war with Austria and
Prussia.[31]

His experiences in Artois were crucial to Robespierre's understanding of how
incomplete the Revolution was and just how serious was the threat posed by
anti-revolutionary and counter-revolutionary attitudes. If a region close to Paris
could be in such a state of disunity and unpreparedness at a time of open
hostility from foreign powers, what might this mean for other, more distant frontier regions? His earlier warnings about conspiracies to thwart the people's will
were now reinforced by his experiences. Although some of his contemporaries—and many historians—heard in Robespierre's speeches the obsessions
of a man prone to paranoia about 'the aristocrats', the weeks he spent in
Artois listening and observing provided compelling evidence that the threats
were real.

The dilapidated state of the barracks in Bapaume, and friction in garrisons at
Arras and Lille, convinced him that the increasingly bellicose noises of the
Jacobin members of the newly elected Legislative Assembly could expose France
to war at a vulnerable time. While he was in Artois, he received a letter from an
acquaintance, Marie-Jeanne ('Manon') Roland, from her husband's estate in
Theizé, in the Beaujolais hills east of Villefranche-sur-Saône. It was written at
harvest time, when 'an extraordinary drought had added all that it is possible to
imagine to the barrenness of an ungrateful and stony soil'. It was a warm and
solicitous letter to one among 'the small number of courageous men, ever
faithful to their principles'. She admitted that she had no particular reason to
write, but 'I believed in the interest with which you would receive news of two
beings whose souls are made to feel for you and who want to express to you an
admiration they accord only to those who place above everything the glory of
being just and the happiness of being sensitive.' Like Robespierre, she had been
surprised at the level of opposition to the Revolution she had encountered, this
time in Lyons, and worried about the vulnerability of the masses to rumour or
manipulation: 'the masses everywhere are good … but they are seduced or
blind'.[32] Manon Roland's letter would have confirmed Robespierre's judgement
about the precarious road the Revolution had to travel before it would reach
secure ground in the provinces. He had been friendly with the Rolands on their
arrival from Lyon earlier in 1791, and was a guest at the regular salon conducted

by Manon. Her offer of closer friendship was undermined, however, by the knowledge that her husband was one of those elected to the new Legislative Assembly who was voicing the belief that the answer to internal division lay in war with the crowned heads of Europe.

Robespierre wrote to 'his brother and friend' Maurice Duplay on 17 November to inform him that he would be back in Paris within a few days, and was delighted to hear of Jérôme Pétion's election as mayor of Paris; again he asked Duplay to give his 'tender and unchanging affection to your ladies'. In fact he delayed his return until the end of the month, having decided quickly to spend three days (24–26 November) in Lille as the guest of its Society of Friends of the Constitution.[33]

In all, Robespierre had spent forty-six days in Artois and Picardy. He wrote afterwards to a friend:

> If I come back to Artois, Béthune would be the place where I'd live with most pleasure. Certainly, the presence of my numerous and implacable enemies does not suit me at all. But to live in Béthune, I would need to find a position which would make this possible for me. If I was appointed president of the district tribunal, it seems to me that the objective would be met. I leave it to you, my dear friend, to reflect on the idea, and I count on your discretion.[34]

Of course, this was at a point when Robespierre was no longer in the Assembly and when, for all he knew, the Revolution and his role in it were essentially complete. The Constitution had been promulgated and the new Legislative Assembly elected. Well might Robespierre have contemplated life after Paris, even the possibility of resigning his new position as public prosecutor there. His like-minded colleague Philippe-Antoine Merlin had recently returned to a position as judge of the criminal court in his home town of Douai to the east of Arras.

We do not know whether it was simply the lack of a suitable post in Pas-de-Calais that made up Robespierre's mind that he needed to return to Paris, or whether these were simply the musings of someone not really serious about returning home. Whatever the case, his six weeks in Artois were a turning point. His decision to return to Paris was the most important of his life, and would embroil him in politics in a way that quickly banished any possibility of a calm career in Béthune.

CHAPTER 8

'The Vengeance of the People'
PARIS 1791–92

Two days after his return to Paris on 28 November 1791, Robespierre wrote glowingly to Antoine Buissart in Arras about the affection showered on him at the Jacobin Club and in public.[1] On the day of his return, he had gone directly to the Club, where he was made its president on the spot. In particular, he had been delighted to see his friend Jérôme Pétion, victorious over Lafayette in elections for the new mayor of Paris: 'I supped the same evening at Pétion's. With what joy we saw each other again! With what delight we embraced! . . . The burden with which he is charged is enormous, but I have no doubt that the love of the people and his qualities will give him the means to bear it. I will have supper at his house this evening.'

Despite the warmth of his welcome, Robespierre found a changed political environment in the capital. Simmering discontent about the viability of the political compromise with Louis XVI after his failed flight in June had been further exacerbated by the open hostility of Europe's crowned heads. But whereas in Artois Robespierre had encountered anxiety about a possible war, in Paris he heard a crescendo of warmongering from many of the new deputies.

The mounting hostility of opponents of the Revolution inside and outside France focused the deputies' concern on the counter-revolution centred on Coblenz, where the king's two brothers had created a court in exile. The officer corps of the royal army had begun to disintegrate, with over 2,100 noble officers emigrating between 15 September and 1 December 1791, and six thousand in all across the year. On 9 November the Legislative Assembly had passed a draconian law, effectively declaring the *émigrés* outlaws should they not return by the start of the new year: 'they will be declared guilty of conspiracy; as such they will be prosecuted, and punished with death'. Louis used his suspensive veto to block the legislation three days later.

Events in the rich Caribbean colonies further convinced the deputies of the insidious intentions of France's rivals, England and Spain. Robespierre, and others from the Society of Friends of the Blacks, had warned of the dangers of refusing to extend civic rights to all in the colonies, and in August 1791 hundreds of thousands of mulattoes and slaves in St Domingue (modern-day Haiti) had risen in revolt. Within the next ten days, slaves had taken control of most of the north, surrounding planters in their isolated camps. From the outset this was a particularly bloody civil war: perhaps one hundred thousand slaves joined the revolt and killed two thousand whites, who retaliated by killing rebel slaves taken prisoner.[2]

In this context the increasingly anxious deputies of the Legislative Assembly, who had originally been committed to the Feuillants' goal of stabilizing the Revolution under the king and Constitution, found compelling the agitated rhetoric of a group of Jacobins led by Jacques-Pierre Brissot, who blamed the Revolution's difficulties on internal conspiracies linked to external enemies. His supporter Maximin Isnard spoke of 'a volcano of conspiracy about to explode'. The level of corruption and conspiracy became evident on 20 November, when even Mirabeau's dealings with the court started to become clear.[3] If the towering revolutionary of 1789 had been prepared to betray the people's cause in this way, where might duplicity end?

The day after Robespierre's rapturous welcome at the Jacobin Club, he delivered a blunt warning of the perils inherent in religious reform, and counselled against any attack on religious customs, in this case the confession: 'it is undesirable to clash directly with religious prejudices beloved of the people; it's better that time matures the people and imperceptibly places them beyond prejudice.'[4] War could only make things worse. He was still immensely popular in the capital, but in the Legislative Assembly there were few who opposed the idea of a war of internal purification and external liberation. Deprived of a voice in the Assembly, Robespierre needed to use the Jacobin Club and his journalism to make his views known. It was at the Club that he delivered a series of speeches warning of the dangers of an ill-prepared external campaign while

internal problems remained unresolved. His stance was conditioned by his
sobering experience in Artois of increasing division and the armed forces' lack
of preparedness. He was convinced as well that internal opponents of the
Revolution, especially the court, would welcome a war that would provide
the occasion for its enemies to purge France of revolutionary contamination.
'Let us overcome our enemies within and then march against our foreign foes, if
any still exist,' Robespierre urged the Jacobins on 18 December. Not only was
the Revolution far from complete, but precipitate, ill-prepared war would expose
the nation to the danger of military rule: in turbulent times, 'army chiefs become
the arbiters of the fate of their country and tip the scales in favour of the
party they have embraced. If they are Caesars or Cromwells, they grab power
themselves.'[5]

Despite Robespierre's insistence that he was not opposed to war—as long
as it was a properly prepared, defensive war—his speech was controversial.
Brissot responded on 29 November, insisting that the new nation must declare
war 'for its honour, external security, domestic peace, to restore our finances
and public credit, to put an end to terror, betrayals and anarchy ...'. In his
second major speech on the war, at the Jacobin Club on 2 January, Robespierre
repudiated Brissot's analogy with the American War of Independence, for in
that case the colonists had fought a defensive war against the English king's
army on their own soil.[6] In contrast, 'nobody likes armed missionaries: and the
first advice nature gives to prudence is to repel them as enemies. . . . The declaration of rights is not a ray of sunshine which strikes everyone at the same
moment ...'.

Rather than an ill-prepared invasion of Austria, he argued for the rapid
arming of the National Guard as a people's militia to defend the homeland, and
called for measures 'to stifle domestic and foreign war'. Among them were public
education, festivals and theatre:

> provided that the spirit of liberty governs them and that equality, the people
> and humanity are the only divinities honoured with the homage of the
> citizens. . . . why do we not imitate those sublime institutions of the Greek
> peoples, those solemn games where artists and poets, orators who had made
> their country famous and lit in the hearts of their fellow citizens the sacred
> flame of virtue and liberty. . . .[7]

For Robespierre, the urgent task was civic regeneration: a state of war could only impede, even threaten, its creation.

A gulf had opened up between former allies and had taken on a sharp personal edge, since the implication of Robespierre's analysis was that Brissot and his supporters were putting the Revolution at risk. For their part, the Brissotins accused Robespierre of putting himself above the people by claiming he was their 'defender'. He was indignant:

> I have never claimed that gaudy title; I am of the people, I have never been anything else, I want only to be that . . . .

> Nobody has given us a truer picture of the People than Rousseau, because nobody loved it more: 'the People always wants what is good, but it does not always perceive it' . . . but its natural goodness predisposes it to being duped by political charlatans. These men are well aware of this and take advantage of it.[8]

At the Jacobin Club on 20 January, Brissot urged Robespierre to end their differences, and a club member asked them to embrace as a sign of their mutual esteem and friendship. In the words of the journalist of the *Ami des citoyens*, 'Brissot and Robespierre flung themselves into each other's arms. Thus pride instantly gave way to sentiments of peace and fraternity, which are the mark of true citizens. The Assembly, moved to tears, warmly applauded . . .'. Robespierre immediately made it clear, however, that his demonstration of affection for Brissot in no way changed his opinion about the issue, and gave notice of his intention to deliver another major speech on the war. He again chastized Antoine-Joseph Gorsas, the editor of the *Courrier des 83 départements*, for misrepresenting him by implying that he had rallied to Brissot's point of view.[9] 'What is true in this account', wrote Robespierre, is that 'we cordially embraced'. But he made clear that this did not mean agreement: 'let us fight like free men, with candour, even energetically if need be, but with consideration and friendship'.

The fraternal embrace between Robespierre and Brissot was quickly forgotten. On 26 November Robespierre asked 'is this truly a fight between the people and their despots?' and rounded on the logic of the Brissotins: 'the majority of soldiers are patriots, I know; but are the majority of officers?' When Leopold II

of Austria rebuffed the ultimatum from the Legislative Assembly to disperse the
émigré camps, and singled out the Jacobin Club for special opprobrium,
Robespierre made it plain to the Club that Leopold was also speaking for 'all
those inside France who are enemies of equality, enemies of the revolution,
enemies of the people, they are the ones who are declaring war on the Jacobins'.
The king's inclusion of Brissotins, including Jean-Marie Roland, in a new
ministry in late March only increased Robespierre's suspicion of the motives of
the court: no doubt 'there was more talk of war than of the means of waging it
successfully'. But he was in a tiny minority, even at the Jacobin Club, and his jibe
resulted in a meeting there breaking up in 'the utmost disorder'.[10]

Between 28 November 1791 and 20 April 1792, Robespierre spoke sixty-five
times at the Jacobin Club, at most of its meetings held four times each week. But
he had few supporters of his repeated warnings about war and his pleas to
complete the Revolution instead through a programme of far-reaching political
and social reform. He had become an object of scorn. A Prussian visitor to Paris,
J. F. Reichardt, attended a meeting of the Club and wrote a letter on 18 March
1792 describing how Robespierre, 'after haughtily seating himself on a chair on
its own, near the door, sat motionless, legs crossed, throwing back his well-
curled head. He did not take the least part in the debates. . . . His face was
smooth, as if flattened, his shifty look made the impertinence of his attitude even
more provocative.' The next day, General Dumouriez—the new Minister for
Foreign Affairs and closely linked to the Brissotins now in the king's ministry—
made a bellicose speech at the Jacobin Club wearing a red liberty cap. As
Robespierre rose to respond, a club member pushed a cap onto Robespierre's
head; discomfited and affronted, Robespierre threw it to the floor.[11]

This was a lonely and difficult period for Robespierre, and Reichardt's description of the silent and isolated man at the Jacobin Club points to the personal
anguish he was experiencing. True, he had loyal friends, none more so than
Marguerite Chalabre, who wrote in support after his key speeches and continued
to express her invitation to friendship. After his January speech against the war,
she castigated 'the cruel war party, who are mad for it as crows for carrion. If they
succeed, there is no hope for the country.' She was scathing about the new
ministry of Brissotins and the offer of 'a kiss of peace' for 'the Incorruptible'. Only
Robespierre's genius gave her 'a single ray of hope', and she offered to delay dinner
until two o'clock the next day in the hope that he would come.[12]

Other women who sought to be close to Robespierre made him more uncomfortable. In late September 1791, Manon Roland had written a long letter to Robespierre from her estate at Theizé in Beaujolais, seeking his friendship and lauding his political acumen and constancy. The day after the formation in March of the ministry headed by her husband she invited Robespierre to her house, because she considered him 'the leader of the wise patriots'. But he did not come and she did not forgive him. So by early April he had fallen out with Brissot and the new ministry, and his erstwhile friend Manon Roland.[13]

On 15 February 1792 he was sworn in as public prosecutor in the Paris Criminal Tribunal, the position to which he had been elected in June 1791. His plan was to devote the day to his new position, and his evenings to wider revolutionary activities, but he admitted to the Jacobin Club that he was now feeling physically frail: 'if my strength and my health are not great enough for this double work, I declare that I shall consider myself obliged to choose'. And choose he did: even though the position was lucrative—a salary of 8,000 *livres*— he resigned on 10 April. He offered no explanation, but it is as likely that he felt compromised working under a Brissotin cabinet as much as physical concerns about over-working. His Brissotin opponents now accused him of 'desertion'. The influential *Feuille villageoise*, allied in outlook to the Brissotins and directed at the leadership in rural communities across the country, attacked Robespierre on 3 May for his decision to resign, claiming he preferred to be the 'perpetual inquisitor' of men of substance: 'believing in his good faith, we excused his ridiculous pride, and his fanatical verbiage, but he is more of a charlatan than a fanatic . . .'.[14]

The Jacobin Club had long anticipated a reception to celebrate the arrival of amnestied soldiers from the Châteauvieux regiment who had been summarily punished for mutiny in 1790 by the Marquis de Bouillé, now an *émigré*, and to whose garrison at Metz the king had tried to flee in June 1791. The soldiers were invited to the Legislative Assembly on 9 April. The Jacobins' discussion on how to mark their arrival gave Robespierre the opportunity to launch an attack on Lafayette, Bouillé's cousin and defender, whom he accused of delaying the arrival of the soldiers and whom he had already targeted as a highly untrustworthy general: 'the most dangerous of all, because he still retains a mask of patriotism sufficient to keep a considerable number of uneducated citizens loyal to him'.[15]

But in this atmosphere of war fever few people were listening to Robespierre. On 20 April war was declared on Austria. Only seven deputies voted against. With the reforms to the Church in mid-1790, the declaration of war was a major turning point of the Revolution. For Maximilien Robespierre, it was his lowest ebb. Leading Brissotins now went on the offensive against him. The journalist and poet André Chénier dismissed Robespierre as 'a talker, known for his demented ferocity and for an inexplicable hatred for a general of whom one could not imagine being jealous . . .'. On 27 April Robespierre again felt impelled to utter the distinctive phrase at a meeting of the Jacobin Club: 'I am neither the messenger, nor the mediator, nor the tribune, nor the defender of the people; I am of the people myself [*je suis peuple moi-même!*]'. He here again identified himself with the people, but so alone did he now feel that he referred to his preparedness for martyrdom.[16] Within six months Robespierre's insistence on the folly of listening to the siren songs of war had placed him sharply at odds with the mass of Parisians who had formerly showered him with adulation.

At the start of May news arrived of a major military reversal in the north. The first two armies in the field, advancing towards Tournai and Mons, had been shattered. Their Irish-born General Dillon, nephew of the *émigré* Archbishop of Narbonne, was murdered by his troops in retribution. In such a situation, Robespierre became a scapegoat for anxious Brissotins. The 28 April issue of Condorcet's *Chronique de Paris* even suggested Robespierre was a secret agent of the court, and the *Révolutions de Paris* insinuated that he had resigned from his position as public prosecutor following a meeting with Marie-Antoinette. Among Robespierre's defenders was Jean-Paul Marat, who was infuriated and devoted an entire issue of his *Ami du peuple* to defending Robespierre. For Marat, it was Robespierre's constancy and consequent popularity that had aroused the Brissotins' rage. At the same time, Marat acknowledged that he had his own differences with Robespierre because of his own angry, often bloodcurdling journalism. During one meeting in January, probably at the Duplays, Robespierre had reproached him for having 'partly destroyed the prodigious influence my paper had on the Revolution by dipping my pen in the blood of the enemies of freedom, by speaking of ropes, of daggers'. His 'absurd and violent propositions', recalled Robespierre, disgusted 'patriots' as much as the aristocracy.[17]

Despite the needling, Robespierre was still addressing the Jacobin Club at least twice a week. Even then, however, his influence was restricted by Brissotin control of its correspondence committee. In May 1792 he began to edit a paper entitled the *Défenseur de la Constitution*, in order to defend himself against his scapegoating as news came in from the front.[18] The *Défenseur*, a substantial weekly of between 48 and 64 pages, was largely written by Robespierre himself, with news items and letters sent by correspondents from the provinces and the armies. A few deputies and other revolutionaries occasionally collaborated, in particular his Versailles ally and now deputy Laurent Lecointre, who received frequent reports from the borders which he passed to Robespierre. Other contributors included fellow Jacobins such as Collot d'Herbois, a popular actor and pamphleteer, and a new friend Georges Couthon, confined to a wheelchair, probably as a result of meningitis, and with whom Robespierre frequently worked in the evenings in his room in the Duplays' house.

Now that the war against Austria had begun, he used the first issue of the newspaper to set out the essentials for ensuring that this would be a genuine 'people's war', fought to the death for the triumph of universal principles in Europe: 'the war we have engaged in began with a reverse; it must end in the triumph of liberty or the disappearance of the last Frenchman on Earth.' It must be a war against tyrants, not against peoples:

> Why have no manifestos intended to foster the People's rights and the princi-
> ples of freedom been translated by the government into the German and
> Belgian languages and spread beforehand among the People and the Austrian
> army? Why have they not been given a formal guarantee of the manner in
> which we propose to conduct ourselves with regard to the political affairs of
> that land after our conquest?

Robespierre named the leaders of the faction he was targeting, those who had assured the people that the war would be as brief as it was necessary: Brissot and Condorcet, supported by influential deputies from Bordeaux, such as Guadet, Vergniaud and Gensonné.[19]

Other issues were distancing Robespierre from Brissot and his followers. Robespierre had argued since July 1789 that only the completion of the Revolution would obviate the need for violent popular retribution. On 3 March

1792 Jacques Simonneau, mayor of Étampes, thirty miles southwest of Paris, was shot and stabbed to death outside his town hall as he tried to prevent a furious crowd from fixing the cost of wheat at a lower price (*taxation populaire*).[20] Simonneau, proprietor of a tannery with about sixty employees, was also a member of his local Jacobin Club. Despite the declining value of the *assignat*, widespread food shortages among wage earners, and fears of war, he was prepared to impose martial law to protect the free market in foodstuffs and, after seven hours of unrest in the markets from locals and peasants from surrounding villages, asked the local cavalry officer to have his eighty troops armed and at the ready. The troops had, however, refused to load their muskets and fled once shots were fired at Simonneau. Others fired on and battered his dead body before leaving to shouts of 'Vive la Nation!'

Simonneau was not the first mayor to be killed by his fellow citizens.[21] But he was more obviously exercising his official functions, the Constitution had been passed, and the majority in the Legislative Assembly was determined to enforce the rule of law and the freedom of commerce. A horrified Assembly decided to honour Simonneau's courage with a Festival of Law. On 3 June sixty battalions of National Guards and deputations from the forty-eight sections of Paris marched through the capital to the Champ de Mars in front of an estimated two hundred thousand spectators, a scene that was captured on a massive canvas by Jacques-Louis David.

Robespierre relied instead on the views of Pierre Dolivier, parish priest of Mauchamps to the north of Étampes, already well known for calling for a republic. Dolivier's petition damning Simonneau was signed by forty citizens of Étampes and claimed that the 'natural law of the right to survive' had to take precedence over economic freedom: 'it is revolting that the rich man and all that surround him, people, dogs and horses, lack nothing in their idleness, while those who live by working, men and animals, succumb under the double burden of work and hunger'. Dolivier's plea found little echo in the Assembly, apart from Robespierre, who published the petition with a long commentary in the *Défenseur de la Constitution* on 7 June.[22]

'I am far from justifying any breach of the law,' Robespierre insisted, and 'God forbid that we should attempt to lessen the indignation the murderers of the mayor of Étampes deserve.' But Simonneau had been prepared to ask for troops to fire on fellow citizens who only wanted food at a reasonable price: he should have been prepared to make a personal sacrifice. Already, in a speech of 19 February 1792 at the Jacobin Club, Robespierre had outlined a programme of far-reaching political and social reform. Certainly, he stopped far short of Dolivier's call for property redistribution, but he made it clear that the 'right to survive'—'society's obligation to assure for its members necessities and subsistence through work'—precedes all others:

> Simonneau was no hero ... he was guilty before he was a victim; and the misfortunes of his homeland and the violence for which his compatriots are blamed were largely of his doing.

> Leonidas died fighting the immense army of Xerxes, felled by the enemies of Greece; and Simonneau fell ordering his unarmed fellow citizens, who had gathered to stop a trade in wheat which alarmed them, to be fired upon; the difference is without doubt too great to allow us to place these two men on the same level.

In the next issue of the *Défenseur*, Robespierre tried to clarify his position on 'the respect due to the law and constituted authorities'.[23] Here he stepped onto dangerous ground, but insisted that, however misguided, a law made by the majority required obedience. On the one hand he recognized that, 'for as long as the majority requires the maintenance of the law, any individual who breaks it is a rebel. No matter whether it is wise or absurd, just or unjust; his duty is to uphold it.' But he insisted equally that 'I obey all laws; but I love only the good ones. Society has the right to demand my loyalty, but not the sacrifice of my reason.'

Robespierre's almost innate mistrust of the officers of the *ancien régime* made him wary of any military activity that might offer them, or their foreign counterparts, a way of re-establishing privilege: even victories for French generals might be dangerous. In mid-1792 he increasingly singled out for opprobrium arguably the most influential man in the kingdom, General Lafayette, the French hero of the American War of Independence and a supporter of the Brissotin majority in the Assembly.[24]

Lafayette had written from his frontier camp at Maubeuge northeast of Paris to the Legislative Assembly, condemning the Jacobin Club, which 'has caused all our disturbances. . . . Organized as a separate empire within the metropolis and the associations which are affiliated to it, it usurps all powers.' On 18 June, with Desmoulins, Robespierre lambasted the general, describing him as a devious and dangerous man who hid his ambitions behind a veil of moderation: 'This is how Cromwell surreptitiously acquired great power, until he raised himself on the ruins of freedom.' Lafayette then publicly attacked Robespierre and the Jacobins, and left his garrison of his own volition to appear before the Assembly after the *journée* of 20 June, when Louis had been forced by *sans-culottes* to don a red liberty cap.[25]

'General,' warned Robespierre, 'I bow before so much grandeur: but I feel intimidated neither by your power nor by your threats.' Lafayette's reputation as a friend of George Washington mattered less in Robespierre's eyes than the fact that the general had subsequently married into the Noailles family, prominent in the court aristocracy. In August 1790 he had supported the violent repression of the military insurrection of the Nancy troops by his cousin, the Marquis de Bouillé. He had also declared martial law on the Champ de Mars in July 1791. Such was Robespierre's hostility to Lafayette that he asserted wildly that as many as '1,500 peaceful citizens' had been assassinated there on 17 July.[26] Lafayette's decision to leave the threatened garrison at Maubeuge to address the Legislative Assembly was inexcusable, and Robespierre pounced with his distinctive use of classical allusion:

> Ajax, King of the Locrians, had left such a high opinion of his valour that his fellow citizens still kept his tent in the centre of their camp; this hero's very shade still won battles. . . . M. Lafayette's tent is in the middle of the camp he commands, and like that of the Greek king, it is often deserted. . . . The only difference between the shades of Ajax and M. Lafayette is that the latter does not win battles.[27]

The losses did continue. The military defeats of the spring and summer of 1792 suggested to anxious patriots that Robespierre's warnings about the perils of war had been prescient. As Prussia entered the war (13 June), the Legislative Assembly declared 'the homeland in danger [*la patrie en danger*]' on 11 July. Later that day Robespierre read to the Jacobin Club a draft address to the Marseilles soldiers (*fédérés*) arriving in Paris en route to the front, which was printed, posted up in the city, and distributed to deputies in the Assembly, members of the Jacobin Club and its branches. The real dangers do not come from the invaders, he argued, but rather from the court and its henchmen, like Lafayette.[28] That did not mean he was prepared to add his voice to the chorus of voices calling for a republic, which had become more insistent since the killings on the Champ de Mars on 17 July 1791. Robespierre was bothered that this would play into the hands of those attacking the radicalism of the Revolution. Just as he warned Jacobins about the scare campaign being whipped up by imagined threats to property, in particular by the 'agrarian law' or forced redistribution of land, so he counselled caution in advocacy of a republic. 'I know that it is in republics that all the great spirits, all noble and generous sentiments have arisen,' he argued, but it was for 'the general will, enlightened by more mature experience', to demand such a change.[29]

But Robespierre also had intellectual qualms about a republic. His revolutionary models were not contemporaries such as Pascal Paoli or George Washington but rather heroic figures from the past: Algernon Sidney (who had fought against both Cromwell and Charles II), Lycurgus, Lucius Brutus, and especially Cato the Elder (Marcus Porcius Cato), Roman soldier, statesman, orator and author, whose stern morality in office as well as in his private life became proverbial. Robespierre had spent his teenage years being steeped in the classics, particularly Plutarch, Tacitus, Livy and Cicero, but also a host of other writers chosen for their lessons on virtuous behaviour. From these he took more than the rich store of historical allusions with which he studded his speeches. He had also absorbed the knowledge that the survival of republics was least likely in large states characterized by difficulties of communicating with and assembling citizens, and that durable republics were founded on a virtuous citizenry. Revolutionary France was vulnerable on both counts. So he hesitated as others called for a republic after Louis' abortive flight in June 1791, and even in July 1792.[30]

In the opening editorial of the *Défenseur*, Robespierre had admitted that 'I am a republican' but

> I would rather see a popular representative assembly and free and respected citizens with a king than a People enslaved and degraded under the whip of an aristocratic senate and a dictator. I do not like Cromwell any better than

Charles I. . . . Does the solution to the great social problem reside in the term *republic* or *monarchy*?[31]

This was a moral rather than constitutional vision of a healthy polity. The founding rights of man are 'those principles of justice and morality which lie at the root of human society'; they are inscribed on the hearts of all man, but can only be read by 'he who has a pure heart and a virtuous character'. Good government was that which pursued these basic, indelible principles:

The declaration of rights, freedom of the press, the right of petition, that of peaceful assembly; worthy representatives, stern towards the great, unrelenting towards conspirators, lenient towards the weak, respectful of the people, ardent protectors of patriotism, scrupulous guardians of public decorum . . .

Only such a government could minimize the chances of popular vengeance against those in power, reminded Robespierre, stressing that, 'more than anyone, I fear those bloody scenes, the horrible and deadly cure for the greatest of evils to which a people can be exposed'.[32]

As debate raged about the monarchy, Robespierre sought to make his position clear while avoiding calls for a popular insurrection which, if unsuccessful, could only result in massive bloodshed and a reinforcement of the rule of his opponents. On 29 July he used a speech at the Jacobin Club to call for the deposition of the king by the Assembly and the election of a democratic legislature, 'wiping out these harmful distinctions which measure the virtues and rights of men according to their taxes'.[33]

The matter was brought to a head the next day. Robespierre was in the presidential chair at the Jacobin Club on 30 July when it received a manifesto issued on the 25th by the commander-in-chief of the Prussian armies, the Duke of Brunswick, threatening summary justice for the people of Paris if Louis and his family were harmed: 'they will exact an exemplary and ever-memorable vengeance by delivering the city of Paris to military punishment and total destruction, and the rebels who are guilty of outrages to the punishments they deserve'. In Paris the right-wing press had been publishing lists of 'patriots' the Prussians would execute when they reached Paris, coupled with lurid images of the Seine choked with Jacobins and streets red with the blood of *sans-culottes*.[34]

The vitriol of this counter-revolutionary rhetoric added to the popular conviction that Louis was complicit in the defeats being suffered by the army. In
response, the forty-eight neighbourhood 'sections' of Paris voted to form a
Commune of Paris to organize insurrection and an army of twenty thousand
sans-culottes from the newly democratized National Guard. Robespierre passed
on the news of the arrival of the Marseillais *fédérés* to Antoine Buissart in Arras:

> French Brutuses are now in Paris. If they leave it without saving the fatherland,
> all is lost. Rather than fail for want of taking the most extreme measures, we
> will all die in the capital. Indescribable events are brewing.
>
> Till we meet again, or perhaps farewell.[35]

The Marseillais, on their way to the front, were showing the way to all patriots:
'Sparta conquered and preserved freedom for herself and the small region which
surrounded her. Marseilles . . . seems to be dragging the rest of France towards
freedom, almost despite itself.'[36] The *fédérés* joined with the *sans-culottes* in the
assault on the Tuileries Palace and the overthrow of the monarchy on 10 August.

Once it was clear that the insurrection could be interpreted as an expression
of the people's will, Robespierre did not hesitate to support it, calling for a new,
democratic National Convention. On the afternoon of the 10th, he urged a
thinly attended Jacobin Club to ensure that their local neighbourhood sections
made the Legislative Assembly aware of their support and 'to set up and maintain links with the popular societies, to admit all citizens to their meetings, all
citizens, without discrimination.'[37] Robespierre became closely involved with
the politics of his own Section des Piques and was one of its six delegates sent to
form the assembly of the sections' delegates on 12 August. On the 13th he was
elected to the Paris Commune and attended its meetings for a fortnight,
supporting it against moves by the Legislative Assembly to dissolve it altogether
as a rival source of authority.

In the battle with the Brissotins over the legitimacy of the Commune,
Robespierre insisted that, 'of all the people's mandatories, they alone have been
the people [*eux seuls ont été peuple*]'. That is, the Commune alone could be
understood as the sovereign people expressing the general will, recalling his
famous 27 April statement to the Jacobin Club: 'I am the people myself! [*je suis*

peuple moi-même!]'. This understanding that the people of Paris had the capacity
to interpret the general will of the sovereign people explains too why they could
act on behalf of all the French, as in 1789. The Commune nevertheless decided
it would be prudent to send envoys to the provinces to explain their actions. At
the same time, on 27 August, Robespierre succeeded in gaining the Commune's
support for the election of a National Convention: the general will and the
people's representatives needed to be brought into closer alignment.[38]

For Robespierre, the Revolution of 10 August demonstrated the progress
made since 1789. Then, the people of Paris had risen to free themselves
from despotism: liberty was but a vague notion. Now, the people had risen
again, to 'put into practice the principles proclaimed three years earlier by its
first representatives'. This time, however, the presence of the *fédérés* meant that
it was the French people rather than the Parisians alone who had risen: 'thus
began the most beautiful revolution ever to honour humanity; let us say more,
the only one which had an object worthy of mankind, that of finally setting up
polities according to the immortal principles of equality, of justice and of
reason.'[39]

This 'beautiful revolution' had a very ugly side. Six hundred Swiss Guards, the
main defenders of the Tuileries Palace, were killed in the fighting or subsequently in bloody acts of retribution after the king took refuge in the nearby
Legislative Assembly. To charges that the slaughter of Swiss Guards and others
after the victory of 10 August had sullied the people's cause irreparably,
Robespierre retorted with reports of civic behaviour towards property, and again
compared popular vengeance with the extent of violence against the people. He
cited examples in which the insurgents had themselves punished their own if
caught stealing from the palace.[40] We do not know whether he regretted the
killing of one of his former fellow students at Louis-le-Grand, the royalist activist
and editor of the *Actes des Apôtres*, François Suleau, singled out to the *sans-
culottes* by the republican and campaigner for women's rights, Théroigne de
Méricourt.

On 15 August Robespierre called successfully for the creation of an
'extraordinary tribunal', with jurors 'chosen from each section, sovereign and
without further appeal' to judge counter-revolutionary 'conspirators'. In its
declaration to the nation, the Assembly itself, he argued, had only spoken of
crimes committed on the 10th, and the existing courts represented only

narrow interests: 'that puts too great a restraint on the vengeance of the people, for the crimes go back much further.... It wants the guilty punished, and rightly so.'[41]

This new Revolutionary Tribunal was Robespierre's final break with the Brissotins, for they were now among the most vulnerable. John Moore, a Scottish doctor sympathetic to the Revolution who had arrived in Paris in mid-August, rushed to attend meetings of the Jacobin Club. On the 17th he was startled by the violent speeches against 'Roberspierre', despite the attempts to drown out the speakers by his supporters, including the 'abundance of women in the galleries'.[42] The Brissotins' successful campaign to launch a short-term war of national defence had exposed the nation to invasion and heightened the hopes of all those who opposed the Revolution. It had also exposed the Brissotins to the charge that they were colluding with Lafayette, who went into exile on the 19th, and even the king, in the hopes of preventing power slipping into the hands of Parisian radicals, including Robespierre. The creation of the Revolutionary Tribunal in a context of bloodletting, recrimination and uncertainty destroyed any chance of a rapprochement between the former allies.

On 20 August, less than nine months after he had embraced Maximilien so warmly on his return from Arras, Pétion was struggling to maintain the friendship. But try he did: 'you would have to stop loving liberty', he wrote in a personal letter, 'to make me stop liking you.... To disagree on a few points which don't go to the heart of the matter doesn't make us enemies ... we will not be in opposing parties, we have the same political faith.... Look after yourself, let's be in the frontline [*marchons de front*], we're in a menacing enough situation to make us think only of the public good.'[43] Manon Roland, too, was despairing about what she saw as Robespierre's intolerance and furious with his refusal to see her, writing to him on 25 August:

I know excellent citizens who have opinions contrary to yours, and I have never found you to be esteemed the less for seeing things from a different point of view. I have bemoaned your prejudices ... you promised me to explain them to me; you were to come to my house. You have avoided me, you have told me nothing, and in this interval you raise public opinion against those who do not think like you. I am too frank not to acknowledge to you that this course did not seem right to me.[44]

At the same time, the news from the front was terrifying. Austrian armies were advancing towards Lorraine with a view to linking up with Prussian forces at Châlons before marching on Paris. Longwy fell on 23 August. John Moore was struck by the power of the rumours about prison plots sweeping through the streets of Paris by late August; early on 2 September they became more charged with the news that Châlons had been taken by the Prussians.[45] The same day, news reached Paris that the great fortress at Verdun, just 140 miles from the capital, was about to surrender to Brunswick's troops. The news generated an immediate, dramatic surge in popular fear and resolve. Convinced that 'counter-revolutionaries' (whether nobles, priests or common-law criminals) in prisons were waiting to break out and welcome the invaders once the volunteers had left for the front, hastily convened popular courts sentenced to death about 1,200 of the 2,700 prisoners brought before them, including 240 priests. They were killed immediately, often with extreme cruelty.[46]

From the day of the storming of the Bastille on 14 July 1789, violence and debate about its legitimacy had been central to the Revolution. The role of violent, collective behaviour in securing the Revolution of 1789—from the battle at the Bastille to the attacks on *châteaux* during the Great Fear, to the forced return of the royal family from Versailles to Paris in October—had made such expressions of the people's will heroic. However, once the principle of popular sovereignty and political freedoms were enshrined in the Declaration of the Rights of Man and of the Citizen and subsequent legislation, many felt that the need for extra-legal insurrection had passed. Rioting and even collective homicide continued none-theless, and individual politicians found ways of equivocating over its repression by the law. For example, the prominent Brissotin Pierre Vergniaud had supported an amnesty for 'patriots' involved in horrific killings at La Glacière in Avignon in October 1791 on the grounds that his fellow deputies could not 'deliver up to the executioner's steel those who have constantly been of service to you.'[47]

Until the bloody summer of 1792, however, violent popular reprisals had been either limited or explicable. The massive and ongoing upheavals in the countryside had been remarkably free of personal violence, or it had been kept within ritualistic confines. Certainly, there had been large-scale urban violence in Nîmes and Montauban in southern France, but this had been of a sectarian nature that could be explained away as vestiges of *ancien régime* intolerance. Violence in Avignon had been far more troubling. But, however heroic the actions of *sans-culottes* and Marseillais on 10 August 1792, how could one justify the massacre afterwards of so many Swiss Guards? Far worse were the killings in the streets of Paris and elsewhere in early September. Brunswick's bloodcurdling ultimatum could only go so far as an explanation for the fear and fury.

Robespierre's opponents sought afterwards to implicate him directly in the killings. The charge is that, once he heard that prisoners judged by self-appointed 'courts' as guilty of being in league with the enemy—no matter how tenuous the connection—were being put to death, he sought to have Brissot and Jean-Marie Roland arrested. The claim was made by Pétion, Louvet and Manon Roland, who in the following months launched an all-out campaign against Robespierre, with the purpose of bringing him before the Revolutionary Tribunal. Already by 5 September Manon Roland was writing to her admirer Bancal des Issarts claiming that 'we are under the knives of Robespierre and Marat', sure that the arrest warrants were to deliver her husband and Brissot up to the killers. Only the intervention of Georges Danton, the firebrand Minister of Justice, had stopped the warrants being served.[48] The only supporting evidence for this is that Robespierre had declared that Brissot and Jean-Louis Carra were aiding the enemy (the latter had suggested that Brunswick or the Duke of York could be a new king of France), and he had obtained warrants from the Commune for the arrest of Brissot and Roland, but this was before the massacres began.[49]

In the weeks between the overthrow of the monarchy and the outbreak of the massacres, it was leading Brissotins who were as panic-stricken as anyone, and called in Gorsas' words for 'the punishment of the guilty ... a few drops of impure blood would have satisfied its just revenge, and now waves of blood will be spilled'. During the massacres themselves, Gorsas, Roland, Carra, Condorcet and Louvet used their newspapers to support the killings as necessary, or deliberately said nothing. On 3 September, Gorsas reported on 'a terrible justice, but necessary, *but necessitated*'. On the 5th, Carra used the *Annales patriotiques* to assure his readers that 'the innocent have been spared. All those who have been slaughtered had given well-known proof of lack of civic virtue, and perhaps that is a crime worthy of death at a time when the homeland must be saved.'[50]

There is no evidence that Robespierre incited or connived at the killings.[51] We know that on 3, 4 and 5 September he was at the meetings of the Electoral Assembly for Paris choosing deputies for the new National Convention. The

Assembly did not refer to what was happening in the streets. All Robespierre did was to follow the Commune's instruction to visit the Temple (the royal family's prison) to ensure that order was not being disturbed there. Robespierre does not seem to have spoken at the Jacobin Club during the week of the massacres; in any case, the Club proceeded as if nothing was happening. It is almost as if its members, like the Paris Commune itself, felt powerless to intervene. Nevertheless, Robespierre and other political leaders in Paris knew that the killings were going on—if not the horrific details—and do not appear to have tried to stop them. In particular, Pétion was mayor of Paris at the time of the massacres, and Roland was Minister of the Interior, and the massacres therefore were primarily their responsibility. Indeed, Charlotte Robespierre later claimed that her brother and Pétion fell out irrevocably over the latter's inability to curtail the killings.[52]

Robespierre later deplored the excesses of the prison massacres, for which the Brissotins deftly fixed the full responsibility on him and Marat. Robespierre conceded that it was natural to 'weep for the victims, including those among them who were guilty'. But he also wanted France's citizens 'to save some tears for [the victims of] other, nay greater calamities, particularly the countless millions who through the ages had suffered the torments of political and social oppression . . '.[53] Several months later he returned to the issue in a major speech to the National Convention: 'I learned what was going on in the prisons only through general rumours and later, no doubt, than did most citizens; for I was either at home, or else in those places to which my public duties called me . . '.[54] Long afterwards, in the 1840s, when Louis Blanc was undertaking research for his monumental History of the French Revolution, he interviewed Robespierre's doctor, Joseph Souberbielle, then very ill but remarkably lucid, who insisted that 'Robespierre had never spoken to him of the September massacres other than with horror, and one day he shouted . . . "Blood! Still more blood! Ah! They'll end up drowning the Revolution in it, these wretches!" '[55]

The killings hung over the elections for the National Convention early in September 1792. This time all men aged twenty-one who were resident in their commune for a year and lived from their income or work could vote: only domestic servants were excluded. To be eligible to be a deputy one had also to be twenty-five years old. Robespierre's campaign in 1789–91 for universal male suffrage was now vindicated. These were still indirect and cumbersome elections, however, where a small number of electors was chosen to make the final decision, one that could take many days. Across France, a combination of factors—farm work at harvest time, preoccupation with war, opposition to the Church reforms and the overthrow of the monarchy—meant that fewer than 10 per cent (700,000 of 7.5 million) voted.

In Paris, 990 representatives of the districts and suburbs convened on 2 September, and Robespierre succeeded in having those with a royalist past (in particular, Feuillants) excluded. Méhée de la Touche, the acting secretary of the Paris municipality and a writer for the Brissotin *Patriote français*, sent a stinging attack on Robespierre to all the sections, warning them of 'a great menace' in the person of Robespierre, 'who I believed the purest lover of liberty and the people, and whose name is on everyone's lips . . . [but] why is the electors' rostrum only open to him and his friends? . . . By what fatality has he become the arch-saint whom one cannot touch without being struck dead?'[56]

But Robespierre's campaign against the war, which had isolated him from public sentiment and made him prey to the Brissotins, had now been vindicated. He was as popular as he had been a year before. On 4 September he was unanimously elected vice-president of the electoral assembly, then chosen as the first deputy (with 338 votes of 525) on the 5th. Robespierre defeated Pétion for first place, and the latter withdrew. Danton was then elected second, Desmoulins sixth, Marat seventh, and Jacques-Louis David twentieth. A furious Pétion decided to stand with Brissot in Eure-et-Loir.

In Pas-de-Calais the 775 electors met in Calais on 2 September to elect eleven deputies and four substitutes. Robespierre was elected first, with 412 of the 724 votes on 5 September. Lazare Carnot was elected on the second round, and later Philippe Lebas and Thomas Paine. Maximilien's brother Augustin, who had been a prosecuting lawyer at the Arras tribunal, was not elected. Elected elsewhere, with Robespierre's active support, was Louis-Antoine St-Just, who had befriended him through their correspondence since 1790. Bursting with ambition and punitive zeal, and just turned twenty-five, St-Just would become Robespierre's closest political ally.[57] Another familiar face was the Abbé Yves-Marie Audrein, the master who had found Maximilien in the toilet at Louis-le-Grand with a 'bad book', who had become the constitutional bishop of the department of Morbihan and was elected to the Convention from there.

The Pas-de-Calais electors had immediately despatched a courier to Paris 'to inform this incorruptible man' of their choice, but Robespierre had decided that he would be a deputy for Paris. His preference for Paris is significant. His uncompromising support for universal male suffrage and preference for a proliferation of smallholdings had put him at odds with his former power base among the tenant farmers who dominated Artésien rural society, even though he never supported action by government to force land redistribution. Henceforth he had very little to say about the countryside. His reception in his home province in October 1791 had been warmest in urban centres. This is a critical reason why he opted to be a deputy for Paris: his standing in the capital was at odds with the mixed reception he had encountered in his home province.[58]

Despite his lack of electoral success in Arras, Augustin would in fact join his brother in Paris, for he was finally elected as deputy to the Convention on 17 September, nineteenth on the list of twenty-four deputies. This could only have been because of Maximilien's standing among the Paris electors. A week later—25 September—Augustin left Arras to take his seat in the Convention. Charlotte did not want to be alone in their house and came with him. Arriving in Paris, they stayed initially at the Duplays in unfurnished rooms looking onto the Rue St-Honoré. The three young adults were together again.[59]

CHAPTER 9

'Did you want a Revolution without Revolution?'

PARIS 1792–93

Several weeks after the 'September massacres', revolutionary armies won their first great victory, at Valmy, just one hundred miles east of Paris, and near where Louis XVI had been recognized and arrested in June 1791. As news arrived of the victory, the new National Convention, elected by universal male suffrage, was convening in a capital haunted by the livid memory of recent slaughter in the prisons and the imminent Prussian threat. Refugees from border regions to the north and east jostled with young volunteers who had responded to the call that 'the homeland is in danger' and were on their way to the front. The streets were crackling with a potent mixture of rumour, optimism and suspicion.

The 750 deputies of the Convention were mostly from middle-class backgrounds, with only about seventy men from the former privileged orders. There was significant experience—about two hundred had been in the Legislative Assembly and more than eighty in the National Assembly of 1789–91, including Robespierre—and most of the remainder had been active in local office. They were also democrats and republicans: immediately on convening, they abolished the monarchy and proclaimed France a Republic on 21 September.

The militant Jacobins were dominant in Paris, and Robespierre was in tune with popular rage against those who had unleashed the miseries of war as well as against the invading armies who must now be defeated. In response, the vituperation from Brissot and his followers towards Robespierre in particular was understandable.[1] These were the political leaders who had sung the siren songs of war during the winter of 1791–92, dismissing the discordant warnings of

Robespierre, but whose reassurances of easy victory had dissipated into a morass of defeat and desertion. The Brissotins were vulnerable, angry and frightened. Had Robespierre sought to deliver up Roland and Brissot to the vengeance of the killers during the prison massacres? No, but they believed he had.

The presence of troops from Marseilles among those who had overthrown the monarchy on 10 August enabled Robespierre to claim that this second revolution was indeed a national one. But the issue remained the place of Paris in political decisions, and 'Paris' signified more than just the capital. To Brissotins it also represented popular upheaval, threats to commercial interests, and menaces to personal security. Their self-presentation as the party of France rather than of Paris was more a reflection of their unpopularity in the capital—where only one of the twenty-four deputies was sympathetic to them—than a reality, for the Jacobin deputies, too, had been elected from all over the country.

Robespierre decided in late September 1792 to resume his journalism, which had been interrupted for a few weeks by the elections. The *Défenseur de la Constitution* changed its cover from red to grey, and its title. The full title is revealing of Robespierre's national agenda, *Lettres de Maximilien Robespierre, membre de la Convention nationale de France, à ses commettans*. By his *commettans* (constituents), Robespierre made it explicit that he meant 'all the French', that all deputies represented all the people. Deliberate, too, was his inclusion of letters from provincial correspondents—for example, from Toulouse, Arras and Manosque—critical of the Brissotins, whom he thereby stigmatized as an anti-Parisian faction rather than representative of the national will.[2]

In its first issue Robespierre was ebullient that 'the reign of equality begins'; there is no limit to 'the extent of the glorious path the human spirit opens before you'. While the signpost along this path was that 'the people are good', he admitted that the end-point of their 'full dignity' was some way off. He insisted that the soul of a Republic is *vertu*—that is, a patriotism in which private interests are subordinate to the public good. But how could *vertu* be created? Robespierre's concern that the revolutionary changes made since 1789 were far from being embedded was coupled with a concern that civic bonds needed to be expressed in new ways, and strengthened by public festivals along the lines of those in ancient Greece. This would be a political culture in which classical allegory was diffused as a ready reference for elevating behaviour beyond the spontaneous and often wild displays of popular festivals.[3]

Robespierre had hesitated to embrace the calls for a Republic in the first months of 1792 because he was certain that republican institutions required a culture of civic virtue, a regenerated society. He knew that the people were inherently good; he also knew that they had been corrupted by centuries of poverty and ignorance.[4] So he had felt that it was too early for France to become a Republic, just as it had been too early on in the Revolution's transformation of France to contemplate a war of emancipation across Europe. Now that the Republic was a *fait accompli*, however, there was no choice but to launch a project of civic regeneration and education. At the same time that the war had to be conducted as a people's war to save the Revolution, so those fighting it had to understand what they were fighting for and how to conduct themselves.

A new civic culture could not immediately replace Christian ritual or belief. The Bordeaux lawyer Marguerite-Élie Guadet had accused Robespierre of propagating 'superstition' at the Jacobin Club in March 1792 after he had thanked 'Providence' for the death of Leopold II of Austria on 1 March and with it the chance of avoiding war. Robespierre had passionately defended his belief in an 'Eternal Being'.[5] Now in mid-November 1792 the Jacobin Club debated a proposal from Joseph Cambon to abolish all public funding of the Church. Robespierre reminded deputies that their key responsibilities were to 'make fast in our midst liberty, peace, abundance and the rule of law' and to be 'economical with the blood, the tears and the gold of the nation':

> as far as religious prejudices are concerned, our situation seems very good and public opinion very advanced. The influence of superstition is almost ended . . . and all that remains in people's minds are the imposing tenets which lend support to morality and the sublime and touching doctrine of virtue and equality which the son of Mary taught in olden times to his citizens.

It would be needlessly alienating to attack the Church, he argued: the people 'links to this form of worship at least some of its moral framework'.[6]

The euphoria of 21 September was ephemeral. Now that the news from the front was more positive, leading Brissotins began to accuse Robespierre and others of being 'septembriseurs' responsible for the massacres, denying their own role in excusing the killings. Over the next few days Brissot and his supporters directly confronted Robespierre with charges that he was seeking a 'triumvirate' (with Danton and Marat) to rule France and what they saw as the undue influence of Paris and 'anarchists' wanting to attack property rights.[7] On the 24th, François Buzot asked for an emergency departmental guard to be organized to protect the Convention. The next day Merlin de Thionville demanded that 'those who know of men in this Assembly so perverse as to call for a triumvirate or dictatorship, show them to me that I may stab them'. The Marseilles deputy François Rebecqui identified Robespierre, who felt obliged to reply with a justification of his actions across four years: 'undoubtedly many citizens have defended the rights of the people better than I have done, but I am the one honoured by having attracted more enemies and more persecution'.

A deputy from Deux-Sèvres, Michel Lecointe-Puyraveau, interrupted: 'Robespierre, don't tell us what you did in the Assembly, just tell us whether you aspired to dictatorship and the triumvirate.' Robespierre's denial did not convince the Brissotins. A deputy for Tarn-et-Garonne, Julien Mazade-Percin, wrote home to Castelsarrasin on 26 September that one of the two parties in the Convention 'aspires to a tribunicial or triumvirate dictatorship'. 'We must be worried,' he added, 'that the soul of the party I have just mentioned may be citizen Robespierre, otherwise so commendable for his services to us.' During October, Buzot and Lanjuinais returned to their demand for a departmental guard, as a physical reminder that Paris could no longer act on behalf of the nation: the Revolution must end. For Robespierre this was a spurious distinction: 'as if the Frenchmen of Paris were a different breed from those who lived in other parts of France . . . it was not the citizens of Perpignan or Quimper who could wield that happy dominance over the views of the public about actions which take place in Paris'.[8]

The Brissotins did not relent. On 29 October the Convention heard new charges against Robespierre from Roland as Minister of the Interior, Lanjuinais and especially Louvet, holding him responsible for the September massacres and claiming that he was aiming at dictatorship. This was a highly charged moment. William Wordsworth, present in the galleries, later recalled in *The Prelude* how, in the arcades outside the Manège, he could hear

Shrill voices from the hawkers in the throng,
Bawling, 'Denunciation of the Crimes
Of Maximilien Robespierre'; the hand,
Prompt as the voice, held forth a printed speech . . .[9]

The speech was Louvet's: 'I accuse you of having continually presented yourself as an object of idolatry; . . . that you are the only virtuous man in France, the only one who can save the homeland . . . I accuse you of working obviously towards supreme power'. He called for the Assembly to pass a law whereby Robespierre could be banished. Danton intervened to save a thoroughly startled Robespierre, who at least had the wits to ask to be given a week to prepare a response.[10]

On 3 November six hundred troops, both from pre-revolutionary regiments and including some of the *fédérés* from Marseilles, marched through Paris calling for 'the heads of Marat, Robespierre, Danton, and all who defend them! Long live Roland! No trial of the king!' The Brissotins had openly called for physical support from the provinces, and within weeks there were as many as sixteen thousand men roaming the streets of Paris and guarding the Convention.[11]

On 5 November the galleries of the Convention were packed, with many having spent the night camped outside; entry tickets were fought over. Robespierre went on the attack:

> Citizens, did you want a revolution without revolution? . . . The French, friends of freedom, meeting in Paris last August, acted on this matter on behalf of all departments. We must approve or disapprove them altogether. To make a crime of a few apparent or real misdemeanours, inevitable during such a great upheaval, would be to punish them for their devotion. . . .

Again, Robespierre insisted that he had not known what was going on in the prisons and that, in any case, the fall of Verdun had terrified Parisians into believing that Brunswick was about to make good his bloody promises. The real grieving should be for the hundred thousand victims of the *ancien régime*; those criticizing the popular justice of August–September were logically calling the storming of the Bastille illegal.[12]

The speech was a triumph for Robespierre: when Louvet asked for the right to reply, the Convention decided to move on to other business. In the evening Robespierre received a triumphant reception at the Jacobin Club, and his speech was printed and sent to its affiliates in the provinces. But the triumph brought him increased vituperation as well. Henceforth, a mortal enmity divided Robespierre and his followers from the Brissotins. They loathed him. Their mouthpiece the *Patriote français* published a *Reply to the Vindication of Robespierre* by Olympe de Gouges, a campaigner for women's rights and defender of Louis XVI. 'I resent and detest you,' she declared: 'I propose that you should take a bath with me in the Seine; but in order to wash away entirely the stains with which you have covered yourself since the 10th [of August], we will fasten cannon-balls—size 16 and 24—to our feet, and we will throw ourselves together in the waves.' A few days later she accused him of wanting to climb to power on the bodies of the followers of Brissot, but warned him that his 'throne will be the scaffold': 'your breath befouls the pure air we now inhale: your twitching eyelid exposes the turpitude of your soul, and every hair on your head is criminal'.[13]

But large numbers of Parisian women admired Robespierre. When he defended himself on 5 November, the *Patriote français* reckoned that there were up to eight hundred women packing the galleries and applauding him, as well as two hundred men, and that he was besieged by women there and at the Jacobin Club. Despite his own support for the rights of women, the *philosophe* Condorcet, now a Brissotin, fell back for an explanation on female vulnerability to a messiah. In the *Chronique de Paris* he sneered that

> Robespierre preaches, Robespierre censures, he is furious, grave, melancholy, shamming exaltation, logical in his thoughts and conduct; he thunders against the rich and the great; he lives frugally and feels no physical needs; he has but a single mission, which is to speak and he speaks almost all the time . . . .

> He has all the characteristics, not of a religious leader, but of the leader of a sect; he has built up for himself a reputation for austerity which borders on sainthood, he mounts his soapbox, he speaks of God and Providence, he says he is the friend of the poor and the weak and he attracts a following of women and the easily led [*faibles d'esprit*]. . . . Robespierre is a priest and will never be anything else.[14]

The Scottish doctor John Moore agreed that 'Robespierre's eloquence is said to be peculiarly admired by the [female] sex'. At the same time, he noted that this fierce man with a 'disagreeable countenance' like a 'tiger-cat' was recognized by all as motivated by 'popularity, not avarice'. The imagery was echoed by Louvet, who now published a long and dense version of his speech, attacking Robespierre in personal terms for 'his presumptuous ambition; his insolent domination', claiming that he ruled by trickery, force, 'terror', his eyes constantly flicking across the meetings of the Jacobin Club.[15]

The battle for supremacy confused and divided Jacobin Clubs across the country, for Roland had formidable resources at his disposal as Minister of the Interior. Robespierre found his name linked to Marat's, and provincial affiliates denounced him as 'miserable' (Cognac), and his 'vomitings' (Villeneuve-sur-Yonne) as a sign of 'false virtue' (Dieppe). Many others remained loyal to 'the Incorruptible', but by the end of the year pro-Brissotin sentiment clearly prevailed in provincial Jacobin Clubs.[16]

Robespierre was sustained by his personal relationships. The Duplays provided the extended family life he had never been able to enjoy, and it may be that the older couple were able to replace—or at least compensate for the absence of—Antoine and Charlotte Buissart. Maurice Duplay was a committed Jacobin, and successful in his tender to undertake carpentry work in the Manège, the Convention's debating chamber.[17] Maximilien's evenings were enlivened by visits from well-known political friends: Desmoulins, Élisabeth Duplay's fiancé Philippe Lebas, St-Just, the artist Jacques-Louis David and Couthon. There were others, less well-known: Lohier, the Duplays' grocer, Robespierre's doctor Souberbielle, a Corsican cobbler from Arras named Calandini, and Didier, a locksmith who lived next door. Sometimes Lebas would sing a few lines from Italian opera or Robespierre would recite a favourite poem from Corneille or Racine, or a passage from Rousseau. There were occasional evenings at the Théâtre Français. Maximilien had brought his dog Brount back with him from Arras in November 1791 and made a habit of walking him through the Champs-Élysées with members of the Duplay family. He was fond of the Duplays' nephew Simon, who had been wounded at the battle of Valmy and hobbled on a wooden leg. On rare days of repose, Robespierre would take a bag of his beloved oranges and walk Brount in the countryside around the capital, often with Françoise Duplay, or eat with her relatives in nearby Choisy.[18]

Augustin and Charlotte, who had followed Maximilien from Arras, lived at first with him at the Duplays, where Charlotte found the women intolerable in their suffocating devotion to Maximilien. 'I tried to make him understand that in his position, and occupying such a high rank in politics, he ought to have a home of his own.' He finally agreed, and moved with Charlotte to rented rooms nearby in the Rue St-Florentin. It was in this apartment that Maximilien became ill after the speech of 5 November: he did not speak at the Convention again until the 30th. Charlotte recalled no details of his illness, except that 'it was not dangerous'. Forty years later she could still recall the scene that erupted when Françoise Duplay came to visit them and found him ill. To Charlotte's eternal regret, he relented and returned to the Duplays: 'they like me so much, he said to me, they show so much regard and kindness to me, that it would be ungrateful to rebuff them'. Charlotte remained consumed with resentment and the two women entered into a battle for Maximilien's affections. Françoise allegedly once returned the jams and preserved fruit that Charlotte had lovingly prepared, with the message that she did not want to poison the great man.[19]

Robespierre had some other new friends. In January 1792 he had received a letter from a Parisian draper, François-Pierre Deschamps. In a eulogy flattering 'the zeal and the probity of an incorruptible lawmaker', Deschamps asked Robespierre whether he would be the godfather of a son about to be baptized with his name. He consented, and at the baptism struck up a friendship with the family and with the godmother Rosalie Vincent, who, like the mother Catherine, was from the village of Fontenay-aux-Roses just to the south of Paris. In February 1793 Deschamps became a member of the Republic's Commerce and Supplies Committee and won a clothing contract for the army. He used the proceeds to rent the former seigneur's house at Maisons-Alfort, a village just a few miles southeast of the capital. There he installed Catherine and Rosalie, and he seems to have occasionally welcomed Robespierre as a visitor. They in turn visited Robespierre at the Duplays, Rosalie taking him a pot of 'cailler' (yoghurt).[20]

Robespierre's opponents, and some historians, later claimed that he constructed a 'shrine' to himself in his room from all the statuettes, portraits and other objects sent to him in homage. The claim was not made while he was alive, and other evidence suggests that his room was sparsely furnished, and bulging with his books and papers.[21] It would indeed be surprising were Robespierre to have constructed a living museum to himself given his involvement in the Jacobin Club's decree that 'no bust of any living man shall be placed in its chamber'.

There were, however, several busts of dead men in the Jacobin Club. Mirabeau's remains had been taken to the Panthéon in April 1791 on Robespierre's urging and his bust was on display in the Club. Mirabeau's secret dealings with the court were uncovered in November 1791, and on 5 December 1792 the Convention

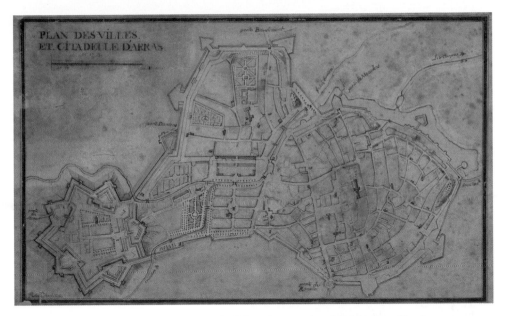

1 Arras in the late eighteenth century. To the left is the army 'citadelle', separated by the narrow Crinchon River from the 'administrative town' and cathedral, top centre, and the new 'Basse Ville', lower centre. The old heart of Arras is at right, dominated by the Abbey of St-Vaast, with the two main squares at lower right.

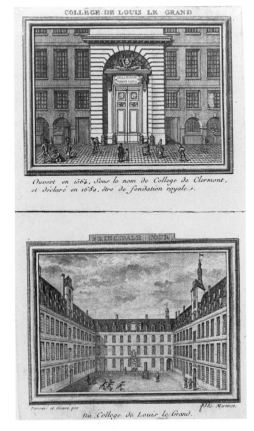

2 *The College of Louis-le-Grand, c.* 1780. The main entry to the College, on the Rue St-Jacques opposite the Sorbonne, and the inner courtyard where the boys took their recreation, surrounded by classrooms and the dining room. The chapel is at the rear. Maximilien lived here for twelve years.

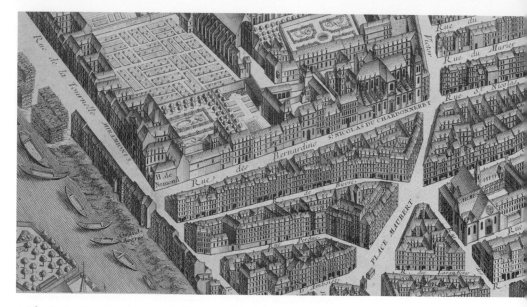

3 The Latin Quarter. The remarkable map of Paris by Louis Bretez, *c.* 1739 (known as the 'Plan de Turgot'), shows the College of Louis-le-Grand (here still the Collège des Jésuites) at bottom right. It was a short walk down the Rue St-Jacques through the Latin Quarter to the Île de la Cité, or up the hill to the city walls and the countryside. Bretez has deliberately widened the streets.

4 *Maximilien de Robespierre*, 1783. The young Louis-Léopold Boilly (1761-1845) painted this portrait while studying under Dominique Doncre in Arras after 1778. The young barrister may be flushed with his recent success in the case of the lightning conductor. Maximilien always enjoyed the companionship offered by dogs.

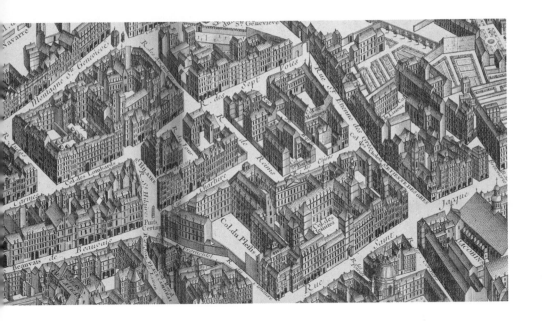

5 *Charlotte Robespierre.*
This portrait of Charlotte
(1760–1834) was
probably completed in
1792–94 by Jean-Baptiste
Isabey (1767–1855), a
pupil of Jacques-Louis
David's. Isabey would
later have a long career
as a court painter.

6 *Louis-Hilaire de Conzié*. Conzié (1732–1805) was Bishop of Arras from 1769; Dominique Doncre's portrait dates from 1775. Conzié appointed Robespierre a magistrate in his ecclesiastical court in 1782, but by 1788 the rupture between them was complete. Conzié fled the Revolution in 1790.

7 *Ferdinand Dubois de Fosseux*. Dubois (1742–1817), the eminent and genial Secretary of the Academy of Artois, was painted by Louis-Léopold Boilly in 1783. Although Dubois was a wealthy and powerful noble, the strained relations with Robespierre in 1788–89 did not terminate a long friendship.

8 *Bon-Albert Briois de Beaumez*. Briois (1759–*c*. 1801) was president of the Council of Artois after 1785 and a noble deputy at the Estates-General, where he became a trenchant opponent of Robespierre. He emigrated in 1792, took United States citizenship, and probably died in India in 1801.

9 Robespierre's house in Arras. An early nineteenth-century view of the house at 9 Rue des Rapporteurs, close to the Council of Artois and the Town Hall, into which Maximilien and Charlotte moved in 1787. The facade has since been altered. The street has recently been named the Rue Robespierre, and the building houses a small museum.

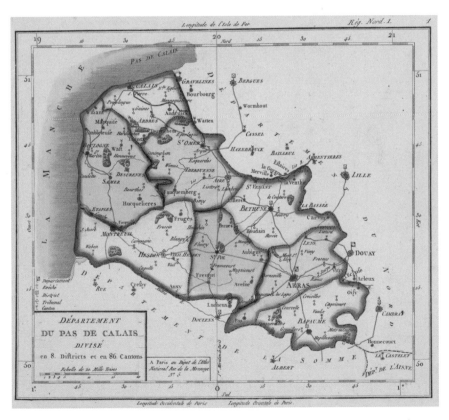

10 The department of Pas-de-Calais. The new department, with Arras as its capital, was created in 1790 from the ancient province of Artois and coastal regions of Picardy.

11 The Arras Society of Friends of the Constitution. The Society was founded in 1790, here proclaiming its motto 'To Live Free or Die'. After 1792 it became the Jacobin Club.

12 *Festival of Federation at Arras.* On 14 July 1790 the mayor of Arras, Dubois de Fosseux, and the bishop, Conzié, made speeches for the Festival of Federation on the Grand Marché, in front of National Guards and soldiers from the garrison. The image has been devised to be shown as a slide.

13 Robespierre in 1789. This engraving of Robespierre was produced by F. G. Fiesinger in 1789, based on a sketch by Jean-Urbain Guérin. It would become the template for later images.

14 Robespierre's home in 1791–94. Maximilien's room was on the first floor above the tap in the courtyard of the Duplays' home in the rue St-Honoré. The second floor was a later addition.

15 *Éléonore Duplay*. Éléonore (1768–1832) studied painting during the Revolution; this pastel is probably a self-portrait. Although it is highly unlikely that she and Maximilien were lovers, she would be referred to after 1794 as 'the widow Robespierre'.

16 *The Paris Jacobin Club*, 1791. The Society of Friends of the Constitution, or Jacobin Club, here engraved by Louis Masquelier, was Robespierre's preferred forum throughout the Revolution.

17 *Maximilien Robespierre*, 1791. This oil portrait by Pierre Vigneron (1789–1872) is likely to have been painted from a sketch (now lost) for a portrait by Adélaïde Labille-Guiard (1749–1803) shown in the Salon of 1791. Maximilien may have deliberately dressed again in the formal black garb of a deputy of the Third Estate in 1789.

18 Augustin Robespierre.
Maximilien's younger brother
(1764–94), from one of a series of
engravings of deputies in the National
Convention done by F. Bonneville.
The misspelling of the family name
was common, especially early in the
Revolution. The caption post-dates
his death.

A. P. J. ROBERSPIERRE, *le Jeune*
Né à Arras Dépt. du Pas de Calais.
Député à la Convention Nationale en 1792,
décapité le 10 avec son frere.

19 Revolutionary Festival in Arras, 1793. Citizens fill the Petit Marché, now
the Place de la Fédération, on 19 Vendémiaire Year II (10 October 1793), to
celebrate the revolutionary calendar. The elderly man is likely to have been
singled out for honour as Arras' oldest citizen.

20 *Robespierre, c.1792.* The most famous portrait of Robespierre, with his striped jacket and waistcoat, and high cravat, by an unknown artist.

21 The centre of Revolutionary Government. From July 1791, Robespierre's life in Paris was lived within a small area between the Jacobin Club (lower left), the Duplays' home on the Rue St-Honoré, and the National Convention, housed until 10 May 1793 in the Manège (bottom), then in a theatre within the Tuileries Palace (top). The Committee of Public Safety met on the left-hand side of the Tuileries. Maximilien used to walk his dog in the gardens. His life ended on the Place de la Révolution at lower right.

22 *Robespierre at the Rostrum.* This anonymous contemporary sketch of Robespierre speaking in the Convention captures his precision and careful dress; it has omitted his glasses, however, and he rarely spoke without a lengthy text before him.

23 Revolutionary debates. Before the Revolution the Salle du Manège in the Tuileries Gardens had housed the royal equestrian school. Now it became the chamber for the Assemblies' debates. Under the Convention, the Jacobins, or 'Mountain', had the habit of sitting to the left, the Girondins to the right: the 'Plain' deputies moved between them. The accoustics were poor and the galleries crowded.

24 Robespierre's 'catechism'. Probably in June 1793, Robespierre sketched out his strategy to achieve 'the goal: the implementation of the Constitution in favour of the people', by winning the foreign and civil wars and 'enlightening the people' (see pp. 158–59).

25 *Camille and Lucile Desmoulins with their son Horace.* Maximilien had been a witness to the Desmoulins marriage in December 1790. Horace was born in July 1792 and was wet-nursed for a time with Danton's son in the Paris countryside. This portrait is attributed to Jacques-Louis David or his school.

26 *Robespierre in the Convention*. François Gérard (1770–1837) made this sketch in the Convention, probably with an oil portrait in mind, since attached notes refer to 'green eyes, pale complexion, Nankin jacket of green stripes, vest blue strips on white, cravat red stripes on white'. Gérard was one of Jacques-Louis David's students; he would become a court painter under Napoleon.

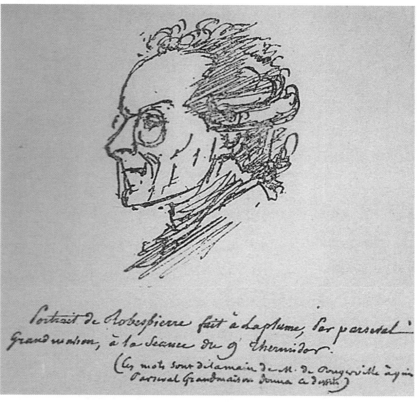

27 Robespierre under attack, 9 Thermidor. This extraordinarily powerful sketch was made of Robespierre, as the caption indicates, during the tumult of 9 Thermidor by François-Auguste de Parseval-Grandmaison (1759–1836), a former student of David's.

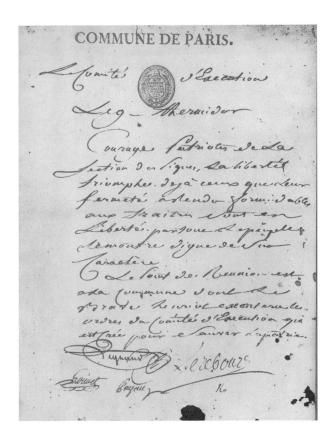

COMMUNE DE PARIS.

28 Robespierre's call to arms, 10 Thermidor. Robespierre had written only the first two letters of his name when gendarmes burst into the Town Hall. The unfinished signature remains the subject of debate (see p. 219).

29 Robespierre lying wounded in the meeting room of the Committee of Public Safety. The engraving by Pierre-Gabriel Berthault was based on a painting by a major artist of the revolutionary period, Jean Duplessi-Bertaux (1750–1818).

30 'Robespierre, after having had all the French guillotined, beheads the executioner with his own hand'. This rapidly became a common Thermidorian cliché. Robespierre is here shown trampling underfoot the Constitutions of 1791 and 1793; the caption identifies separate guillotines for all groups in French society, from Girondins, nobles and priests to 'the elderly, women and children'.

31 *The Triumvir Robespierre*. The engraver Jean-Joseph Tassart has used an earlier common likeness to depict Robespierre squeezing a human heart. An accompanying verse claims that 'nothing can be heard in his favour'. This Thermidorian image refers to a triumvirate that Robespierre allegedly formed with Couthon and St-Just.

received a number of documents seized from the Tuileries that further compromised Mirabeau's memory. That evening, at the Club, Duplay, Robespierre's landlord, asked that the Society remove the bust of Mirabeau. Robespierre supported this motion, and added Helvétius, Rousseau's 'persecutor': 'I see here only two men worthy of our homage, Brutus and Jean-Jacques Rousseau.' The busts of Mirabeau and Helvétius were thrown from their pedestals and smashed. Not for the first time, Robespierre took umbrage at perceived slights in the press, chiding Louis-Marie Prudhomme, editor of the *Révolutions de Paris*, on 15 December 1792, for reminding readers that it was he who had moved to honour Mirabeau in the Panthéon.[22]

What rankled most about Prudhomme's article was his claim that Robespierre's views were not so different from those of the mayor of Paris, Jérôme Pétion. One year after Robespierre's delight in being able to dine with Pétion on the evening of his return from Arras on 28 November 1791, the friendship was in tatters and Pétion publicly rounded on his friend. After Pétion had been unable to deliver a prepared speech in support of Louvet during the debate on 5 November, he decided to publish it:

Robespierre's character accounts for what he has done. Robespierre is very touchy and mistrustful; he sees plots, treachery, precipices everywhere. His bilious temperament ... never forgiving anyone who has wounded his pride, and never recognizing his misdeeds ... wanting more than anything the approbation of the People, constantly courting it ... which may have led to the belief that Robespierre aspired to the heights and wanted to usurp the powers of a dictator.[23]

In his 30 November 1792 issue of *Lettres à ses commettans*, Robespierre responded with a long, scathing critique of Pétion's discomfort with the revolutionary actions of *sans-culottes* on 10 August, and claimed that Pétion's chagrin at Robespierre's popularity had led him to opt to sit as a deputy from Eure-et-Loir, with Brissot:

rather than suffer the affront of seeing priority given to another citizen, you chose to be the third man in Chartres over being the second in Paris. ... I admit my sins; although others, more easily able to judge, say that I am as easy-going, as good-natured in private life as you find me touchy in public life; you have had long experience of this and my friendship towards you has long survived conduct which offended most of my sentiments.

The men of the Convention were imbued with the lessons of the past, especially from classical antiquity, and Robespierre was brilliant in his deadly use of historical parallels. The great heroes of history had been Agis of Sparta, Cato, Marcus Brutus, Algernon Sidney and 'the son of Mary'; Pétion, in contrast, had fallen under the thrall of Lafayette and would never be a hero. 'You know how hard you had to work to tear from my eyes the blindfold which [esteem] had placed there': the friendship and political alliance were over.[24]

The Jacobin deputies' habit of sitting together on the upper left-hand benches in the Convention earned them the epithet of the 'Mountain'. The tension with the Brissotins—now often labelled 'Girondins' because some key individuals were from Bordeaux, capital of the department of Gironde—also spilled over into the streets. The long-awaited opening of Jean-Louis Laya's *Amis des Lois* at the Théâtre Français on 2 December occasioned scuffles between the theatregoers and the Paris Commune's agents bent on closing it down. In the play Robespierre was depicted as a malevolent Nomophage ('eater of the laws') unmasked by a virtuous, moderate former aristocrat.[25]

The next day Robespierre delivered his first speech on the fate of Louis XVI, now on trial for treason by the Convention. Like his new friend St-Just, he argued that the Constitution of 1791, in which the king's person was inviolable, was no longer operable because Louis himself had violated it, and that, the people already having declared Louis guilty, the Convention should simply decide his punishment and not try him:[26]

> What penalty will we impose on Louis? . . . For myself, I abhor the death penalty lavishly imposed by your laws, and I feel neither love nor hatred for Louis; I hate only his crimes. I have asked for the abolition of the death penalty . . . it can be justified only in cases where it is necessary to the safety of individuals or society. But Louis must die because the homeland must live.

Robespierre's reasoning had few supporters, and the thrust of the Jacobin argument during a dramatic, eloquent debate was that to spare Louis would be to admit his special nature: for them 'Louis Capet' was a citizen guilty of treason.[27] The Girondins, in contrast, sought to placate the rest of Europe by a sentence of exile or mercy. On 27 December, Girondin deputies proposed that the final question of Louis' fate should be left to a popular plebiscite (*appel au peuple*) on two questions: 'Shall Louis be put to death? Shall Louis be imprisoned?' In his newspaper Robespierre attacked Vergniaud, Gensonné, Brissot and Guadet over their proposal for a plebiscite: 'the people have already spoken twice on the subject of Louis XVI'. Given their history of suspicion of popular democracy, the Girondins were indeed on shaky ground in calling for the 'appel au peuple'. As Robespierre noted in an open letter to his opponents in early January, this would 'parody sovereignty, by pushing it to the furthest excesses of absolute democracy, such as never before existed among any people, even in Sparta or Athens'.[28] The Convention had to act for the people.

The tension in the Convention was palpable and, when it erupted into open antipathy, Robespierre was the favourite target. On 6 January 1793 the Girondins tried unsuccessfully to end the 'permanence' of the Parisian sections as 'a revolutionary instrument', endangering public order. When Robespierre tried to speak, reported the *Gazette nationale*, there were

> *Cries of Order, Censure him! Lynch him! interrupt him. Several members address him in violent terms. Sarcastic remarks, the noise of individual altercations ring out from one end of the room to the other.* Is it permitted *yells a member* to treat an honest man esteemed by France in this way! (*Gales of laughter from some sixty members from one end muffle this exclamation) Robespierre endeavours to continue.* Chambon: Ah! Robespierre! We do not fear your daggers . . .[29]

On the evening of 16 January the roll call began on the question 'What penalty is to be imposed on Louis?' Robespierre was the first of the Paris delegation to vote, arguing again that there was no contradiction between his earlier stand on capital punishment and his vote for death, without delay.[30] On the 18th the president announced the result of the ballot: of 749 representatives (of whom 28 were absent or did not vote), 387 voted unconditionally for death, 334 for other sentences. Louis went to the scaffold on 21 January, evidently with calm courage. His execution marked another turning-point in the Revolution: not only did it make unbridgeable the gulf between republicans and royalists, it engulfed all of Europe in the war against France.

Right-wing attacks on Robespierre now multiplied. A royalist play published in March 1793 repeated the accusation that he was related to Damiens. So did the Abbé Claude Fauchet, constitutional Bishop of Calvados and a member of the Convention, once known for his social radicalism but firmly monarchist after 1791: 'Who will reign over me? Will it be the viper from Arras, the offshoot of Damiens, this man dried up by his venom, whose tongue is a dagger and whose whisper is poison?'[31] Others disagreed. In February 1793 Maximilien, Augustin and Charlotte went to dine with the family of Marc-Antoine Jullien, a Jacobin deputy from Drôme. Rosalie Jullien, an admirer of Robespierre's journalism, wrote to her son that Robespierre 'is about as suited to be a party chief as to clench the moon with his teeth. He is abstracted, like a thinker; dry, like a man of affairs; but gentle as a lamb; and as gloomy as the English poet, Young. I see that he lacks our tenderness of feeling, but I like to think that he wishes well to the human race, more from justice than from affection.'[32]

The angry polarization of attitudes towards Robespierre personified wider divisions over the Revolution. With the entry of England, then Spain, into the war following Louis' execution, the very survival of the Revolution was at stake. The head of the administration in Arras, the former secretary of the Academy, Ferdinand Dubois, wrote to Robespierre early in 1793 of the 'terrifying struggle' in which liberty and despotism were involved. Robespierre agreed. As he put it in *Lettres à ses commettans*, 'the salvation of the republic depends on two things':[33]

1.   The triumph of liberty at home,
2.   The course of the war.

These two things are intimately linked. . . . The success or the end of the war depends less on the extent of our preparations and the number of soldiers we will put into the field than on the spirit of the government and of the republican principles which will reign over us. . . .

In such a situation political difference could readily be understood as 'factionalism', one of the most serious of charges, since it implied that the factious were splintering the nation's unity. Robespierre insisted on freedom of the press and of opinion, and sought to distinguish between personal enmity and matters of principle but, as the military situation became more critical, divisions over politics and the economy hardened into a battle about who represented the collective will.

At the core of the conflict between Jacobins and Girondins was the question of popular unrest and its causes. In November 1792 Robespierre had targeted the prominent Girondin Marc-David Lasource, who 'claims that a revolution must not spill one drop of blood; and when it flows, he attributes this misfor-tune, not to tyrants, *but to anarchists and agitators*'. On 30 November the Convention heard a disturbing account of the subsistence crisis in Eure-et-Loir, supported by reports from administrators that they were under popular pressure to impose fixed prices. After the Convention had discussed a range of reasons for the unrest, Robespierre spoke on 2 December:

> no man has the right to build up mountains of wheat, beside his fellow man dying of hunger. What is the first object of society? It is to maintain the inalien-able rights of man. What is the first of those rights? That of existence.

> The first law of society therefore is that which guarantees all members of society the means of existence; all the rest are subordinate to that one . . .[34]

But Robespierre was not advocating total control of the grain supply or the market; nor did he advocate forced redistribution of property. Farmers should not only receive 'the price of their work', they should be able to sell any surplus above subsistence needs on the 'free market'. Above all, the surest way to guar-antee subsistence was to facilitate the free movement of goods: 'let circulation of goods across the breadth and length of the republic be protected, and let us take precautions to ensure that circulation occurs'. Nevertheless, the Girondins succeeded in convincing the Convention to re-establish the martial law first introduced in October 1789 but suspended in August 1792. In Robespierre's words, they wanted 'unlimited freedom of commerce, and bayonets to calm troubles and appease hunger'.[35]

Robespierre had reified 'the people' into the purest expression of the general good, despite the excesses of August–September 1792. His consistent stand on the people's behalf in 1789–92 had brought him deep support, even adulation, while in opposition; as the Jacobins became the dominant power in the Convention in early 1793, however, it became more difficult to excuse all popular actions against authority. As he had ever since 1789, Robespierre identified behind some popular unrest the malevolence of those perverting public opinion. Now this was evident even in Paris.

On 12 February petitioners in the Convention demanded that it impose price controls. Robespierre told the Jacobin Club that evening 'there is in the people's hearts a justifiable feeling of indignation. I have maintained in the midst of persecution, and without support, that the people are never wrong.' At the same time, he was bothered that popular unrest in Paris should focus on groceries such as coffee, sugar and soap, at a time of relative security of the bread supply, and wondered whether this was playing into aristocrats' hands: 'I am not saying that the people are guilty … but when the people rise, must they not have a goal worthy of them? Must paltry goods be of concern to them? … The people must rise up, not to collect sugar, but to bring down the tyrants.' Robespierre was asked to draft an explanatory letter to the provincial affiliates. This time, he was more confident that there were sinister forces behind the unrest, in particular 'Pitt's gold': the English enemy was to blame. Had not shouts of 'Long live Louis XVI!' been heard; had not the rioters singled out 'patriotic' rather than 'Fayettiste' shopkeepers?[36]

But he was just as concerned to target those who used the disturbances to rail against Parisian 'anarchy' as he was to recognize the importance of action. Why did not the Girondins criticize unrest in the provinces rather than Paris? 'Is it because it gave birth to the Republic and sent the tyrant to the scaffold? … Ah! Who could doubt it?' In any case, he was deeply suspicious of the motives of this 'unlawful assembly of women, led by the lackeys of the aristocracy, valets in disguise'. There were only two solutions. One was the repression of 'counter-revolutionaries', among whom he now counted 'stock-gamblers.'[37] 'The second way is to ease public poverty. Disturbances can only become dangerous when the enemies of freedom can make the words famine and poverty ring in the ears of a starving or hopeless people. … Let us make beneficent laws, conducive to bringing the price of commodities into line with that of poor people's labour.'

The power held by Roland as Minister of the Interior, who circulated not only instructions and news but a particular interpretation of events to the provinces, rankled with Robespierre and other Jacobins. In late November 1792 Robespierre had criticized actions by Roland in seizing documents distributed by post as threatening freedom of the press. But the entry of England and Spain into the war changed everything: this was now a European war to the death calling for emergency measures, which extended to controls on the press and freedom of speech. 'How can we get out of this situation?', asked Robespierre, naming the editors of the key royalist newspapers the *Ami du roi*, the *Gazette de Paris* and the *Journal général de la Cour et de la ville*: 'we must consign all the scoundrels I have denounced to public opprobrium. Name me the republic in which one can assume the right to defame patriots at the very moment when they are threatened from every side? . . . tell me under what régime, in what times they should not be denounced, and punished as criminals guilty of treason.' But he was prepared to 'confront the faction: it can assassinate me.'[38]

By the second week of March the military situation in the northeast was becoming desperate. The survival of the young Republic was at stake. The problem was, announced Robespierre, that in a year when we 'must see the death of all tyrants; . . . see freedom establish itself more strongly on the ruins of tyranny of every kind', the war effort was still being undermined at home. But if emergency laws needed to target conspirators, who were they? Robespierre clarified this to the Jacobins, to loud applause: 'authors of writings inclined to refer to the ardent, the true friends of liberty as anarchists; writings designed to disseminate civil war, to cause uprisings by private armies in the departments . . .'. A few days later, the Convention heard of the defeat of Dumouriez at Neerwinden, and Robespierre insisted to the Convention that swingeing measures against internal enemies were imperative: 'the time has come to save the State . . . . we too closely resemble the flighty Athenians, indifferent, presumptuous, who slumbered through the sound of the swords with which their ears were assailed.'[39]

While Robespierre publicly expressed his hope that the execution of Louis would be the last capital punishment meted out by the Revolution, the die was cast by Dumouriez' defection to the enemy on 5 April. Robespierre now described capital punishment as the appropriate penalty for 'every attempt made against the security of the State, or the liberty, equality, unity, and indivisibility of the Republic'. How could the Republic expect its soldiers to kill or be killed by France's external enemies while at home the internal enemies could attack with impunity? For Dumouriez had targeted the *sans-culottes* and Jacobins in an open letter to the Convention before his defection, just as his Girondin allies did daily.[40]

The Revolutionary Tribunal had been closed on 29 November, at the start of the king's trial. Now in late February, Danton demanded its reintroduction after having seen at first hand the state of the war in the northeast. The jury-based criminal tribunals established in 1791 had represented a dramatic improvement in transparency, equity and punishment inflicted on the guilty, but rates of acquittal in trials for political offences, including armed rebellion, were very high, whether because of public sympathy for the accused or concern that the obligatory punishments were too severe. Like most in the Convention, Robespierre hesitated before agreeing that a new Revolutionary Tribunal was necessary, with capital punishment for crimes against the security of the state.[41] The removal of such trials from the competence of the criminal tribunals marked a major departure from earlier revolutionary practice.

As the military situation deteriorated in the northeast, Robespierre called for the Convention to delegate an emergency cabinet representative of all groups. On 25 March it established a twenty-five-member Commission of Public Safety. Policing powers were delegated to a Committee of General Security. Both were to be re-elected monthly.[42]

On 24 February the Convention had ordered a levy of 300,000 conscripts. In the west this provoked massive armed rebellion and civil war, known, like the region itself, as 'the Vendée'.[43] Erupting as it did at a desperate time for the young Republic, the insurrection was seen by Jacobins as a 'stab in the back' at the moment of the Revolution's greatest crisis. By early May the progress being made by the Vendéan insurgents led the Convention to plan the recruitment of an emergency army from Paris. To repeated applause, Robespierre argued to the Jacobin Club that the Vendéan insurrection was in its deeds a 'detachment' of the Austrian army commanded by the Prince of Saxe-Coburg:

> I declare that we must not only exterminate all the rebels in the Vendée but all the rebels against humankind and the French people. . . .

> There are only two parties, that of corrupt men and that of virtuous men. Do not distinguish men according to their fortune and their state, but according to their character. There are only two classes of men: the friends of liberty and

equality, defenders of the oppressed, friends of the indigent and the sinful, rich, unjust men and tyrannical aristocracy. That is the division which exists in France.[44]

Ultimately, the civil war was to claim more than 100,000 lives on each side, as many as the external wars of 1793–94. The particularly brutal nature of much of the killing on both sides was to etch hatreds deep into the memories of all those involved.

On 17 April news arrived that Spanish troops had crossed the Pyrenees into Roussillon, then the Basque country. The young Republic seemed in peril of being overrun from all directions. The increasingly desperate military situation exposed to danger those who had brought on the war or attacked the Republic. Marie-Antoinette and her family were especially vulnerable, but so were the Girondins, particularly once their ally Dumouriez deserted to the enemy.

The Girondins had been extraordinarily inept for, as the military crisis worsened dramatically and the Vendéan rebellion swelled in size and menace, they sought scapegoats in the Parisian *sans-culottes*, and the capital itself, in terms recalling the Duke of Brunswick. While Pétion called on 'respectable men of means . . . to drive these poisonous insects back into their dens', Robespierre regretted that the 'hard and merciless' rich had prevented the people from reaping 'the fruit of their labours'.[45] The Girondins launched their campaign against Robespierre and Marat, against Parisian radicalism and 'anarchy', at the worst possible moment. At the very time that their leaders decided that 'Paris' was the problem, their close ally General Dumouriez had deserted and the Vendée had rebelled.

The Jacobins were never clearly in the majority in the Convention—estimates range from 215 to 300 of the 750 deputies—but by the spring a similar number of 'neutral' deputies (such as Grégoire, Barère and Carnot) were swinging their support behind them. On 5 April a reconstituted Committee of Public Safety completely excluded Girondin deputies: the Convention had swung to the Jacobins. It acted to supervise the army through 'deputies on mission'. It passed decrees declaring *émigrés* 'civilly dead', providing for public relief and placing controls on grain and bread prices (4 May). In the provinces, too, majority support had swung back behind Robespierre and the Mountain within the network of Jacobin Clubs, following the trial of the king, Dumouriez' desertion, and the energetic proselytizing of eighty-two deputies-on-mission, largely Jacobins, sent out by the Convention in March. By May three-fifths of the provincial clubs were pro-Jacobin, especially in the north, southeast and centre.[46]

In the midst of military crisis, the Convention also had to turn its attention to the framing of a new, republican Constitution. The Convention had decided that deputies who were also editors of newspapers would need to choose between that profession and their parliamentary mandate. In what would be the final issue of *Lettres à ses commettans*, Robespierre published his own draft Declaration of the Rights of Man and of the Citizen that he had read to an enthusiastic Jacobin Club on 21 April. The Declaration was marked by a restatement of his internationalism—the rights of man were 'the universal code of all nations' and 'men of all countries are brothers who should assist each other'—but warned that those who make war to enslave others—the coalition—should be treated like 'brigands and assassins'.[47]

The Declaration was Robespierre's clearest statement of the underpinnings of a republican polity, once the peace was won:

I.   The aim of every political association is to maintain the natural and inalienable rights of man and the development of all his faculties.

II. The principal rights of man are to provide for the conservation of his existence and liberty.

Like the Declaration of 1789, it guaranteed 'the right of peaceful assembly, the right to free expression of opinions, whether through the press or any other avenue'. Only in 'times of revolution' might it be necessary to curtail such freedoms for the nation's safety. In contrast, however, the Declaration of 1793 set out a distinctively Jacobin model of social welfare and the limits to property:

VII. Property is the right guaranteed to every citizen by law to enjoy and dispose of his goods. The right to property is limited, like all others, by the obligation to respect the rights of others. . . .

X.   Society is obliged to see to the needs of all its members, either by finding them work, or by ensuring the means of survival for those unable to work.

XI.   Society must assist with all its power the progress of public wisdom [*raison*] and put education within the reach of every citizen.

Popular sovereignty was to be the expression of a unified general will, a democratic transformation of the *ancien régime* postulate that the king personified the kingdom. Equally, Robespierre also set out to clarify the relationship between popular sovereignty and the right to revolt, and between the people and their representatives, in terms redolent of Rousseau. On the one hand, laws were to be the free expression of 'the will of the people' (article XIII) and citizens must obey those charged with executing them (XXII). On the other, however, the people could not only change governments but could also recall their representatives (XV). The right to resist oppression was guaranteed; indeed, 'when the government oppresses the people, insurrection of the whole people and of every part of the people is the most sacred of duties' (XXII).

The Declaration of 1789 had as its overarching goal the enjoyment of 'inviolable' individual freedoms; now that of 1793 saw the enjoyment of 'general well-being' (*bonheur commun*) as the objective. While both declarations understood the exercise of their primary goal as being limited by respect for the equal rights of others, there was a stark difference between the two that was at the heart of the revolutionary project of Robespierre and other Jacobins. For 'general well-being' was not simply the sum of the happiness of individuals, but was rather the overall health and harmony of society. This could not be achieved, Robespierre argued repeatedly, in a society where there were very rich and very poor: that is why the first of all rights was that of existence and why he was hostile to great wealth and to finance capitalism in particular. His ideal society was one close to that of *sans-culottes* and peasants, in which households lived in a modest comfort based on their labour as artisans and farmers. The role of the state—'society'—was to ensure that all were guaranteed a 'fair share' through rights to education, social welfare and participation. If 'liberty, the first of man's possessions, the most sacred of the rights he derives from nature', must be limited by the need to respect the liberty of others, so must property, for example, through progressive taxation.

While Robespierre's views on democracy drew heavily on Rousseau, especially the *Discourse on the Origin and Basis of Inequality among Men* and the *Social Contract*, his vision of politics and society and the impulses necessary to achieve that were also heavily influenced by his reading of the Spartan ideal. His admiration for Sparta extended to its use of the idea of a supreme being, the limited application of capital punishment rather than public opprobrium, and the absence of rewards other than honour for achievements. Despite his fascination with Plutarch's description of Lycurgus' Sparta and its forced equality of landholdings, however, he was intransigent in his opposition to the idea of the 'agrarian law' applied to rural property or to restricting manufacture and commerce. Controls on the economy were essential for the war effort and to provide security for the poor, but the well-to-do could only be penalized by the law if their activities were demonstrably antisocial or illegal. He did not wish to 'throw the French Republic into the mould of Sparta'. As he put it, 'it is much more a matter of making poverty honourable than of proscribing opulence; Fabricius's cottage need not begrudge the palace of Crassus.' 'Virtuous' behaviour would both create and sustain his ideal Republic, not wholesale property seizure and redistribution. On this issue there would be an ongoing tension with the more militant of the *sans-culottes*, whatever the general similarity of their social outlook.[48]

Only republican institutions could ensure the regeneration of the people and protect them from the tyranny of those with undue wealth and power, whether officials, employers or politicians. Even the Convention's chamber should be more 'democratic'. Robespierre had criticized the Manège for allowing only a few hundred spectators and had called for a chamber designed to permit twelve thousand people to be as one with their deputies. On 10 May the Convention moved its sittings from the Manège to the vast 'salle des machines' theatre in the Tuileries. This was no longer a two-sided debating chamber but rather a semi-circular amphitheatre constructed to hold up to four thousand people. This was far from Robespierre's ideal; even so, its accoustics made effective oratory well-nigh impossible.[49] His allies in the newspaper press and his network of correspondents were more important than ever.

On 10 May 1793 the Convention adopted the preamble and Article 1 of the new Constitution: 'The French Republic is one and indivisible'. Robespierre then delivered a major speech on the objectives and context of the new charter, echoing Rousseau. 'Man is born for happiness and freedom; and everywhere he is enslaved and unhappy,' he regretted. If there was a major cause of the Revolution's struggle to change society, it lay in deep-seated social prejudice: 'should we be surprised that so many stupid shopkeepers, so many selfish middle-class people retain towards craftsmen that insolent disdain that the nobility lavished on the middle-class and the shopkeepers themselves?'[50]

By early May 1793 Robespierre was again feeling the physical and mental effects of overwork and stress. Writing to his friend François-Victor Aigoin in Montpellier, he admitted that 'I have been both indisposed and extremely busy':[51]

Never, my friend, allow yourself to doubt my loving friendship. After my fatherland, I love nothing so much as men such as yourself. . . . Be brave and let your good citizenship itself be your consolation for the persecution it has brought on you. Rely on my loving attachment, but make some allowance for the state of weariness and despondency into which my painful work sometimes plunges me.

But there was to be no respite, for militant *sans-culottes* were now insisting—as in Robespierre's draft Declaration of Rights—that they had the right to recall 'unpatriotic' deputies. They wanted revenge against the leading Girondins.

As the Montagnard deputies were those most likely to be absent from the Convention on military or other missions, the Girondins were at times still able to use the Convention to their ends. On 12 April, in a debate there on the release of those imprisoned for debt, the Minister for Justice Pétion had deviated to threaten that 'it is time for the traitors and the slanderers to go to the scaffold; and I promise here to pursue them to the death', evidently including Robespierre. When Robespierre interjected to tell him to 'stick to the facts!', Pétion promised that 'It's you I'll be pursuing.' In fact it was Marat who was the Girondins' target that day: it voted 226 to 93 to indict him. Three days later the Convention was interrupted by delegates of the Paris sections with a petition in retaliation, denouncing the conduct of twenty-two prominent Girondin deputies.[52]

In late December 1792 Robespierre had intervened in the Convention's debate about the immunity of deputies, a response to popular demands in Paris that 'unpatriotic'—that is, Girondin—deputies be replaced.[53] For Robespierre, only 'the people' could recall deputies, and only then after due process; the Convention could not itself expel deputies: 'each deputy belongs to the people, not his colleagues'. He had accordingly opposed the indictment of Marat by the Convention in April. In March and April, Robespierre was adamant that an insurrection against the Girondin deputies—however legitimate the popular wrath against them—would make the 'national representation' too vulnerable.

After the Girondins organized on 1 May a demonstration in which shouts of 'Vive la loi!' were mingled allegedly with 'Vive le roi!', the talk in the sections of a mass petition against the 'wicked mandatories' had hardened, according to police reports, into desire for 'imminent insurrection' against them.[54] By the end of May, Robespierre had finally come to agree with the militants, just as he had on 10 August 1792. The immediate prompt was given by the reading at the Jacobin Club on 26 May of letters that Vergniaud had written to the people of Bordeaux in which he called on them to avenge him if he died: 'men of the Gironde! Do you tremble before these blood-sodden monsters, whose wickedness is equal to their cowardice? If you remain apathetic, crime will reign and liberty will be annihilated.' Uncomfortable as Robespierre felt with the sections of Paris dictating the expulsion of leading Girondins as the 'people's mandatories', he rationalized their action as a legitimate expression of the 'general will', and the only way to break the deadlock in the Convention.[55]

By then the Girondins had embarked on a legislative and judicial campaign to break the power of the sections. On 28 May the Girondins still had the numbers (279 to 239) to establish a Commission of Twelve to investigate the looming insurrection. For Robespierre and other Jacobins, the issue now became how to expel the leading Girondins without expelling them all and turning the National Convention into a mere rump vulnerable to the Paris Commune. Robespierre hence opposed the targeting of all those who had voted against the death of the king rather than 'the really guilty'.[56]

On 31 May, Barère, in the name of the Committee of Public Safety, presented a draft bill putting the armed forces at the disposition of the Convention and abolishing the Commission of Twelve. Petitioners from the forty-eight sections then flooded into the Convention, sitting on the benches of the Mountain, to the indignation of the Girondins. As Robespierre addressed Barère's bill, Vergniaud snapped at him to 'finish up!' Robespierre retorted:

> Yes, I will conclude, and against you; against you who, after the revolution of 10 August, wanted to send to the gallows those who had made it; against you who have not ceased to provoke the destruction of Paris; ... against you who pursued with the same relentlessness those patriots whose heads Dumouriez

was demanding; ... Well! My conclusion is the decree of accusation against Dumouriez and against all who have been named by the petitioners.[57]

The National Convention was surrounded with sufficient numbers and menace to force the nominated Girondin deputies to resign or the Convention to expel them. Finally, on 2 June, the Convention voted the arrest of twenty-nine deputies and two ministers. Robespierre said nothing once the *sans-culottes* surrounded the Convention or for several days thereafter, nor did he intervene over how many deputies should be expelled.

On 6 June, Barère presented a report on the *journées* of 31 May–2 June and how the Convention should interract with the departments whose deputies were under detention, for principles of popular sovereignty, if not revolutionary democracy, had been breached. Robespierre was in no mood for reconciliation with a counter-revolution 'plunging a dagger into the hearts of the worthiest citizens', and defended the action of the sections. The Convention subsequently approved on 13 June the motion of Georges Couthon to declare to the nation that the Paris Commune and its sections had effectively saved 'the liberty, unity and indivisibility of the Republic'. Robespierre asked that the vote be put immediately, and 'a large majority' agreed.[58]

Among the Girondin leaders who went into hiding were Buzot, Pétion, Barbaroux and Louvet. Most of the Girondin deputies placed under house arrest fled the capital and joined their departments, where administrations were openly rejecting the authority of the National Convention and Committee of Public Safety.[59] At this most critical moment in the history of the Revolution, the coincidence of military defeat on the frontiers and the expansion of the Vendéan insurrection meant that Girondin actions were necessarily seen as counter-revolutionary. Not only would the foreign coalition slaughter revolutionaries and end the Revolution, but Girondins now known as 'Federalists' would hand over to them a nation that had disintegrated. The Federalist revolts were seen as the ultimate proof of Girondin treachery.

One of those most involved with the purge of the Convention was the Abbé Jacques Roux, a firebrand whose rhetoric had earned him the epithet of 'the red priest' among the militants known as 'Enragés'. Robespierre was no friend of the Abbé, whom he regarded as violently vindictive. Roux addressed the Convention on 25 June, targeting the 'commercial aristocracy': 'freedom is only a chimera when one class of men can starve another with impunity'. He was there denounced by Robespierre. Roux had support within the Cordeliers Club, and on the 30th Robespierre and Collot d'Herbois were among those delegated by the Jacobins to attend a session of the Cordeliers. They must have been persuasive, since Roux and his ally Leclerc were expelled from the Cordeliers on the spot, Collot accusing them of 'fanaticism and perfidy'.[60] This was a critical encounter, for Robespierre and his closest colleagues were making it clear that the Jacobin-dominated Convention and the Committee of Public Safety would henceforth be the initiators of policy: neither the anti-Parisian commercialism of the Girondins nor views on redistribution presented by menacing Enragés would be tolerated.

Ever since July 1789 French revolutionaries had had to confront the central challenge of all revolutions: at what point did the violent popular insurrection that had created and legitimized abrupt change cease to be an expression of the general will against its oppressors? Despite his personal horror of the violence of revolt, Robespierre had argued that it was intrinsic to revolution; indeed, the Constitution of 1793 explicitly guaranteed it as a right, even a duty. The outcome of the purge of Girondin leaders was for him that the Convention and the popular will were aligned, that the threat of popular insurrection was no longer necessary. On 8 July Robespierre felt able to inform the Jacobin Club that 'the present National Convention no more resembles that perverted assembly, corrupted by hypocrites [and] traitors than liberty resembles slavery and virtue resembles vice. Since I have seen it liberated from the police spies, the Brissots, the Guadets, I maintain that the Mountain is in the majority in the Convention.' At least for the duration of the crisis, Robespierre had now concluded that the Convention and its committees were the faithful expression of the 'general will', and that those who claimed to act against them in the people's name were at best misled and at worst in league with the enemy.[61]

Within a week of the expulsion of the Girondins, Hérault de Séchelles produced a draft of the new Constitution on behalf of the Committee of Public Safety. In its concern with democratic freedoms, social welfare and education, it mirrored Robespierre's Declaration of Rights. While his hopes for limits on private property were not met, and he failed in a bid to have the heading for decrees and laws changed from 'French Republic' to 'French People', he was delighted with the document. He looked forward to the time when the

Convention could 'leave to individuals, leave to families the right to do whatever does not harm others; leave to towns the power to regulate their own affairs in any matter that does not directly concern the general administration of the Republic. In a word, give to individual liberty whatever does not belong naturally to public authority.'[62] But by the time the Constitution was passed by the Convention on 24 June, the Republic and the nation itself were in danger of internal collapse and external defeat: public safety would have to take precedence over such individual freedoms.

CHAPTER 10

'A complete regeneration'
PARIS, JULY–DECEMBER 1793

In the summer of 1793 the Republic faced an overwhelming crisis. The unchecked insurrection in the Vendée was absorbing much of the military capacity of the nation at the same time as foreign armies were advancing across the southwest, southeast and northeast of the country. An English naval blockade had isolated the Republic from its colonies and American allies. As many as sixty of the eighty-three departmental administrations had withdrawn their recognition of the authority of the Convention in outrage at the arrest of leading Girondin deputies. The decline in the purchasing power of the *assignat* and the need to provision the armies were aggravating food shortages in Paris and other cities. The nation was literally disintegrating in the face of what seemed insuperable obstacles.

Robespierre was on the edge of collapse, too. On several previous occasions he had admitted that he was worn out; he was particularly susceptible after protracted periods of great stress. This was the case after the purge of leading Girondins on 2 June, which he had plainly found to be an intellectual as much as a physical crisis. He confessed to the Jacobin Club on 12 June that 'I no longer have the strength to battle the aristocracy's intrigues. Exhausted by four years of difficult and fruitless work, I sense that my physical and moral resources are no longer at the level required by a great revolution, and I am announcing that I am going to resign.'

Somehow he managed to recoup his strength and, around the same time, sketched out for his own use his general principles in what was later to be dubbed his 'catechism':[1]

A single will is essential [*Il faut une volonté une*].

It must be republican or royalist.

To defeat the provincial bourgeois whom he blamed for the Federalist revolts, 'it is essential that the People allies itself with the Convention, and that the Convention makes use [*se serve*] of the people'. In fulfilling the Revolution's aim—'the use of the constitution for the benefit of the people'—there were three great obstacles to overcome: the people's ignorance, their poverty and 'the war at home and abroad'. The 'rich and corrupt', 'treacherous pens and tongues', 'traitors and conspirators' had to be punished 'by making a terrible example of all the criminals who have outraged liberty, and spilt the blood of patriots'.

This was a blunt statement of Robespierre's judgement that victory in the crisis of the summer of 1793 would mean censorship, arrests and punishment of opponents as much as full-scale organization for war. He had come to the conclusion that only unrelenting commitment to creating unity of purpose, 'a single will', could save all that had been won since 1789 and all that remained to win. His world was now polarized into traitors and patriots. The approach of the like-minded, in government and across the Republic, would be a mobilization of all resources—military, economic, emotional—and an unremitting pursuit of internal and external enemies: the Republic would be 'one and indivisible'. This was now a war to the death.

On 27 July ill-health obliged a member to resign from the Committee of Public Safety. The Convention accepted Robespierre as the Committee's preferred replacement.[2] For the first time, he entered a government, but he entered it at the most dangerous moment. He had just turned thirty-five. Whereas other members of the Committee were usually chosen because of particular expertise, Robespierre was effectively a member without portfolio, chosen by the Convention because of his experience, standing and popularity. His reputation was at its height, but the challenges faced by him and his peers seemed overwhelming.[3]

Expectations of the Committee of Public Safety were formidable. Members usually gathered in the Pavillon de l'Égalité (the former Pavillon de Flore of the Tuileries Palace) at 7 a.m. to read and respond to dispatches; after attending the Convention between 1 p.m. and its closure at 4 or 5 p.m., some would attend the Jacobin Club before reconvening at the Committee at 7 or 8 p.m. Its nine

members were finally increased to twelve with replacements and the appointment of other Jacobins—Carnot, Prieur de la Côte-d'Or, and the more militant
Billaud-Varenne and Collot d'Herbois—in August and September. It was subject
to re-election each month, but had extraordinary powers: it could issue arrest
warrants (28 July), had control of secret-service expenditure (2 August), nominated the members of special committees (13 September), supervised generals
and public servants (10 October) and conducted foreign policy (4 December).
Finally, on 17 April 1794, the council of ministers was replaced by executive
commissioners responsible to the Committee. Only the police was not under its
control, but it met with the relevant Committee of General Security on twenty
occasions.[4]

The Duplay home continued to be the place where Robespierre prepared
speeches for the Convention and Jacobin Club, received visitors and relaxed. He
had become close to Philippe Lebas, also from Artois, and saw much of him
there; on 26 August 1793, Lebas married Élisabeth Duplay on her twentieth
birthday. In later life she would recall of Maximilien that 'we loved him like a
good brother! He was so nice! . . . He was so virtuous! He revered my father and
mother. All of us felt tender towards him.' One of the other visitors was Filippo
Buonarroti, who was placed by Robespierre in charge of organizing expatriate
Italian revolutionaries and accorded French citizenship in May 1793. He later
recalled the deep affection that infused the Duplays' relationships with
Maximilien: 'he was temperate, incorruptible, industrious and good. These
qualities endeared him to all who knew him well.' On rare days of repose he was
content to visit villages just to the south of Paris to eat with friends: with
Marguerite Chalabre at Vanves, and others at Issy, Créteil, Choisy, Fontenay-
aux-Roses and Maisons-Alfort. These were places already familiar to him from
his weekly excursions as a schoolboy at Louis-le-Grand.[5]

Robespierre was enormously popular in Paris but, unlike other Jacobins who
identified with the *sans-culottes*, he continued old rituals with his morning toilet,
refusing to adopt revolutionary forms of dress or to dispense with his wig. Was
this a mark of the deeply engrained habits of a reserved and serious man or, as
the biographer Max Gallo would have it, his way of 'denying his body by covering
it . . . his unconscious way of expressing his self-love and denying man's carnal
animal aspect'?[6] Similarly, a former nobleman and now Jacobin deputy, Paul
Barras, would later claim that Robespierre never used the familiar 'tu' in

addressing friends, reinforcing the image of a repressed man unable to shed *ancien régime* habits. But this was not in fact the case: although he had previously used the formal 'vous' with everybody but his family, even Antoine Buissart, by 1793 he was addressing familiarly Buissart, friends such as Danton, Camille and Lucile Desmoulins, and Jacobins close to him: Collot, St-Just, Marc-Antoine Jullien, Joseph Lebon, François Chabot, Stanislas Fréron, André Dumont, Armand Guffroy and others.[7]

Despite his domestic stability, Robespierre's closest family relations continued to trouble him. The Committee of Public Safety had entrusted Augustin and the deputy Jean-François Ricord with a political mission to the southeast in the aftermath of the Federalist revolt. Ricord took his young wife Marguerite with him; Augustin decided to take Charlotte. As the deputies were harried and sometimes humiliated by locals hostile to the Jacobins, Charlotte fell out with her companions, accusing Marguerite of seducing her brother. She returned alone and bitter to Paris; her relationship with Augustin never recovered.[8] The news was also troubling from Arras, where the war was but a short distance from the town. Robespierre's ally, Lebon, had left the priesthood and had won a seat in the Convention when the deputy Antoine Magniez resigned in protest after 2 June 1793; now in August 1793 Lebon was sent on a mission back to the departments of Pas-de-Calais and Nord after the fall of Valenciennes on 28 July. He conscripted 6,800 men in Pas-de-Calais, to crush an uprising known as the 'Petite Vendée'—and began an uncompromising repression about which Maximilien's old friends soon began complaining.[9]

The Convention appointed 'deputies-on-mission' like Lebon from its own number to supervise the war effort. It passed emergency decrees, such as those declaring the 'civil death' of *émigrés*, and placed controls on grain and bread prices. The Jacobins sought to create a rural–urban alliance by a mixture of intimidation, force and policies aimed both at meet popular grievances and placing the entire country on a war footing. In June–July the Convention passed a series of laws designed to address some of the essential grievances of the peasantry. On 3 June *émigré* property was put up for sale in small lots, with specific assistance given to the poorest to acquire a plot, and on the 10th the Convention decreed that the division of communal lands would take place by head if the community wished to proceed. Then, on 17 July, seigneurial dues were abolished without compensation: the feudal regime was finally dead.[10] In return, on

23 August all single males between eighteen and twenty-five years of age were conscripted by a 'levée en masse'.

The flight of thousands of priests, and the death or imprisonment of many others, had created an almost complete breakdown of primary-school education.[11] Successive assemblies had received but not implemented radical plans for a total reform of primary education in accordance with the Revolution's regenerative impulses. The most recent, in April, was fatally compromised by Condorcet's authorship. On 13 July, Robespierre outlined to the Convention the draft education policy developed by the eminent noble-turned-Jacobin Michel Lepeletier, assassinated on 20 January after voting for Louis' death. With the Constitution and the law code, he argued that this policy was one of the three 'monuments which the Convention owes to History': he was convinced of 'the need to bring about a complete regeneration, and if I may put it like this, to create a new people'.[12] On the very day Robespierre called for this 'regeneration', Jean-Paul Marat was assassinated at his home by Charlotte Corday, a Girondin sympathiser. Counter-revolution now threatened Parisian deputies in the very heart of the capital.

The proposal Robespierre outlined was remarkably bold and wide-ranging, with an emphasis on the 'Spartan' virtues he had absorbed from Plutarch's *Life of Lycurgus*.[13] The system was all-encompassing, ranging from civic study, physical exercise and manual work to clothing and food. Like Lycurgus' *agoge*, the French Republic would also remove children from their parents for six or seven years. 'The objective of national education will be to strengthen children's bodies, to develop them through gymnastic exercise, to accustom them to manual labour, to inure them to fatigue of every kind, to shape their hearts and minds through useful information and to give them the knowledge necessary to all citizens whatever their profession.' Girls and boys would learn to read, write and count; they would learn patriotic songs and the lessons of history; they would acquire 'the basics of morality and domestic and rural economics', and 'the basics of their country's constitution'. But boys alone would learn 'measuring and carpentry'; girls would learn 'to spin, to sew and to bleach'. All children would perform manual work and—in contrast to the system at Louis-le-Grand—there would be no servants. The children would receive 'healthy but frugal meals; suitable but coarse clothing; their bedding will be uncushioned, so that, whatever profession they follow, in whatever circumstances they may find themselves during their lives, they will be used to being able to do without comforts and excess, and despise artificial needs'.

Robespierre was the only deputy who advocated the adoption of the report in its entirety: others baulked at the pivotal measure of compulsory boarding. The next day, the Convention suspended further consideration of the decree, preferring the far more pragmatic approach of Gabriel Bouquier at the end of the year.[14] Robespierre was more in tune with the Convention when he sang the praises of martyrs for the *patrie*: in particular Lepeletier, the Lyonnais Jacobin Chalier, and the child soldiers Joseph Viala and Joseph Bara. It was young patriots like Bara whose example the French should emulate, a reminder of the stoicism of Spartan children. The fourteen-year-old boy had supposedly cried out 'Long live the Republic!' as Vendéan rebels goaded him into shouting 'Long live the King!' Robespierre eulogized him to the Convention on 28 December as the 'model to arouse in young hearts the love of glory, of the homeland and of virtue'.[15]

The Jacobins who now dominated the Convention and the Committee of Public Safety also sought to realize their vision of a regenerated society through festivals worthy of the grandeur of the Revolution.[16] On 10 August 1793, the anniversary of the overthrow of the monarchy was celebrated as the Festival of the Unity and Indivisibility of the Republic. Symbols of monarchy were burned on public squares in Paris, then, during an immense republican picnic of loaves and fishes, members of the Convention drank fluid symbolizing the milk of liberty spurting from the breasts of a statue of the Goddess of Liberty. From this 'fountain of regeneration' were then released three thousand doves, each with tiny banners attached to their feet proclaiming 'We are free! Imitate us!' The new Constitution had been put to a referendum and the results (1.8 million 'yes' votes to 11,600 against) were made public at the celebrations. The Constitution was then carried in a cedar casket from the site of the Bastille to the Convention. It was to be opened once the crisis was over.

A combination of radical Jacobin reforms and popular initiatives created an extraordinary force for republican 'regeneration'. Supporters of the Revolution— 'patriots', as they were most commonly known—marked their repudiation of the old world by attempting to eradicate all of its traces, giving children names drawn from nature, classical antiquity or contemporary heroes, and purging place names of religious or royal connotations. In Arras street names had been changed to recognize earlier revolutionaries, such as the second-century BC Roman land reformer Tiberius Gracchus and the English poet and republican John Milton; the two great squares became the Place de la Fédération and the Place de la Liberté. Most radically, in order to mark the magnitude of what had been achieved since the proclamation of the Republic on 21 September 1792, the Convention introduced a new calendar that replaced the Gregorian calendar and its saints' days and religious cycles with a decimal calendar based on *décadi* of ten days, the names of which were drawn from nature and the virtues. The calendar was inaugurated on 21 September 1793: the first day of the Year II of liberty and equality.[17]

The Committee, although without the formalities of a council of ministers, acted like a war cabinet, and the nature of its decisions reflected its preoccupations with the mobilization and supply of the army, and military strategy. Spheres of responsibility were clear. In the final four months of 1793, the Committee issued 920 decrees, of which authorship may be confidently ascribed in 272 cases to Carnot (military matters), in 244 to Barère (foreign policy) and in 146 to Prieur de la Côte d'Or (munitions). Robespierre, by no means expert in military matters, was responsible for just 77.[18] He never visited the front, and was content to leave organizational and strategic decisions to those with real military experience. While Carnot and Prieur were with those who understood that it would be the massed, rapidly deployed new armies which might succeed, Robespierre consistently supported measures to remind the rank and file that they were the backbone of the nation, that promotion should be strictly on merit, and that it was officers who were responsible for setting an unimpeachable example of courage.[19]

Even though only Prieur and St-Just were younger, Robespierre's standing on the Committee was such that he exerted a powerful overall sense of purpose and direction. There were many specific matters on which he did not have his way, but the key political statements were his. He had always been fastidious about his correspondence and this, combined with his political popularity and the renown of his major speeches, made him in people's eyes the leader of the Committee. He received letters from all over France in these months—from Bayonne to Montmédy, Perpignan to Coutances—on everything from requests for better army supplies to denunciations and proposals for new reforms.[20] Robespierre was approached about—and blamed for—everything. Since November 1792, for example, Anne-Marguerite Andelle had been appearing at the Duplay home seeking a meeting with 'the republican leader' in order to detail conspiracies even further than in her long letters, albeit for payment of a hefty fee. When finally arrested she offered information on prison plots in the Salpêtrière (as well as about 'the horrors of which even Sodom was unaware'). There is no evidence that Robespierre ordered her incarceration, but she later blamed him for all her woes.[21]

Although many of the practices of war and its support necessarily represented continuity with those of the *ancien régime*, this was to be warfare on a massive scale, not simply for territorial self-defence but for the survival of the Republic and the Revolution. Invading armies and their counter-revolutionary supporters were inevitably described in Manichean terms: like their enemies, the Jacobins readily referred to 'extermination' or 'annihilation' of the enemy. While this was rhetoric, the magnitude of the struggle being waged with external and internal armies meant that the ordinary rule of law did not apply. As Jean-François Carteaux's troops mopped up the Federalist insurrection in and around Marseilles at the end of August, Robespierre, then president of the Convention, was satisfied: 'let the traitors die, so that the spirits of the murdered patriots are appeased, Marseilles is purified, liberty is avenged and strengthened against the blows of her cowardly foes!'[22]

The charge given to the Committee of Public Safety was crushing in its scale. With the benefit of hindsight, 'the Terror' it applied appears as a monolith, with Robespierre as its architect. At the time, however, those in the National Convention who haphazardly put in place its building blocks had no such prescience. Indeed, all the evidence suggests that they were living on borrowed time. It was the desperate nature of the crisis of mid-1793, and the lack of resources or institutions to deal with it, that forced the deputies into reluctant suspension of civil liberties they would normally have seen as untouchable.[23]

There was no one moment at which the National Convention decided upon a system of government that they called 'the Terror': the closest they came to this was to support a delegation from the forty-eight sections and the Jacobin Club, which demanded that it 'make terror the order of the day' on 5 September 1793. Rather, since October 1792 the Convention and its committees had pieced together a series of emergency measures designed to defeat the invading armies and counter-revolution in all its guises, to meet the continuing grievances of

urban and rural people, and to control the actions of militants who claimed to
represent the people's will. These included a Revolutionary Tribunal, the mass
mobilization of human and material resources for the army, controls on prices,
wages and production, a definitive abolition of seigneurialism, and an
emergency executive with sweeping powers. The period from the entry of
Robespierre onto the Committee is more accurately described as one of rigorous
governmental measures to win a civil and foreign war, rather than as 'the Terror',
a descriptor first used only afterwards.[24]

In their references to the need to intimidate or arouse 'terror' in the minds of
counter-revolutionaries, Jacobins were casting back to historical precedent
rather than forward: as recently as the 1770s proponents and opponents of royal
power had accused each other of imposing terror in the image of the religious
wars of a century earlier.[25] In fact, much of the violence later grouped under the
organizing trope of 'the Terror' consisted of attempts by the government to
channel popular fury and division into a national will that could secure victory
in the extreme violence of the wars—both foreign and civil—being fought out
on French soil.

The military crisis preoccupied the Convention and Committee of Public
Safety, but it was linked to a second emergency. How could rapidly expanding
armies be supplied at the same time as the subsistence needs of the cities,
especially Paris? Despite the new harvest, the provisioning of the armies
in particular meant that the people of Paris were faced with shortages of
consumer goods, especially bread. The law of 4 May 1793 required departments
to ensure that the trade in essential goods like grains would be free and the
provisioning of cities assured, but little was arriving from the great wheat belt
surrounding Paris.

In the wake of renewed direct pressure on the Convention on 4 and
5 September, when Robespierre was president of the Convention, deputies felt
compelled to pass a law detaining suspects, and to impose a 'general maximum'
on 29 September that pegged the prices of thirty-nine commodities. An *armée
révolutionnaire* of six thousand Parisian *sans-culottes*—and ultimately as many as
fifty-six provincial *armées*—would have as a mission the requisitioning of
food for cities and the armies, the payment of taxes, the purging of counter-
revolutionaries, the search for deserters from the military, the seizure of metals
from churches for the war effort, and the maintenance of revolutionary zeal.[26]

The new state apparatus that was put in place across 1793 was also a way of controlling the violence and direct action to which governments were vulnerable in Paris. The horror of the massacres of September 1792 hung heavily over the Convention, and the insurrection of May–June 1793 reminded every deputy of the power of the *sans-culottes* to impose their will at the expense of the people's representatives. Revolutionary *journées* had made the Revolutions of 1789 and 1792; now, with a democratically elected republican government under siege, could the nation's representatives any longer be simply the mandatories of the Parisians? In September 1793 the latest challenge to the Convention's authority led the government to decide to reimpose state control over public space.[27]

On 9 September the Convention accepted a motion from Danton and the Committee of Public Safety to cut the number of section meetings to two per week; needy citizens who attended would receive two days' pay as reimbursement for the work time lost. This ended the permanence of sections that had been proclaimed for the whole of France on 25 July 1792. The decree excited strong opposition from militant members of the Paris sections, for whom it amounted to an attack on popular sovereignty. Claiming to speak for them, Jean Varlet confronted the Convention on 17 September: 'are you trying to close the eyes of the People, to cool their watchfulness?' Basire, Jeanbon St-André and Robespierre rejected the accusation, the latter charging that too often it was 'the rich, the schemers, the dandies' who could afford to spend time in the meetings. With only two meetings each week, 'the craftsmen and honourable class of workers' would be able to take their place.[28]

Robespierre and the Convention were also under pressure from militant women. He was president of the Convention on 26 August when Claire Lacombe presented a petition on behalf of the Society of Revolutionary Republican Citizenesses, founded in May. The Society demanded the introduction of the new Constitution, the exclusion of the former nobility from all employment, the purging of all government administrations and the creation of extraordinary tribunals. Robespierre agreed with their views in general, but felt defensive about the implication that the Convention was dilatory or complacent: 'There are in this Assembly men of true patriotism; there are many and this Assembly is above all suspicion.' On 5 September the Citizenesses won the Convention's backing to require women to wear the tricolour cockade. But their zeal was making enemies of influential Jacobins who were nervous about the way their ally Jacques Roux's demands were alienating the Convention. Roux was arrested the same day. While the Citizenesses supported the new 'general maximum', they continued to make allegations of corruption against prominent Jacobins such as Chabot and Basire, and called for further purges. Lacombe confronted the Convention in late October about 'monsters without number of the masculine sex'; Robespierre jotted in a notebook, 'close down the RRC'. They and another thirty women's clubs were closed down across the country in the general crackdown on popular societies. The Citizenesses had aroused vitriolic opposition from prominent Jacobins such as Amar in terms of biology and nature: 'each sex is called to that kind of occupation which is proper to it, its action is circumscribed within a circle which cannot be broken'. For Robespierre, in contrast, it was simply a question of politics.[29]

September was a turning point in Robespierre's approach to the concentric circles of crisis surrounding the Convention and its committees. The private jottings in his journal—the most personal of all the evidence we have, since they were written for himself alone—make this clear, as do his speeches and actions in response to the interrelated military, economic and political crises starkly confronting the government. By late October he was starting to articulate attitudes and practices that were 'terroristic': that trials before the Revolutionary Tribunal need not last more than three days if the jurors 'were clear in their consciences', and that suspects need not be provided with explanations for their arrest.[30]

Then, as now, governments and authorities turned to networks of people known to them to staff critically important functions; the pressure to do so was the more acute in the face of national crisis. In Robespierre's case, his networks extended from those whom he knew already in Artois to the hundreds of acquaintances and friends he had made in Paris. In September 1793 members appointed to the Revolutionary Tribunal included individuals known to him from Artois—its President Herman and the judges Le Fetz and Lanne—or from Jacobin politics in Paris, including his landlord Duplay and the young Joachim Vilate, who were among the sixty jurors. On 9 December (19 Frimaire Year II, according to the new calendar) Carnot wrote to Robespierre's old friend Antoine Buissart to appoint him as head of the administration at Arras, reassuring him that 'you owe this less to our friendship than to your republican principles and your ability'. Dubois de Fosseux, well known to Robespierre for his prodigious work as secretary of the Academy of Arras, was offered, but refused, the position of secretary-general of the Committee of Public Safety. Marc-Antoine Jullien, the eighteen-year-old son of personal friends from Drôme, was given an extra-ordinary role of special agent for the Committee of Public Safety, travelling through Brittany, the Vendée and Bordeaux.[31]

It was probably at this time that Robespierre drew up several lists of 'patriots having more or less talent'. They were a heterogeneous group, including artisans and shopkeepers as well as lawyers and politicians, and ranged in age from Jullien (18 years), St-Just (26) and Claude Payan (28) to Martial Herman (44) and Maurice Duplay (57). The institutional basis of the regime was underpinned by the assumption that revolutionary agents and the Revolutionary Tribunal were stacked with patriots like them whose virtue was matched by competence and humanity. Robespierre is supposed to have asked Duplay one day what was happening at the Tribunal; when he replied 'Maximilien, I've never tried to find out what you do at the Committee of Public Safety,' Robespierre shook his hand warmly.[32] Robespierre's belief that Duplay would protect the judicial process from political pressure belied other evidence that revolutionary authorities were not always so scrupulous. He assumed that the just implementation of repression could rely on the probity of its agents, but there is no doubt that scores were settled and atrocities committed.

In 1791 Robespierre had been one of the most outspoken defenders of freedom of the press, seeing in widespread 'calumny' a lesser evil than that of controlling free expression of opinion. The bitterness of the conflict with the Girondins during the winter of 1792–93, and in particular the preparedness of Roland when Minister of the Interior to use public funds to disseminate attacks on the Jacobins, had led him to reconsider. In the context of the desperate military crisis and armed counter-revolution, the Law on Suspects of 17 September would now be used explicitly to detain or intimidate those who 'by their conduct, relations, words, or writings show themselves to be partisans of tyranny and federalism and the enemies of freedom'.[33] The arrest of 'suspects' by surveillance committees was directed at those who, by word, action or status, were associated with the *ancien régime* or who were charged with anti-revolutionary words and acts, criticizing the government or hoarding of produce.

Nevertheless, there was not a monolithic, censored press in the way that the epithet 'dictatorship' would suggest, just as within the Convention deputies continued to voice their displeasure. Certainly the number of newspapers in Paris declined in 1793–94, from almost sixty to about fifty, but many of these continued to be critical of the regime, even from a royalist point of view, through selective reporting and nuance. Several royalist papers continued under changed titles well into 1794. They had campaigned hard for Louis XVI during his trial at the start of the year; now they did so for Marie-Antoinette and the arrested Girondins. While they could not openly advocate a victory of the rebels in the Vendée or of the Federalists, they achieved their end by publishing the manifestos of the uprisings as reportage, to state their case.[34]

Nor was the Committee of Public Safety immune from open criticism. On 25 September a deputy from the department of Nord, Philippe Briez, who had been in Valenciennes in July when the town capitulated, upbraided the Committee for not having taken the necessary precautions. The opposition within the Convention seized on the opportunity, adding Briez to the Committee, but he refused, claiming lack of ability. Robespierre was furious, and attacked Briez for having abandoned the troops at Valenciennes. People had every right to criticize the Committee, but not someone who had not done his duty:

> over two years a hundred thousand men have been slaughtered through treachery and weakness; it is weakness towards traitors which is destroying us. People feel sorry for the greatest criminals, for those who are giving the homeland up to the enemy's swords; me, I can pity only the unfortunate and virtuous [la vertu malheureuse]; I can pity only oppressed innocence; I can pity only the fate of a generous people who are being slaughtered with so much wickedness.

Briez was not arrested for his outburst, and it took all Robespierre's powers of persuasion to convince the Convention to renew the Committee's mandate. Not for the first time, the stress of managing a highly charged political confrontation, combined with a crushing workload, had physical consequences. Robespierre appears to have had further brief periods of illness on 19–23 September and 26 September–3 October.[35]

The questions of the term of office of the Committee of Public Safety and the status of the suspended Constitution always hung over the head of the Convention. On 8 October, Robespierre was forced to argue against a move to implement sections of the Constitution: 'partial enactment of the Constitution would cripple the revolutionary measures and deliver France up to our enemies by fulfilling all their wishes. Hear their cry: *Let's split the patriots, let's bring on the dissolution of the Convention*. Citizens, let us wait for calm before we enact, in its entirety, a Constitution which will be admired by future generations.' This tension between measures to defeat counter-revolution and the continuing commitment of the deputies to the values embedded in the Constitution of 1793 was to be at the heart of the politics of the Year II.[36]

The arrested Girondins were particularly vulnerable. Had they not issued the siren calls of war in the winter of 1792? Had not a Girondin general, Dumouriez, defected to the enemy? Had they not sought to prevent the execution of Louis? And were they not the instigators of the Federalist revolt at the moment of gravest military crisis? The role of Girondin deputies in the Federalist revolt exposed those under arrest in Paris to the charge that their goal had been the overthrow of the Republic at a time of internal and external crisis. The shock news of the surrender of Toulon on 27 August, made public in Paris on 2 September, prompted calls for their immediate trial. Nevertheless, as other Jacobins, led by Desmoulins, Billaud and Amar, unleashed a concerted attack on more than sixty Girondins accused of being guilty of systematic conspiracy against the Republic, Robespierre acted to mitigate the consequences. He opposed Billaud's motion to force the Convention to vote on the Girondins' fate, on the grounds that it would polarize the nation's representatives, and argued successfully that the seventy-five other deputies in custody for signing a protest against the arrests should not go on trial. He insisted that 'among the men who have been arrested, there are many of good faith who have been led astray by the most hypocritical faction ever seen in all of history'.[37]

On 14 March 1793, Robespierre had argued for a more rigorous test of 'conspiracy', lest the Revolutionary Tribunal be consumed by the claims of rival factions. Yet, if conspirators used dissimulation and false proclamations about their love of the 'patrie' to disguise their perfidy, how could relevant evidence be found and used? It was one thing to know that the generals Lafayette and Dumouriez were counter-revolutionaries, since they had defected to the enemy, but how was one to know how wide their tentacles of influence still spread inside the Republic? In the context of the trial of Brissot and the Girondins in October, Robespierre and others drew on a rich historical analogy, the attempt to seize power by an aristocratic faction under Catilina in first-century BC Rome, and the prompt and severe action taken by Cicero. Cicero's own account, a staple of the education in the classics imbibed by Robespierre's generation at Louis-le-Grand, emphasized the perversity and duplicity of the Catiline conspirators.[38]

The Revolutionary Tribunal, re-established on 10 March, had already sentenced more than fifty people to death before Robespierre joined the Committee of Public Safety. But numbers increased in the last three months of 1793: 177 of the 395 accused before the Revolutionary Tribunal were guillo-tined. Increasing numbers were convicted at political trials of prominent oppo-nents, not only of the Revolution but of the dominant Jacobins. Marie-Antoinette was executed on 16 October, followed on the 31st by nineteen Girondins accused of responsibility for all the Revolution's vicissitudes. Olympe de Gouges was executed on 3 November; Louis XVI's cousin Philippe-Égalité on the 7th. In August 1792, Manon Roland had voiced her despair at Maximilien's aloofness from her. A year later, now in prison, she vented her spleen on the 'timid' and 'jealous' man, a 'very atrocious being' with a 'vulgar voice', whom she deemed responsible for her woes.[39] She was guillotined on 8 November; two days later, her husband committed suicide in a country lane outside Rouen, where he had been in hiding. Other executions followed: Bailly, who had administered the 'Tennis Court Oath' in June 1789, was guillotined on 11 November, Barnave on the 29th, and two other prominent Girondins accused of conspiring to restore the monarchy, Jean-Paul Rabaut St-Étienne and Armand Kersaint, on 5 December.

From October onwards, Robespierre's mental universe was crowded with unrelenting conspiracies: vice and virtue were the 'opposing spirits'. He now saw the external and internal enemies of the Republic as in league, and he argued at one point that, ever since the beginning of the Revolution, the real counter-revolutionary factions in France had been tied to Austrian and Anglo-Prussian plots. In 1793 the common thread in everything from military defeat to food riots was Pitt, in league with all the 'false patriots' of whatever guise. Robespierre was far from alone in such convictions.[40]

France's long tradition as a refuge for all foreigners seeking asylum for what-ever reason was always to be tested at a time of war, including for those who were political refugees. Article 120 of the 1793 Constitution, under which the 'French people offered asylum to those banished for the cause of liberty', had been suspended with the rest of the Constitution. The ranks of foreigners living in France had been swollen by refugees from Liège and elsewhere in the northeast and deserters from invading armies. Robespierre had earlier welcomed political refugees from across Europe, but by late 1793 he had concluded that hostile foreign governments had 'vomited on France all the clever scoundrels who are in their pay. Their agents still infect our armies . . . they deliberate in our adminis- tration, in our section assemblies; they've infiltrated our clubs; they've even sat in the sanctuary of the national representative body; they are directing and will always direct the counter-revolution in this way.' There were many individual exceptions, and pro-revolutionary Belgians were treated less harshly than other foreigners: he had always seen the revolutionary movements in Liège and elsewhere as an extension of the French Revolution.[41] But the 'foreign plot' consumed him.

On 27 Brumaire (17 November), Robespierre made his first major speech for several months, a 'Report on the Political Situation of the Republic' on behalf of the Committee of Public Safety. It was above all the English government that he singled out, accusing it of everything from wanting to replace Louis XVI with the Duke of York (who had placed Dunkirk under siege) to seeking to drive the south of France into a federation just as in the United States. He even accused the Girondins of being in league with the English to arm the slaves of St-Domingue and destroy the French colonies.[42] Robespierre regretted the lack of strong support from other peoples, for which he blamed the malevolence of Brissot's diplomat appointees to the United States and English manoeuvres in Turkey, 'the useful and faithful ally of France'. Austria had plans to annex Lorraine, Alsace and French Flanders if France was defeated; 'elsewhere, Roussillon, French Navarre and the departments bordering Spain have been promised to His Catholic Majesty'. As was now to be the case with key statements of policy, the decree and report were to be 'printed and translated into all languages, dissemi- nated throughout the whole Republic and in foreign countries, to demonstrate to the world the principles of the French Republic and the attacks by its enemies on the general safety of all peoples'. Copies of the speech were published in English, German, Italian and Spanish; English translations, for example, were published in London, Belfast, New York, Philadelphia and Boston.[43]

On 15 Frimaire (5 December), Robespierre again reported to the Convention on behalf of the Committee of Public Safety, this time to respond to the manifesto of Europe's crowned heads that theirs was a defensive alliance against the 'immorality' of the French Revolution. He mocked 'the conjugal fidelity of Catherine' but, again, it was the British who most outraged him: 'insolent and vile people, your so-called representation is venal in your eyes and by your admission. You yourselves adopt their favourite saying; that the talents of your deputies are industrial commodities, like the wool of your sheep and the steel of your factories . . . and you dare speak of morality and freedom!' From the nation that he had once admired for its fierce defence of liberty, England had become both the cradle of all the foreign plots and a 'despicable meteor which the republican star would make disappear'. There were times when Robespierre's fury with the English government spilled over into general antipathy—'I don't like the English'—but he insisted to the Jacobin Club on 30 January 1794 that 'when we see this people free itself, then we will extend all our esteem and friendship'.[44]

Although Robespierre left no memoirs or diaries, among his papers is a notebook compiled in the last few months of 1793: a list of prompts for actions needed by the Committee of Public Safety.[45] Most of the headings referred to individuals and groups to be appointed or to be brought to account. Others referred to pressing economic and social needs in the interests of the people: 'guarantee assistance for widows and children of defenders [of the Republic]; tax the big wholesalers so that retailers can sell'. Above all, he was concerned with four 'essential points' of government: subsistence and provisioning; war; public spirit and conspiracies; and diplomacy. Overarching all this work was the task of strengthening civic spirit and unmasking those undermining unity, 'the only way to promptly terminate the Revolution to the benefit of the people'.

He also felt that it was urgent to stall the outbreak of anti-Christian vengefulness, jotting down 'annul the decree from the municipality [of Paris] outlawing Mass and Vespers'. 'De-Christianization' had first been implemented by Fouché in the departments of Nièvre and Allier, and it accelerated once the Convention decreed on 16 Brumaire (6 November) that a commune had the right to renounce Catholic observance.[46] Robespierre's attitude to de-Christianization and the rights of the faithful was essentially pragmatic: the excesses of the former were a self-destructive and needless response to popular faith. He had no particular desire to defend Catholicism per se. In a circular in November from the Committee of Public Safety to all popular societies he referred to 'the convulsions of dying fanaticism' but counselled that those 'left behind require encouragement to advance in their turn. To frighten them is to invite them to regress.'[47]

On 20 Brumaire (10 November), on the initiative of the Paris Commune, a Festival of Liberty took place in the former Cathedral of Notre-Dame. A fortnight later the Commune sanctioned a *fait accompli* in deciding to close all Paris churches. Two days before the closure, Robespierre delivered an impassioned and successful speech to the Jacobins about the dangers. The Convention, he urged, should not allow 'peaceful ministers of religion to be persecuted.... Priests have been denounced for saying Mass! They'll say it even longer if they are prohibited from doing so. He who seeks to prevent them is more fanatical than he who says the Mass.' He admitted that 'I have, from college days, been a fairly bad Catholic,' but accepted that, 'if God did not exist, it would be necessary to invent Him.'[48]

He agreed that it was necessary to requisition useful material for the war effort: scores of thousands of bells from France's sixty thousand steeples had been seized and melted down. But too often such seizures had been coupled with behaviour that would needlessly antagonize neutral foreign countries and huge numbers of the faithful in France itself. On 14 Frimaire (4 December), Couthon had reported with satisfaction of his mission to Lyons and Puy-de-Dôme that he had overseen 'a complete victory over fanaticism and religion': at Issoire, for example, the 'Popular Society' had organized an auto-da-fé of two hundred statues of saints. While he insisted that it was 'the pride of priests and the error of the people' that were attacked, and not God, the danger was clear to Robespierre. Two days later, he presented a draft bill on freedom of religious observance to the Convention, which was immediately passed. The bill now promised that authorities would be as severe against those who threatened this freedom as it was against 'those who might try to use religion as a pretext for compromising the cause of freedom.'[49]

Robespierre had a useful exemplar close at hand in the Prussian noble-turned-Jacobin Jean-Baptiste du Val-de-Grâce, Baron de Cloots, better known as Anacharsis Cloots, and often referred to as the 'orator of mankind'. One of those made a French citizen in September 1792 and elected to the Convention from Oise, he had become personally involved with the de-Christianization campaign. Cloots was under a cloud because of alleged dealings with the Vandenyvers, bankers condemned to death for criminal corruption by the Revolutionary Tribunal on 17 Frimaire (7 December). Robespierre fulminated against Cloots at the Jacobin Club on 22 Frimaire (12 December), demanding successfully 'the exclusion from the Jacobins of all nobles, priests, bankers and foreigners'. 'Can we regard a German baron as a patriot? Can we regard a man with an income of more than a hundred thousand *livres* as a *sans-culotte*?'[50]

The attack on the de-Christianizers was part of a wider set of actions by Robespierre and Danton designed to undermine the political power of the Paris Commune and its militant officials, such as Jacques Hébert. It included the Law on Revolutionary Government of 14 Frimaire (4 December). While ostensibly designed to ensure effective supervision of public officials, more importantly it asserted the primacy of central authority. Anxiety in the Committee about the role of the *armées révolutionnaires* in spreading de-Christianization and needlessly alienating rural populations saw the armies' demise embedded in the legislation.[51]

Across 1793 the Convention had put in place a raft of emergency measures designed to place the nation on a war footing, repress internal counter-revolution, and exert central control over political initiative. The achievements were dramatic by the end of the year. Republican forces led by a young artillery officer, Napoleon Bonaparte, had recaptured Toulon, and foreign armies had suffered major reverses in the northeast, at Wattignies on 16 October, and in the south, at Peyrestortes, just north of Perpignan, on 17 September. The Vendéan rebellion had been contained and other revolts crushed, both at a huge cost in lives. Though the 'general maximum' had not been fully implemented, the economic slide had been reversed and the purchasing power of the *assignat* had climbed back to 48 per cent of its 1790 face value from 36 per cent a few months earlier.

Rebellion simmered and flared in many departments, but there were many regions of the country where the constant demands of the Committee and Convention were met with acquiescence, if not alacrity. In departments such as the Yonne, Aude, Tarn-et-Garonne, Lot-et-Garonne, Creuse and Dordogne, deputies-on-mission succeeded in imposing relative calm in the most difficult of circumstances by equitable rationing and judicious use of measures against suspects.[52] Another role of the deputies-on-mission was to establish Jacobin Clubs and 'popular societies', of which about three thousand of the more than 5,300 across the nation were set up in these months. Robespierre was overwhelmingly popular in the language of these clubs, although in some areas no doubt out of judicious choice rather than sincerity.[53]

At the same time, news was filtering back to the Convention and its Committees that the price of success had been inordinately high. From Nantes, Lyons and even Arras came reports of wholesale and indiscriminate killing. Worse, some of those responsible seemed to believe that such slaughter was legitimate. Was anything permitted for the public's safety? The visceral response to the internal enemies of the Revolution drew its strength from a panic that the nation itself was falling apart but, as Jacobins and the armies reclaimed cities and regions from the Girondins and counter-revolutionaries, there were vengeful, and at times appalling, episodes of punishment, always accompanied by a language of extermination.[54]

One of Maximilien's acquaintances in Arras had been Joseph Fouché, a teacher at the College. Fouché had swung with the winds of change from the Girondins to the militant supporters of Hébert, and in Allier and Nièvre had led the de-Christianization campaign. In Lyons he had organized with Collot d'Herbois a horrific repression, and on Fouché's return to Paris Robespierre demanded an account of his behaviour. Paul Barras accompanied him to Robespierre's rooms, and decades later could still recall Robespierre's icily dismissive reception. The repression, including 1,800 executions, was the most unchecked anywhere except for the Vendée. The Committee and Convention had given Collot and Fouché *carte blanche* 'to punish militarily and without delay the counter-revolutionaries of Lyons'. Whether the vagueness of the decree, which also ordered the destruction of all the houses of the rich, was designed to be an example to other centres of rebellion, the deputies-on-mission took it at face value, with local Jacobins urging them on.[55]

At the very time when the greatest gains were being made, but all still remained in the balance, two of Robespierre's closest and most admired allies—Georges Danton and Camille Desmoulins—decided that the time was right for a change of direction. The struggle was unleashed when François Chabot—a former monk, now a militant Jacobin under a cloud for marrying the sister of suspect Austrian bankers—went to Robespierre's lodgings in person on 14 November and spun a story of a breathtakingly wide conspiracy designed to corrupt leading Jacobins. The next day he and Basire claimed to the Committee of Public Safety that the Baron de Batz, a noble financier suspected (with reason) of being a key foreign agent, was using funds from the liquidation of the East India Company to pay Hébert and his followers to undermine the Republic through deliberate excesses. Worse, Chabot implicated Georges Danton, who rushed back from his home in Arcis (Aube) with his new bride within days.[56]

Robespierre had had to defend his old ally Danton repeatedly against charges that his behaviour and personal ties were questionable. In July he had responded to a charge that Danton had favoured a corrupt official from Marseilles by warning of the dangers of calumny against a man who had given his 'whole life to the cause of liberty'. In August Robespierre had had to speak up for Danton against the Enragés Roux and Leclerc, claiming that 'new men, one-day patriots, want to ruin his oldest friends in the eyes of the People'. Then, when Danton returned, he had to intervene to prevent the Jacobin Club from expelling him on the spot.[57] In turn, Danton supported Robespierre's attack on de-Christianization but also called for greater 'economy in the blood of men'. As others grumbled against Danton, Robespierre defended him once again: true, he could have acted sooner against Dumouriez, Brissot and their accomplices, but

> we owe many victories over the enemies of the People to him. I state this in relation to politics; I have watched Danton . . . I have seen him always the same and I have always met him on the same patriotic path. . . . the difference between us came only from the difference in our temperaments . . .[58]

Of equal standing to Danton was Camille Desmoulins. The day following the Law of 14 Frimaire (4 December), Desmoulins launched his newspaper the *Vieux Cordelier*.[59] The first two issues, approved by Robespierre, targeted the Hébertists and de-Christianization, but Desmoulins was attacked in the Jacobin Club on 24 Frimaire for having written sympathetically of the Girondins that 'they die as republicans, as Brutus died'; Robespierre again felt impelled to defend a friend and revolutionary. Yes, he had been too close to Mirabeau and the Lameths: 'I knew Camille in college, he was a fellow student, he was then a talented young man without mature judgement. Since then Camille has developed the most ardent love of the Republic; . . . one must not look only at one point in his moral life, one must take the whole; one must examine him as a whole.'[60] He recalled his courage in advocating a Republic in 1788, in

La Philosophie au peuple français: 'at that time, in the depths of the provinces, I learned with a secret pleasure that the author was one of my fellow collegians'.

The pressure to relax the constraints on personal freedoms—particularly the detention of large numbers of suspects—came from another direction. On the evening of 22 Frimaire (12 December) a number of women came to protest at the bar of the Convention against the detention of their husbands. On 30 Frimaire a larger, diverse group of perhaps fifty appeared, including women from Commune-Affranchie (formerly Lyons) and a delegation of mothers, wives, daughters and sisters of detainees in Paris. The women sought 'freedom for all innocent detainees and victims of error or human passions', recalling that the Convention charged its Committee of General Security to present it with a report on the 22 Frimaire petition within three days, and that eight days had now elapsed. The pressure was so strong that Robespierre proposed that the Convention create a commission from the two governing committees to examine all detentions promptly and to free the innocent. A week later Robespierre and Barère were still disagreeing on the composition of the commission; the former was sure that 'Mr Pitt' would be delighted and remained unconvinced that there were innocent patriots in prison. Finally, Billaud opposed its establishment and the idea was abandoned.[61]

The tone of the third issue of the *Vieux Cordelier* on 25 Frimaire (15 December) was different, full of satire and classical allusions, and posing the awkward question as to whether despotic regimes had the policy that 'it is better to execute several innocent people rather than [let] a guilty person go free'. Robespierre's famous aphorism was mocked by inversion. Desmoulins drew brilliantly on Tacitus to insinuate that the revolutionary government was like Tiberius' despotism. In the Convention there were calls to change the membership of the Committee and to open the prisons.

The fourth issue of the paper, which was dated 30 Frimaire but did not appear until 4 Nivôse (24 December), was even more explosive. While responding to the counter-attack of the Hébertists, Desmoulins now also made a ringing call for clemency: 'you want to remove all your enemies by means of the guillotine! Has there ever been such great folly? Could you make a single man perish on the scaffold, without making ten enemies for yourself from his family or his friends?' The really dangerous enemies of the Revolution were now dead or in exile: the crisis was now over. 'I think quite differently from those who tell you that terror must remain the order of the day.' The paper also contained a direct appeal to Robespierre to remember their days together at Louis-le-Grand: 'Oh, my old comrade from college! You whose eloquent speeches will be read again by posterity! Remember the lessons of history and philosophy, that love is stronger and more durable than fear ...'. The issue was laced with brilliant allusions to classical history, which would not have been lost on his former schoolmate.

The campaign of Desmoulins and Danton was courageous and humane, but stunningly inept, since the crisis was plainly far from over. General Hoche's troops had suffered a major reverse at Kaiserslautern in late November. There were hundreds of towns and villages on France's borders whose inhabitants were directly under the control of occupying armies. One of them was Collioure, at the other extreme of France from Arras, most of whose 2,300 Catalan inhabitants subsisted from winegrowing, fishing and the coastal trade within the Mediterranean.[62] They had welcomed the Revolution of 1789 for its articulation of rights and the subsequent abolition of privilege and seigneurialism, even if the reforms to the Church had resulted in the flight of its ten priests and monks. Colliourencs, like the Flamands, Alsaciens, Provençaux and Basques of other frontier regions, had then lived through the privations of the Republic's desperate struggle for survival. With the local French garrison, the people of Collioure had resisted a Spanish siege from May 1793 before the town succumbed and was occupied by Spanish troops on 20 December. Although a public meeting during the siege in late June had formally condemned the expulsion of the Girondin deputies (including the local deputy Birotteau), in late July the Jacobin Constitution of 1793 was translated into Catalan and approved unanimously by 135 citizens in the parish church. Local resistance in Collioure had been led by Jean-Paul Berge, one of the remarkable network of correspondents sustained by Dubois de Fosseux as secretary of the Academy of Arras before the Revolution. Dubois had his own anxieties in late 1793 as Lebon imposed violent repression in Arras; Berge died fighting the Spanish at the Col de Banyuls on 12 December. The siege of Collioure was devastating: crops were destroyed; the port was blockaded; and hundreds of people were dying prematurely. Like other French citizens on the frontiers, Colliourencs would have found Desmoulins' proposition that the crisis was over perplexing indeed.

For Robespierre and republican politicians and officials across the country, every day was a swirl of uncertainty, confusion and fear, matched only by resolve and hard work. On the morrow of Desmoulins' appeal, Christmas Day 1793 (5 Nivôse), Robespierre delivered a major policy speech on the 'theory of revolutionary government', 'the war of liberty against its enemies':

> The principal concern of constitutional government is civil liberty, and that of revolutionary government, public liberty. Under a constitutional government, it is almost enough to protect individual liberties against abuses from the state; under a revolutionary government, the state is obliged to defend itself against the factions which attack it. Revolutionary government owes good citizens the protection of the state; to the enemies of the people, it owes only death.

The question was whether Danton and Desmoulins had become part of a faction, 'enemies of the people'.

CHAPTER 11

'Men with changing tongues'
PARIS, JANUARY–JUNE 1794

Desmoulins did not learn his lesson from Robespierre, but nor did he want to. On 18 Nivôse (7 January) he was called to the Jacobin Club to justify the praise lavished on Pierre Philippeaux in issue no. 5 of the *Vieux Cordelier*. Philippeaux, a deputy from Sarthe, was increasingly under suspicion for his public attacks on the severity of the repression in the Vendée, especially by the deputy Jean-Baptiste Carrier, and of Collot d'Herbois' bloodletting in Lyons.[1] Robespierre was caught between his loyalty to government colleagues and his fury that Philippeaux might be right, but criticized Desmoulins for opening his columns to 'the slanders of Philippeaux against the revolutionary government and the patriots'. In the end, however, Robespierre continued to try to see in Desmoulins a brilliant but occasionally wayward patriot:

> Desmoulins does not deserve the acts of severity certain people have whipped up against him; I even think that seeming to want him punished like the great criminals goes against freedom . . .

> I am happy for liberty to treat Desmoulins like a hare-brained child who used to be well-disposed and has been misled through bad company; but we must insist that he prove his repentance for all his stupidities . . . I would not have told these truths had Desmoulins not been so pig-headed . . .

Robespierre asked that copies of the newspaper be destroyed, to which Desmoulins retorted: 'that's very well spoken, Robespierre, but I will answer you like Rousseau, "to burn is not to answer".[2] Robespierre was stung, and indignant, and drew on their shared education in Tacitus and Cicero to launch his own barb: 'how dare you still try to justify works which are the delight of the aristocracy? Learn, Camille, that were you not Camille, people would be less indulgent towards you.... Desmoulins, seduced by the consonance of the words, thinks that Philippeaux wrote the *Philippics*, but let him not be mistaken, they are but *Philippotics*.' Danton leapt to the defence of Desmoulins and underlined the importance of freedom of the press. The next day the Jacobin Club began to examine the various issues of the *Vieux Cordelier*. There was little point, concluded Robespierre:

> with his redoubtable bludgeon [Camille] deals the most dreadful blow to our enemies; with the most biting sarcasm he rips apart the worthiest patriots. Desmoulins is a strange mixture of truths and untruths, of policy and idiocies, of sensible views and fanciful and personal plans.... I am not taking anyone's side, Camille and Hébert are equally wrong in my eyes. Hébert is too preoccupied with himself, he wants all eyes upon him, he does not think enough about the national interest.[3]

Desmoulins' refusal to change the editorial slant of his newspaper had exasperated Robespierre. On 21 Nivôse (10 January) he supported Desmoulins' expulsion from the Jacobin Club. Over the next few days Robespierre drafted a speech in which he sought to make sense of the accusations swirling through Paris. The speech was never delivered, but his identification of 'two rival coalitions'—'moderantism' and 'excess'—was to inform his tactics for the future: 'one wants to take us to the Tropics, the other to the Arctic'. Shortly afterwards, the sixth issue of the *Vieux Cordelier* appeared. It only mentioned Robespierre in passing, but insisted that, even if, 'in time of revolution, the people's safety might require restraints on the liberty of the press, one must never take away the free expression of opinion from the representatives'.[4]

As Hébert's followers used the *Père Duchesne* and Danton's used the *Vieux Cordelier* to exonerate themselves by targeting each other, ever more sweeping and alarming claims were made about the level of intrigue.[5] As was the case in other claims of conspiracy, there was enough evidence of malpractice to make a wider plot believable. Fabre d'Églantine—designer of the revolutionary calendar and a close friend of Danton—and Chabot were alleged to be involved in profiting from the liquidation of the East India Company, and both claimed knowledge of a wider 'foreign plot' in an attempt to implicate others and save themselves.

The position of the 'moderates' or 'Indulgents' was further undermined on 19 January, when the Convention heard that Austrian troops had entered the region around Cambrai, allegedly burning crops, disembowelling women and even butchering and eating children. Long-standing Austrophobia, focused on Marie-Antoinette, rivalled Anglophobia, and during the winter of 1793–94 they became entwined in the 'foreign plot'. As the two factions heaped epithets and denunciations upon each other, the evidence seemed to accumulate that both 'factions' had compromising connections with the sordid world of financial speculation. They were linked, and linked each other, with individuals who had seen in the Revolution an opportunity for financial gain, men such as the Dutch banker de Kock (an acquaintance of Dumouriez), Vandenyver (the banker for Madame du Barry, with whom he was guillotined in December 1793), Berthold Proli and the Frey brothers. The Dantonists were particularly vulnerable, since an associate of Chabot had links with both the Gascon nobleman Jean Batz, who had tried to rescue Marie-Antoinette from prison, and the Freys, once suppliers to the Austrian army and who, with others, were charged with profiting from the sale of the East India Company.[6]

As the armies slogged through a war of attrition with the invading forces during the European winter of 1793–94, the conflict in the Caribbean was also reaching a climax. The Committee of Public Safety had already offered freedom to slaves who joined the army of the Republic; now the issue of slavery itself was confronted. On 24 April 1793, in outlining his views on 'the principles of property' for his draft Declaration of the Rights of Man and of the Citizen, Robespierre had linked slavery with serfdom and hereditary wealth:

> Ask a merchant of human flesh what is property; he will answer by showing you that long coffin he calls a ship, in which he packs in tightly men who still seem alive: there is my property, I've bought them for so much a head. Ask a gentleman who has lands and vassals or who believes the universe has been turned upside down since he has them no longer . . .[7]

Robespierre was absent from the Convention on 16 Pluviôse (4 February) when it voted to abolish slavery. He had been present, however, at a meeting of the Society of People of Colour in June 1793, which passed a motion against slavery, and also at the Jacobin Club on 19 June where there was general support for the decree. He later signed orders putting it into effect.[8]

Robespierre was instead preoccupied with a speech he was to give on the morrow, 17 Pluviôse (5 February 1794), the most portentous of his life: a 'Report on the Principles of Political Morality'. 'What is the goal towards which we are heading?', he asked the Convention. The goal was clear—'the peaceful enjoyment of liberty and equality'—but this would necessitate a moral revolution. Consciously or not, he drew on a speech familiar to him from his teenage years, Cicero's second oration against Lucius Catilina. Like Cicero, who had contrasted the virtues of the Roman Republic—honour, modesty, chastity, equity, temperance, fortitude, prudence, piety—with the vices of tyranny— wantonness, sordidness, fraud, wickedness, baseness, lust—so Robespierre insisted that

> We seek an order of things in which all the base and cruel passions are enchained, all the beneficent and generous passions are awakened by the laws; ... and where commerce is the source of public wealth rather than solely the monstrous opulence of a few households.
>
> In our land we want to substitute morality for egotism, integrity for [formal codes of] honour, principles for customs, a sense of duty for one of mere propriety, the rule of reason for the tyranny of fashion, scorn for vice for scorn for the unfortunate ... the charm of happiness for the tedium of pleasure, the greatness of man for the pettiness of the great, a people who are magnanimous, powerful, and happy, for a kindly, frivolous, and miserable people—which is to say all the virtues and all the miracles of the republic for all the vices and all the absurdities of the monarchy.[9]

Only a democratic and republican government could achieve such a state of virtue. Robespierre deliberately marked his distance from the most militant of the *sans-culottes*: the deputies were no longer simply their 'mandatories'. 'Democracy is not a state in which the people, continually meeting, regulate for themselves all public affairs.... Democracy is a state in which the sovereign people, guided by laws which are of their own making, do for themselves all that they can do well, and by their delegates do all that they cannot do for themselves.'

Like Cicero, Robespierre insisted 'how frivolous it would be to regard a few victories achieved by patriotism as the end of all our dangers'. The armies' victories in late 1793 did not mean the crisis was over. The gravest dangers now were domestic, but 'are not the enemies within the allies of the enemies without?' 'One of these two factions pushes us toward weakness, the other toward excess. The one wants to change liberty into a bacchante, the other into a prostitute':

> In this situation, the first maxim of your policy ought to be to lead the people by reason and the people's enemies by terror. If the mainspring of popular government in peacetime is virtue, amid revolution it is at once *virtue* and *terror*: virtue, without which terror is fatal; terror, without which virtue is impotent. Terror is nothing but prompt, severe, inflexible justice ...

In a world in which there are only republicans and their enemies, 'there are no citizens in the Republic but the republicans'. Their enemies would feel only 'the avenging blade of national justice'.

Robespierre's speech of 5 February 1794 was his attempt to find a way to respond to the 'Indulgents' by appeals to 'terror' as virtue's necessary companion. Throughout the Revolution, its partisans and opponents had all used a vocabulary of binary opposites, of friends and enemies, to explain their triumphs and vicissitudes. To common epithets of 'patriots' and 'counter-revolutionaries', *sans-culottes* and 'aristocrats', 'Montagnards' and 'Federalists', 'Jacobins' and 'Girondins', there corresponded many others. Across the span of the Revolution, such opposites had narrowed in range; now, in the spring of 1794, the 'patriot' took on two opposites from within the Jacobin movement: 'Indulgents' and 'Ultra-revolutionaries'.[10]

Shortly after this pivotal speech Robespierre again fell ill. He was able to reappear at the Jacobin Club and Convention in the middle of the month but collapsed again on 19 February and did not resurface until 12 March. Couthon was also sick. Across the next few days Parisian sections sent delegations to enquire about their health. On 1 Ventôse (19 February) the daily police report noted that 'near the Jardin des Plantes a large group of men talked about Robespierre's illness. The people were so grieved by it that they said that, if

Robespierre happened to die, all would be lost.' The next day, as news spread that Robespierre had been up and about, there was widespread relief: 'as a deputy he is a treasure to the people; he loves them, and they trust him'. A week later, on 9 Ventôse, there were rumours of poisoning.[11]

Robespierre had never been physically robust, and had admitted to the Jacobin Club on 15 February 1792 to a concern that 'my strength and my health are not great enough'. He had thrown himself with extraordinary energy into the role of articulating the meaning and destiny of the Revolutions of 1789 and 1792. Across 1793 he had made almost four speeches a week—101 in the Convention and 96 to the Jacobin Club—on the themes of patriotism, sacrifice and the virtues, and their mortal enemies, greed, conspiracy and egotism.[12] His entry onto the Committee of Public Safety increased the pressure immeasurably. His confrontation in the winter of 1793–94 with two of the men he most admired and liked had taken a serious toll.

We cannot be certain about the nature of the illnesses that Robespierre suffered with increasing frequency. The Duplays' doctor, Joseph Souberbielle, was a frequent visitor to the house and accepted the task of attending to a varicose ulcer on Robespierre's leg. Unfortunately, Souberbielle did not speculate on the nature of his more serious illnesses. It may well be that Robespierre's decision to sacrifice his health for the Revolution through a relentless commitment to work meant that periods of great stress like the winter of 1793–94 made him susceptible to bouts of anaemia and a psychosomatic disorder. His abstemious diet would only have made him more vulnerable to such exhaustion, and explains why Robespierre several times admitted publicly that he was at the end of his physical strength. A German who had sought out information about Robespierre before publishing his account in May 1794 described a Spartan regime:

He rises very early. . . . Then he does a few hours' work, without taking anything but a glass of water. . . . Meanwhile, he reads the gazette or pamphlets of the day and takes his lunch, which consists of a little wine, bread and a few pieces of fruit. . . . He dines at his host's table, and it is always he who says grace before the meal. . . . After the meal, he has coffee served to him, stays home for an hour waiting for visits, then, normally, he goes out. . . . He comes home extraordinarily late; he often works till nearly midnight at the Committee of Public Safety.[13]

He had his personal confidants—St-Just, the Duplays, Augustin, probably several police agents—and their daily reports as he recuperated would have given him a distorted view of what was happening during his absence from the Committee and the Convention. By the time Robespierre returned to full participation in the daily grind of considering reports, issuing decrees and writing letters and speeches, he had internalized a Manichean vision of the state of the Revolution and what remained to be done. His speeches thereafter became more agitated and even apocalyptic; his personal and tactical judgement, once so acute, seems to have deserted him. From March, his capacity for leadership was at odds with his status and respect.

By then Robespierre was convinced of the conspiracy that had been put in place in 1789. Throughout the Revolution he had seen those whom he had trusted betray that trust by compromise or treachery. From the hopes he had placed in Louis and Mirabeau at the outset, through the desertion of generals like Dumouriez and Lafayette, to the compromises with monarchy he witnessed in Pétion and Brissot and, worst of all, the backsliding of Danton and Desmoulins, the years after 1790 had been a long betrayal of the people's cause. Continuing military crisis exposed both 'Indulgents' and 'Ultras' to the most serious conspiratorial charges of all, that they were somehow implicated in a 'foreign plot' more dangerous than the coalition's armies. Were not the tentacles of the plot sliding into the Convention itself, even into the Committees? There was more than enough evidence of links between Danton, Chabot and foreigners fishing in the well of bank loans, army supplies and clandestine diplomacy to make claims of dangerous alliances plausible.[14]

On 14 Ventôse (4 March) the deputy Carrier, whom Robespierre had recalled to Paris because of reports of atrocities in Lyons and Nantes, and Hébert convinced the Cordeliers Club to declare a state of insurrection in an attempt to recapture the initiative, but only two neighbourhood sections in the capital were prepared to support them. When Robespierre and Couthon were able to return to the Convention on 22 Ventôse (12 March), after an absence of five weeks, 'all the members and citizens on the benches showed by their applause their satisfaction at seeing the two patriots once more'. The following day Robespierre admitted his frailty in front of the Jacobin Club, and focused on the Hébertist plot. 'Would to God that my physical powers were equal to my moral powers,' he regretted, and called on others to take up the fight against the 'frightful plot' aimed at the Convention and Jacobins.[15]

On 28 Ventôse (18 March) a delegation from the Cordeliers Club sought to defuse the situation, but Robespierre and others rounded on them. These were 'corrupt men, men with changing tongues who disavow one day what they said the day before ... the sword of justice shall strike them all'.[16] That day the Convention formally charged the deputies compromised by the East India Company scandal and sent them to the Revolutionary Tribunal. At the same time, however, Robespierre intervened to shield the signatories of two royalist petitions (of eight thousand and twenty thousand names) from the wrath of the Jacobin Club. The self-serving charge by Chabot (which would ultimately prove fatal for him, too) that the Hébertists were involved with foreign spies and conspirators deepened Robespierre's antipathy. Also on trial with the Hébertists were their associates, the Dutch banker de Kock, the Belgian Proli and the former Prussian noble Anarchasis Cloots. Making Cloots and Proli even guiltier in Robespierre's eyes was their enthusiasm for de-Christianization.[17]

After the guillotining of the 'Ultras', or Hébertists, on 4 Germinal (24 March), the Indulgents became more openly opposed to the Committee of Public Safety. In a seventh issue of the *Vieux Cordelier* that Desmoulins had prepared, he was sharply critical of the Committee and mocked 'le jansénisme de républicain': Robespierre was a republican puritan in a Church of virtue.[18] Others continued to put their trust in 'the Incorruptible'. Jean d'Yzèz, a deputy from the department of Landes, wrote home to a friend that he was sure Robespierre would not be a Cromwell, and hoped he would prove to be a Solon or Lycurgus:

He directs all deliberations. Public opinion grants him authority and grants it to him alone. Everything he says is an oracle. Everything he condemns is an error. ... I have followed trustingly in his footsteps. The reason for this is simple. I believed I saw in him a man who truly loved liberty, who was passionate about it. The means he used seemed to me closest to the true path.[19]

The removal of the 'Ultras' enabled the Committee to adjust economic policy away from Hébertist demands. Neither the law of 26 July 1793, providing for the death penalty against hoarders, nor the 'general maximum' had been successful: they had discouraged open trade and thereby penalized both retailers and consumers. The revised scheme of the maximum in March 1794 fixed prices at 1790 levels plus 5 per cent for the producer, 10 per cent for the retailer and the cost of transport. A new law of 12 Germinal (1 April) effectively abolished constraints on the retail trade in order to encourage better provisioning of markets. The aim of the law, in Robespierre's words, 'is to prevent fraud but not discourage trade'.[20]

But the fate of the 'Indulgents' was still to be resolved. In late March there were desperate meetings between Robespierre and Danton as pressure mounted for arrests. Robespierre remained hesitant—what exactly was Desmoulins' offence?—but Billaud and Collot, worried by what the proscription of Hébert and his allies might mean for them, were unrelenting. According to Billaud, Robespierre had to be cajoled into adding his signature to those of the Committee members who had decided to act. But sign he did. During the night of 9–10 Germinal (29–30 March), Danton, Desmoulins and Philippeaux were arrested. The next day, Legendre moved that those arrested be brought before the bar of the Convention 'where you will hear them and where they will be accused or absolved by you. I think Danton is as pure as I am.' Robespierre retorted, 'in what way is Danton superior to Brissot, to Hébert, to his close friend Fabre d'Églantine?' Legendre's motion was not passed.[21]

Now that the die was cast, the political risk was that men of the fame of Danton and Desmoulins might use the Revolutionary Tribunal as a platform to overthrow the government. Convinced, Robespierre made lengthy notes that he passed on to St-Just for his speech denouncing Danton. Of the long list of charges, many were spurious (such as political connections Danton had early in the Revolution) or aimed at Danton's allegedly dissolute private life. Robespierre accused Danton of proposing that an alliance be forged with the United States by transferring to it the Caribbean colonies. He was even accused of sparing the guilty from 'the vengeance of the people' in September 1792. Only the charge that, while a minister, he had enriched Fabre from public funds had genuine substance. In fact, what Robespierre did not know about Danton's venality and corruption was even more serious than he suspected.[22]

They were charged with 'a conspiracy aiming at the re-establishment of the monarchy and the destruction of the national representation and the republican government'. When Danton spotted another Montagnard, Cambon, among the witnesses for the prosecution, he mocked: 'Do you believe that we're conspirators? Look, he's laughing! He doesn't believe it. Write down that he laughed.' But there was just enough evidence to make Robespierre's suspicions self-evidently true. His doctor, Souberbielle, was a member of the Revolutionary Tribunal and later recalled that, although he regretted sending Marie-Antoinette to her death, 'during the trial of Danton, who was a friend of mine, I dared not meet his eyes, for I was determined to condemn him, because I possessed absolute proof that he was planning the overthrow of the Republic'.[23]

When Danton's first wife had died in February 1793, Maximilien had written a beautiful letter to his friend: 'if in the only misfortunes that can crush such a soul as yours the certainty of having a loving and devoted friend may offer you some consolation, I offer it to you. I love you more than ever and until death. At this moment, I am yourself. Do not close your heart against the words of a friendship which feels all your pain.' In April 1794, by contrast, Robespierre's allegations against his former friend and ally went beyond charges of financial corruption to moral impropriety, accusing him of sneering over dinner that virtue was what 'he practised every night with his wife'.[24] Similarly, in December 1790, Robespierre had been a witness to the marriage of Camille and Lucile Desmoulins. But in April 1794 not even Robespierre's memory of holding their son Horace on his knee could save Camille, or Lucile herself. (Nor would Fouquier-Tinville, prosecutor at the trial, show any leniency to his cousin Camille.)[25]

The executions of 5 April created the political context in which the Committee could make the control of dissent more tightly centralized. By then there were as many as six thousand suspects incarcerated in Paris and as many as eighty thousand across the nation, one person in every 350. On 23 Ventôse (13 March) a People's Commission had been established to clarify why so many suspects were being held under vague charges. St-Just was proposing to establish two categories of 'suspects'—one of the unjustly detained, another of 'enemies of the Revolution', to be imprisoned until the peace, then banished.[26] The Commission had never been put in place; now a new policy to resolve the problem of the guilt or innocence of 'suspects' was implemented. New police laws in April expelled foreigners from Paris and frontier towns and centralized all political trials in Paris. St-Just established a new Bureau of Police on 4 Floréal (23 April) and, when he went to the Army of the North on a mission ten days later, Robespierre effectively took it over. Provincial tribunals were dissolved, except in Cambrai and Orange: henceforth detainees were to be brought to Paris for trial.[27] Discontent simmered on the streets of Paris in the spring of 1794 as patriots sought to make sense of the veracity of the charge that revolutionaries such as Hébert, Desmoulins and Danton had been in fact in league with the external enemies.

Robespierre had oversight of the police bureau in May and June, although he only authored about thirty of its decrees. The bureau received detailed reports amid hundreds of denunciations of both counter-revolutionaries and Hébertists. Robespierre made clipped marginal notes in his distinctive handwriting: 'when you denounce, you must provide names', 'why denounce suspects rather than arresting them?', 'forward to Carnot', 'forward to Herman' and, commonly, 'more information needed'. Rarely did he order an arrest personally, but it was a convenient commonplace to assume that he did.[28]

He started appointing people he knew and trusted to the Revolutionary Tribunal: Duplay, Lebas' cousin Laveyron of Créteil, Souberbielle, several neigh-bours. Robespierre was close to Martial Herman, the son of the former registrar of the Estates of Artois and himself a lawyer within the Council of Artois, and whom Robespierre had met at dinners at his old school in Arras. He described him as 'a man of enlightenment and integrity, capable of the most senior posts'. Entering the Revolutionary Court in August 1793, Herman had presided at the trial of Marie-Antoinette and the Girondins. He was promoted after the Danton trial from president of the Revolutionary Tribunal to the Commission for Civil Administration and Police (equivalent to Minister of the Interior), which oversaw it. He was replaced at the Tribunal on 8 April 1794 by René-François Dumas ('a man of integrity and energy, capable of the most important tasks') from Jura.[29]

Robespierre was also close to and trusting of the twenty-eight-year-old Claude Payan, from a Valence family of Jacobins credited with having prevented the Federalist revolts in Marseilles and Lyons from joining forces along the valley of the Rhône. In September 1793, Payan became a member of the Revolutionary Tribunal as well as editor of the Committee's mouthpiece, the *Antifédéraliste*. Payan had fewer scruples than Robespierre, admitting to his brother Joseph that the duke of Orléans was innocent but that it was 'expedient' for him to die.[30] On 10 Germinal (30 March) the Committee appointed him to succeed Pierre Gaspard Chaumette as its 'national agent'—effectively as chairman—on the Paris Commune, and he quickly set about ensuring that its members were 'patriotic' in his own style.

With the elimination of both the Hébertists and Dantonists in the spring of 1794, Robespierre and his followers were at the summit of their power; Robespierre's own status was dominant within the Committee of Public Safety. Even then, however, this power was dependent on continuing support within the National Convention. There was a growing gulf between Robespierre's view of the purpose of the emergency measures—of the Revolution itself—and that of the majority in the Convention, not to mention 'the people' at large. During Robespierre's illness, in late February 1794, St-Just had introduced the 'Ventôse decrees', which were aimed at broadening landownership and tackling poverty by distributing the property of suspects. The proposals, never implemented, were as vague as they were unsettling for the men of the Convention, wedded as the latter were to the rights of private property as well as to legal propriety.[31]

Opposition to Robespierre and the dominant Jacobins continued to be expressed despite more stringent threats to dissenters. Robespierre had become hostile to journalists in general, but newspapers that had been openly, even personally, critical of him, such as the *Feuille villageoise*, survived into 1794. There were still more than fifty newspapers available in June 1794.[32] More widely, the unremitting sacrifices for war, coupled with confusion at the widespread purge of erstwhile patriots, generated bewilderment and lassitude. A worker in an armaments factory was heard to announce 'We've had it! (*C'est foutu!*).... We're going to die of hunger. We're being fooled by fine words.' One Marie Dumesnil shouted on the Place de Grève: 'Vive le Roi! The Republic can get fucked! I shit on the Nation!' An informant reported on 7 Germinal (27 March) that a 'true *sans-culotte*', while listening to a child recite a few articles of the Constitution, 'said that he preferred a bottle of wine to all that. What support can the Republic expect from such men?', he lamented.[33]

Of the 542 decrees of the Committee of Public Safety signed by Robespierre, 124 were written in his own hand, and these along with the 47 others that he signed first were largely to do with policing and arrests. At the same time, it is true that he was personally repelled by violence and horrified by the behaviour of Carrier, Fouché and others. Charlotte Robespierre recollected forty years later how outraged her brother was by reports of the 'torrents of blood' that Fouché had made run through Lyons.[34] She recalled her brother's horror at having to sentence a man to death in Arras before the Revolution. He never seems to have lost a squeamishness about physical violence; indeed, he avoided it repeatedly. It is unlikely that he witnessed the handful of public killings immediately after the Bastille fell in July 1789 or the far greater retribution meted out to many hundreds of Swiss Guards after 10 August 1792, or to priests, nobles and common criminals early the following month, even though he was close by. He never left Paris to visit the killing fields on the frontiers or in the Vendée. There is no evidence that he attended guillotinings.

But the war had fundamentally changed Robespierre's attitude to bloodshed—whether or not after judicial process—in the name of the Revolution. Horrific though he would have found the slaughter of August–September 1792 in Paris, he accepted it as 'the people's justice' and refused, at least in public, to accept that many innocent lives had been lost. Within a year, however, with 'la patrie en danger', he moved with others on the Committee and in the Convention to close down the capacity of 'the people' to impose its will on the government. Henceforth, political killings were to be part of the machinery of government.

The confrontation with two men whom he regarded with affection as well as respect had consumed his emotional and physical resources over the winter of 1793–94. He never fully recovered. These were also months when the daily pressures on the Committee of Public Safety were relentless. By the time he had resolved the issue—that Danton and Desmoulins were as much a threat to the victory of the Revolution as were the Hébertists—he was again in a state of mental and physical collapse. On 30 Germinal (19 April) he could no longer appear in public, and did not do so again until 18 Floréal (7 May). From 9 February he was exhausted and often ill, and was absent more often than not. More than 630 times across five years he had lectured the Assembly or Jacobin Club about the virtues, but in the first seven months of 1794 he made only sixteen speeches in the National Convention, compared with 101 in 1793.

Robespierre had turned just thirty-six the day before he returned to work on 18 Floréal, but contemporaries would have thought him older: he was physically, emotionally and intellectually worn out. Years later Paul Barras described a visit he made with Stanislas Fréron to see Robespierre at the Duplays' house around this time. Barras had reasons for exaggeration, even distortion, but his recollection of Robespierre's appearance may be accurate enough to indicate the physical toll taken by his mental exhaustion: 'his eyes, dim and myopic, fastened on us in a fixed state. His face was mean-featured and ghostly pale with veins of a greenish hue; it worked constantly. His hands too, clenched and unclenched as if from a nervous tic; his neck and shoulders twitched spasmodically.'[35]

From Artois, as elsewhere, came reports of excesses for which Joseph Lebon was responsible. In the northeast there had been emigration by thousands of nobles and priests in particular, and foreign armies were only a few miles from towns like Arras and Cambrai. The recapture of Tourcoing on 29 Floréal (18 May) was rare good news. Lebon had the daunting task of controlling requisitioning and counter-revolution; in the process, some of the worst excesses were committed. In Arras itself, Lebon oversaw a merciless repression. Some 298 men and 93 women from Pas-de-Calais were guillotined on the small square in front of the fine new theatre 'à l'italienne' near the judicial quarter.[36] This was only a few steps from where Maximilien and Charlotte had lived in 1787–89; indeed, Maximilien must have known that Lebon's executions could have been seen from his front windows.

Robespierre and his colleagues were caught between reliance on the zeal of militant Jacobin deputies and continuing evidence that in particular cases zeal had slipped into arbitrary persecution of innocent citizens. At one point Antoine Buissart wrote from Arras that he and his wife Charlotte were 'outraged by your silence': 'we've been warning you for more than four months. Do I have to repeat what I've told you a hundred times?' Finally Charlotte herself wrote on 26 Floréal (15 May) complaining that the town had been subjected for months to the viciousness of Lebon and that 'virtuous beings' were calling for Robespierre to intervene. Presumably only her husband's standing had deterred Lebon from arresting Antoine as well. 'Permit an old friend to address to you a faint and brief picture of the evils with which the fatherland is burdened. You advocate virtue. For six months we have been persecuted and governed by every vice. . . . Our ills are very great, and our fate is in your hands. All virtuous minds implore you.' Robespierre had already personally drafted a frosty letter to Lebon, recognizing 'the energy with which you have suppressed the enemies of the Revolution', but recalling him to Paris: 'come back as soon as possible'. But Lebon was not relieved of his position for almost two months. Surely a personal friend and representative of the nation could not be guilty of atrocity?[37]

Robespierre had used the time spent recuperating to draft a major speech. He was more aware than ever before of the gulf between his certainty of the essential goodness of the people, which had been the motor of his actions, and the actuality of the values and behaviour of the French people. On 18 Floréal (7 May) he made perhaps the greatest speech of his career, on the relationship between republican principles, religion and morality, addressing the nature of popular festivals and establishing a Cult of the Supreme Being.[38] Like his other major speeches, this too was to be translated 'into all languages'.

There is no doubt that Robespierre believed in God and the afterlife, and was personally affronted by de-Christianization. At the same time, he had pragmatic political reasons for seeking to establish a republican spirituality that might unite a wide spectrum of society divided not only by religiosity but also by social and economic views. His religious beliefs were an amalgam of the Catholicism into which he had been inculcated in the first twenty-three years of his life and of the cult of nature he had encountered as a student in Paris and among his literary friends in Arras. He was by no means alone in seeing in the Supreme Being the source of the highest values and aspirations of humanity; indeed, the 1789 Declaration of the Rights of Man had been 'under the auspices of the Supreme Being'.[39]

Robespierre's speech on the Cult of the Supreme Being insisted that 'this delightful [délicieuse] land that we inhabit ... is made to be the land of liberty and happiness':

Nature tells us that Man is born for freedom, and the experience of the centuries shows us Man enslaved. His rights are inscribed in his heart, and his humiliation in history.... Sparta shines like a flash of lightning amid vast shadows ...

Everything in the physical order has changed; everything must change in the moral and political order. Half of the revolution has already occurred; the other half must also be accomplished. ...

How different is the God of Nature from the God of priests! ... The priests have created God in their image: they have made Him jealous, capricious, greedy, cruel, implacable.... They have relegated Him to Heaven as if to a palace, and have called Him to Earth only to ask for tithes, riches, honours and the pleasures of power for themselves.

The decree both established the revolutionary cult—'the French People acknowledge the existence of the Supreme Being and the immortality of the soul'—and guaranteed freedom of worship to all. The cult was both a political strategy and an expression of Robespierre's sincere belief that the inculcation of the highest values of morality and civic spirit would be accelerated through worship and festivals. To festivals celebrating the great revolutionary days–14 July 1789, 10 August 1792, 21 January 1793, 31 May 1793—would be added thirty-six others on each *décadi*, at the end of the ten-day weeks of the revolutionary calendar. These would honour the Revolution's goals (Liberty, Equality, the Republic, World Freedom, Happiness), the revolutionary virtues (Truth, Justice, Modesty, Friendship, Frugality, Courage) and Robespierre's idealized family characteristics: Love, Conjugal Fidelity, Paternal Love, Maternal Tenderness and Filial Piety.

With his educational programme, the Cult of the Supreme Being represented Robespierre's attempt to resolve the central conundrum in his understanding of the Revolution. On the one hand, his conviction was unshakeable that the people's impulses were good, and the Republic would be based on civic virtue; on the other hand, the masses were vulnerable to seduction by the malevolent, and evidence of corruption and self-seeking was everywhere. So, across the eight months after November 1793, Robespierre's ten major speeches were primarily about 'virtue' (with 119 references) rather than 'terror' (28 references), the latter mostly in the speech of 17 Pluviôse (5 February).[40] The cult was to be Robespierre's way of finally achieving the regeneration he had craved since 1789 and which the corrupters of the public spirit—whether royalists, spies or the factions—had contrived to thwart. Instead of the cruel God of the Catholic religion, this would be a people's cult with its own martyrs and values reflecting the birth of a new era, the era of equality. He even suggested that he might be one of those martyrs: 'Oh! Sublime people! Receive the sacrifice of all my being. Happy is he who was born in your midst! Even happier is he who can die for your happiness'.[41]

On 16 Prairial (4 June), Robespierre was unanimously elected president of the Convention (with 485 votes) for a fortnight and in that capacity delivered two speeches at the Festival in Honour of the Supreme Being on the 20th (8 June). It was no coincidence that the day chosen was Pentecost, commemorating the descent of the Holy Spirit upon the Apostles and other followers of

Jesus—sometimes described as the 'Birthday of the Church'. He then headed a procession to the Champ de la Réunion (the former Champ de Mars).[42] For the first time, he was to make a speech in public rather than in the Convention or Jacobin Club, and people struggled to hear him as disgruntled deputies chattered. He first addressed the people gathered in the 'National Garden' and defined the essence of the Supreme Being: 'it is He who instills remorse and terror in the bosom of the triumphant oppressor and tranquillity and pride in the heart of the innocent . . . it is He who makes the maternal heart beat with tenderness and joy; it is He who bathes with delightful tears the eyes of a son pressed to his mother's breast . . .'. Then, on a constructed 'Mountain', he spoke as 'Atheism', 'this monster whom the spirit of kings had vomited over France', was consumed by flames to be replaced by 'Wisdom': 'let us be . . . terrifying when under military attack, modest and vigilant in our triumphs; let us be generous towards good people, compassionate towards the unfortunate, inexorable towards the wicked, just to everyone'.

The reactions to the festival highlight two of the myths about these months: first, that this was a dictatorship devoid of popular support; and second, that the deputies had been intimidated into silence by a tyrant. The Cult of the Supreme Being had the uncanny property of appealing both to popular elements of Catholicism (especially at a time when most of the clergy had deserted the people) and to those who wanted a cult of Reason or Nature. The crowds were vast: the promise of renewed harmony seemed to have struck a deep chord. An estimated half a million people—most of the population of Paris—turned out for the celebration, but the sneers and innuendos from some of them were audible. Certain deputies were irritated by Robespierre's pre-eminence and said so; others guffawed at the heavy-handed symbolism of the choreography. Bourdon de l'Oise menaced that 'there is but one step from the Capitol to the Tarpeian Rock' (referring to the rock from which traitors were thrown in ancient Rome), and Robespierre's former ally, Lecointre from Versailles, now a bitter enemy, snapped that 'I scorn you as much as I detest you.' Jacques Thuriot, a former ally of Danton who had resigned from the Committee of Public Safety in September 1793, was heard to mutter: 'Look at the bugger. It is not enough for him to be master. He has to be God.' In the 1840s Élisabeth Lebas reportedly told the republican writer and politician Alphonse Esquiros that on returning home after the festival Robespierre had said to her that 'You won't see me for much longer.'[43]

Certainly the pre-eminent role that Robespierre had played at the festival was a serious miscalculation. In matters of detail, too, his judgement had become impaired: for example, the honour of constructing the wooden amphitheatre had been allocated to his landlord Maurice Duplay.[44] Robespierre's self-identification with the Revolution and the way he used speeches to deliver panegyrics had made him increasingly vulnerable to rumour: he was accused both of being responsible for the death sentence passed on 10 May on Louis XVI's sister Élisabeth, even though he had opposed it in the Committee of Public Safety, and of wanting to marry Louis' daughter to start a new dynasty. But some 1,235 written addresses poured into the Convention from across the country congratulating it, and Robespierre in particular, on the Festival and Cult. The Jacobin Club of Nay, in the Pyrenees, decided that it would have a reading every evening from one of Robespierre's speeches. A young Jewish merchant in Bordeaux, Isaac Rodrigues, quoted the speech enthusiastically to his close friend and fellow Jacobin, Isaac Pereyre, serving in the Army of the Western Pyrenees in Bayonne, and it reminded him to be, 'in Robespierre's words, "terrifying when under military attack, modest in our triumphs"'. At Montignac (Dordogne), in contrast, the secretary was only halfway through reading the speech on the Supreme Being when, 'the room being quite deserted, the president adjourns the meeting'.[45]

A core element of Robespierre's vision for the Cult of the Supreme Being was the place of public festivals, and particularly the role of women:

> You will be there, young citizenesses, to whom victory must soon return brothers and lovers worthy of you. You will be here, mothers and wives, whose husbands and sons are making trophies to the Republic from the rubble of thrones. O, Frenchwomen . . . what need you envy the women of Sparta?[46]

Among the new festivals to be celebrated were those honouring Conjugal Fidelity, Paternal Love and Maternal Tenderness. From his youth Robespierre had articulated a vision of marriage and the family which was idealized and heartfelt, perhaps in reaction to the family life that he had not known. Earlier in the Revolution, perhaps in 1791, Robespierre was reported to have shouted at his erstwhile friend Pétion, who had teased him that he needed a wife to make him more sociable at dinner parties, that 'I will never marry!'[47] Whatever the temptation Robespierre might have felt to experience intimacy through marriage to Éléonore Duplay, he resisted. His doctor, Souberbielle, was later recorded as insisting:

> All the historians assert that he carried on an intrigue with the daughter of Duplay, but as the family physician and constant guest of that house I am in a position to deny this on oath. They were devoted to each other, and their marriage was arranged; but nothing of the kind alleged ever sullied their love. Without being affected or prudish, Robespierre disliked loose conversation. His morals were pure.[48]

But, while the family life he knew at the Duplays provided a daily stability to his increasingly tortured existence, Robespierre was the focus of other female attentions ranging from adulation to rage. Some of the letters he received from women may have been self-seeking, such as one from a distant relative of Mirabeau, on 30 Germinal (19 April), offering to teach gratis, including the 'Catechism of Nature'. 'I shall be virtuous, and follow your advice and your example … firm and unchangeable, you are an eagle scouring the heavens.' Others were as obsessive as they were adulatory. One written on 13 Prairial (1 June) by a young woman of Nantes, Louise Jaquin, who claimed to have lost her husband fighting in the Vendée, offered marriage and a life of ease: 'You are my god, and I know no other on earth. I look upon you as my guardian angel, and I wish to live only under your laws; they are so gentle.'[49] This was a private letter; other female adulation of him was public. On 12 May the Committee of General Security ordered the arrest of Catherine Théot, a self-styled prophet who claimed that Robespierre had a divine mission as a mouthpiece of the Supreme Being.[50] The case did not become public until late June, but rumours were rife.

Other women were uncomplimentary about a man they had admired but from whom they now felt distanced, such as 'citizeness laundrywomen' who fulminated to the commander of the National Guard François Hanriot that he could deal with (*danser à vie*) 'all the Robespierres and the fucking idiots [*foutu jean foutre*] of the gang who are going to kill all our children and make us die of hunger'.[51] Still other women were among those who evidently wanted Robespierre dead. On 5 Prairial (24 May), a sixteen-year-old girl, Cécile Renault, armed with two small knives, was arrested as she tried to enter the Duplay house where Robespierre was living, 'to see what a tyrant looked like'. Prolonged applause greeted Robespierre when he arrived safely at the Jacobin Club on the morrow and delivered an 'energetic speech shining with true bravura, greatness of republican spirit, the most generous devotion to the cause of freedom and the most pronounced philosophy'.[52]

A more serious threat to Robespierre's life had been averted the day before Renault's attempt. On 4 Prairial, Henri Admirat, an employee at the National Lottery, having lain in wait all day for Robespierre, had fired two pistol shots at Collot instead. Popular outrage exploded when news of Admirat's attempted assassination, and the wounding of Geffroy, a locksmith who had gone to Collot's aid, became known. Across the next two months 218 deputations from sections and popular societies went to the Convention to express their anger and admiration for Geffroy; another 244 written addresses were received.[53]

Robespierre had long been aware of reports of people wishing him dead. Now he was unnerved. After Admirat's attempt, he made a fevered speech to the Convention in which he seemed certain of his impending death. He began with a litany of the weapons of the wicked: 'calumnies, treasons, fires, poisonings, atheism, corruption, famine, assassinations, have all lavished their crimes; there still remains assassination, and then assassination, and then again assassination. In saying these things, I sharpen daggers against me ...'. Joachim Vilate, a twenty-six-year-old militant from central France who had taken the classical Roman name Sempronius-Gracchus and won the trust of Robespierre and other key Jacobins, recalled that, after the Festival of the Supreme Being, he had bumped into Robespierre and found him ecstatic: 'for the first time, joy shone on his face. . . . He was drunk with enthusiasm.' Within weeks, however, the assassination attempts made him sombre and suspicious: 'he could talk only of assassination, once again of assassination, always of assassination. He was frightened his own shadow would assassinate him.' An innocent remark by a soldier that 'it won't be long until a woman assassinates Robespierre' resulted in him having his house sealed and searched.[54]

Robespierre was now being assailed constantly with claims and counter-claims about conspiracies and perfidy. Personal letters flooded in, seeking employment and favours, complaining of unfair treatment, or flattering 'the Incorruptible'. Some of the letters were anonymous and personally threatening. One claiming to be from a member of the Convention reproached him for Danton's death: 'but will you be able to avoid the blow from my hand or that of twenty-two others, like me as determined as Brutus and Scaevola?' An anonymous, detailed letter warned that 'I can never tell you often enough how numerous the conspirators are and the worst of all is that they have their people in both your Committee of Public Safety and Committee of General Security . . .'.[55] The evil was sapping his energy. He admitted to the Jacobin Club on 31 May that 'I no longer have the strength necessary to combat the intrigues of the aristocracy.'

The Admirat assassination attempt in particular seems to have thoroughly unsettled him. Two days after the Festival of the Supreme Being, Robespierre— still president of the Convention—pressured a reluctant Convention to pass the Law of 22 Prairial (10 June). It was drafted by Couthon and instituted a system whereby the sixty jurors of the Revolutionary Tribunal working in relays were to be the judges of whether evidence was admissible or even needed. The Law contained an article doing away 'with any provisions of previous laws inconsistent with the present decree'.[56] The law established open-ended categories of 'enemies of the people', from those who had taken up arms or conspired to overthrow the Republic to those who had simply criticized the government:

Those who have spread false news to divide or disturb the people;

Those who have sought to mislead opinion and to prevent the instruction of the people, to deprave morals and corrupt the public conscience, to impair the energy and purity of revolutionary and republican principles . . .

The work of the Revolutionary Tribunal was to be much more straightforward: 'the penalty for all offences within the cognizance of the Revolutionary Tribunal is death'.

Although the Law of 22 Prairial seems at first glance to be the antithesis of the Declaration of the Rights of Man and of the Citizen of 1789 and its guarantees of individual freedoms, in fact the Declaration had hedged the exercise of rights by reference to their limits being set by 'the law' as the expression of 'the general will' defining what was 'harmful to society'. In the electric atmosphere of June 1794 it seemed that Robespierre and Couthon had decided that they and the Revolutionary Tribunal could interpret that general will. However, the Committee of General Security and most of the Committee of Public Safety were not consulted about the law. Robespierre's reassurances in the Convention sounded flippant: 'A man is brought before the Revolutionary Tribunal. If there are material proofs against him, he is condemned; if there are no material proofs, in this case witnesses are called.' More than one quarter of the deputies were barristers by profession; few spoke out. A few brave deputies voiced outrage at the imprecise and ambiguous terms of the law. Pierre Ruamps, one of those who had challenged Robespierre two days earlier at the Festival of the Supreme Being, shouted: 'if this law passes, there's nothing for us to do but blow our brains out!'[57] Many deputies had never forgiven or forgotten the role of the Committee, and Robespierre in particular, in removing the parliamentary immunity of Danton and Desmoulins. The Law of 22 Prairial seemed a further menace to them all. Next day (11 June) the Convention passed a motion declaring 'the exclusive privilege of the national representation to impeach and try its own members', and that particular article was dropped.

Robespierre and the Committee may have felt impelled to push through such open-ended legislation because of the desirability of trying Carrier, Fouché and the others expeditiously.[58] Another reason for the Law was the overcrowding in Paris prisons, where there were now as many as 7,300 'suspects'. After the Law of 22 Prairial, the level of capital sentences was 79 per cent, although it had in any case been increasing since February and was already seven in ten. The Law was designed to centralize and expedite trials, while ending the chaotic disparities in the way provincial courts were operating.[59] It is highly likely that the personal intervention of the Buissarts back in Arras contributed in that regard.

In Robespierre's great speech of 18 Floréal (7 May) establishing the Cult of the Supreme Being, he had called on the National Convention to simultaneously revive public morality and to 'rain thunderbolts on the guilty': there was no inconsistency with proposing the Law of 22 Prairial two days after the Festival of the Supreme Being. The Festival, after all, was designed to inculcate moral regeneration; the Law of 22 Prairial aimed to intimidate or annihilate those who would sap that regeneration. As Robespierre had insisted in his great speech of 5 February, in revolution 'the mainspring of popular government . . . is at once *virtue* and *terror*. . . . Terror is nothing but prompt, severe, inflexible justice . . .'. By June 1794 the motors for generating virtue and terrifying its enemies had been centralized in the Committees and their bureaucracies; rumour and rancour were also in greater concentration there. And Maximilien Robespierre was now an object of fear, loathing and jealousy for increasing numbers of people at the same time as he admitted that he was at the end of his physical and mental capacities.

CHAPTER 12

'The unhappiest man alive'
PARIS, JULY 1794

The Festival of the Supreme Being and the Law of 22 Prairial were Robespierre's final, desperate attempts to link the inculcation of virtue with merciless intimidation and punishment of those who would undermine it. Two days after the passage of the law, on 12 June 1794, he made a speech referring to conspirators past and present, even among those sitting with the Mountain in the Convention. When Bourdon de l'Oise interjected, 'I challenge Robespierre to prove...', Robespierre was evasive but menacing:

> I will name them when I need to. At every moment of the day, at every moment even of the night, there are plotters working to insinuate in the minds of the men of good faith who sit on the Mountain, the falsest ideas, the most atrocious slanders. . . . If you knew everything, citizens, you would know that one might more justly have accused us of weakness . . . for not having shown enough severity towards the enemies of the homeland.[1]

Robespierre was claiming the right to be trusted as the embodiment of virtue who would name the guilty when the time was ripe. Deputies such as François Bourdon de l'Oise had good reason to be fearful, for he was one of five about whom Robespierre had written scathing personal notes: 'he covered himself in crime in the Vendée, where he allowed himself . . . the pleasure of killing volunteers with his own hand. He combines perfidy with fury.' At the Festival of the Supreme Being, Bourdon had been heard to utter 'the grossest sarcasm'. The other Bourdon, Léonard, was despised for his vulgarity, as well as his indecency in the Convention, 'speaking without taking off his hat, and wearing ridiculous clothes'.[2]

Members of the Committee of General Security had never forgiven Robespierre and St-Just for establishing a new police bureau that cut across their own powers. They made Robespierre pay. Their inquiry into the self-styled prophet and admirer of Robespierre, Catherine Théot, painted her as a pawn of the English enemy, and diminished Robespierre by association. Théot, known popularly as the 'Mother of God', had claimed that her reading of Ezekiel revealed that Robespierre was one of two new messiahs. On 27 Prairial (15 June), Marc Vadier, on behalf of the Committee, presented the Convention with his report, which mocked religious 'superstition' and pointedly identified only five people to be arrested. He also sneered at Robespierre's moral austerity by claiming that one of Théot's rules was that 'abstinence from earthly pleasures is required of the chosen of the Mother of God'.[3] The Théot affair seriously compromised Robespierre's objective in creating the Cult of the Supreme Being, and further convinced those who had alleged that he imagined himself the cult's 'pontiff'. Robespierre's subsequent request on 26 June to Fouquier-Tinville not to proceed with a trial confirmed many in their belief that his powers were boundless.

Robespierre had always been reluctant to accept that the desperate pleas of petitioners for clemency were anything other than the despair of relatives of the guilty, even when the numbers going to the guillotine appeared excessive. The procedures of the Revolutionary Tribunal seemed to him beyond reproach, especially when they included a number of people personally known to and appointed by him. A week after the passage of the Law of 22 Prairial about sixty people considered to be linked to Cécile Renault in the alleged assassination attempt of 24 May were executed as a group, all wearing the red shirt of parricide: had they tried to kill the 'father' of the Republic? Was this an attempt by his enemies to so nauseate public opinion by mass executions (*nausée de l'échafaud*) that it would turn against him? If so, it is odd that the guillotine would be moved from the Tuileries to less prominent locations, the Place Antoine on 9 June and the distant Barrière du Trône on the 14th. But by then Robespierre was nauseated too, from illness and despair.

Across the month of Prairial (20 May–18 June), the Committee of Public Safety continued its core work, battling its own exhaustion and divisions. Of the

608 orders (of a total of 762) in that month for which personal authorship may be ascribed, 207 were from Lindet (183 on military transport), 177 by Carnot (130 on the armed forces) and 157 from Prieur (de la Côte-d'Or; 114 on munitions). Robespierre authored just 14, on a variety of subjects.[4] The mass guillotining of the 'red shirts', 17 June, occurred on the same day that the Republic's armies took Ypres, and a series of military victories unfolded in the northeast: Charleroi on 25 June, Fleurus on the 26th, Ostende and Tournai on 4 July, then Brussels on the 8th. By then the Spanish armies had been pushed back to the border in the south. In particular, the victory at Fleurus, which ended the threat of Austrian troops on French soil, exposed the sharp contradictions between the objectives of those who had put in place or merely accepted the draconian controls of the Year II. Was the objective simply to do whatever was necessary to make the Republic safe from military threat, or was it to create the foundations of a regenerated society?

The workplaces, streets and meeting places of Paris were seething with a potent mixture of optimism for the future but dread of the present. Even with the reception of the news of Fleurus, Robespierre's allies in the Convention, its key Committees, the Paris Commune and the Jacobin Club were not convinced that the Republic was safe: there were still internal enemies to crush and, for some at least, the moral regeneration had only begun. Robespierre was still widely trusted as 'the Incorruptible'. On 4 Messidor (22 June), William Augustus Miles, an English liberal who had spent two years in Paris, wrote to an acquaintance in London advising him that this 'extraordinary man . . . is beyond the reach of gold'. 'Robespierre's countrymen are convinced of his incorruptibility': 'he may be assassinated or summarily condemned, but he will never be destroyed by a regular process . . .'.[5]

Robespierre's revolutionary career had been characterized by both a capacity to articulate the overarching goals of the Revolution and an adroit pragmatism: supporting the war only once it had been declared, supporting a Republic only once the monarchy had been overthrown, accepting street protest until he entered government. Now in the early summer of 1794 his tactical judgement deserted him. The coincidence of the assassination attempts and his exhaustion prevented him from being able to see the victory at Fleurus as the signal that explicit undertakings could be given that the crisis was almost over. The failure of Robespierre and those close to him in government to indicate when the vision that had been articulated on 5 February—a Republic safe for virtuous citizens—could be achieved by encouragement rather than intimidation was to prove fatal.

Instead, when Robespierre's fortnight as president of the Convention ended on 30 Prairial (18 June), before the news of Fleurus, he virtually disappeared from public life. He signed six of the Committee's decrees that day, twelve on 19 June and eleven on the 20th, but only another thirty over the next five weeks, presumably brought to his residence. He signed few decrees at the Committee of Public Safety after 25 June. He ran the police bureau until the 29th, when he effectively withdrew from the Committee of Public Safety, and St-Just took over. He attended the Committee on only two or three further occasions. He made no further speech at the Convention until 26 July, almost a month later, and few of any substance at the Jacobin Club.[6]

We know little of how Robespierre spent his time after 18 June. It is probable that his health had again failed, exacerbated as it was by fears of assassination, and bitterness at the rumours and slanders engulfing him. He would not, of course, be the last wartime leader to succumb to overwhelming pressure.[7] Once again, it was the stress of deep conflict that caused physical collapse, just as it had after the confrontation with Beaumez in mid-1790, with Louvet and the Girondins in November 1792, with the Paris militants in September 1793, and with Danton and Desmoulins in February and April 1794.

His family life had also fallen apart. The deadly atmosphere of escalating executions, conspiracy and threats further poisoned the relationship between Charlotte and her two brothers, or with Augustin at least. She and Augustin had fallen out badly during their official travels in Provence in the autumn of 1793, and in May 1794 Lebon had been recalled to Paris to escort her to Arras. Augustin unleashed a tirade against his sister: she 'does not have a drop of blood which resembles ours. . . . We must make her go to Arras and thus distance ourselves from a woman who is the despair of us both. She would like to give us the reputation of being bad brothers, that is the aim of the slanders she spreads about us.'[8] Charlotte wrote a grief-stricken letter to Augustin on 18 Messidor (6 July), a copy of which she kept until her death: 'to be hated by my brothers, whom I desire to cherish, that is the only thing able to make me as wretched as I am. . . . I do not know yet what I am going to do; but that which seems very urgent is that you should get rid of an odious sight.' She could only hope that the hatred in Augustin's eyes would fade: 'wherever I may be, even beyond the seas, if I can be useful to you in any way, let me know, and I will come to you at once'.[9]

Charlotte may have departed from the immediacy of Maximilien's life, but Arras came back to haunt him. Just as his sister agreed to return home, another Charlotte arrived in Paris from Arras to complain of the horrors Lebon was inflicting on the town. Maximilien's oldest friends, Antoine and Charlotte Buissart, had been made alternately fearful and frustrated by his silence. Antoine complained on 10 Messidor (28 June) that 'over the month since I last wrote to you, it seems to me, Maximilien, that you are asleep and are allowing patriots to be slaughtered'. Such was the Buissarts' concern that Charlotte and her son now came in person to see Robespierre, and stayed with the Duplays.[10]

Maximilien's withdrawal from public life was well known, a former classmate from Louis-le-Grand warning him from Amiens early in July that 'your efforts for the public good, of which you are the best friend . . . make us fear for your life and you have become, so it's said, inaccessible at this time of personal danger'. Another who felt that 'Robespierre no longer exists for his friends' was Régis Deshorties—whose sister Anaïs had been courted by Maximilien in the late 1780s—who wrote to Augustin at the same time. 'The human race . . . owes endless obligations' to men like Maximilien, he stressed, but confessed that 'earth would be a desert for him if it had none but men of this character for inhabitants'. Other letters were anonymous and threatening. One claimed that 'you are becoming a dictator. . . . Is there anyone in history more tyrannical than you? . . . Won't we deliver our homeland from such a monster?'; another described him as a 'tiger soaked in the purest blood of France . . . your country's executioner'. He is said to have commented to his tobacco-seller, Mme Carvin, early in Thermidor that 'we'll never get out of this mess; I'm worried sick [*bourrelé*]; I'm going crazy [*j'en ai la tête perdue*].'[11]

By late June there was loud grumbling in the Paris neighbourhoods about the meaning of increased executions, including of prominent *sans-culottes* activists, despite military successes. There were still copies of Louvet's October 1792 'Accusation' against Robespierre being sold; and police reported a brochure entitled 'True and salutary political principles opposed to the false and fanatic system' of the Convention and Robespierre.[12] More seriously, timber-workers in state workshops went on strike in late June in the face of rising food prices and shortages. As crops ripened it was reported that six thousand harvesters had gathered near Meaux to insist on higher wages.[13] Was it virtuous to take advantage of the absence of able-bodied men serving in the armies to go on strike?

Divisions were apparent between the two Committees, even within the Committee of Public Safety itself. Billaud and Collot felt themselves particularly vulnerable because of their links with the Hébertists and Fouché. Those preoccupied with the war effort found the talk of regeneration and virtue tiresome: at a stormy joint meeting of the two Committees on 11 Messidor (29 June), Carnot was alleged to have shouted at St-Just that he and Robespierre were 'ridiculous dictators'.[14] After this altercation Robespierre stopped participating directly in the deliberations of the Committee of Public Safety. Lack of attendance at the Convention, Committee and even the Jacobin Club now distanced him from those who might have been able to penetrate his despair.

Despite Robespierre's repeated insistence that priests, the well-to-do and even former nobles could be good republicans, he had always been prone to understanding the revolutionary world in terms of a binary opposition: the good and the evil, 'patriots' and 'counter-revolutionaries'. Robespierre was as vulnerable as anyone to explanations that imputed misfortune to conspiracy. Such was the extent of perceived malevolence by the summer of 1794 that he insisted on 13 Messidor (1 July) the conspiracy was so vast that he could only begin to outline it. In an emotional address to the Jacobin Club on the political tensions and his own position, he complained that there were people trying to revive the Indulgents' faction 'to exempt the aristocracy from the justice of the nation'. 'If Providence has seen fit to snatch me from the hands of murderers, it is to commit me to employing the moments that remain to me usefully.' Slanders were constantly assaulting him: 'you would shudder if I told you where', no doubt referring to Carnot's jibe. He had been accused of setting up the Revolutionary Tribunal 'to slaughter patriots and members of the Convention', that he had had Cécile Renault's entourage guillotined to hide a love affair. But when a Club member shouted in support, 'Robespierre, you have all Frenchmen on your side', he responded simply, 'I want neither partisans nor praise: my defence is in my conscience.'[15]

Only through sporadic attendance at the Jacobin Club did Robespierre continue to intervene in an increasingly noisy cascade of charge and countercharge. On 21 Messidor (9 July) he returned to the Club to outline what he saw as the threats to revolutionary government stemming from calls to relax its vigilance. That could only occur when it had achieved the 'execution of the laws of nature, which require that every man be just, and in virtue, the fundamental basis of society'.[16] Only then could 'the fruit of our victories be liberty, peace, happiness and virtue'. His listeners were perplexed that he still did not specify the source of 'the perfidious insinuations of certain people'.

A week later, on 28 Messidor (16 July), he returned to the Jacobin Club: this time he had in his sights the shortcomings of the popular societies. He began with despair over a decision of the Bayonne affiliate to expel a member for failure to pay debts, and warned about unnecessary purges lest 'the true patriot, if he be guilty of some slight error or minor fault, is stripped of the title of good citizen'. But he also had in mind the widespread incidence of 'fraternal banquets' in the Paris sections, popular gatherings organized to celebrate the victory at Fleurus and the fifth anniversary of the taking of the Bastille on 26 Messidor (14 July). They were also an opportunity for new 'Indulgents' to call for an end to revolutionary government and its controls. He warned that 'the momentary success of the so-called patriotic banquets springs from the general feeling of civic virtue enlivening the entire People. . . . [but] their enemies are not yet defeated, and virtue, vigilance and courage alone can strengthen the Republic'.[17] For their part, the banqueters simply wanted to celebrate military triumph.

There were 796 death sentences in Messidor (19 June–18 July). Whereas about half those brought before the Revolutionary Tribunal in 1793 had been acquitted, under the Law of 22 Prairial only one person in five was freed. The numbers of executions escalated relentlessly: in Floréal (20 April–19 May) there had been an average of eleven each day, sixteen a day in Prairial (20 May–18 June), but now twenty-six a day in Messidor. Many people—and increasing numbers of them—went to the guillotine for offences which, in ordinary times, would have led to trials for criminal conspiracy (fraud, peculation, profiteering), prison terms for petty theft or assault on public officials, or even just to angry political exchange. Fourteen nuns and lay sisters, and two servants, from a former Carmelite convent in Compiègne, northern France, were accused of living in a religious community in 1794. They were arrested by the local surveillance committee on 22 June and imprisoned in a former Visitation convent in Compiègne. There they openly resumed their religious life. The Committee of General Security charged them with having royalist correspondence, and sent them before the Revolutionary Tribunal. On 29 Messidor (17 July) they were guillotined at the Barrière de Vincennes (nowadays Place de la Nation) in Paris.[18]

As the prisons were emptied through the jaws of the Revolutionary Tribunal, they not surprisingly became cauldrons of 'suspects' attempting to escape by whatever means. In turn, the authorities became obsessed with 'prison plots': seventy-three prisoners from Bicêtre were executed on 28 Prairial and 8 Messidor; and 146 from the Luxembourg on 19–22 Messidor. Among those most terrified were seventy-three Girondin deputies who had protested against the expulsion of their associates in June 1793, and whom Robespierre had saved from death; they now repeatedly expressed their gratitude by extolling 'his loyalty, his love of justice and humankind' and asked him to defend them again as they observed the accelerated executions around them. He did.[19]

A further joint sitting of the two Committees on 3 Thermidor—from which Robespierre was absent—sent the Revolutionary Tribunal a list of 318 people to be judged immediately. He was also absent from the Committee of Public Safety on 4 Thermidor when it further centralized the work of the Tribunal through four 'people's commissions'. He was being inundated with letters of denunciation of individuals, of prison plots, and of personal threats: he was described in public as a 'fucking rogue and scoundrel [*foutu gueux et sçelérat*]'. An anonymous letter writer claimed that 'you are tending towards dictatorship, and you want to kill the liberty you created'. Most were neither menacing nor anonymous. One letter vaunted him as the 'flame, column, and corner-stone of the edifice of the Republic', another from the town of L'Égalité (formerly Château-Thierry) as 'the messiah whom the eternal being promised us to reform everything'. 'Your principles are those of nature, your language that of humanity ... you are regenerating humankind, your genius and political wisdom are saving liberty', but 'do look after your health'.[20]

On 7 Messidor (25 June) Robespierre ordered the arrest of the Dantonist and former noble Alexandre Rousselin and others who had led a thoroughgoing purge in the department of Aube; then, on the recommendation of one of Aube's deputies, Antoine Garnier, on 30 Messidor (18 July) he ordered the release of 320 'suspects' who Rousselin had imprisoned. Whatever Robespierre's precise motives, this, and the earlier recall of nine other deputies-on-mission and the expulsion of Fouché from the Jacobin Club, convinced many that a new purge was impending of those seen to have been excessive in their repression. Garnier

later reported a conversation with Robespierre, who had not denied the rumour
that a list of thirty names was being prepared of deputies who had 'betrayed' the
Convention.[21]

Despite the best endeavours of Robespierre and his allies, the victory at
Fleurus had cut the knot tying together the strands of revolutionary government. In the Convention powerful deputies such as Carrier, Fouché, Barras,
Fréron and Tallien felt vulnerable to insinuations that they would be called to
account for their merciless repression of counter-revolution in the provinces. All
wondered why the great victory at Fleurus had not resulted in clarity about the
end of revolutionary government. Most of the deputies, after all, had supported
authoritarian measures as a pragmatic response to military crisis and social
upheaval. One of the Paris sections opened a register on 1 Messidor (19 June)
calling for support for the implementation of the Constitution of 1793: in ten
days it had two thousand signatures but the Committee of General Security
closed it down.[22] But why could not the Constitution of 1793 now be put into
effect? With the military situation eased and the sections tamed, why were
executions escalating in a context of vague threats to unnamed deputies?

Still the guillotinings increased. There were 342 in the first nine days of
Thermidor: a daily average of thirty-eight compared with eleven in Floréal, three
months earlier, before the military crisis had begun to ease. The Revolutionary
Tribunal was meeting its brief of determining the guilt of 'suspects' with ghastly
efficiency. 'Prison plots' continued to be uncovered: forty-six people from the
Carmes prison were executed on 5 Thermidor (23 July), and seventy-six from
St-Lazare over the following three days. Robespierre was effectively absent
from public life after 11 Messidor (29 June): the dramatic acceleration in July of
guilty verdicts and executions under the Law of 22 Prairial therefore cannot be
imputed directly to him.[23] There is no doubt, however, that, though rarely
present at meetings of the Committee, he ordered arrests: he often met with
Herman and Dumas, president of the Revolutionary Tribunal, and St-Just and
Simon Duplay took files to him at the Duplays. Robespierre's dilemma was
always his trust in the competence and judgement of the fellow Jacobins who sat
on the Revolutionary Tribunal. But we cannot know with certainty the answer
to the most troubling question: was he directly implicated in the bloodbath that
Paris suffered, or was it unleashed to discredit him? The most likely answer is

that, in his absence, his enemies were jumping at shadows, and he was the perfect scapegoat for their panic to kill as many suspects as possible.

There were occasions when Robespierre intervened personally to protect individuals. At mid-year he removed the most draconian elements of a police regulation requiring even pre-revolutionary and classical plays to substitute 'citizen' and 'citizeness' for titles such as monsieur, madame, baron and count. Similarly, he moved to protect refugees from the failed revolution in Liège, accused of having had dealings with General Dumouriez in 1792–93. One of them, Fyon, was arrested on 18 July, and others were already in prison. It was Robespierre who intervened to have them released. Jean-Nicolas Bassenge was due to have a meeting with Robespierre to discuss the possibility of a French war of liberation for Liège and Belgium on 8 Thermidor (26 July).[24]

Dissension became louder and more diverse. On 1 Thermidor (19 July) the Jacobin Club was consumed by an angry debate about the veracity of claims of persecution, with Robespierre making ambiguous noises about 'oppressed inno-cence'. On 5 and 6 Thermidor (23 and 24 July) noisy demonstrations by women had disrupted the sitting of the Convention.[25] But there was division on the Committee of Public Safety, too, with the 'professionals' (Carnot, Lindet, St-André, the Prieurs) dismissive of the utopianism of Robespierre and St-Just, and Collot and Billaud expressing personal hostility towards him. St-Just and Barère tried to act as peacemakers between the two Committees, and Robespierre attended the second of two joint sittings on 5 Thermidor (23 July), but still he rejected attempts to smooth over his differences with individuals on both Committees.[26]

He spent these days in stressed exhaustion and fear of assassination, receiving second-hand reports from his close allies about doings in the Convention, the Committees and on the Revolutionary Tribunal. As Robespierre slowly recov-ered his strength during July, however, he began to prepare a breakthrough speech to be delivered to the Convention on 26 July (8 Thermidor).[27] At last it seemed that the terrifying uncertainty about the winding down of emergency controls would be resolved. He began by referring to his exhaustion and absence: 'for the last six weeks, at least, my so-called dictatorship has ceased to exist, and I have exercised no sort of influence on the government. ... Has the country been any happier?' He decided to erase a confession of despair from this speech: 'but for my conscience, I should be the unhappiest man alive'.

He affirmed his belief in virtue and defined it, insisting that he felt it in his soul:

> Virtue is a natural passion, no doubt; ... this profound horror of tyranny, this sympathetic zeal for the oppressed, this sacred love of the *patrie*, this most sublime and most holy love of humanity ... you can feel it at this very moment burning in your souls; I feel it in mine. ...

But the crisis was not over: 'our enemies retreat, but only to leave us to our internal divisions'. He insisted repeatedly that 'there is a criminal conspiracy', yet named only three deputies (Cambon, Mallarmé and Ramel, key members of the Finance Committee) apart from vague assertions that conspiracy reached into the Convention and even the governing Committees. Again and again he denied that he was responsible for throwing innocents into prison or sending them to the guillotine, while noting that his enemies' rallying cry was 'it's all Robespierre's doing!' The rambling, emotional speech of almost two hours was vague to the point of incoherence because by then almost everyone was suspected of conspiring: Robespierre even confessed to 'doubting this virtuous republic whose image I had traced for myself'; he seemed to be courting martyrdom.[28]

There was just enough precision in the speech to make those suspected of excesses fear that they had been identified as the ones spreading 'terror and calumny': 'impure agents have been excessive in making unjust arrests; destructive projects have threatened every modest fortune, and brought despair upon a countless number of families attached to the Revolution'. In the debate that followed, Étienne-Jean Panis, a Parisian Jacobin previously on the Committee of General Security, leapt to his feet 'to pour out my broken heart': 'I reproach Robespierre for having expelled whatever Jacobins he liked. I wish that he had no more influence than anyone else; I wish that he would say if he has proscribed our heads, whether mine is on the list which he has drawn up.' Robespierre's friend André Dumont had also had enough: 'no-one wants to slaughter you', he shouted, 'it's you who are slaughtering public opinion!' Cambon and Robespierre, already divided by animus stemming from the former's protection of competent *ancien régime* treasury officials, engaged in a protracted exchange. Cambon's alarm stemmed from fear, but he was as perplexed as alarmed, since he had overseen prodigious work in trying to restore order to the system of government bonds used by individuals as life annuities, but whose volume was potentially crippling for the Republic's finances.[29]

Since his physical collapse at the time of the trial of the Indulgents in early April, Robespierre had made a series of errors of judgement, beginning with his acquiescence in the decision to include Desmoulins on a list of those to be arrested along with men who were charged with serious financial malpractice at the expense of the Republic. His decision to hold the Festival of the Supreme Being during his term as president of the Convention exposed him to mutterings about his omnipotence. Pushing through the Law of 22 Prairial two days later (10 June) had turned those mutterings to fearful agitation. He had been unable to use the turnaround in the Republic's military fortunes over the next few weeks to map out a pathway to the return to constitutional rule. Now his failure to name those deputies to be brought to trial was a crucial mistake.[30] He may only have had five or six men in mind, but there were many more with reason to be terrified. At a time when heads were falling like slate tiles, the Convention had had enough. Jean-Henri Voulland, a member of the Committee of General Security, wrote home to the southern town of Uzès on 9 Thermidor (27 July) that

> Robespierre's speech, thrown into the midst of the Convention yesterday, made a most painful impression. . . . no-one on either of the two committees has ever conspired against the Republic, nor against any individual devoted to its interests. Robespierre was singularly deceived when he let himself be persuaded that a plan to ruin him or to accuse him had been conceived . . .[31]

Robespierre delivered the same speech that evening at the Jacobin Club, despite attempts by Collot and Billaud to prevent him, and a shouted warning— 'We want no dictators here!'—from Claude Javogues, another deputy with reason to be anxious about being called to account. Dumas, president of the Revolutionary Tribunal, strongly supported Robespierre, describing his opponents as the remnants of the Hébertists and Dantonists. At the end of his speech, Robespierre startled the Club by adding, as if in premonition, 'my friends, you have just heard my last will and testament'.[32] The Club's president ordered a message to be sent to provincial affiliates that a new 'foreign plot' had been revealed by Robespierre, 'who seeks only the prize of the unanimous esteem of his fellow citizens and their will to punish traitors'. Perhaps Robespierre had been lulled into a false sense of security by his extraordinary esteem within the Club. Perhaps he was in such a state of mental collapse that he no longer had the capacity to imagine how his language might be heard. Despite the rumblings in the Convention and even the Jacobin Club, he was evidently unable to comprehend the potential menace, and it seems that he had arranged to have dinner with his friends the Laveyrons in Créteil on 10 Thermidor (28 July).[33]

Ever since Louis XVI's bungled attempt to flee the country in June 1791, Robespierre and other Jacobins had been vulnerable to fears that the murderous opposition of counter-revolutionaries inside France was only part of a wider foreign conspiracy. There had always been enough evidence to reinforce these fears, even if the full extent of these conspiracies had rarely materialized. Now, on 8 Thermidor, Robespierre had insisted that there was another conspiracy, this time within the Convention. And this time at least, he was totally correct. Collot and Billaud had been expelled from the Jacobin Club, and met with Fouché and Tallien. Fouché and another key player, Carnot, had six years earlier enjoyed poetry and wine with their fellow 'Rosati' Maximilien in a field outside Arras, but now felt in mortal danger.

There were four key groups of deputies with good reason to kill or be killed. First among them were the recalled deputies-on-mission, such as Carrier, Fouché, Tallien, Fréron and Dubois-Crancé, all of whom would have shuddered when Robespierre referred to those guilty of excess.[34] A second group were those on the Committees who had been close to the Hébertists, including Collot, Billaud, Amar and Vadier. The latter two were also smarting because of the sidelining of the Committee of General Security, evident in Vadier's handling of the Théot affair. Similarly, a third group linked to Danton were inevitably unsettled by Robespierre's references to laxity, men such as Lecointre, Thuriot, Legendre and Bourdon de l'Oise. Finally, the 'technocrats' on the Committee of Public Safety, such as Lindet, Prieur de la Côte-d'Or and Carnot, heard implied menace in his speech, recalling the disastrous meeting a week earlier. To these four groups, Robespierre's speech had added the influential Cambon to the list of those impelled to act.

No one was safe when Robespierre was now plainly unable to distinguish between dissent and treason. His opposition was forced to act in concert. There were so many factions and fears that no one knew to end the fear except by using Robespierre as a scapegoat. As the Jacobin deputy Marc-Antoine Baudot later reflected, 'the struggle of 9 Thermidor wasn't a question of principles, but of killing . . . the death of Robespierre had become a necessity'.[35]

On 9 Thermidor (27 July) the meeting of the Convention began at 11.00 a.m. as usual, with the reading of correspondence and hearing of petitioners. About midday St-Just mounted the rostrum, intending to defend Robespierre: 'he does not, it is true, explain himself with sufficient clarity; but some allowance may be made for his withdrawal from the scene and the bitterness of his soul.' Why should he be accused of 'seeking to enslave men's minds'? 'Is sensibility a thing of evil?'[36] He was then prevented from speaking on a point of order from Tallien. The meeting continued in an uproar of shouted accusations and denials. With Thuriot occupying the president's chair, Billaud then began the indictment and proposed the arrest of Hanriot and Robespierrist officers in the National Guard: 'everything demonstrates at this instant that the National Convention is threatened with slaughter'.

At this point Lebas made a desperate and unsuccessful attempt to seize the rostrum. Billaud then turned on Robespierre 'for having distanced himself from the Committee of Public Safety only because he could not do as he pleased there'. He accused Robespierre of 'always talking about virtue, while defending crime. . . . there is no representative of the people who wants to live under a tyrant'. Members of the Convention shouted 'No, no!' in support of Billaud, ignoring his earlier criticism of Robespierre as too lenient; indeed, his signature had appeared on arrest warrants more frequently than Robespierre's. But Billaud had set the scene: this was to be a stampede by guilty men, with the objective being the killing of Robespierre and his allies.

Robespierre then came to the rostrum. According to a reporter, members shouted 'we do not listen to conspirators'. As he started to speak, 'I could recall it to . . .' further shouts were heard of 'down with the tyrant!' As Robespierre tried to continue—'I protest; my enemies are seeking to abuse the National Convention'—he was silenced with cries of 'Down with him! Down with him!' After Tallien had assured the Convention that 'he is armed with a dagger to strike the tyrant were the Convention not disposed to give him the justice due to scoundrels', Barère outlined 'how greatly the forms of the revolutionary government have been changed' and referred to Robespierre's vague accusations: 'false anxieties and real dangers cannot co-exist; enormous reputations and men who are equal cannot long exist together.' Vadier then claimed that there were six spies of Robespierre's who followed members of the Convention every day, and gave Robespierre reports that were used as the basis of denunciations. Bizarrely, Vadier also accused him of being too moderate in seeking to spare 'conspirators' from the guillotine.

As accusations mounted against Robespierre, Tallien alleged that he was a coward, that he 'always hides when the fatherland is in great peril; that at the time of 10 August [1792], he showed himself at the Commune only three days after the fall of the tyrant'. The reporter for the *Journal du soir* noted that 'Robespierre wanted to speak; he was at the rostrum. "Down with the Cromwell!" shouts Cambon. *Vadier*: "I am the first who asked for the decree of accusation against the crowned tyrant. It has cost me to believe Robespierre a tyrant, but I believe it. I call for a decree of accusation against him". ' Robespierre tried repeatedly to speak amidst the general cacophony. Finally he shouted: 'I ask for death.' Another reporter observed that, 'turning to the Mountain, he sends it a look of rage and despair. He lavishes on members who have spoken against him the epithets of bandits, cowards and hypocrites. The tumult grows; the president puts on his hat. Robespierre wants to take the floor; this is opposed. "By what right", he shouts angrily, "does the president protect murderers?"' As Robespierre struggled to speak, a deputy jeered, 'it's Danton's blood that is choking him'. Augustin shouted: 'I also ask for death, I want to die for freedom. I am as guilty as my brother; I wanted to do good for my country; I too want to die at the hand of criminals.'

None of Robespierre's allies was able to make the Convention listen, and it proceeded to order the arrest of Hanriot, Dumas and other Robespierrist officials, then five deputies: the two Robespierres, St-Just, Couthon and Lebas. The deputies were taken before the Committee of General Security, then sent to different prisons. Maximilien was taken to the Luxembourg Prison, where the startled officers refused to process him, then to the mayor's office where again he was greeted by senior police administrators. No one wanted to arrest the deputies or officials. Who would want to take responsibility for interning 'the Incorruptible'? Finally the deputies found their way to the Town Hall. Hanriot, the mayor Lescot-Fleuriot and Payan summoned a special meeting of the Commune, mobilized the National Guard and closed the city gates.

Lescot-Fleuriot called on the people of Paris to save those 'who have made the Republic's armies triumph' against the new conspirators in the National

Convention. But most of the forty-eight sections made no move: only thirteen finally sent battalions to defend the Town Hall against the Convention. Even so, they had considerable force at their disposal, but were immobilized by uncertainty as to whether to march on the Convention.[37] The Convention had declared itself in permanent session and, after a brief adjournment, resumed again at seven in the evening. News arrived that Robespierre and his allies had called on armed support from the sections. The Convention declared the five deputies outlaws. It gathered sufficient armed forces and, headed by Léonard Bourdon, they entered the Town Hall at about half past two in the morning. By then the sections had melted away from the Place de Grève, in front of the Town Hall, and the armed forces were able to make the arrests, including of Augustin, who broke both legs after leaping from a window in an attempt to escape.

When the Convention's forces entered, Robespierre was signing a desperate appeal to his own neighbourhood section:

Commune of Paris, Executive Committee.
9th Thermidor.

Courage, patriots of the Section des Piques! Liberty is triumphant! Already those whose firmness is feared by the traitors are at liberty. Everywhere the People is showing itself worthy of its character. The rendezvous is at the Town Hall, where the brave Hanriot will carry out the orders of the Executive Committee that has been formed to save the country.
Louvet, Payan, Lerebous, Legrand, Ro-

He would not know that his section, a model of careful deliberation and surveillance, had already rebuffed the Commune's request: 'as long as no order has been received from the National Convention, no order will be given to provide armed force'. By the next day it was describing him as a 'scoundrel'.[38]

Robespierre's unfinished signature may have been the result of uncertainty about declaring the Commune to be in a state of insurrection against the National Convention. For was not the Convention the French people itself? The incomplete signature is surrounded by spatters of blood. Lebas had two pistols: some have suggested that he blew his brains out with one and that Robespierre

tried to commit suicide with the other. Others prefer to believe that he was shot
by a gendarme as he was signing the document: he would never have despaired
enough to commit suicide when there was still so much to do.[39]

It was a drawn-out and excruciating agony. The bullet had smashed
Robespierre's jaw at 2.30 a.m. At 3.30 he was placed in the waiting room of the
Committee of Public Safety, where the curious were able to observe his pain.
Two health officers were sent by the Committee of General Security to the
Tuileries at 5 a.m., where they found him lying on a table, 'covered with blood'.
They inspected the wound to his left cheek, which had smashed his teeth and
jaw, and applied bandages to soak up the blood in his mouth, during which 'the
monster did not take his eyes off us, but without uttering a word'. Nicolas
Jomard, an architect attached to the Committee of Public Safety through the
cannon foundries, described the scene as he arrived at the Town Hall after
Robespierre's arrest. There he found him 'shoeless, his stockings had fallen down
to his calves, his breeches were unbuttoned and his whole shirt was covered in
blood'. The curious had already started congregating: 'several of them who were
closest lift his right arm to see his face; one says, "He's not dead, because he's still
warm", another says, "Isn't he a fine-looking king?" Another says, "Even if it were
Caesar's body, why wasn't it thrown on the garbage dump?" '[40]

Robespierre and the others were transferred to the Conciergerie at 11.00 a.m.
and condemned to death. He was unable to do anything other than moan, and
repeated gestures he made for pen and paper were refused. It was only at 6.00 p.m.
that three carts with their twenty-two prisoners began a long and interrupted
journey through taunting crowds along the Rue Honoré and past the Duplays.
'Isn't he a lovely king?' mocked some; 'Is your majesty suffering?' jeered others.[41]

The guillotine had been returned to the west end of the Tuileries, the Place
de la Révolution, for the occasion. At 7.30 p.m. the executions commenced.
Maximilien was the twenty-first to die: his agony had lasted seventeen hours.
After he had managed to climb the steps of the scaffold, his head wrapped in a
bloody and filthy bandage, he had a final torment to endure before execution.
The executioner ripped off the bandage; the lower jaw fell away, eliciting a
hideous roar of pain.[42] The twenty-one other 'Robespierrists' were then buried
with him in a common grave in the Errancis cemetery. It was the evening of the
day that had been set aside for Jacques-Louis David's commemorative spectacle
for the child heroes Joseph Viala and Joseph Bara, now postponed.

From Arras, the senior administrator Régis Deshorties, brother of Maximilien's pre-revolutionary love Anaïs, offered an analysis on hearing the news:

> So he is no more, that man who had for so long walked the path of the most incorruptible patriotism . . . considering himself as the most enlightened of his compatriots, Robespierre believed that he had to be permitted to choose the means by which he could most properly serve them. A man of genius is naturally made to lead others; but in a free country he is a traitor if he employs means contrary to liberty, even if it is to save the homeland.

For Deshorties, both Robespierre's stature and his tragedy stemmed from his heroic dedication to his founding principles, a personal consistency recognized and celebrated in 1791–92, and fatal in 1794. Deshorties himself, just a fortnight earlier, on 30 Messidor (18 July), had written to Augustin regretting that Maximilien's 'unending obligations' in serving 'the *patrie* and the great interests of humanity' had left him no time for friends or private life.[43] No one else was of a mind to reflect on why that seemed to be the case, or on the toll that the personal sacrifice of mental and physical health might have taken on the young man.

EPILOGUE

'That modern Procrustes'

Twenty-one of Robespierre's associates went to the guillotine with him on 10 Thermidor (28 July). The morning after the executions the president of the Convention reassured the deputies about the momentous decision they had taken the day before: 'the new tyrant was Robespierre . . . the fatherland is once more saved'. For the first time, the term 'the system of the Terror' was used, by Barère, who was eager to elevate his role in attacking Robespierre on 9 Thermidor into proof that he had not been a 'terrorist' himself. The following day the Jacobin Club rounded on the 'monster' who had been their most prominent and esteemed member from 1791, denouncing him as a 'hypocritical despot', a new Catilina who had deceived them all for so long by 'the specious pretext of love of the public good'. He was gone, with his 'infinite number of backbiters and especially women backbiters [*clabaudeurs et encore plus de clabaudeuses*]'.[1]

Deputies who had kept their heads down through fear or cowardice now rushed to inform their constituents of the events and their meaning. Julien Mazade, a Girondin deputy from Tarn-et-Garonne who had written letters home glowing with praise for Robespierre, now felt able to express other opinions: 'the tyrant is no more. He was on the point of slaughtering the Convention, our lives hung by a thread. . . . Never attach yourselves to any individual. Idolize only the principles of the homeland.' Thibaudeau, a deputy from Vienne, agreed: those who had overthrown 'the new Cromwell', far from being a fearful alliance of men with guilty consciences, were 'intrepid defenders of the people's rights . . . who thought only of the homeland'.[2]

Seventy-one 'co-conspirators' from the Paris Commune were executed on 11 Thermidor (29 July); others followed over the next few months. François-Pierre Deschamps, the draper who had convinced Robespierre to be the god-father of his son Maximilien, was among the *sans-culottes* who rallied to Robespierre in Thermidor, and he was executed on 5 Fructidor (22 August). Joachim ('Sempronius-Gracchus') Vilate, the young militant from Creuse, was in the last batch to go to the guillotine, on 7 May 1795, along with the state prosecutor Fouquier-Tinville. While awaiting trial, he wrote that he had found Robespierre 'sober, hardworking, irascible, vindictive and imperious', but was sure he was trying to stop the 'devastating torrent' of blood.[3] Hundreds of people labelled 'Robespierre's accomplices' were arrested and tried. At times the evidence was minor: three men were arrested on 11 Thermidor for having shouted abuse at a singer intoning a song against Robespierre. Almost all had excuses prepared. In court, men ranging from prominent Jacobin officials and allies to close friends like Duplay, Herman, Jacques-Louis David and Lohier, sought to distance themselves from a man whose name could not now be uttered unless preceded by 'infamous', 'scoundrel' or 'tyrant'.[4]

Others close to Robespierre suffered in different ways. On 9 Thermidor (27 July), Lebas had proved his loyalty to Robespierre by remaining with him, committing suicide as the troops entered. He left his young wife Élisabeth Duplay with a five-week-old son. Élisabeth's mother Françoise, so devoted to Robespierre, committed suicide or was murdered in her cell on 12 Thermidor (30 July). Her husband Maurice was imprisoned until April 1795 but somehow avoided execution, probably because of the articulate appeals made by his daughters Sophie and Élisabeth. Éléonore was imprisoned with her young brother Jacques and cousin Simon for more than a year. Simon insisted that Robespierre 'deceived me like so many others, and that's my only crime'. Éléonore was finally released and lived a sad life until 1832.[5]

Robespierre's faithful correspondent and friend, Marguerite Chalabre, was arrested on 22 Thermidor (9 August) and spent almost all of the next year in prison, finally deciding to save herself by renouncing him. He was also spurned by his old friend Charlotte Buissart, who wrote home to her husband Antoine in Arras that 'I cannot describe my surprise when I found out all the horrors that this Maximilien had ordered.' Antoine rushed to Paris and succeeded in distancing himself also, so successfully that he was appointed the new president of the main court in Arras. One of his colleagues would be Robespierre's old sparring partner, Guillaume Liborel, who returned from exile to the magistracy and was later awarded the Légion d'Honneur by Napoleon and ennobled by the restored monarchy in 1815.[6]

The year of 'terror until the peace' had polarized France. For those mindful of the magnitude of the counter-revolution, it was a successful emergency regime during which too many excesses had been committed. Others were horrified by what they saw as the unnecessary violence used against the Revolution's opponents, particularly as the military crisis receded. Whatever the case, the overthrow of Robespierre was universally welcomed at the time as symbolizing the end of large-scale executions.[7]

People rushed to repudiate what they now called 'Robespierre's Terror', and for all sorts of reasons.[8] Former Girondins, who had been cowed into acquiescence in 1793–94, were now able not only to blacken Robespierre's name with impunity, but also to rewrite their own role as legalistic 'moderates', despite their complicity, for example, in the September massacres. Just one month after Robespierre's death, his old enemy Méhée de la Touche published *La Queue de Robespierre*, the first in a long series of satires based on Robespierre's supposed will, in which he had left his 'tail' to his followers. One of these satires rehearsed the old obsession with Robespierre's hold over women:

> Robespierre's tail is most in fashion
> To soothe and still the ladies' passion.
> When his tail and his sharp blade
> Penetrate some charming glade,
> I hear a young virgin's plea:
> O how this knife stabs me!
> This Robespierre of a tail
> With blood will gorge and swell;
> Squeeze it if you dare
> Till pleasure wakes up there.
> The murderer's huge tail
> Makes the whole world quail;
> This tail bears a deep stain
> Of pleasure, love, and pain.[9]

Robespierre's name became the repository for the guilt of all consciences. The Convention charged a deputy, Edme-Bonaventure Courtois, with the task of heading a committee to report on the papers found in the dwellings of Robespierre and his 'accomplices'. Courtois was an old friend of Danton from Arcis and was close to being implicated in Danton's trial in April 1794.[10] Courtois made the most of his opportunity, supported by Robespierre's former friend and ally from Arras, Armand Guffroy, now fervent in his denunciation. The committee reported back on 16 Nivôse (5 January 1795) with allegedly damning—but in reality very slight—evidence. The papers seized were mostly a collection of letters Robespierre had received during the Revolution: male and female friends asking favours, offering advice and giving warnings, and enemies making anonymous threats. Courtois chose to report only 153 of 377 items, those most likely to suit his purposes. The others were books of history, law, mathematics and philosophy, and English and Italian dictionaries and grammars.[11]

The most egregious document submitted by Courtois came from one of Robespierre's old school acquaintances, and sometime friend, Stanislas Fréron. Fréron had been chilled by Robespierre's disapproval of the violence of his repression in Marseilles and Toulon in 1793, and was in fear for his life. Fréron offered Courtois whatever he wanted by way of character assassination, beginning with his schooldays in Paris. Although four years older than Robespierre, Fréron claimed to remember him well:

> He was as we have known him since: sad, bilious, morose, jealous of the success of his comrades.... His face had already developed the convulsive grimaces we know. . . . He was never known to have laughed. He never forgot a slight; he was vindictive and treacherous. . . . He did all right academically. . . .
>
> Robespierre was choked with bile. His complexion showed it and at Duplay's he was always served oranges which he devoured avidly. One could always see where he had been seated at table by the orange rinds . . .

Fréron claimed, fancifully, that he drank too much, always carried pistols, and was surrounded by bodyguards. He was attracted to a feline image of Robespierre: 'He has a face like a cat and his handwriting is like the scratching of a claw.'[12]

One of the readers of the Courtois report was Captain Watkin Tench, recently returned to England from taking one of the first vessels of British convicts to Australia. He was captured off the Breton coast near Quimper in November 1794 and held in the prison ship the *Marat*. He had read Courtois' report with care, and advised his readers that 'nothing bearing the marks of an arranged plan for mounting a throne, or erecting himself into a dictator, was found'.[13] Tench, an intelligent and keen observer, was curious to note that those who had 'prostrated themselves like reptiles' before Robespierre now blamed him for 'all the assassinations and misery': 'it is impossible to pronounce the word *guillotine*, without associating with it its grand mover Robespierre'. Tench, a man of Robespierre's age and who, like him, had had a classical education, described him as 'that modern Procrustes', drawing on the classical story of the blacksmith from Attica who stretched or shortened people to force them to fit his iron bed. But Tench was scathing about Robespierre's erstwhile allies: 'to screen themselves from odium, all the subordinate tyrants fix upon him, and attribute to his orders, the innumerable butcheries and acts of oppression which they have perpetrated'.

An avalanche of accusations was published shortly after Robespierre's death, describing the year of Terror as the work of a personal tyranny by a monster. The feline image became commonplace. The Jacobin deputy Merlin de Thionville, once a close ally, described how 'Danton had a mastiff's head, Marat that of an eagle, Mirabeau that of a lion, and Robespierre that of a cat. But this face changed its physiognomy: at first it was the worried but tender look of a domestic cat; then the untamed face of a wild cat; finally the ferocious face of a tiger-cat.' Merlin was said to have responded later to a question about why he had helped overthrow him, 'if you'd seen his green eyes, you'd have killed him too'.[14] Similar themes were taken up across the Channel, where in August 1794 Robert Southey and Samuel Taylor Coleridge rushed to write a three-act play, *The Fall of Robespierre*.

None of these memoirs was as bitter as those of Robespierre's fellow Arrageois, the Abbé Proyart, whom Maximilien had encountered at the College of Louis-le-Grand. At the time Proyart published his *Life and Crimes of Robespierre* in 1795, he was an *émigré* at Augsburg, and all the clerical and seigneurial structures on which his family's position had been based were in ruins. Proyart concluded that Robespierre's wickedness had been produced by his schooling as much as by his vicious character. He described Robespierre as 'a more atrocious being than any known to the barbarism of antiquity', and blamed the exiling of the Jesuits and the proliferation of scholarships to Louis-le-Grand for the schooling of him and other 'monsters' in Paris. The 'charlatans' who had educated them had taught them about botany, mathematics and geography, but not 'the geography of his own heart' and the road to salvation.[15]

While positive images of Robespierre were kept alive among republicans in the first half of the nineteenth century, it was not until the 1860s that the first wholly positive biography appeared, a massive work by Ernest Hamel, like his hero a politician from the northeast. For Hamel, Robespierre was 'not only one of the founders of democracy' but 'one of the greatest men of good who has appeared on earth'. He had but one reproach: the Law of 22 Prairial was a 'huge mistake', a 'pernicious' law born of his desire to bring the Terror to a prompt conclusion.[16] A positive assessment of Robespierre was at its peak in the first half of the twentieth century, particularly in the context of two world wars and the rise of fascism in Europe. In France this rehabilitation was particularly the work of the left-wing historians Albert Mathiez, Gérard Walter and Georges Lefebvre. For them Robespierre personified the uncompromising realization of the principles of 1789 and the heroic defence of the Republic against counter-revolutionary Europe in 1792–94. In a famous lecture—'Why are we Robespierrists?—given shortly after the First World War, Mathiez described him as the 'most noble, most generous and most sincere face of the French Revolution'.

Georges Lefebvre, Professor of the History of the French Revolution at the Sorbonne, wrote the foreword to a collection of Mathiez's essays in 1958, the bicentenary of Robespierre's birth. Lefebvre's own view of Robespierre was also coloured by his personal context, this time during the Second World War, when his brother Théodore, a geography teacher, had been beheaded for his resistance by the occupying German army. In 1947 Lefebvre had admitted that he shook with emotion every time he read Robespierre's speech of 25 September 1793 in which he blamed the lack of resolve and virtue at the highest levels of military command for the slaughter of scores of thousands of republican soldiers. Lefebvre concluded that 'Robespierre should be described as the first who defended democracy and universal suffrage ... the intrepid defender of the Revolution of 1789 which destroyed in France the domination of the aristocracy'. He was a great and peaceable man driven by circumstance to actions—such as support for the death penalty and press censorship—which he would normally have found repellent.[17]

Historians' judgements have commonly been a function of their own political views and the context of their own times. The American R. R. Palmer's classic study of the Committee of Public Safety, *Twelve Who Ruled*, was completed in the darkest days of the Second World War, in 1941. Like Lefebvre, Palmer was sympathetic to Robespierre, 'one of the half-dozen major prophets of democracy', because of the parallels with the time in which he was writing: 'since 1940 it is no longer so laughable as it once was to say that democracy is founded upon virtue. As we read through the catalogue of changes which Robespierre announced that the Revolutionary Government wished to see in France, we sense a certain similarity to what we might have read in the morning paper.'[18]

A parallel story unfolded in Arras. Robespierre was for long blamed personally for the 159 executions of townspeople, and by the end of June 1794 the prisons of the city held 1,328 'suspects', among them the former mayor, Dubois de Fosseux. Robespierre's name became anathema in the town for generations: he was assumed to have given Lebon his orders, even though he had in fact been horrified by his excesses. The first local historians of the Revolution damned Robespierre.[19] It was not for more than a century that a concerted attempt was made to clear his name in Arras, by a lawyer and member of the Rosati, Émile Lesueur, and by Mathiez and his colleagues at the Sorbonne. The Société des études Robespierristes, established at the Sorbonne by Mathiez in 1908, presented Arras with a commemorative plaque in 1923 for the house where Maximilien and Charlotte had lived in 1787–89, but it disappeared two years later. Passions were reignited in 1933 when the socialist municipal council received a delegation from Paris, led by Georges Lefebvre, with a bust of Robespierre. The dedication of the bust had to take place inside the Town Hall, away from the turbulence outside: rivers of red paint had been spread over the Place du Théâtre where three symbolic guillotines had been erected.[20] The bust has remained under lock and key.

With the passage of time, however, Robespierre's name no longer excites such division in Artois. In 1958 the renaming of the Lycée des Garçons in Arras as the Lycée Robespierre was proposed on the bicentenary of his birth, and was finally decreed in 1969. In 1990 a new Lycée in Lens was also given the name. On the bicentenary of the battle of Fleurus, 26 June 1994, a plaque was attached to the

Carraut house in the Rue Ronville. The Rue des Rapporteurs where Maximilien and Charlotte lived has been named after Robespierre, and their house bears a plaque and is known as the 'Maison Robespierre' for the purposes of tourism.[21] In 2008 the Town Hall hosted a ceremony to mark the 250th anniversary of his birth, with the recital of selections of his poetry and speeches and the laying of a wreath at his bust (still locked away), and a small but particularly good exhibition on his early life. Much of the rehabilitation had been the work of a local organization, the Friends of Robespierre for the Bicentenary of the Revolution, established in the lead-up to the bicentenary of 1789 'to make known to the public how Robespierre incarnated the most generous ideas of the French Revolution, and that his work was interrupted by those who sought to limit the emancipation of the people'.[22]

In France today there are well over fifty streets, schools, buildings and businesses (among them a pizzeria, a dry-cleaner and a pharmacy) carrying Robespierre's name. Elsewhere, the linen company Robespierre Europe produces a 'revolutionary' collection of sheets covered in erotic prints; the Brooklyn rock band 'Team Robespierre' plays 'synth-punk'.[23] The Amis de Robespierre have also had a plaque placed on the facade of the building in Paris that today occupies the site of the Duplays' house where he lived from July 1791 until his death. There is a statue of Robespierre in St-Denis, near the royal basilica, and a metro station in Montreuil has carried his name since the Popular Front in 1936.[24] Unlike its working-class suburbs, however, the city of Paris continues to keep its distance. On 30 September 2009, 220 years after the Revolution of 1789, the city council voted narrowly against a motion from a left-wing city councillor to name a street or square after Robespierre. The councillor argued, unsuccessfully, that Robespierre was 'first and foremost a revolutionary formed by the ideals of the philosophy of the Enlightenment' and not a 'caricature of a bloodthirsty executioner'.[25]

In our own times the use of the terms 'Terror' and 'war on Terror' have become so highly charged that a calm consideration of French revolutionaries in 1793–94 who adhered to a policy of 'terror until the peace' has become almost unachievable. Fanciful parallels have been drawn between Robespierre and Tony Blair on the one hand and Osama Bin-Laden on the other, and scholars continue to make wildly erroneous statements about Robespierre. The Terror was not his work, but a regime of intimidation and control supported by the National Convention and 'patriots' across the country, yet books on contemporary terrorism commonly refer to him as wholly responsible for the tens of thousands of deaths in 1793–94.[26] In 2009 some historians on a BBC production *Terror! Robespierre and the French Revolution* explicitly elided Robespierre's name with the Terror and likened France to the Gulag and the Third Reich. He has been wrongly accused of dismissing the scientist Lavoisier's wish to have his execution delayed in order to complete an experiment with the infamous quip that 'the Republic has no need of chemists'.[27] Others have asserted that, by articulating the virtue of unremitting repression of the Revolution's enemies, Robespierre provided the logic for 'genocide' in the Catholic west.[28]

Robespierre's imagined personality has inspired similar antipathy. Few biographers have, like Ruth Scurr, 'tried to be his friend and to see things from his point of view', but she did not try very hard, and found him a 'mediocre figure strutting and fretting on the historical stage', narcissistic and 'remarkably odd'.[29] Many have described him as physically repellent and emotionally cold, with no capacity for sexual intimacy. Indeed, he has been cast as a narcissistic ascetic, whose self-identification with the Revolution was a classic case of Freudian 'displaced libido'.[30] An obsessive personality is seen to be revealed by his fastidious appearance and toilet, a horror of bodily corruption which would render physical intimacy repellent to him.[31] It has been claimed that his misspelling in an electoral pamphlet of a shoemaker's name Lantillette as Languillette ('baby eel') shows a longing to cut off the penis: Robespierre was apparently a repressed homosexual with a castration complex, a misogynist and pathological narcissist constantly searching for a good father and an all-powerful mother.[32] Others have understood him as a paranoiac who, at a time of generalized belief in the malevolent power of conspiracy, was consumed by the omnipresence of counter-revolutionary plots and his certainty that a new world could be created by rhetoric.[33]

One of those who led the charges against Robespierre on 9 Thermidor (27 July) was Bertrand Barère. However, after returning in 1832 from his exile as a regicide, Barère remembered how fortunate the young Republic had been to have Robespierre's leadership, but 'we didn't understand this man. He was nervous, bilious; his mouth was pursed. He had the temperament of great men, and posterity will give him that title. . . . He was pure, a man of integrity, a true republican. His vanity, his irascible sensitivity and his unjust mistrust of his colleagues brought him down. . . . It was a great calamity!'[34] Was Robespierre brought down by these deep flaws in his personality, a moral rigidity masked by a grim idealism that prevented him from compromising with human inadequacies? Was his a 'fatal purity'? Was his decision to round on fellow revolutionaries in the spring of 1794 an acute example of the deadly psychological sequence, in Peter Gay's words, 'in which frustration is translated into rage and assuaged by revenge'?[35]

This biography has argued instead that Maximilien Robespierre may best be understood as a child and youth formed by his family life and social contexts in Artois and Paris; and as a young revolutionary who then found himself involved with others in remaking a world in a particular direction and against massive odds. Certainly, since biographers are involved in inferring motives from observable behaviour by their subjects—actions and decisions, letters and speeches—we must engage with psychological categories and inferences. But such reflection should remind us above all that Maximilien was once a small and vulnerable child and that when children become adults they do not grow into saints and devils, but into men and women. We should be wary of applying psychoanalytic categories crudely in an attempt to explain someone's actions, as have those who have exaggerated the psychological damage that may have been done to a small boy by the sad circumstances of his mother's death.[36]

Few individuals in the past have been written about so voluminously as Robespierre, and even fewer so tendentiously. Despite the vast records from his public life, and the richness of anecdotes from those who encountered him, we should be honest enough to admit the gaps, silences and ambiguities. There is abundant evidence that he gave and received affection; we will never know, however, why such emotions evidently did not result in a fully intimate relationship. What we can say with some confidence is that Robespierre's experiences had formed in him strong views about the rights of children and the ideal values of marriage, which were to inform his attitude to reforms to property rights, education and the family.[37] These reforms were at the heart of the Revolution, and Robespierre brought to them values learnt as a little boy and young man in a world in which his mother in particular, then his sisters, aunts and grandmothers, were of unusual importance. Far from the emotionally stunted, rigidly puritanical and icily cruel monster of history and literature, this was a passionate man.

Too often he has been written about as if a brain on stilts, as the mouthpiece of a cohesive, omniscient ideology, not as a young man full of fervour and bewilderment, both resolute and uncertain, caught between the national stage and a longing to be 'home'. We know that his life ended on 28 July 1794 in excruciating pain following a gunshot the day before, which had blown away half his jaw. We can certainly chart a dramatic narrative from May 1789 that leads inexorably to that day—but only with hindsight.

Robespierre was formed both by the difficult circumstances of his upbringing and by his adult experience of the distinctive social structures of his province; he was closely familiar with the vast noble and Church patrimony that underpinned a complex of hierarchical relations in Artois, and yet he was outside the system as a scholarship boy raised by a family of brewers. This was a world of sharp class antipathies similar to neighbouring Picardy, which produced some of the most radical Jacobins: Desmoulins, Fouquier-Tinville, St-Just and Babeuf. This context was to underpin Robespierre's ideology and political trajectory for the rest of his life.

In late 1789 Robespierre sent an open letter to the people of the northeast, which he began with a statement of his credo, cited earlier:

1. The aim of society is the happiness of all.
2. All men are born free and with equal rights, and cannot cease to be so.
3. The principle of sovereignty resides in the nation; all power emanates and can emanate only from it.[38]

His personal journey thereafter may be understood as a negotiation between these certainties and the realization that 'the people are good but do not always know what is best' in the context of revolutionary upheaval, invasion and counter-revolution, and bloodshed on a massive scale. The gap between ideal and actual was filled by the war between virtue and conspiracy. Unlike most of his peers in the revolutionary Assemblies, he was not prepared to compromise the principles of 1789 in order to achieve stability, and in that lay his greatness and his tragedy. The fundamental tension for him was that only a virtuous citizenry could enable a true democracy to thrive. If there was a gulf—as there was bound to be—between public behaviour and virtuous actions, then it was evident that malign forces were to blame: not only centuries of prejudice and oppression, but conspiracy.

There is nothing in the evidence we have of Robespierre's actions and beliefs before May 1789 that would enable one to predict that, in particular circumstances, he would find in repression and capital punishment the answer to dissent. The crowds that chaired him from the National Assembly in September 1791 to shouts of 'Long live the Incorruptible!', or that a few days later welcomed him home on what he did not know was to be his last visit to Arras, were of the view that he personified the principles of individual dignity, democracy and civic equality. But it was his certainty that 'the people' needed only to have their false friends unmasked to know instinctively the path to a golden age that made his role at a time of war and civil war so desperate and ultimately deadly.

There were some close to him whose affection and admiration remained unalloyed. In the early 1860s a Parisian doctor, Poumiès de la Siboutie, wrote an intriguing volume of memoirs based on diaries he had kept during his career. He had come to know Robespierre's doctor, Joseph Souberbielle, who had died in 1846, and recalled Souberbielle's admiration: 'I would have given my life to save Robespierre, for whom I cherished the affection of a brother. No one knows better than I do how sincere, disinterested, and thorough was his devotion to the Republic. He was the scapegoat [*bouc émissaire*] for the Revolution but was worth more than all of them together.' When the historian and radical social theorist Louis Blanc visited Souberbielle in those years, he found him very ill, but the mere mention of Robespierre's name caused him to sit bolt upright and recite the end of the last speech of 8 Thermidor (26 July), finishing by exclaiming 'how could he have said it better, the poor devil?'[39]

Maximilien's sister Charlotte was just as loyal, although she never had the chance to enjoy Souberbielle's personal rehabilitation and life of ease. She was arrested on 9 Thermidor (27 July) and imprisoned for a fortnight, and in hindsight might have felt fortunate to have fallen out with Augustin and returned to Arras. She spent the rest of her life in straitened circumstances in Paris, on a modest state pension. She was drawn into print in 1830, following the publication of a fanciful and prejudiced volume purporting to be the *Mémoires de Maximilien Robespierre*. 'I belong to a family which has not been accused of venality. . . . As for my brothers, history must pronounce definitively on them; it is for history to recognize one day whether Maximilien Robespierre is really guilty of all the revolutionary excesses of which he was accused by his colleagues after his death.' In her memoirs she recalled Maximilien's early essay for the Royal Academy of Metz on the injustice whereby an entire family suffered because of the alleged crimes of one member: that had been her lot, she noted with some bitterness. Charlotte died in August 1834, aged seventy-four.[40]

Other women, far away, were involved in preserving a positive memory of her brother. In distant Collioure, where Jacobin armies had finally freed the town from Spanish occupation in May 1794, Robespierre remained the personification of republicanism, and his name re-emerged with the proclamation of the Second Republic in 1848. The new mayor was the grandson of Dubois de Fosseux's correspondent in the Arras Academy, Jean-Paul Berge, who had died fighting the invading Spanish on the border in December 1793. As 'reactionaries' challenged the new Republic, they were warned to 'fear the sons of Robespierre'. In March 1851, a time of Bonapartist political crackdown, two young Catalan women used the Mardi Gras festivities to dress as Marianne, goddess of the Republic, and were 'carried in triumph throughout the town'. Arrested and fined, the women returned to Collioure in June in a cart decorated with laurel to wild acclamation, including from members of a clandestine republican club that met under Robespierre's portrait.[41]

Who knows what Maximilien Robespierre would have made of these two young Catalan women parading in his name on Mardi Gras sixty years later? It is a thought to savour. No doubt he would have been incensed to learn that the Second Republic would be overthrown by Louis-Napoleon's military *coup d'état* a few months later, just as his own Republic had been by Louis-Napoleon's uncle. Collioure was one of many places to rebel against the coup of December 1851. The Second Republic reintroduced universal male suffrage, but other policies that Robespierre saw as intrinsic to a Republic in 1793—free and secular education, social welfare for the sick, unemployed and frail—would take many decades to achieve. Ultimately, however, the French Revolution succeeded in entrenching the core promises of 1789—popular sovereignty, constitutional government, legal and religious equality, the end of corporate privilege and seigneurialism—through the Republic's visceral and successful response to its enemies in 1793–94.[42] Robespierre and the Committee of Public Safety had led the Republic and the Revolution to security. Their achievement was enormous; so were the human costs. But by the time the Republic was safe in 1794, Robespierre was ill, exhausted, irrational and in despair.

Chronology

Italicized entries are the general chronology of the Revolution; others pertain more particularly to Robespierre.

6 May 1758	Birth of Maximilien Robespierre in Arras
16 July 1764	Death of mother Jacqueline
1766–69	School in Arras
1769–81	College of Louis-le-Grand in Paris
1781–89	Lawyer in Arras
1784	Elected to Royal Academy of Arras
8 May 1788	*Reforms to reduce power of parlements*
8 August	*Estates-General convoked for 1 May 1789*
27 December	*Royal Council decrees doubling of the number of representatives to the Third Estate*
January 1789	Publishes *To the Artois Nation*
March–April	*Elections to the Estates-General; formulation of 'cahiers'*
April	Publishes *The Enemies of the People Unmasked* and a second edition of *To the Artois Nation*
24–29 April	Elected deputy for the Third Estate of Artois

THE ESTATES-GENERAL

(5 May 1789–27 June 1789)

5 May	*Opening of the Estates-General at Versailles*
May	Joins Breton Club
6 June	First speech criticizes wealth of bishops
17 June	*Declaration of the National Assembly*
20 June	*'Tennis Court Oath'*

THE NATIONAL CONSTITUENT ASSEMBLY

(28 June 1789–30 September 1791)

14 July	*Taking of the Bastille*
17 July	Accompanies Louis XVI to Paris
Late July–early August	*Municipal revolutions, peasant revolts (Great Fear)*
4–11 August	*August Decrees on feudalism*
27 August	*Declaration of the Rights of Man and of the Citizen*
7 September	Opposes royal veto
11 September	*National Assembly grants suspensive, rather than absolute, veto to the king*
5–6 October	*March of the Parisian women on Versailles; royal family brought back to Paris*
October 1789–July 1791	Lodges at 30 Rue Saintonge in Paris
21 October	Opposes decree on martial law
22 October	Opposes exclusion of 'passive' citizens from electoral assemblies
2 November	*Church property placed at the disposal of the nation*
November	Participates in creation of Society of Friends of the Constitution in the Jacobin convent, Rue St-Honoré
14 December	*Decree establishing municipalities*
19 December	*First issue of 'assignats'*
23 December	Advocates civil rights for Jews, actors, Protestants
24 December	*Grant of religious liberty to Protestants*

28 January 1790	*Sephardi Jews granted equal rights*
February	Opposes repressive measures against peasant riots
13 February	*Decree prohibiting monastic vows in France*
26 February	*Decree dividing France into departments*
March	Opposes seigneurial rights on common land
31 March	Elected president of the Jacobin Club
May	Opposes the king's right to declare war, supports clerical marriage
April–June	Conflict with Beaumez over taxation and provincial exemptions
22 May	*National Assembly renounces wars of conquest*
31 May–16 June	Likely period of illness
19 June	*Decree abolishing hereditary nobility and titles*
12 July	*Civil Constitution of the Clergy*
14 July	*Festival of Federation*
August–September	Defends mutinous troops at Nancy and elsewhere
October	*Revolt of slaves and former slaves in St-Domingue*
November	Urges annexation of Avignon
27 November	*Decree requiring the clerical oath*
February 1791	Supports trials by jury with eligibility of 'passive' citizens
April	Opposes property qualification for deputies; defends freedom of speech; demands open membership of National Guard; supports changes to inheritance laws
May	Defends right to petition and freedom of the press; supports free 'men of colour' in the colonies; opposes death penalty
15 May	*Children of free blacks in colonies granted equal rights*
16 May	Proposes 'self-denying ordinance' for deputies in outgoing National Assembly
June	Brief period of illness
9 June	Elected public prosecutor in Paris (resigned April 1792)
14 June	*Le Chapelier law on associations*
20 June	*The king's declaration and flight from Paris*
21 June	Calls for deposition of the king in Jacobin Club
5 July	*The Padua Circular*

17 July	*Petition and 'massacre' on the Champ de Mars*
Late July	Moves to Duplay home, 366 Rue St-Honoré
15 August	*Creation of Revolutionary Tribunal*
27 August	*Declaration of Pillnitz*
14 September	*Louis XVI accepts the Constitution of 1791; annexation of Avignon and the Comtat-Venaissin*
28 September	*Ashkenazi Jews granted equal rights*
29 September	Opposes Le Chapelier law outlawing popular societies from intervening in public debate
30 September	Popular acclamation in Paris at the conclusion of the National Assembly

THE LEGISLATIVE ASSEMBLY

(1 October 1791–20 September 1792)

1 October	*Legislative Assembly convenes*
14 October–28 November	Visit to Artois and Picardy
9 November	*Decree against émigrés (vetoed by the king on 12 November)*
29 November	*Priests refusing to take oath to Constitution suspended from functions*
December 1791–May 1792	Speeches against war in Jacobin Club
9 February	*Decree nationalizing émigré property*
15 February	Admission of his physical frailty to Jacobin Club
February	Defends mutinous soldiers of Châteauvieux regiment
March	Declares belief in God to Jacobin Club
April	Opposes Assembly's tribute to Simonneau, mayor of Étampes, killed in food riot
20 April	*Declaration of war on Austria*
17 May– 20 August	Edits *Défenseur de la Constitution*
27 May	*Decree on deportation of non-juring priests (vetoed 19 June)*
12 June	*Dismissal of Girondin ministers*
13 June	*Prussia declares war on France*

20 June	*Invasion of the Tuileries by Paris demonstrators*
11 July	*Declaration of the 'patrie en danger'*
25 July	*Publication of the Brunswick Manifesto*
29 July	Calls for deposition of the king
1 August	Calls for election of National Convention
10 August	*Storming of the Tuileries and overthrow of the king*
11 August	Member, General Council of the revolutionary Paris Commune for his Section des Piques
13 August	Elected to Paris Commune
19 August	*Defection of Lafayette to Austrians*
23 August	*Fall of Longwy to Prussians*
2 September	*Fall of Verdun to Prussians*
2–6 September	*'September massacres' in the prisons of Paris*
5 September	Elected deputy for Paris and Pas-de-Calais to National Convention; opts for Paris

THE NATIONAL CONVENTION

(20 September 1792–28 July 1794)

20 September	*Victory at Valmy*
21 September	*Proclamation of the Republic*
October 1792– April 1793	Edits *Lettres . . . à ses commettans*
5 November	Confrontation with Girondins in Convention
6 November	*Victory at Jemappes*
6–30 November	Illness
December 1792– January 1793	Speeches on trial and execution of the king
14–17 January	*King's trial*
21 January	*Execution of Louis XVI*
1 February	*French declaration of war on England and Holland*
24 February	*Decree for a levy of 300,000 men*
25 February, 1 March	Criticizes food riots in Paris
7 March	*Declaration of war on Spain*

10 March	*Reintroduction of Revolutionary Tribunal; creation of Surveillance Committees*
10 March	Calls for strong central government
10–11 March	*Outbreak of Vendéan insurrection*
19 March	*Decree on public relief*
28 March	*Decree against émigrés*
4 April	*Defection of Dumouriez to the Austrians*
6 April	*Decree on the formation of a Committee of Public Safety*
9 April	*Decree establishing 'deputies-on-mission'*
21 April	Presents draft of new Declaration of the Rights of Man and of the Citizen
4 May	*First law of the Maximum*
10 May	Speech on new Constitution
26 May	Supports insurrection against leading Girondin deputies
31 May–2 June	*Expulsion of leading Girondins from the Convention*
28 May, 12 June	New admissions of physical exhaustion
June	*Federalist revolts in Bordeaux, Calvados and elsewhere*
24 June	*Constitution of 1793*
25 June	Denounces Jacques Roux
13 July	Presents Lepeletier's plan for Public Education
13 July	*Assassination of Marat*
17 July	*Execution of Joseph Chalier in Lyon*
27 July	Appointed to Committee of Public Safety
1 August	*Decree establishing a uniform system of weights and measures*
23 August	*Decree establishing the levy en masse*
27 August	*Toulon surrenders to the British navy*
5 September	Robespierre president of the Convention; popular pressure forces vote on 'terror as the order of the day'
17 September	*Law of Suspects*
17 September	Supports restriction of meetings of sections to two per week with payment to attendees
19 September– 3 October	Periods of illness
29 September	*Law of the General Maximum*
8 October	Supports suspension of the Constitution of 1793

9 October	*End of Federalist insurrection in Lyon*
10 October	*Declaration of Revolutionary Government*
	(19 Vendémiaire Year II)
16 October	*Victory at Wattignies; execution of Marie-Antoinette*
24–31 October	*Trial and execution of leading Girondins*
17 November	Speech on the conduct of diplomacy and war
21 November	Condemns 'atheism' to Jacobin Club
4 December	*Law on Revolutionary Government (Law of 14 Frimaire)*
6–7 December	Speech on freedom of worship
8 December	*Decree concerning Religious Liberty (18 Frimaire)*
24 December	*Desmoulins uses the* Vieux Cordelier *no. 4 to attack*
	government and Robespierre
25 December	First speech on principles of revolutionary government
10 January 1794	Breaks with Desmoulins
4 February	*Abolition of slavery in French colonies*
5 February	Second speech on principles of revolutionary government
6 February–	Illness
11 March	
26 February	*Introduction of The Ventôse Decrees (8 Ventôse II)*
13–24 March	*Arrest and execution of Hébertists*
March–April	*Revisions to economic policies and the Maximum*
30 March–6 April	*Arrest and execution of Dantonist 'Indulgents'*
19 April–6 May	Illness
23 April	*Creation of new Bureau of Police*
7 May	Speech on Cult of the Supreme Being
23, 24 May	Two attempts on Robespierre's life
31 May	Renewed admission of exhaustion to Jacobin Club
4 June	Elected president of National Convention
8 June	*Festival of the Supreme Being in Paris*
10 June	*Law of 22 Prairial*
12 June	Attacks 'intriguers' in Convention; ceases attending
17 June	Execution of 'red shirts'
26 June	Advocates mercy for Catherine Théot
26 June	*Victory at Fleurus*
29 June–26 July	Absence from Committee of Public Safety; illness

1, 9 July	Speeches against 'intriguers' to Jacobin Club
16 July	Opposes 'popular banquets'
22–23 July	Failure of attempted reconciliation between the two Committees
23 July	*Introduction of new wage regulation in Paris*
26 July	Speeches in Convention and Jacobin Club
27–28 July	Refused hearing in Convention, arrested and executed with Couthon, St-Just and nineteen others
29 July	Execution of seventy-one 'co-conspirators'

Notes

Epigraphs

1. *Oeuvres de Maximilien Robespierre*, vol. III, tome II, pp. 170–72.
2. Marc Bloch, *Apologie pour l'histoire, ou métier d'historien*, Paris: Armand Colin, 1949, p. 70.

Introduction: 'Clay in the hands of writers'

1. *Oeuvres*, vol. III, pp. 57–59: undated letter bearing the note 'received 9 November 1789'. My italics.
2. ARBR, *Bulletin*, 7, 56. My italics.
3. William Doyle and Colin Haydon, 'Robespierre: After Two Hundred Years', in Haydon and Doyle (eds), *Robespierre*, Cambridge & New York: Cambridge University Press, 1999, pp. 3–16, is a good summary of the historiographical debate. See, too, *Actes du colloque Robespierre, XIIe congrès international des sciences historiques*, Paris: Société des études Robespierristes, Paris, 1967; François Crouzet, *Historians and the French Revolution: The Case of Maximilien Robespierre*, Swansea: University College of Swansea, 1989; George Rudé, *Robespierre: Portrait of a Revolutionary Democrat*, London: Collins, 1975, Part II; Michel Vovelle, *Combats pour la Révolution française*, Paris: Éditions la Découverte/Société des études Robespierristes, 1993, Part I; J. M. Thompson, *Robespierre*, Oxford: Blackwell, 1935, pp. 595–633.
4. Maurice Agulhon, 'Robespierre posthume: le mythe et le symbole', in Jean-Pierre Jessenne, Gilles Derégnaucourt, Jean-Pierre Hirsch and Hervé Leuwers (eds), *Robespierre: de la nation artésienne à la République et aux nations. Actes du colloque, Arras, 1–2–3 Avril 1993*, Villeneuve d'Asq: Centre d'histoire de la région du nord et de l'Europe du nord-ouest, Université Charles de Gaulle-Lille III, 1994, pp. 443–44. See the excellent analysis by Steven L. Kaplan, *Farewell, Revolution: Disputed Legacies*, Book 3, ch. 5; and *Farewell, Revolution: The Historians' Feud, France 1789/1989*, both Ithaca, N.Y.: Cornell University Press, 1995.
5. Eli Sagan, *Citizens and Cannibals: The French Revolution, the Struggle for Modernity, and the Origins of Ideological Terror*, Lanham, MD & Oxford: Rowman & Littlefield, 2001, ch. 22. See, too, John Hardman, *Robespierre*, London & New York: Longman, 1999, for example, pp. x, 214. Adam Gopnik describes him as a 'mass-murdering nerd—a man who, having read a book, resolves to kill all the people who don't like it as much as he does': *New Yorker*, 5 June 2006.

6. Hilary Mantel, 'If you'd seen his green eyes', *London Review of Books*, 20 April 2006, pp. 3, 8. Mantel's novel is *A Place of Greater Safety*. Acerbic judgements about Robespierre's personality are to be found in Thompson, *Robespierre*, pp. 113, 591–92; idem, *Robespierre and the French Revolution*, London: English Universities Press, 1952, pp. 2, 29, 161; and Richard Cobb, *Tour de France*, London: Duckworth, 1976, pp. viii, 53, 63.

7. Lynn Hunt, 'For Reasons of State', *The Nation*, 29 May 2006, p. 28; David Andress, *The Terror: Civil War in the French Revolution*, London: Little, Brown, 2005, pp. 375–76; Dan Edelstein, *The Terror of Natural Right: Republicanism, the Cult of Nature, and the French Revolution*, Chicago: University of Chicago Press, 2009, pp. 271–72. On Assange, see http://www.oursisthefury.com/2010/julian-assange-a-robespierre-for-our-time/ accessed 28 October 2010.

8. Slavoj Žižek, *Slavoj Žižek Presents Robespierre: Virtue and Terror*, London: Verso, 2007, referring to Ruth Scurr, *Fatal Purity: Robespierre and the French Revolution*, London: Chatto & Windus, 2006.

9. Michel Vovelle, 'Pourquoi nous sommes encore Robespierristes?', in *Combats pour la Révolution française*, pp. 349–59. See Kaplan, *Farewell, Revolution: Disputed Legacies, France 1789/1989*, pp. 456–63.

10. Claude Mazauric, 'Présentation', *Oeuvres*, vol. 1, Paris: Phénix Éditions, 2000, pp. xviii–xxix; idem, 'Robespierre', in Albert Soboul (ed.), *Dictionnaire historique de la Révolution française*, Paris: Presses universitaires de France, 1989, p. 921. A recent statement of the continued relevance of 'Robespierrisme' is by Yannick Bosc, Florence Gauthier and Sophie Wahnich, *Pour le bonheur et pour la liberté*, Paris: Éditions La Fabrique, 2000.

11. Janet Malcolm, 'A House of One's Own', *New Yorker*, 5 June 1995, pp. 74–75.

12. See Mazauric, 'Présentation', pp. i–xviii, on the history of the century-long publication of Robespierre's works and the historiographical context.

13. Frank Tallett, 'Robespierre and Religion', in Haydon and Doyle (eds), *Robespierre*, pp. 92–108; Colin Lucas, 'Robespierre: homme politique et culture politique', in Jessenne et al., *Robespierre*, p. 13.

14. This ambiguity is explored imaginatively in Norman Hampson, *The Life and Opinions of Maximilien Robespierre*, London: Duckworth, 1974.

15. Patrice Guennifey, 'Robespierre', in François Furet and Mona Ozouf (eds), *Critical Dictionary of the French Revolution*, translated by Arthur Goldhammer, Cambridge, MA: Harvard University Press, 1989, p. 299. See, too, David P. Jordan's fine 'intellectual biography', *The Revolutionary Career of Maximilien Robespierre*, New York: Free Press, 1985.

16. Note the discussion in William M. Reddy, *The Navigation of Feeling: A Framework for the History of Emotions*, Cambridge: Cambridge University Press, 2001, esp. pp. 173–99.

Chapter 1 A 'serious, grown-up, hardworking' little boy: Arras 1758–69

1. Archives Départementales [hereafter AD] Pas-de-Calais, 5M1 41, R17; ARBR, *Bulletin*, 2.

2. AD Pas-de-Calais, 5M1 41, R8. A brilliant attempt at writing about François is by Claude Manceron, *The Men of Liberty: Europe on the Eve of the French Revolution 1774–1778*, translated by Patricia Wolf, London: Eyre Methuen, 1977, pp. 520–27.

3. Abbé Lievin Bonaventure Proyart, *La Vie et les crimes de Robespierre, surnommé le Tyran, depuis sa naissance jusqu'à sa mort: ouvrage dédié à ceux qui commandent, et à ceux qui obéissent*, Augsbourg: n.p., 1795, p. 20. Note the comments on the 1850 edition by Thompson, *Robespierre*, pp. 599–602.

4. This did not prevent Robert being permitted to succeed his father Martin in the post of royal notary at Carvin in 1720.

5. Émile Lesueur, 'Avertissement', *Oeuvres*, vol. I, pp. 197–205; Auguste Joseph Paris, *La Jeunesse de Robespierre et la convocation des États généraux en Artois*, Arras: Rousseau-Leroy, 1870, Livre I; A. Lavoine, *La Famille de Robespierre, ses origines, le séjour des Robespierre à Vaudricourt, Béthune, Lens, Harnes, Hénin-Liétard, Carvin et Arras, 1452–1764*, Arras: Archives d'Arras, 1914; Bernard Nabonne, *La Vie privée de Robespierre*, Paris: Hachette, 1943, Part I, chs 1–4.

6. Yves DRobespierre of Carvin registered a coat of arms in 1697: a single silver wing and black band on a gold background.

7. Thompson, *Robespierre*, pp. 1–3. The 1725 inheritance deed from Maître Yves DRobespierre listed rents from eight farms.

8. ARBR, *Bulletin*, no. 11.

9. AD Pas-de-Calais 5M1 41, R16 (28 December 1761, 22 January 1763); 5M1 41, R17 (6 May 1758); Gérard Walter, *Robespierre*, 2 vols, Paris: Gallimard, 1961, vol. 1, pp. 14–15.

10. Hector Fleischmann, *Robespierre and the Women He Loved*, translated by Angelo S. Rappoport, London: John Long, 1913, p. 18.

11. Walter, *Robespierre*, vol. 1, pp. 15–17.

12. Max Gallo, *Robespierre the Incorruptible: A Psycho-Biography*, translated by Raymond Rudorff, New York: Herder & Herder, 1971, pp. 25, 66. See, too, Michèle Ansart-Dourlen, *L'Action politique des personnalités et l'idéologie jacobine. Rationalisme et passions révolutionnaires*, Paris & Montréal: Harmattan, 1998, p. 96; Jean-Philippe Domecq, *Robespierre, derniers temps: biographie. Suivi de La fête de l'Être suprême et son interprétation*, Paris: Pocket, 2002, p. 21. As a rejoinder to such assertions, see Hampson, *Robespierre*, ch. 1.

13. Laurent Dingli, *Robespierre*, Paris: Flammarion, 2004, pp. 11–19, 23, 35, 435. For a discussion of possible readings of Robespierre's childhood, see Joseph I. Shulim, 'The Youthful Robespierre and His Ambivalence toward the Ancien Regime', *Eighteenth-Century Studies*, 5 (1972), pp. 398–420; and 'Robespierre and the French Revolution', *AHR*, 82 (1977), pp. 20–38.

14. See the discussion in Colin Heywood, *Growing up in France: From the Ancien Régime to the Third Republic*, Cambridge: Cambridge University Press, 2007, chs 6–7.

15. Charlotte Robespierre, *Mémoires de Charlotte Robespierre sur ses deux frères, précédés d'une Introduction de Laponneraye*, Paris: Présence de la Révolution, 1987; Gabriel Pioro and Pierre Labracherie, 'Charlotte Robespierre et "Ses Mémoires"', *La Pensée*, 88 (1959), pp. 99–108.

16. Charlotte Robespierre, *Mémoires*. See Marilyn Yalom, *Blood Sisters: The French Revolution in Women's Memory*, New York: Basic Books, 1993, ch. 6. The republican politician and fervent 'Robespierriste' Ernest Hamel later claimed to have met a school friend of Maximilien, aged ninety-six, who corroborated Charlotte's account: *Histoire de Robespierre, d'après des papiers de famille, les sources originales et des documents entièrement inédits*, 3 vols, Paris: Lacroix, 1865–67, vol. 1, p. 13.

17. The description that follows draws primarily on Alain Nolibos, *Arras: de Nemetucam à la communauté urbaine*, Lille: La Voix du Nord, 2003, pp. 86–101, and 'Un tableau général d'Arras au XVIIIe siècle', in *Arras à la veille de la Révolution, Mémoires de l'Académie des Sciences, Lettres et Arts d'Arras*, 6e série, 1 (1990), pp. 15–34.

18. Nigel Aston, *Religion and Revolution in France, 1780–1804*, Basingstoke: Macmillan, 2000, p. 3; John McManners, *Church and Society in Eighteenth-Century France*, Oxford: Clarendon Press, 1998, vol. 1, p. 479.

19. Some historians, would later make the charge that Maximilien himself had added 'de' to his name as evidence of pretentiousness or a desire to pass himself off as a noble. For example, see William Doyle, *The Oxford History of the French Revolution*, Oxford: Clarendon Press, 1989, p. 26; Norman Hampson, *Danton*, Oxford: Blackwell, 1978, p. 23. I have myself repeated this mistake elsewhere.

20. Proyart, *Vie et crimes de Robespierre*, p. 20; Nolibos, *Arras*, pp. 102–3.

21. Augustin Deramecourt, *Le Clergé du diocèse d'Arras, Boulogne et Saint-Omer pendant la Révolution (1789–1802)*, 4 vols, Paris: Bray et Retaux/Arras: Imprimerie du Pas-de-Calais, 1884–86, vol. 1, especially pp. 50–55, 148–54, 452–53, 482–86.

22. Nolibos, *Arras*, pp. 97–99; Aston, *Religion and Revolution in France*, p. 26; McManners, *Church and Society*, vol. 1, p. 216.

23. André Mervaux, 'Les Militaires en garnison à Arras de 1788 à 1790', in *Arras à la veille de la Révolution*, pp. 99–125.

24. Proyart, *Vie et crimes de Robespierre*, p. 23; Philippe Marchand, 'Le Collège d'Arras', in *Arras à la veille de la Révolution*, pp. 165–80; Marie-Madeleine Compère and Dominique Julia, *Les Collèges français: 16e–18e siècles*, vol. 2, Paris: INRP-CNRS, 1988, pp. 57–69.
25. There is no reason to suppose that the scholarship was awarded on anything but merit: cf. Tallett, 'Robespierre and Religion', pp. 93–94.
26. Nabonne, *Vie privée de Robespierre*, Part I, ch. 4.

Chapter 2 'An extremely strong desire to succeed': Paris 1769–81

1. G. Lenôtre, *Robespierre's Rise and Fall*, translated by R. Stawell, London: Hutchinson, 1927, p. 279.
2. Quoted in Daniel Roche, *The People of Paris: An Essay in Popular Culture in the 18th Century*, translated by Marie Evans, Berkeley & Los Angeles: University of California Press, 1987, p. 10.
3. Charlotte Robespierre, *Mémoires*, p. 34; Richard Mowery Andrews, *Law, Magistracy and Crime in Old Regime Paris, 1735–1789*, vol. 1, *The System of Criminal Justice*, Cambridge: Cambridge University Press, 1994, pp. 1–22.
4. Much of what follows is based on R. R. Palmer, *The School of the French Revolution: A Documentary History of the College of Louis-le-Grand and its Director, Jean-François Champagne 1762–1814*, Princeton, N.J.: Princeton University Press, 1975; Nabonne, *Vie privée de Robespierre*, Part I, chs 5–8; Andrews, *Law, Magistracy and Crime*, vol. 1, pp. 241–49; and the institutional history by Gustave Dupont-Ferrier, *Du Collège de Clermont au lycée Louis-le-Grand: la vie quotidienne d'un collège parisien pendant plus de 350 ans*, 3 vols, Paris: E. de Boccard, 1921–25, vol. 1.
5. In general see Charles R. Bailey, 'French Secondary Education, 1763–1790: The Secularization of Ex-Jesuit Colleges', *Transactions of the American Philosophical Society*, 68 (1978), pp. 75–83; McManners, *Church and Society*, vol. 2, ch. 45; Dale Van Kley, *The Jansenists and the Expulsion of the Jesuits from France*, New Haven, CT, & London: Yale University Press, 1975, ch. 7.
6. Harvey Chisick, 'Bourses d'études et mobilité sociale en France à la veille de la Révolution: bourses et boursiers du Collège Louis-le-Grand (1762–1789)', *Annales*, 30 (1975), pp. 1,562–84.
7. Palmer, *School of the French Revolution*, pp. 25–26, 45–47; William J. Murray, *The Right-Wing Press in the French Revolution: 1789–1792*, London: Royal Historical Society, 1986, pp. 35–40, 58–60, 65–66. There is no evidence that Royou ever taught Robespierre: Harvey Chisick, *The Production, Distribution and Readership of a Conservative Journal of the Early French Revolution: The Ami du Roi of the Abbé Royou*, Philadelphia, PA: American Philosophical Society, 1992, pp. 42–43.
8. Proyart, *Vie et crimes de Robespierre*, pp. 24–28; Palmer, *School of the French Revolution*, pp. 55–56.
9. Palmer, *School of the French Revolution*, pp. 16–18, 27–29; Bailey, 'French Secondary Education', pp. 88–90.
10. Claude Mossé, *L'Antiquité dans la Révolution française*, Paris: Albin Michel, 1989, ch. 2.
11. Harold T. Parker, *The Cult of Antiquity and the French Revolutionaries: A Study in the Development of the Revolutionary Spirit* (1937), New York: Octagon, 1965, ch. 2.
12. 'Second Oration against Lucius Catilina: Addressed to the People', *M. Tullius Cicero. The Orations of Marcus Tullius Cicero, literally translated by C. D. Yonge, B. A.*, London: Henry G. Bohn, 1856. See Thomas E. Kaiser, 'Conclusion: Catilina's Revenge—Conspiracy, Revolution, and Historical Consciousness from the Ancien Régime to the Consulate', in Peter R. Campbell, Thomas E. Kaiser and Marisa Linton (eds), *Conspiracy in the French Revolution*, Manchester: Manchester University Press, 2007, pp. 191–92, 200.
13. Palmer, *School of the French Revolution*, pp. 29–30, 43–44, 53–54, 58; Bailey, 'French Secondary Education', pp. 90–102.
14. Palmer, *School of the French Revolution*, pp. 59–67, 70.
15. Abbé Proyart, *L'Écolier vertueux, ou vie édifiante d'un écolier de l'Université de Paris*, Tours: Alfred Mame, 1866, pp. 31–33; Marisa Linton, *The Politics of Virtue in Enlightenment France*,

Basingstoke: Palgrave Macmillan, 2001, pp. 183–84. Proyart's book was in print from the early 1770s.

16. Palmer, *School of the French Revolution*, pp. 66, 70.
17. Charlotte Robespierre, *Mémoires*, p. 34; Palmer, *School of the French Revolution*, pp. 68–69.
18. ARBR, *Bulletin*, 2; Dingli, *Robespierre*, pp. 23, 548, n. 36.
19. Charlotte Robespierre, *Mémoires*, pp. 34–35.
20. *Oeuvres*, vol. I, 224–25. The surname was blotted out throughout the poem, presumably part of a later attempt by Charlotte to avoid losing the poem were her private papers to be searched.
21. Proyart, *Vie et crimes de Robespierre*, p. 43; *Oeuvres*, vol. III, p. 22.
22. Proyart, *Vie et crimes de Robespierre*, pp. 46–48. Cf. John Laurence Carr, *Robespierre: The Force of Circumstance*, London: Constable, 1972, p. 14, who dates 'the grooming of the martyr' from that moment.
23. Fleischmann, *Robespierre and the Women He Loved*, p. 23; Georges Lizerand, *Robespierre*, Paris: Fustier, 1937.
24. *Oeuvres*, vol. III, p. 21.
25. *Oeuvres* vol. III, pp. 22–23.
26. Sarah Maza, *Private Lives and Public Affairs: The Causes Célèbres of Pre-Revolutionary France*, Berkeley, CA: University of California Press, 1993, pp. 233–55; William Doyle, 'Dupaty (1746–1788): A Career in the Late Enlightenment', *Studies on Voltaire and the Eighteenth Century*, 230 (1985), p. 35.
27. Palmer, *School of the French Revolution*, pp. 76–80.
28. For Paris in the 1780s, see Roche, *People of Paris*; David Garrioch, *Neighbourhood and Community in Paris 1740–1790*, Cambridge: Cambridge University Press, 1986, and *The Making of Revolutionary Paris*, Berkeley, CA: University of California Press, 2002; Richard Andrews, 'Paris of the Great Revolution: 1789–1796', in Gene Brucker (ed.), *People and Communities in the Western World*, vol. 2, Homewood, IL: Dorsey Press, 1979, pp. 56–112.
29. On the study of law in general, see Francis Delbeke, *L'Action politique et sociale des avocats au XVIIIe siècle. Leur part dans la préparation de la Révolution française*, Louvain: Librairie universitaire & Paris: Recueil Sirey, 1927, ch. 2; David A. Bell, *Lawyers and Citizens: The Making of a Political Elite in Old Regime France*, New York & Oxford: Oxford University Press, 1994, ch. 1; Hervé Leuwers, *L'Invention du barreau français. La Construction nationale d'un groupe professionnel*, Paris: Éditions de l'École des hautes études en sciences sociales, 2006, esp. ch. 1.
30. Aston, *Religion and Revolution in France*, chs 1–2.
31. Bailey, 'French Secondary Education', p. 95; Robert Darnton, *The Literary Underground of the Old Regime*, Cambridge, MA: Harvard University Press, 1982.
32. Proyart, *Vie et crimes de Robespierre*, pp. 36, 49–51; Maza, *Private Lives and Public Affairs*.
33. *Oeuvres*, vol. 1, pp. 211–12. According to Charlotte Robespierre, Maximilien did meet Rousseau in person: *Mémoires*, p. 35. Hamel, *Histoire de Robespierre*, vol. 1, pp. 21–22, agrees. This is highly unlikely: see Nathalie-Barbara Robisco, 'Le mythe de la rencontre avec Rousseau dans la formation du jeune Robespierre', in Jessenne et al. (eds), *Robespierre*, pp. 35–43; Carol Blum, *Rousseau and the Republic of Virtue: The Language of Politics in the French Revolution*. Ithaca, N. Y. & London: Cornell University Press, 1986, pp. 153–62.
34. *Oeuvres*, vol. II, pp. 1, 17–18; Andrews, *Law, Magistracy and Crime*, vol. 1, pp. 246–49.
35. Palmer, *School of the French Revolution*, p. 72; Louis Jacob, *Robespierre vu par ses contemporains*, Paris: A. Colin, 1938, pp. 20–21. Desmoulins was awarded 200 *livres* in 1783: Bailey, 'French Secondary Education', p. 97.
36. *Oeuvres*, vol. III, p. 98.

Chapter 3 'Such a talented man': Arras 1781–84

1. Palmer, *School of the French Revolution*, p. 72; Jacob, *Robespierre vu par ses contemporains*, pp. 20–21.

2. *Oeuvres*, vol. II, pp. 18–19.

3. This section draws on Nolibos, *Arras*, pp. 89–92.

4. Marie-Laure Legay, *Les États provinciaux dans la construction de l'état moderne aux XVIIe et XVIIIe siècles*, Geneva: Librairie Droz, 2001.

5. *Oeuvres*, vol. II, pp. 2–6; Philippe Sueur, *Le Conseil provincial d'Artois (1640–1790). Une cour provinciale à la recherche de sa souveraineté*, Arras: Commission départementale des monuments historiques du Pas-de-Calais, 1978, pp. 54–64; Nolibos, *Arras*, pp. 95–98; Nigel Aston, *The End of an Elite: The French Bishops and the Coming of the French Revolution*, Oxford: Clarendon Press, 1992, pp. 13, 39, 86.

6. Aston, *Religion and Revolution in France*, pp. 15–16.

7. Léon-Noël Berthe, *Dubois de Fosseux, secrétaire de l'Académie d'Arras, 1785–1792 et son bureau de correspondance*, Arras: CNRS, 1969.

8. Paris, *Jeunesse de Robespierre*, pp. 35–36; Shulim, 'The Youthful Robespierre'.

9. *Oeuvres*, vol. II, pp. 19, 41–43, 121.

10. *Oeuvres*, vol. II, pp. 19–20; Dingli, *Robespierre*, p. 24; Walter, *Robespierre*, vol. 1, pp. 31–33; Charlotte Robespierre, *Mémoires*, p. 45.

11. 'Notes et glanes', *AHRF*, 5 (1928), 470–1.

12. *Oeuvres*, vol. III, pp. 23–24.

13. Proyart, *Vie et crimes de Robespierre*, p. 51.

14. Jacob, *Robespierre vu par ses contemporains*, pp. 21–22; *Oeuvres*, vol. XI, p. 12.

15. *Oeuvres*, vol. II, pp. 24–25; Charlotte Robespierre, *Mémoires*, ch. 2.

16. *Oeuvres*, vol. II, p. 25, vol. XI, p. 11.

17. ARBR, *Bulletin*, 37; Louis Jacob, 'Un ami de Robespierre: Buissart (d'Arras)', *Revue du Nord*, 20 (1934), pp. 277–78. For Jean Artarit, *Robespierre, ou, l'impossible filiation*, Paris: Table Ronde, 2003, pp. 64–66, 74, Antoine was one in a line of surrogate fathers, and Charlotte the castrating, all-powerful mother he craved.

18. *Oeuvres*, vol. II, pp. 129–35, 199–201; Jessica Riskin, *Science in the Age of Sensibility: The Sentimental Empiricists of the French Enlightenment*, Chicago & London: University of Chicago Press, 2002, ch. 5; Marie-Hélène Huet, *Mourning Glory: The Will of the French Revolution*, University Park, PA: University of Pennsylvania Press, 1997, pp. 10–21.

19. Jacob, *Robespierre vu par ses contemporains*, pp. 22–23; *Oeuvres*, vol. XI, pp. 11–15.

20. *Oeuvres*, vol. III, p. 29. The significance of Franklin and the American experience has been strongly restated by Annie Jourdan, *La Révolution, une exception française?* Paris: Flammarion, 2004, Part 2, ch. 4.

21. Within a year, however, Vissery had died and the municipality demolished his contraption: Riskin, *Science in the Age of Sensibility*, p. 186.

22. *Oeuvres*, vol. I, pp. 205–9 (it has also survived as a letter to Buissart himself: *Oeuvres*, vol. III, pp. 24–28); Émile Lesueur, 'Avertissement', *Oeuvres*, vol. I, pp. 204–5; Dingli, *Robespierre*, pp. 27–34.

23. See Anne Vincent-Buffault, *L'Exercice de l'amitié. Pour une histoire des pratiques amicales aux XVIIIe et XIXe siècles*, Paris: Seuil, 1995.

24. Eugène Déprez, 'Introduction', *Oeuvres*, vol. I, pp. 5–19; Odile Barubé, 'La Vie culturelle à Arras à la veille de la Révolution', in *Arras à la veille de la Révolution*; Dingli, *Robespierre*, pp. 78–79, 81.

25. *Oeuvres*, vol. I, pp. 5–19; Andrews, *Law, Magistracy and Crime*, pp. 47–49.

26. *Oeuvres*, vol. 1, pp. 20–63. See Norman Hampson, *Will and Circumstance: Montesquieu, Rousseau and the French Revolution*, London: Duckworth, 1983, pp. 131–33.

27. *Oeuvres*, vol. III, p. 30; Jacob, *Robespierre vu par ses contemporains*, pp. 28–29. On Lacretelle, see Maza, *Private Lives and Public Affairs*, pp. 271–84.

28. *Oeuvres*, vol. I, pp. 28–29.

29. Déprez, 'Introduction', pp. 81–87; *Oeuvres*, vol. I, pp. 88–115.

30. Jacob, *Robespierre vu par ses contemporains*, pp. 30–31.

Chapter 4 'Bachelorhood seems to encourage rebelliousness': Arras 1784–89

1. *Oeuvres*, vol. II, pp. 279–311, vol. III, pp. 31–33, 98.
2. *Oeuvres*, vol. II, pp. 226–54.
3. Norman Hampson, 'Robespierre and the Terror', in Haydon and Doyle (eds), *Robespierre*, p. 155; Thompson, *Robespierre*, p. 38; *Oeuvres*, vol. I, p. 275; vol. II, pp. 325–26.
4. Léon-Noël Berthe, 'Robespierre et le fonds de Fosseux', *AHRF*, 172 (1963), pp. 189–91. Despite the assiduous work of Dubois, the weekly, then monthly, sessions of the Academy held in his mansion were thinly attended: Barubé, 'La Vie culturelle à Arras', in *Arras à la veille de la Révolution*, pp. 141–42.
5. Babeuf was sent Robespierre's speech on the 'rights of bastards': Marcel Reinhard (ed.), *Correspondance de Babeuf avec l'Académie d'Arras (1785–1788)*, Paris: Institut d'histoire de la Révolution française, 1961, p. 8. See also R. B. Rose, *Gracchus Babeuf: The First Revolutionary Communist*, London: Edward Arnold, 1978, ch. 3; Léon-Noël Berthe, *Dictionnaire des correspondants à l'Académie d'Arras au temps de Robespierre*, Arras: Chez l'auteur, 1969; V. M. Daline, 'Robespierre et Danton vus par Babeuf', *AHRF*, 32 (1960), pp. 389–90.
6. *Oeuvres*, vol. XI, pp. 137–83. See Hampson, *Will and Circumstance*, pp. 134–36.
7. Proyart, *Vie et crimes de Robespierre*, pp. 51–63.
8. Marcel Reinhard, *Le Grand Carnot*, vol. 1, *De l'ingénieur au conventionnel 1753–1792*. Paris: Hachette, 1950, pp. 91–101.
9. *Oeuvres*, vol. XI, pp. 185–201. See also *Oeuvres*, vol. XI, pp. 129–35; *ARBR, Bulletin*, 41, 42; Léon-Noël Berthe, 'Un inédit de Robespierre: sa réponse au discours de réception de Mademoiselle de Kéralio–18 avril 1787', *AHRF*, 46 (1974), pp. 261–83; Alyssa Goldstein Sepinwall, 'Robespierre, Old Regime Feminist? Gender, the Late Eighteenth Century, and the French Revolution Revisited', *JMH*, 82 (2010), pp. 1–29.
10. Jacob, *Robespierre vu par ses contemporains*, pp. 24–28; Émile Lesueur, 'Avertissement', pp. 215–22.
11. *Oeuvres*, vol. I, pp. 187–89, 232. On Robespierre's panoply of heroes, see Annie Jourdan, 'Robespierre and Revolutionary Heroism', in Haydon and Doyle (eds), *Robespierre*, pp. 54–74.
12. Louis Madelin, *Fouché 1759–1820*, 2nd edn, 2 vols, Paris: Plon, 1903, vol. 1, p. 16. Fouché was transferred by the Oratorians to their college at Nantes in October 1790.
13. Werner Krauss, 'Le Cousin Jacques: Robespierre et la Révolution française', *AHRF*, 32 (1960), pp. 305–8.
14. *Oeuvres*, vol. III, pp. 30–34; Scurr, *Fatal Purity*, pp. 46–49.
15. *Oeuvres*, vol. III, pp. 30, 34–35. This is according to Charles Vellay's note with the letter reprinted in *Annales révolutionnaires*, 1 (1908), pp. 107–9.
16. *Oeuvres*, vol. I, pp. 222, 241–44.
17. Only a few portraits show his green-tinted glasses and it may be that he also needed to place a larger pair over them when he needed to see into the distance. On Robespierre's much-debated physical appearance, see Henri Guillemin, *Robespierre: politique et mystique*, Paris: Éditions du Seuil, 1987, pp. 21–28.
18. Proyart, *Vie et crimes de Robespierre*, pp. 62–63.
19. Charlotte Robespierre, *Mémoires*, p. 39.
20. Guennifey, 'Robespierre', p. 303.
21. Claude Mazauric, 'Présentation', *Oeuvres*, vol. I, pp. xiv–xv; vol. II, p. 26. Arras was a rare case of stability in numbers of barristers after 1770: see Leuwers, *Invention du barreau français*, p. 40; cf. Richard L. Kagan, 'Law Students and Legal Careers in Eighteenth-Century France', *P&P*, 68 (1975), pp. 38–72. Robespierre's name still appears in court records in February 1790, but he could not have been present.
22. See *Oeuvres*, vol. III, p. 34: a warm letter from Robespierre to the keeper of the Lille poorhouse about the 'irreproachable' conduct of Catherine Calmet.
23. *Oeuvres*, vol. XI, p. 148.
24. *Oeuvres*, vol. II, p. 10.

25. On the history of 1788–89 in Arras and Artois, see E. Lecesne, *Arras sous la Révolution*, 3 vols, Arras: Sueur-Charruey, 1882–83, vol. 1, pp. 1–62; Legay, *États provinciaux*, pp. 484–508; Hervé Leuwers, Annie Crépin and Dominique Rosselle, *Histoire des provinces françaises du nord. La Révolution et l'Empire. Le Nord—Pas-de-Calais entre Révolution et contre-révolution*, Arras: Artois Presses Université, 2008, ch. 1. In general, see William Doyle, *Aristocracy and its Enemies in the Age of Revolution*, Oxford: Oxford University Press, 2009, chs 5–6.

26. Lesueur, 'Avertissement', pp. 155–60; *Oeuvres*, vol. III, pp. 22–23; Maza, *Private Lives and Public Affairs*, pp. 246–55; Doyle, 'Dupaty', pp. 82–106; Barry M. Shapiro, *Revolutionary Justice in Paris, 1789–1790*, Cambridge & New York: Cambridge University Press, 1993, p. 8.

27. *Oeuvres*, vol. I, pp. 160–81.

28. Jean Sgard (ed.), *Dictionnaire des journaux 1600–1789*, Paris: Universitas, 1991, notice 8.

29. On the Dutch Revolution and its refugees, see Joost Rosendaal, ' "Parce que j'aime la liberté, je retourne en France". Les réfugiés bataves en voyage', in Willem Frijhoff and Rudolf Dekker (eds), *Le voyage révolutionnaire. Actes du colloque franco-néerlandais du Bicentenaire de la Révolution française, Amsterdam, 12–13 october 1989*, Hilversum: Verloren, 1991, pp. 37–47; Greg Burgess, *Refuge in the Land of Liberty: France and its Refugees, from the Revolution to the End of Asylum, 1789–1939*, Basingstoke: Palgrave Macmillan, 2008, pp. 11–15; Nicolaas C. F. van Sas, 'The Patriot Revolution: New Perspectives', in Margaret C. Jacob and Wijnand W. Mijnhardt (eds), *The Dutch Republic in the Eighteenth Century: Decline, Enlightenment, and Revolution*, Ithaca, N.Y., & London: Cornell University Press, 1992, pp. 91–122.

30. Aston, *The End of an Elite*, pp. 78–79, 86, 135. See, for example, the memoir by Augustin Théry, priest of Camblain, against the Abbey of Mont-St-Éloi in 1766, in Deramecourt, *Le Clergé du diocèse d'Arras*, vol. 1.

31. *Oeuvres*, vol. XI, pp. 205–45; Legay, *États provinciaux*. A succinct statement of the resonance of 'virtue' in the political debates of 1787–89 is by Marisa Linton, 'The Intellectual Origins of the French Revolution', in Peter R. Campbell (ed.), *The Origins of the French Revolution*, Basingstoke: Palgrave Macmillan, 2006, pp. 156–59.

32. Nabonne, *Vie privée de Robespierre*, pp. 97–98.

33. Michael Burrage, *Revolution and the Making of the Contemporary Legal Profession: England, France and the United States*, Oxford: Oxford University Press, 2006, pp. 67–79.

34. *Oeuvres*, vol. VI, Introduction, pp. 6–9. Those 'new' nobles excluded from the meetings of the Second Estate protested successfully to the Finance Minister, Jacques Necker, about their second-class status; however, they then joined their fellows in insisting on the privileges of their order. See Norman Hampson, 'The Enlightenment and the Language of the French Nobility in 1789: the Case of Arras', in D. J. Mossop, G. E. Rodmell and D. B. Wilson (eds), *Studies in the French Eighteenth Century Presented to John Lough*, Durham: University of Durham, 1978, pp. 81–91.

35. Jacob, *Robespierre vu par ses contemporains*, p. 24.

36. We do not know the outcome: *Oeuvres*, vol. II, pp. 274–352; XI, p. 52; Hampson, 'Robespierre and the Terror', pp. 156–57.

37. *Oeuvres*, vol. XI, pp. 53, 111–12, 117–18, 121.

38. Marie-Laure Legay, *Robespierre et le pouvoir provincial: dénonciation et émancipation politique*, Arras: Commission départementale d'histoire et d'archéologie du Pas-de-Calais, 2002, pp. 15–21; Jean-Pierre Jessenne, 'Les Enjeux artésiens ou l'inévitable prise de distance', and Bruno Decriem, '1788/1789 en Artois: un candidat en campagne électorale, Maximilien de Robespierre', in Jessenne et al. (eds), *Robespierre*; Jessenne, *Pouvoir au village et révolution: Artois, 1760–1848*, Lille: Presses universitaires de Lille, 1987.

39. *Oeuvres*, vol. XI, pp. 205–45.

40. Paris, *Jeunesse de Robespierre*, p. 281; *Oeuvres*, vol. XI, pp. 275–77.

41. Sueur, *Conseil provincial d'Artois*, p. 339; Leuwers, *Invention du barreau français*, p. 76.

42. *Oeuvres*, vol. VI, Introduction, p. 7.

43. *Oeuvres*, vol. VI, Introduction, pp. 10–13; Paris, *Jeunesse de Robespierre*, p. 43; Jacob, *Robespierre vu par ses contemporains*, pp. 34–35.

44. *Oeuvres*, vol. VI, Introduction, pp. 13–16.
45. *Oeuvres*, vol. IX, Introduction, p. 9.
46. Jacob, *Robespierre vu par ses contemporains*, p. 36. In his speech to the Jacobins on 28 April 1792, Robespierre recalled that 'I urged them to respond to the Artois nobility simply that nobody had the right to give the people what already belonged to it.... thus had I been formed by Nature to play the role of an ambitious tribune and dangerous agitator of the People!'
47. Proyart, *Vie et crimes de Robespierre*, pp. 69–74.
48. François Wartelle, 'Les Communautés rurales du Pas-de-Calais et le système fédodal en 1789–1790', *Cahiers d'histoire de l'Institut de recherches marxistes*, 32 (1988), pp. 100–21.
49. Proyart's views are echoed by Simon Schama, *Citizens: a Chronicle of the French Revolution*, New York: Knopf, 1989, p. 577; François Furet, *The French Revolution 1770–1814*, translated by Antonia Nevill, Oxford: Blackwell, 1992, p. 143; Patrice Guennifey, 'Robespierre', in Annie Jourdan (ed.), *Robespierre—figure-réputation*, Amsterdam & Atlanta, GA: Rodopi, 1996, p. 2; Scurr, *Fatal Purity*, p. 8.
50. On the extent of commoner alienation from noble elites in 1787–88, see Vivian R. Gruder, *The Notables and the Nation: The Political Schooling of the French, 1787–1788*, Cambridge, MA: Harvard University Press, 2007.
51. Walter, *Robespierre*, vol. 2, pp. 408–09; Hampson, 'Robespierre and the Terror', p. 158. The comments are handwritten, dated 1 May 1789 and appended to the Bibliothèque nationale copy of *À la nation artésienne*.

Chapter 5 'We are winning': Versailles 1789

1. Fleischmann, *Robespierre and the Women He Loved*, p. 80; Proyart, *Vie et crimes de Robespierre*, p. 79.
2. See Bell, *Lawyers and Citizens*, pp. 187–89; Michael Fitzsimmons, *The Parisian Order of Barristers and the French Revolution*, Cambridge, MA: Harvard University Press, 1987, ch. 2.
3. Jules Claretie, *Camille Desmoulins and his Wife; Passages from the History of the Dantonists Founded upon New and Hitherto Unpublished Documents*, translated by Cashel Hoey, London: Smith, Elder, 1876, pp. 77–80.
4. *Oeuvres*, vol. III, pp. 36–42.
5. Like Desmoulins, Target had his family roots in Guise: Jean-Paul Bertaud, *Camille et Lucile Desmoulins. Un couple dans la tourmente*, Paris: Presses de la Renaissance, 1986, p. 55.
6. Edna Hindie Lemay, *La Vie quotidienne des députés aux Etats Généraux, 1789*, Paris: Hachette, 1987, p. 56; F. A. Aulard, *La Société des Jacobins. Recueil des documents pour l'histoire du Club des Jacobins de Paris*, 6 vols, Paris: Librairies Jouaust, Noblet et Quantin, 1889–97, vol. 1, p. viii.
7. Étienne Dumont, *Souvenirs sur Mirabeau et sur les deux premières assemblées législatives*, Paris: Librairie de Charles Gosselin, et chez Hector Bossange, 1832, pp. 250–51.
8. Dumont, *Souvenirs sur Mirabeau*, pp. 59–62. Early drafts of some of his speeches, replete with crossings-out, are among the papers aquired at auction by the Archives Nationales in May 2011 from the estate of Philippe Lebas.
9. Thompson, *Robespierre*, p. 53; Barry M. Shapiro, *Traumatic Politics: The Deputies and the King in the Early French Revolution*, University Park, PA: Pennsylvania State University Press, 2009, pp. 87–88.
10. *Oeuvres*, vol. III, pp. 42–50.
11. Jacob, *Robespierre vu par ses contemporains*, p. 53.
12. On the question of violence in July, see Timothy Tackett, *Becoming a Revolutionary: The Deputies of the French National Assembly and the Emergence of a Revolutionary Culture (1789–1790)*, Princeton, N.J.: Princeton University Press, 1996, pp. 165–69; Micah Alpaugh, 'The Politics of Escalation in French Revolutionary Protest: Political Demonstrations, Non-violence and Violence in the *grandes journées* of 1789', *FH*, 23 (2009), pp. 336–59.
13. *Oeuvres*, vol. VI, pp. 39–40.

14. *Oeuvres*, vol. VI, pp. 48–50. See Jeffrey Larrabee Short, 'The Lantern and the Scaffold: The Debate on Violence in Revolutionary France, April–October 1789', Ph.D. thesis, State University of New York at Binghamton, 1990, ch. 3.

15. Jean-Clément Martin, *Violence et Révolution: Essai sur la naissance d'un mythe national*. Paris: Éditions du Seuil, 2006, p. 15.

16. For a discussion of whether Barnave ever used these words, see Short, 'The Lantern and the Scaffold', pp. 168–70.

17. Lynn Hunt, 'The World We Have Gained: The Future of the French Revolution', *AHR*, 108 (2003), pp. 4–9.

18. *Affiches d'Artois*, 28 July 1789, in Nolibos, *Arras*, p. 106; Leuwers, Crépin and Rosselle, *Histoire des provinces françaises du nord*, pp. 25–29.

19. In general, see Michael P. Fitzsimmons, *The Night the Old Regime Ended: August 4, 1789 and the French Revolution*, University Park, PA: Pennsylvania State University Press, 2003.

20. *Oeuvres*, vol. VI, pp. 52–53.

21. Legay, *États provinciaux*, p. 490; Hervé Leuwers, 'Des nations à la nation. Obstacles et contradictions dans le cheminement politique de deux hommes des provinces du nord: Robespierre et Merlin de Douai (1788–1791)', in Jessenne et al. (eds), *Robespierre*, pp. 73–87.

22. Dale Van Kley (ed.), *The French Idea of Freedom: The Old Regime and the Declaration of Rights of 1789*, Stanford, CA: Stanford University Press, 1994; Jean-Pierre Gross, 'Robespierre et l'impôt progressif', in Jessenne et al. (eds), *Robespierre*, pp. 279–97; Thompson, *Robespierre*, pp. 55–57.

23. See, for example, Hervé Leuwers, 'Rendre la justice à la nation. Révolution constituante et réforme judiciaire, 1789–1791', in Michel Biard (ed.), *La Révolution française. Une histoire toujours vivante*, Paris: Tallandier, 2009, pp. 123–36.

24. Walter, *Robespierre*, vol. 1, pp. 87–88.

25. Marc Bouloiseau, 'Aux origines des légendes contre-révolutionnaires. Robespierre vu par les journaux satiriques (1789–1791)', *Bulletin de la Société d'histoire moderne*, 57 (1958), pp. 6–8.

26. Jacob, *Robespierre vu par ses contemporains*, pp. 53–54, 213.

27. *Oeuvres*, vol. VI, pp. 86–95.

28. *Oeuvres*, vol. VI, pp. 99–101.

29. *Oeuvres*, vol. VI, pp. 121–23; Riho Hayakawa, 'L'Assassinat du boulanger Denis François le 21 octobre 1789', *AHRF*, 333 (2003), pp. 1–19. The transformation of deputies into revolutionaries in a context of extreme uncertainty is explored expertly by Tackett, *Becoming a Revolutionary*.

30. Robespierre initially worried that these departments 'could easily build an aristocracy of the rich on the ruins of the feudal aristocracy': *Oeuvres*, vol. III, pp. 57–59.

31. *Oeuvres*, vol. VI, p. 46.

32. *Oeuvres*, vol. VI, pp. 130–34; Eric Thompson, *Popular Sovereignty and the French Constituent Assembly 1789–1791*, Manchester: Manchester University Press, 1952; Michael Kennedy, *The Jacobin Clubs in the French Revolution: The First Years*, Princeton, N. J.: Princeton University Press, 1982, pp. 245–88.

33. *Oeuvres*, vol. VI, pp. 167–68.

34. *Oeuvres*, vol. XI, pp. 281–97. Robespierre continued to insist on universal manhood suffrage, for example, in January 1790, and on a National Guard open to all men. See *Oeuvres*, vol. VI, pp. 200–3, 552–53; Raymonde Monnier, *Républicanisme, patriotisme et Révolution française*, Paris: Harmattan, 2005, p. 17.

35. *Oeuvres*, vol. VI, pp. 95, 514. Some of these assumptions were shared across the political spectrum: see Paul H. Beik, 'The French Revolution Seen from the Right: Social Theories in Motion, 1789–1799', *Transactions of the American Philosophical Society*, 46 (1956), pp. 18–19. Robespierre's concern with conspiracy from 1789 is highlighted by Linton, 'Robespierre's Political Principles', in Haydon and Doyle (eds), *Robespierre*, pp. 38–39; Roger Barny, 'Robespierre et les Lumières', in Jessenne et al. (eds), *Robespierre*, pp. 45–59.

36. Thompson, *Robespierre*, pp. 61–62; Lemay, *Vie quotidienne des députés*, p. 206.

37. The chapel was demolished in August 1791. Bouloiseau, 'Robespierre vu par les journaux satiriques'; Pierre Rétat, 'Notes sur la présence de Robespierre dans les journaux de 1789', in Jean Ehrard, Antoinette Ehrard and Florence Devillez, *Images de Robespierre: actes du colloque international de Naples, 27–29 septembre 1993*, Napoli: Vivarium, 1996, pp. 3–10; Murray, *Right-Wing Press*, p. 220; Élisabeth Roudinesco, *Madness and Revolution: The Lives and Legends of Théroigne de Méricourt*, translated by Martin Thom, London & New York: Verso, 1991, pp. 29–32; Olivier Blanc, 'Cercles politiques et "salons" de début de la Révolution (1789–1793)', *AHRF*, 344 (2006), p. 79. On Charles de Lameth, see Edna Hindie Lemay, *Dictionnaire des constituants 1789–1791*, 2 vols, Oxford: Voltaire Foundation, 1991, vol. I, pp. 512–15. It seems that Robespierre often ate at the Lameths in 1789, 'with other deputies whose means did not allow them to live well in Paris'.

38. *Oeuvres*, vol. III, pp. 57–59, undated letter bearing the note 'received 9 November 1789'.

Chapter 6 'Daring to clean out the Augean stables': Paris 1789–91

1. *Oeuvres*, vol. III, pp. 66–67.
2. *Oeuvres*, vol. VI, pp. 217–18. See Jean Bart, 'Droit individuel et droits collectifs', in Jessenne et al. (eds), *Robespierre*, pp. 259–60. In general, see Peter Jones, *The Peasantry in the French Revolution*, Cambridge: Cambridge University Press, 1988.
3. *Oeuvres*, vol. VI, pp. 271–74; vol. XI, pp. 299–300; Wartelle, 'Les Communautés rurales du Pas-de-Calais', pp. 118–20.
4. *Oeuvres*, vol. VI, pp. 227–28, 237–41.
5. *Oeuvres*, vol. VI, pp. 324–25; Bart, 'Droit individuel et droits collectifs', pp. 260–61.
6. Edna Hindie Lemay, 'Poursuivre la Révolution: Robespierre et ses amis à la Constituante', in Jessenne et al. (eds), *Robespierre*, pp. 139–56; Lemay and Alison Patrick, *Revolutionaries at Work: The Constituent Assembly 1789–1791*, Oxford: Voltaire Foundation, 1996, p. 16.
7. *Oeuvres*, vol. III, pp. 69–70, 96–97, 102–3. On Robespierre's developing links with provincial clubs, see Kennedy, *The Jacobin Clubs: The First Years*, pp. 253–58; Aulard, *Société des Jacobins*, vol. 1.
8. *Oeuvres*, vol. III, pp. 85–90.
9. Burgess, *Refuge in the Land of Liberty*, ch. 1.
10. Marc Bélissa, 'Robespierre et la guerre de conquête', in Jessenne et al. (eds), *Robespierre*, pp. 349–58.
11. *Oeuvres*, vol. VI, p. 588; Michael Rapport, 'Robespierre and the Universal Rights of Man, 1789–1794', *FH*, 10 (1996), pp. 303–33; Annie Geffroy, 'Le mot nation chez Robespierre', in Jessenne et al. (eds), *Robespierre*, pp. 89–104.
12. Alan Forrest, 'Robespierre: la guerre et les soldats', in Jessenne et al. (eds), *Robespierre*, pp. 358–68; *Oeuvres*, vol. VI, p. 530; Michael Kennedy, *The Jacobin Clubs in the French Revolution: The Middle Years*, Princeton, N.J.: Princeton University Press, 1988, pp. 115–17.
13. On the rampant forging of *assignats*, see Jean Bouchary, *Les Faux-monnayeurs sous la Révolution française*, Paris: M. Rivière et Cie, 1946.
14. Tallett, 'Robespierre and Religion', pp. 98–99. Robespierre's views were in line with the broad attitudes of 'Jansenists': see William Doyle, *Jansenism: Catholic Resistance to Authority from the Reformation to the French Revolution*, Basingstoke: Macmillan, 2000, ch. 8.
15. *Oeuvres*, vol. III, pp. 81–82; vol. VI, pp. 397–99; Dale Van Kley, *The Religious Origins of the French Revolution: From Calvin to the Civil Constitution, 1560–1791*, New Haven, CT, & London: Yale University Press, 1996, pp. 360–61, 374; Thompson, *Robespierre*, pp. 83–87.
16. *Oeuvres*, vol. 1, p. 222; Bouloiseau, 'Robespierre vu par les journaux satiriques', pp. 7–8; Abbé François-Xavier de Montesquiou-Fezensac, *Adresse aux provinces, ou examen des opérations de l'Assemblée Nationale*, n.p., n.l. 1790.
17. Thompson, *Robespierre*, pp. 91–92.
18. *Oeuvres*, vol. III, pp. 83–84; Claretie, *Camille Desmoulins and his Wife*, p. 14; Bertaud, *Camille et Lucile Desmoulins*, pp. 101–2. Desmoulins had in fact been three years behind Robespierre at school.

19. *Oeuvres*, vol. III, p. 100; Claretie, *Camille Desmoulins and his Wife*, pp. 137–40. On the marriage, see Bertaud, *Camille et Lucile Desmoulins*, ch. 4.

20. Pierre Villiers, *Souvenirs d'un déporté*, Paris: chez l'Auteur, an X [1802], pp. 1–2. Villiers was wounded defending the Tuileries in August 1792. He published his memoirs after he had been deported following the coup of 18 Fructidor Year V. There is disagreement as to whether Villiers actually lived with Robespierre: see Fleischmann, *Robespierre and the Women He Loved*, pp. 84–85; Charlotte Robespierre, *Mémoires*, p. 48; René Garmy, 'Aux origines de la légende anti-robespierriste: Pierre Villiers et Robespierre', in Albert Soboul (ed.), *Actes du colloque Robespierre. XIIe congrès international des sciences historiques*, Paris: Société des études Robespierristes, 1967, pp. 19–33. Villiers claimed that 'nearly every night Robespierre bathed his pillow in blood': for Artarit, *Robespierre*, p. 66, the blood suggests a 'psychosomatic epistaxis with a strong female sexual element'.

21. The letters are reproduced in Fleischmann, *Robespierre and the Women He Loved*, pp. 194–203, who is dismissive of the possibility that Robespierre might have been attracted to an 'old woman' (of thirty-eight years), surrounded as he was by 'fresh young girls'. Albert Mathiez made the revealing statement that 'women felt him different from other men, for they knew instinctively that Robespierre would give himself *completely*, when the day came that he gave himself': *Girondins et Montagnards*, Paris: Firmin-Didot, 1930, p. 26.

22. Norman Hampson, *Saint-Just*, Oxford: Blackwell, 1991, p. 28 and ch. 2; Jacques Guilhaumou, *La Langue politique et la Révolution française: de l'événement à la raison linguistique*, Paris: Méridiens Klincksieck, 1989, pp. 65–69; Marisa Linton, 'The Man of Virtue: The Role of Antiquity in the Political Trajectory of L. A. Saint-Just', *FH*, 24 (2010), pp. 393–419.

23. Geoffrey Cubitt, 'Robespierre and Conspiracy Theories', in Haydon and Doyle (eds), *Robespierre*, 75; *Oeuvres*, vol. VI, pp. 184, 230; Bouloiseau, 'Robespierre vu par les journaux satiriques'.

24. The discourse of conspiracy has been a particular focus of recent scholarship: see especially Campbell, Kaiser and Linton (eds), *Conspiracy in the French Revolution*; Lynn Hunt, *Politics, Culture, and Class in the French Revolution*, Berkeley, CA: University of California Press, 1984, pp. 39–44; Timothy Tackett, 'Conspiracy Obsession in a Time of Revolution: French Elites and the Origins of the Terror, 1789–1792', *AHR*, 105 (2000), pp. 691–713; Patrice Gueniffey, *La Politique de la Terreur: essai sur la violence révolutionnaire*, Paris: Fayard, 2000.

25. *Ami du Roi*, 22 March 1791, cited in J. Gilchrist and W. J. Murray (eds), *The Press in the French Revolution*, Melbourne & London: F. W. Cheshire & Ginn and Co., 1971; Bouloiseau, 'Robespierre vu par les journaux satiriques', pp. 7–8.

26. Peter R. Campbell, 'Conspiracy and Political Practice from the *ancien régime* to the French Revolution', in Barry Coward and Julian Swann (eds), *Conspiracy in Early Modern Europe*, Aldershot, Hants, & Burlington, VT: Ashgate, 2004, pp. 197–212. This concern with the machinations of enemies was not unique to France or the French Revolution: see the classic studies by Bernard Bailyn, *The Ideological Origins of the American Revolution*, Cambridge, MA: Harvard University Press, 1967; and Daniel Field, *Rebels in the Name of the Tsar*, Boston: Houghton Mifflin, 1976.

27. The vituperative attacks on Marie-Antoinette are studied by Lynn Hunt, *The Family Romance of the French Revolution*, Berkeley, CA: University of California Press, 1992; Chantal Thomas, *The Wicked Queen: The Origins of the Myth of Marie-Antoinette*, translated by Julie Rose, New York: Zone Books, 1999; and Thomas E. Kaiser, 'Who's Afraid of Marie-Antoinette? Diplomacy, Austrophobia and the Queen', *FH*, 14 (2000), pp. 241–71. Robespierre seemed immune to such a phobia.

28. *Oeuvres*, vol. VII, pp. 16–17, 346–50, 361–62; Yves Bénot, 'Robespierre, les colonies et l'esclavage', in Jessenne et al. (eds), *Robespierre*, pp. 409–21; Lemay and Patrick, *Revolutionaries at Work*, pp. 102–5; Florence Gauthier, *L'Aristocratie de l'épiderme. Le Combat de la Société des citoyens de couleur, 1789–1791*, Paris: CNRS, 2007. The St-Domingue colonists and their parliamentary allies waged a successful campaign to force the Assembly to repeal the measure, on 24 September 1791. On 24 March 1792, however, this in turn was repealed. By then, St-Domingue was engaged in full-scale civil war.

29. *Oeuvres*, vol. VII, pp. 368–71. See the debate about the import of Robespierre's intervention: Florence Gauthier (ed.), *Périssent les colonies plutôt qu'un principe! Contributions à l'histoire de l'abolition de l'esclavage, 1789–1804*, Paris: Société des études Robespierristes, 2002, pp. 96–97; Frédéric Régent, *La France et ses esclaves. De la colonisation aux abolitions (1620–1848)*, Paris: Grasset, 2007, p. 226.

30. Marcel Dorigny and Bernard Gainot, *La Société des amis des noirs, 1788–1799: contribution à l'histoire de l'abolition de l'esclavage*, Paris: Éditions UNESCO, 1998, pp. 252–53; Gilchrist and Murray (eds), *The Press in the French Revolution*, pp. 259–60.

31. *Oeuvres*, vol. VI, pp. 429–31.

32. *Oeuvres*, vol. VII, pp. 46–48, 63–65, 129–31; Serge Aberdam, 'Curé rouge ou légende noire? Jean-François Carion: une figure emblématique de prêtre révolutionnaire en Sud-Morvan', *AHRF*, 274 (1988), pp. 366–408. See *Oeuvres*, vol. VII, pp. 135–39, for Robespierre's concern at the severe measures against rioters in Douai who had hanged a national guardsman and a merchant on 14 March. In November 1790 one of Robespierre's former fellow students at Louis-le-Grand, Dupont du Tertre, was appointed France's first Minister of Justice.

33. *Oeuvres*, vol. VII, pp. 181–82, 187; Bernard Schnapper, 'Liberté, égalité, autorité: la famille devant les assemblées révolutionnaires (1790–1800)', in Pierre Lenoël and Marie-Françoise Lévy (eds), *L'Enfant, la famille et la Révolution française*, Paris: Olivier Orban, 1990, pp. 325–40; Gross, 'Robespierre et l'impôt progressif', pp. 253–97; Suzanne Desan, *The Family on Trial in Revolutionary France*, Berkeley, CA, & London: University of California Press, 2004, pp. 61, 147. In general, on gender roles and political rights, see Anne Verjus, *Le Cens de la famille: les femmes et le vote, 1789–1848*, Paris: Belin, 2002, and *Le Bon Mari: une histoire politique des hommes et des femmes à l'époque révolutionnaire*, Paris: Fayard, 2010.

34. *Oeuvres*, vol. VII, pp. 18–19, 85, 320–21, 542–43; Hugh Gough, *The Newspaper Press in the French Revolution*, Chicago: Dorsey Press, 1988, pp. 46–47; Lucien Jaume, *Le Discours jacobin et la démocratie*, Paris: Fayard, 1989, pp. 201–3; Jacob, *Robespierre vu par ses contemporains*, p. 78; Murray, *Right-Wing Press*, pp. 40–41, 262–63. Robespierre seems to have changed his mind on the security of the postal service after speaking on 27 July 1789 about the seizing of letters: Short, 'The Lantern and the Scaffold', p. 177; Shapiro, *Revolutionary Justice*, pp. 51–53.

35. *Oeuvres*, vol. VII, pp. 432–37.

36. *Oeuvres*, vol. VII, pp. 383–88. Barry M. Shapiro, 'Self-Sacrifice, Self-Interest, or Self-Defence? The Constituent Assembly and the "Self-Denying Ordinance" of May 1791', *FHS*, 25 (2002), pp. 625–56, argues that the deputies, including Robespierre, were exhibiting psychological projection of their own fears of inadequacy more than engaging in a statement of principles or factional self-interest. For Scurr, *Fatal Purity*, p. 137, this was an example of Robespierre's 'fatal purity' in clinging rigidly to his principles.

37. This has been well captured by Michael P. Fitzsimmons, *The Remaking of France: The National Assembly and the Constitution of 1791*, Cambridge & New York: Cambridge University Press, 1994.

38. *Oeuvres*, vol. III, pp. 105–6, 108–9; Jacob, *Robespierre vu par ses contemporains*, pp. 68–75. In general, see Stephen Clay, 'Vengeance, Justice and the Reactions in the Revolutionary Midi', *FH*, 23 (2009), pp. 22–46.

39. *Oeuvres*, vol. III, p. 109; Étienne Charavay (ed.), *Assemblée électorale de Paris*, vol. 1, Paris: D. Jouaust, Charles Noblet, Maison Quantin, 1890–1905, pp. 589–90, 601; Bouloiseau, 'Robespierre vu par les journaux satiriques', pp. 7–8; Jacob, *Robespierre vu par ses contemporains*, pp. 59–60.

40. *Oeuvres*, vol. III, pp. 109–13; vol. VII, p. 514.

41. On the flight and its repercussions, see Timothy Tackett, *When the King Took Flight*, Cambridge, MA: Harvard University Press, 2003.

42. *Oeuvres*, vol. VII, pp. 553–58; Parker, *Cult of Antiquity*, pp. 38–39, 43–45; Marisa Linton, 'Robespierre's Political Principles', p. 45.

43. Jacob, *Robespierre vu par ses contemporains*, p. 80; Plutarch, *Life of Lycurgus*, translated by John Dryden, Boston: Little, Brown, 1906; Gordon H. McNeil, 'Robespierre, Rousseau, and

Representation', in Richard Herr and Harold T. Parker (eds), *Ideas in History: Essays Presented to Louis Gottschalk by his Former Students*, Durham, N.C.: Duke University Press, 1965, pp. 135–56; Susan Maslan, *Revolutionary Acts: Theater, Democracy, and the French Revolution*, Baltimore, MD: Johns Hopkins University Press, 2005, ch. 3.

44. *Oeuvres*, vol. VII, pp. 591–94.
45. *Oeuvres*, vol. XI, pp. 339–76.
46. Edna Hindie Lemay, 'Robespierre et ses amis à la Constituante', in Jessenne et al. (eds), *Robespierre*, pp. 139–56. On the Feuillants split, see Kennedy, *The First Years*, ch. 15. An example of the reasons given for leaving the Jacobins is in Nicole Felkay and Hervé Favier (eds), *En prison sous la Terreur. Souvenirs de J.-B. Billecocq (1765–1829)*, Paris: Société des études Robespierristes, 1981, pp. 73–75.
47. Lenôtre, *Robespierre's Rise and Fall*, pp. 1–6; Thompson, *Robespierre*, pp. 177–84.
48. *The Correspondence of William Augustus Miles 1789–1817*, London: 1890, vol. I, p. 245.
49. Laura Auricchio, *Adélaïde Labille-Guiard: Artist in the Age of Revolution*, Los Angeles: J. Paul Getty Museum, 2009, pp. 77–79.
50. Jacob, *Robespierre vu par ses contemporains*, pp. 78–81. Oelsner figures prominently in Thomas P. Saine's discussion of German reactions to the French Revolution, *Black Bread–White Bread: German Intellectuals and the French Revolution*, Columbia, S.C.: Camden House, 1988.
51. Jacob, *Robespierre vu par ses contemporains*, pp. 82–84.
52. Thompson, *Robespierre*, pp. 167–68.
53. *Oeuvres*, vol. VII, pp. 754–59.
54. *Oeuvres*, vol. VII, pp. 268, 439; Jourdan, 'Robespierre and Revolutionary Heroism', pp. 56–57; Susan Carpenter Binkley, *The Concept of the Individual in Eighteenth-Century French Thought from the Enlightenment to the French Revolution*, Lewiston, N.Y., Queenstown, Ontario, & Lampeter, Wales: Edwin Mellen Press, 2007, pp. 76–84.
55. *Oeuvres*, vol. VII, pp. 754–59.
56. Tackett, *Becoming a Revolutionary*, pp. 226–34, 321, calculates that 336 of the 766 deputies (of a total of 1,315) who spoke did so only once or twice. Mirabeau's supposed quip is reported in Hamel, *Histoire de Robespierre*, vol. 1, pp. 396–97, but cf. Barbara Luttrell, *Mirabeau*, Carbondale & Edwardsville: Southern Illinois University Press, 1990, p. 237. It may have originated in Thomas Carlyle, *The French Revolution*, vol. I, *The Bastille*, chapter 1.6.II: 'The Constituent Assembly', 1837.
57. *Oeuvres*, vol. IV, Introduction, pp. 1–5; Lemay and Patrick, *Revolutionaries at Work*, p. 29; Kennedy, *The Jacobin Clubs: The Middle Years*, p. 8; Paul Friedland, *Political Actors: Representative Bodies and Theatricality in the Age of the French Revolution*, Ithaca, N.Y.: Cornell University Press, 2002, pp. 279–82.

Chapter 7 'Numerous and implacable enemies': Arras 1791

1. ARBR, *Bulletin*, 28; Walter, *Robespierre*, vol. 1, pp. 95–97, 148–50.
2. *Oeuvres*, vol. XI, pp. 281–97.
3. *Oeuvres*, vol. III, pp. 57–59, undated letter bearing the note 'received 9 November 1789'.
4. On the history of Arras in 1789–91, see Lecesne, *Arras*, vol. 1, chs 1–2.
5. Leuwers, Crépin and Rosselle, *Histoire des provinces françaises du nord*, pp. 29–36, 82–93; Nolibos, *Arras*, pp. 107–8; Leuwers, *Invention du barreau français*, pp. 249–52.
6. *Oeuvres*, vol. III, pp. 66–68.
7. *Oeuvres*, vol. III, pp. 74–83, esp. pp. 82–83; vol. XI, pp. 317–29, 330–36. See Bruno Decriem, '1790: l'affaire des impôts d'Artois' in ARBR, *Bulletin*, 8.
8. Yalom, *Blood Sisters*, p. 103; Hugh Gough, 'Robespierre and the Press', in Haydon and Doyle (eds), *Robespierre*, pp. 111–12; Frédéric Barbier, *Lumières du Nord. Imprimeurs, librairies et 'gens du livre' dans le Nord au XVIIIe siècle (1701–1789)*, Geneva: Droz, 2002, p. 384. Marchand emigrated in January 1792. Fouché later claimed that it was he who lent Robespierre money: *Memoirs*, vol. 1, London: H. S. Nichols, 1896, p. 10.
9. *Oeuvres*, vol. XI, pp. 451–56.

10. See Léon-Noël Berthe et al., *Villes et villages du Pas-de-Calais en 1790: 60 questions et leurs réponses*, vol. 1, *Districts d'Arras et de Bapaume*, Arras: Commission départementale d'histoire et d'archéologie du Pas-de-Calais, 1990; Wartelle, 'Les Communautés rurales du Pas-de-Calais', pp. 100–21.

11. See Jessenne, 'Les Enjeux artésiens', pp. 27–30; *Pouvoir au village*, ch. 1.

12. Leuwers, Crépin and Rosselle, *Histoire des provinces françaises du nord*, pp. 53–55, 80–81.

13. ARBR, *Bulletin*, 55; Leuwers, Crépin and Rosselle, *Histoire des provinces françaises du nord*, ch. 3.

14. *Oeuvres*, vol. III, p. 107; vol. VII, p. 623; Walter, *Robespierre*, vol. 1, p. 201.

15. Walter, *Robespierre*, vol. 1, p. 200.

16. The best sources for Robespierre's stay in Artois are Walter, *Robespierre*, vol. 1; Bruno Decriem, 'Maximilien Robespierre dans l'Artois révolutionnaire', ARBR, *Bulletin*, 5–7.

17. *Oeuvres*, vol. III, pp. 124–26.

18. Charlotte Robespierre, *Mémoires*, pp. 57–58; Jacob, *Robespierre vu par ses contemporains*, pp. 91–94.

19. Hervé Leuwers, 'Révolution constituante et société judiciaire. L'Exemple septentrional', *AHRF*, 350 (2007), pp. 27–47; Sueur, *Conseil provincial d'Artois*, pp. 310–46.

20. *Oeuvres*, vol. VIII, pp. 19–23.

21. *Oeuvres*, vol. VIII, p. 20.

22. Walter, *Robespierre*, vol. 1, p. 202; Auguste Joseph Paris, *La Terreur dans le Pas-de-Calais et dans le Nord: histoire de Joseph Le Bon et des tribunaux révolutionnaires d'Arras et de Cambrai*. Arras: Rousseau-Leroy, 1864, p. 39. Lebon, born in Arras in 1765, already knew Robespierre well enough in 1790 to address him with the familiar 'tu': *Papiers inédits trouvés chez Robespierre, Saint-Just, Payan, etc. supprimés ou omis par Courtois, précédés du rapport de ce député à la Convention nationale*, 3 vols, Geneva: Mégariotis Reprints, 1978, vol. 3, pp. 237–41.

23. Charlotte Robespierre, *Mémoires*, pp. 39, 58; Jacob, *Robespierre vu par ses contemporains*, p. 179.

24. Thompson, *Robespierre*, p. 9, and Blum, *Rousseau and the Republic of Virtue*, p. 156, are of the opinion that the piece dates from 1791; cf. Walter, *Robespierre*, vol. 1, p. 76, who dates it to early 1789.

25. *Oeuvres*, vol. 1, pp. 211–12; Robisco, 'Le Mythe de la rencontre avec Rousseau'. Note Norman Hampson's acerbic comments about Robespierre's obsession with the ideas of Rousseau in *Will and Circumstance*, p. 145; idem, 'Je veux suivre sa trace vénérée: Robespierre as Reincarnation of Rousseau', in Jourdan (ed.), *Robespierre—figure-réputation*, p. 36.

26. Blum, *Rousseau and the Republic of Virtue*, pp. 153–62.

27. Albert Mathiez, 'Babeuf et Robespierre', *Études sur Robespierre (1758–1794)*, Paris: Éditions sociales, 1958, pp. 237–50.

28. *Oeuvres*, vol. III, p. 127.

29. *Oeuvres*, vol. III, p. 126.

30. Georges Sangnier, *Les Émigrés du Pas-de-Calais pendant la Révolution*, Paris: Blangermont, 1959, pp. 29–33.

31. The farmer deputies who had lived with Robespierre in Versailles were already distant: Alexandre Petit would later emigrate, and Charles Payen was guillotined in June 1794.

32. Jacob, *Robespierre vu par ses contemporains*, pp. 65–68; also in Fleischmann, *Robespierre and the Women he Loved*, pp. 172–78. This was one letter that Charlotte kept: Charlotte Robespierre, *Mémoires*, pp. 50–52. On Theizé, see Jeanne-Marie Phlipon Roland, *Private Memoirs of Madame Roland*, translated by Edward Gilpin Johnson, London: Grant Richards, 1901, p. 357.

33. *Oeuvres*, vol. III, pp. 129–30.

34. ARBR, *Bulletin*, 7, 56.

Chapter 8 'The Vengeance of the People': Paris 1791–92

1. *Oeuvres*, vol. III, pp. 130–31.

2. There is a rich recent literature on Haiti: see Robin Blackburn, 'Haiti, Slavery, and the Age of the Democratic Revolution', *William and Mary Quarterly*, 63 (2006), pp. 633–74; Laurent Dubois, *Avengers of the New World: The Story of the Haitian Revolution*, Cambridge, MA: Belknap Press of Harvard University, 2005; John D. Garrigus, *Before Haiti: Race and Citizenship in St-Domingue*, London: Palgrave Macmillan, 2006; Jeremy D. Popkin, *You Are All Free: The Haitian Revolution and the Abolition of Slavery*, Cambridge and New York: Cambridge University Press, 2010.

3. *Moniteur universel*, no. 313, 9 November 1791, vol. 10, p. 325; Michael Sydenham, *The Girondins*, London: Athlone Press, 1961, pp. 101–8; Tackett, 'Conspiracy Obsession in a Time of Revolution'; Munro Price, 'Mirabeau and the Court: Some New Evidence', *FHS*, 29 (2006), pp. 37–75; Olivier Blanc, *La Corruption sous la Terreur (1792–1794)*, Paris: Robert Laffont, 1992, ch. 4.

4. Aulard, *Société des Jacobins*, vol. 3, p. 266.

5. *Oeuvres*, vol. VIII, pp. 47–64. Note the comments of Alan Forrest, 'Robespierre, the War and its Organisation', in Haydon and Doyle (eds), *Robespierre*, pp. 128–30. For the debates on the origins of the war, see Thompson, *Robespierre*, pp. 202–26; Georges Michon, *Robespierre et la guerre révolutionnaire, 1791–1792*, Paris: M. Rivière, 1937; Kennedy, *The Jacobin Clubs: The Middle Years*, ch. 9; Jordan, *Robespierre*, ch. 5.

6. *Oeuvres*, vol. VIII, pp. 74–93.

7. *Oeuvres*, vol. VIII, pp. 178–80. See Maxime Rosso, 'Les Réminiscences spartiates dans les discours et la politique de Robespierre de 1789 à Thermidor', *AHRF*, 349 (2007), pp. 51–77.

8. *Oeuvres*, vol. VIII, pp. 74–93.

9. *Oeuvres*, vol. III, pp. 135–36; vol. VIII, p. 131.

10. *Oeuvres*, vol. VIII, pp. 137–50, 210–12, 229–37.

11. Jacob, *Robespierre vu par ses contemporains*, p. 96; Thompson, *Robespierre*, pp. 213–14.

12. Fleischmann, *Robespierre and the Women He Loved*, pp. 203–09. Chalabre's letters are also in *Papiers inédits trouvés chez Robespierre*, vol. 1, pp. 171–78.

13. Sydenham, *Girondins*, pp. 86–91.

14. *Oeuvres*, vol. III, pp. 139, 144; vol. IV, pp. 12–13; vol. VIII, pp. 193–98; Melvin Edelstein, '*La Feuille villageoise*': communication et modernisation dans les régions rurales pendant la Révolution, Paris: Bibliothèque nationale, 1977, p. 53.

15. *Oeuvres*, vol. VIII, pp. 250–53; Warren Roberts, *Jacques-Louis David and Jean-Louis Prieur, Revolutionary Artists: The Public, the Populace, and Images of the French Revolution*, Albany, N.Y.: State University of New York Press, 2000, pp. 139–44.

16. Saint-Paulien, *Robespierre, ou les dangers de la vertu, 1789–1799*, Paris: Table Ronde, 1984, p. 7; *Oeuvres*, vol. VIII, pp. 311, 315; Jourdan, 'Robespierre and Revolutionary Heroism', p. 71. Jaume, *Discours jacobin*, pp. 68–71, 80–83. Cf. the argument of Pierre Rosanvallon, *Democracy Past and Future*, New York: Columbia University Press, 2006, that Rousseauan revolutionary democracy—identifying a single general will and mistrusting anything that smacked of 'party' or 'faction'—was inherently totalitarian.

17. *Oeuvres*, vol. IV, pp. 202–3; Jacob, *Robespierre vu par ses contemporains*, p. 105, fn. 1. Olivier Coquard, 'Marat et Robespierre: la rencontre de deux politiques révolutionnaires', in Jessenne et al. (eds), *Robespierre*, pp. 157–66. Marat was living further along the Rue St-Honoré with the Évrard sisters.

18. See *Oeuvres*, vol. IV, pp. 8–11; Hardman, *Robespierre*, p. 43; Jack R. Censer, 'Robespierre the Journalist', in Harvey Chisick (ed.), *The Press in the French Revolution*, Oxford: Voltaire Foundation, 1990, pp. 189–96; Michel Eude, 'La politique de Robespierre en 1792, d'après le *Défenseur de la constitution*', *AHRF*, 28 (1956), pp. 1–28. In all, its 12 numbers make up 594 pages from 17 May to 20 August 1792.

19. *Oeuvres*, vol. IV, pp. 83–84.

20. On the Simonneau killing and its wider context, see Sukla Sanyal, 'The 1792 Food Riot at Étampes and the French Revolution', *Studies in History*, 18 (2002), pp. 23–50; R. B. Rose, 'The "Red Scare" of the 1790s and the "Agrarian Law"', *P&P*, 103 (1984), pp. 113–30; David Hunt, 'The People and Pierre Dolivier: Popular Uprisings in the Seine-et-Oise Department,

1791–1792', *FHS*, 11 (1979), pp. 184–214; Maurice Dommanget, *1793: les Enragés contre la vie chère–les curés rouges, Jacques Roux–Pierre Dolivier*, Paris: Spartacus, 1976.

21. Anthony Crubaugh, *Balancing the Scales of Justice: Local Courts and Rural Society in Southwest France, 1750–1800*, University Park, PA: Pennsylvania University Press, 2001, pp. 55–56.

22. *Oeuvres*, vol. IV, pp. 109–36.

23. *Oeuvres*, vol. IV, pp. 144–49.

24. Alan Forrest, 'Robespierre, the War and its Organisation', p. 133; *Oeuvres*, vol. VIII, p. 101.

25. *Oeuvres*, vol. VIII, pp. 377–83; Thompson, *Robespierre*, pp. 246–47.

26. *Oeuvres*, vol. IV, pp. 165–89.

27. *Oeuvres*, vol. IV, pp. 225–42.

28. *Oeuvres*, vol. VIII, pp. 390–94.

29. *Oeuvres*, vol. VIII, p. 212; vol. XI, pp. 381–89.

30. The core concept of 'virtue' and its consequences for political action and strategy have been explored expertly by Marisa Linton: ' "Do You Believe That We're Conspirators?" Conspiracies Real and Imagined in Jacobin Politics, 1793–94', in Campbell, Kaiser and Linton (eds), *Conspiracy in the French Revolution*, pp. 144–45; idem, 'Ideas of the Future in the French Revolution', in Malcolm Crook, William Doyle and Alan Forrest (eds), *Enlightenment and Revolution: Essays in Honour of Norman Hampson*, Burlington, VT, & Aldershot: Ashgate, 2004, pp. 153–68; idem, *Politics of Virtue*; idem, 'Robespierre's Political Principles', esp. pp. 45–46.

31. *Oeuvres*, vol. IV, p. 9. See Raymonde Monnier, 'Républicanisme et Révolution française', *FHS*, 26 (2003), pp. 87–118. Robespierre's words sit oddly with the claim of Dan Edelstein, *The Terror of Natural Right: Republicanism, the Cult of Nature, and the French Revolution*, Chicago: University of Chicago Press, 2009, pp. 19, 249–56, that republicanism and 'terror' were intrinsic to Jacobinism.

32. *Oeuvres*, vol. IV, pp. 13, 23–24.

33. *Oeuvres*, vol. IV, pp. 317–33; vol. VIII, p. 408. See C. J. Mitchell, *The French Legislative Assembly of 1791*, Leiden: E. J. Brill, 1988, pp. 238–41 and ch. 15.

34. *Moniteur universel*, no. 216, 3 August 1792, vol. 13, pp. 305–6. In different ways, the potency of the counter-revolution is stressed in D. M. G. Sutherland, *The French Revolution and Empire: the Quest for a Civic Order*, Oxford: Blackwell, 2003, chs 4–6; Murray, *Right-Wing Press*, chs 9, 12.

35. *Oeuvres*, vol. III, p. 151.

36. *Oeuvres*, vol. IV, p. 336.

37. *Oeuvres*, vol. IV, p. 352 ; vol. VIII, pp. 427–28.

38. Raymonde Monnier, 'Robespierre et la Commune de Paris', in Jessenne et al. (eds), *Robespierre*, pp. 125–37; idem, *L'Espace public démocratique: essai sur l'opinion à Paris de la Révolution au Directoire*, Paris: Éditions Kimé, 1994, pp. 135–37; R. B. Rose, *Tribunes and Amazons: Men and Women of Revolutionary France 1789–1871*, Sydney: Macleay Press, 1998, ch. 12; McNeil, 'Robespierre, Rousseau, and Representation', pp. 135–56.

39. *Oeuvres*, vol. IV, pp. 352–59.

40. *Oeuvres*, vol. IV, pp. 360–66.

41. *Oeuvres*, vol. III, p. 153; vol. VIII, pp. 435–37.

42. J. M. Thompson (ed.), *English Witnesses of the French Revolution*, Oxford: Oxford University Press, 1938, pp. 180–81.

43. *Oeuvres*, vol. III, p. 152.

44. Fleischmann, *Robespierre and the Women He Loved*, pp. 179–82.

45. John Moore, *Journal of a Residence in France, from the Beginning of August to the Middle of December 1792*, vol. 3 of *The Works of John Moore, M.D. with Memoirs of his Life and Writings*, 7 vols, Edinburgh: Stirling and Slade, 1820, pp. 107–9, 135.

46. AN D XLII 5: a list in November 1792 detailed the deaths of 1,079 prisoners of a total 2,616. The standard work on the killings is Pierre Caron, *Les Massacres de septembre*, Paris: Maison du livre français, 1935; an excellent overview is Andress, *Terror*, ch. 4.

47. Cited in René Moulinas, *Les Massacres de la Glacière: Enquête sur un crime impuni, Avignon 16–17 octobre 1791*, Aix-en-Provence: Edisud, 2003, p. 175.

48. Jeanne-Marie Roland de la Platière, *Lettres de Madame Roland*, 2 vols, Paris: C. Perroud, 1900–2, vol. 2, pp. 434–35. For Ruth Scurr this was Robespierre's great compromise with 'the blood lust of the mob': *Fatal Purity*, pp. 200–1. John Hardman relied on the judgement of J. W. Croker, that Robespierre had orchestrated the massacres to kill the Brissotin leaders and to intimidate the electoral process: 'Robespierre', in *Essays on the Early Period of the French Revolution*, London: John Murray, 1857, p. 350. Dingli, *Robespierre*, pp. 272–73, states 'as a fact' that Robespierre sought to have Brissot arrested in September 1792, based on *Mémoires inédites de Pétion*, Paris: C. A. Dauban, 1866, pp. 53, 163. There are similar claims in Hardman, *Robespierre*, pp. 50–52, 56–57; Walter, *Robespierre*, vol. 1, pp. 338–53; Hampson, 'Robespierre and the Terror', p. 163; Sydenham, *Girondins*, pp. 117–18.

49. Andress, *Terror*, pp. 113–14; Édith Bernardin, *Jean-Marie Roland et le Ministère de l'Intérieur (1792–1793)*, Paris: Société des études Robespierristes, 1964, pp. 16–17; Jean Massin, *Robespierre*, Paris: Club français du livre, 1957, pp. 127–37, all argue that there is no incontrovertible evidence; what matters, of course, is the Brissotins' belief that Robespierre had tried to. Alphonse de Lamartine, *Histoire des Girondins*, 6 vols, Paris: Pagnerre, Hachette & Furne, 1860, Livre 25, IV, claimed that a confidant of Robespierre had personally confirmed his role, but provided no evidence for this.

50. Marcel Dorigny, 'Violence et Révolution: les Girondins et les massacres de septembre', in Albert Soboul (ed.), *Actes du colloque Girondins et Montagnards (Sorbonne, 14 décembre 1975)*, Paris: Société des études Robespierristes, 1980, pp. 102–20; Élisabeth and Robert Badinter, *Condorcet: un intellectuel en politique*, Paris: Fayard, 1988, ch. 8.

51. The massacres did not occur under anyone's orders. The fact that they were so widespread—there were more than sixty 'settlings of scores' by murder in thirty-two departments in September—suggests that they were a visceral, panic-stricken response to fear of slaughter by Brunswick's troops. Army volunteers were involved in twenty-nine of the killings. See Caron, *Massacres de septembre*; Paul Nicolle, 'Les Meurtres politiques d'août–septembre 1792 dans le département de l'Orne: étude critique', *AHRF*, 62 (1934), pp. 97–118; Mona Ozouf, 'Massacres de septembre: qui est responsable?', *Histoire*, 342 (2009), pp. 52–55.

52. Charlotte Robespierre, *Mémoires*, p. 49; Aulard, *Société des Jacobins*, vol. 4, pp. 250–68; Charavay (ed.), *Assemblée électorale de Paris*, vol. 3, *2 septembre 1792–17 frimaire an II*, pp. 98–111; Thompson, *Robespierre*, pp. 273–77. Massin, *Robespierre*, pp. 127–37; and Frédéric Bluche, *Septembre 1792: logiques d'un massacre*, Paris: Robert Laffont, 1986, both argue that it was Brissotin leaders themselves—especially Roland—who failed to act decisively.

53. See Arno J. Mayer, *The Furies: Violence and Terror in the French and Russian Revolutions*, Princeton, N.J.: Princeton University Press, 2000, pp. 182–83.

54. *Oeuvres*, vol. IX, pp. 90–91.

55. Louis Blanc, *Histoire de la Révolution française*, Paris: Librairie Internationale, Paris, 1869, vol. 2, pp. 206–7. Blanc believed Souberbielle but condemned Robespierre for not having tried to stop the killings. See Thompson, *Robespierre*, pp. 276–77.

56. Charavay (ed.), *Assemblée électorale de Paris*, vol. 3, *2 septembre 1792–17 frimaire an II*, pp. xxiii–lxv, 162, 612–13. On Méhée, see Blanc, *Corruption sous la Terreur*, pp. 120–23.

57. Lecesne, *Arras*, vol. 1, pp. 271–96; Hampson, *Saint-Just*, pp. 34–35.

58. See Jessenne, 'Les Enjeux artésiens', pp. 27–33; idem, *Pouvoir au village*. Examples of hostility towards prosperous farmers in Pas-de-Calais are in Georges Lefebvre, *Questions agraires au temps de la Terreur. Documents publiés et annotés*, La Roche-sur-Yon: Henri Potier, 1954, pp. 194–98.

59. Fleischmann, *Robespierre and the Women He Loved*, pp. 108–9. Hampson, 'Robespierre and the Terror', p. 163, assumes that Augustin's election was due to Maximilien's 'pulling of political strings'.

Chapter 9 'Did you want a Revolution without Revolution?': Paris 1792–93

1. There were no political parties in the modern sense during the Revolution, and the identification of political and social tendencies within the Convention has long aroused debate: see

Alison Patrick, *The Men of the First French Republic: Political Alignments in the National Convention of 1792*, Baltimore, MD: Johns Hopkins University Press, 1972; Sydenham, *Girondins*, for example, pp. 27–31, chs 8–9; and the forum in *FHS*, 15 (1988), pp. 506–48. On the conflict between 'Girondins' and 'Montagnards', see also Paul R. Hanson, *The Jacobin Republic under Fire: The Federalist Revolt in the French Revolution*, University Park, PA: Pennsylvania State University Press, 2003, ch. 2.

2. For example, *Oeuvres*, vol. V, *Lettres . . . à ses commettans*, nos 3 and 9; Gough, 'Robespierre and the Press', p. 116. Twenty-two numbers of *Lettres* were published between 30 September 1792 and mid-April 1793.

3. *Oeuvres*, vol. V, pp. 15–19. See Michel Vovelle, *Les Métamorphoses de la fête en Provence, de 1750 à 1820*, Paris: Flammarion, 1976, chs 7–8; Mona Ozouf, *Festivals and the French Revolution*, translated by Alan Sheridan, Cambridge, MA: Harvard University Press, 1988, ch. 4.

4. See the reflections of Norman Hampson, 'The Heavenly City of the French Revolutionaries', in Colin Lucas (ed.), *Rewriting the French Revolution*, Oxford: Clarendon Press, 1991, pp. 56–57.

5. *Oeuvres*, vol. VIII, pp. 233–34; Tallett, 'Robespierre and Religion', pp. 96–97; Sydenham, *Girondins*, pp. 190–92.

6. *Oeuvres*, vol. V, pp. 116–21.

7. *Oeuvres*, vol. IX, pp. 13–14; Dorigny, 'Violence et Révolution'. Cf. Sydenham, *Girondins*, ch. 6.

8. *Oeuvres*, vol. IX, pp. 16–22; 31–40; Jacob, *Robespierre vu par ses contemporains*, p. 123. On the divided response of provincial Jacobin Clubs, see Kennedy, *The Jacobin Clubs: The Middle Years*, pp. 302–07.

9. David P. Jordan, *The King's Trial: The French Revolution vs. Louis XVI*, Berkeley, CA: University of California Press, 1979, pp. 53–54; William Wordsworth, *The Complete Poetical Works*, London: Macmillian, 1888, 'The Prelude', Book 10, lines 99–102. John Moore was also there: Thompson (ed.), *English Witnesses*, pp. 210–13.

10. *Oeuvres*, vol. IX, pp. 62–65; Jean-Baptiste Louvet de Couvray, *Accusation contre M. Robespierre*, Paris: Imprimerie nationale, 1792. See Scurr, *Fatal Purity*, pp. 213–17.

11. Jean-Paul Bertaud, *The Army of the French Revolution: From Citizen-Soldiers to Instrument of Power*, translated by R. R. Palmer, Princeton, N.J.: Princeton University Press, 1988, pp. 85–86; Thompson, *Robespierre*, p. 285.

12. *Oeuvres*, vol. IX, pp. 77–78, 86–91. By 10 April 1793 the September massacres had become 'salutaires et actes de bienfaisance': *Oeuvres*, vol. V, p. 322. Note the comments of Bronislaw Baczko, 'The Terror before the Terror? Conditions of Possibility, Logic of Realization', in Keith Michael Baker (ed.), *The French Revolution and the Creation of Modern Political Culture*, vol. 4, *The Terror*, Oxford: Pergamon Press, 1994, p. 30.

13. *Oeuvres*, vol. IX, p. 78; Olympe de Gouges, *Écrits politiques 1792–1793*, Paris: Côté femmes, 1993, pp. 164–73.

14. Jacob, *Robespierre vu par ses contemporains*, p. 126; Marc Bouloiseau, 'Robespierre d'après les journaux girondins', in *Actes du colloque Robespierre. XIIe Congrès international des Sciences historiques*, Paris: Société des études Robespierristes, 1967, pp. 12–13. A miscellany of hostile views of Robespierre's personal life and relations with women is in Dingli, *Robespierre*, pp. 431–48.

15. Moore, *Journal of a Residence in France*, pp. 150, 330, 369; Thompson (ed.), *English Witnesses*, p. 206; Jean-Baptiste Louvet de Couvray, *À M. Robespierre et à ses royalistes, etc.* Paris: Imprimerie du Cercle social, 1792, esp. pp. 9, 13, 21, 31, 34, 47, 50–51.

16. On Roland's propaganda war, see Bernardin, *Jean-Marie Roland*, pp. 387, 515–19; Gough, *Newspaper Press*, pp. 90–92; Kennedy, *The Jacobin Clubs: The Middle Years*, pp. 302–3, Appendix F.

17. AN F13 281A. Duplay was one of about fifteen tradesmen thus contracted, and received 22,460 *livres*.

18. AN W 501; Fleischmann, *Robespierre and the Women He Loved*, pp. 144, 163–64; Stéfane-Pol [Paul Coutant], *Autour de Robespierre: le conventionnel Le Bas, d'après des documents inédits et les mémoires de sa veuve*, Paris: E. Flammarion, 1901, ch. 5, p. 107; Thompson, *Robespierre*, pp. 177–87; Hamel, *Histoire de Robespierre*, vol. 3, pp. 281–99; Richard Cobb, *Paris and its Provinces 1792–1802*, London: Oxford University Press, 1975, pp. 134–35. Brount may well have been the dog Mlle Duhay had raised for him in Béthune.

19. Charlotte Robespierre, *Mémoires*, pp. 52–56. Fleischmann, *Robespierre and the Women He Loved*, pp. 108–9.

20. Sabine Dupuy, 'Du parrainage d'un enfant du peuple aux conciliabules de Charenton: itinéraire d'une amitié chez Robespierre', in Jessenne et al. (eds), *Robespierre*, pp. 117–24.

21. Fleischmann, *Robespierre and the Women He Loved*, p. 133. On the precise layout of the Duplay house, see Victorien Sardou, Preface to Stéfane-Pol, *Autour de Robespierre*. Cf. Hamel, *Histoire de Robespierre*, vol. 3, pp. 281–99. On the decor, see, for example, Scurr, *Fatal Purity*, pp. 10, 207, and Hardman, *Robespierre*, p. 34. Scurr makes the equally unlikely claim that Louis XVI read 250 books during his five months in prison and translated an entire volume from English, while finding time to teach his son Latin and geography and devise games for him. Paul Barras, with every reason to tarnish Robespierre's image, later recalled in detail a visit that he and Fouché had made to his rooms, without mentioning busts: *Memoirs*, translated by Charles E. Roche, 4 vols, London: Osgood, McIlvaine, 1895, vol. 1, pp. 181–87. Nor did those who later searched Robespierre's rooms: AN F7/4774/94—dossier Maximilien Robespierre.

22. *Oeuvres*, vol. III, pp. 155–57; vol. IX, pp. 142–45. Robespierre also paid homage to Algernon Sidney.

23. Jacob, *Robespierre vu par ses contemporains*, p. 127.

24. *Oeuvres*, vol. V, pp. 97–115, 140–59.

25. Martin Nadeau, 'La Politique culturelle de l'an II: les infortunes de la propagande révolutionnaire au théâtre', *AHRF*, 327 (2002), pp. 57–74; Maslan, *Revolutionary Acts*, pp. 61–64.

26. *Oeuvres*, vol. IX, pp. 120–30; On the trial in general, see Jordan, *The King's Trial*; Patrick, *Men of the First French Republic*.

27. Cf. Edelstein, *The Terror of Natural Right*, ch. 3.

28. *Oeuvres*, vol. III, p. 159; vol. V, pp. 189–204; McNeil, 'Robespierre, Rousseau, and Representation'.

29. Rose, *Tribunes and Amazons*, p. 211; *Oeuvres*, vol. IX, pp. 212–15.

30. *Oeuvres*, vol. IX, pp. 228–29.

31. *Louis XVI tragédie en vers et en cinq actes. En Allemagne, mars 1793*, Act 1; Bouloiseau, 'Robespierre vu par les journaux satiriques', pp. 7–8. On Fauchet, see Jules Charrier, *Claude Fauchet, évêque constitutionnel du Calvados*, Paris: Honoré Champion, 1909, vol. 2, pp. 196–98, 232.

32. R. R. Palmer (ed.). *From Jacobin to Liberal: Marc-Antoine Jullien, 1775–1848*, Princeton, N.J.: Princeton University Press, 1993, p. 28.

33. *Oeuvres*, vol. V, pp. 243–64; Hamel, *Histoire de Robespierre*, vol. 2, p. 598.

34. *Oeuvres*, vol. V, pp. 83, 86; vol. IX, pp. 106–18.

35. Florence Gauthier, 'Robespierre critique de l'économie politique tyrannique et théoricien de l'économie politique populaire', in Jessenne et al. (eds), *Robespierre*, pp. 235–43.

36. *Oeuvres*, vol. IX, pp. 274–75, 286–87. See William H. Sewell, 'The Sans-Culotte Rhetoric of Subsistence', in Baker, *Terror*, pp. 265–67; Haim Burstin, *Une Révolution à l'oeuvre: le Faubourg Saint-Marcel (1789–1794)*, Seyssel: Champ Vallon, 2005, pp. 778–80.

37. *Oeuvres*, vol. V, pp. 345–46.

38. *Oeuvres*, vol. V, pp. 75–77; vol. IX, pp. 295–99, 327; Gough, 'Robespierre and the Press', pp. 124–26. In the heat of the struggle Robespierre supported the silencing of 'perverting' journalists: *Oeuvres*, vol. IX, p. 490. See vol. IX, pp. 157, 430, for other references to his 'martyrdom'.

39. *Oeuvres*, vol. IX, pp. 307–17, 332–33.

40. *Oeuvres*, vol. IX, pp. 376–409; Forrest, 'Robespierre: la guerre et les soldats'; Thompson, *Robespierre and the French Revolution*, pp. 95–96.

41. Robert Allen, *Les Tribunaux criminels sous la Révolution et l'Empire, 1792–1811*, translated by James Steven Bryant, Rennes: Presses universitaires de Rennes, 2005.

42. The many thousands of cases that came before the Committee of General Security in 1792–95 are in the 348 boxes held in AN F7 4577–4775. On the response to the military crisis, see Howard G. Brown, *War, Revolution, and the Bureaucratic State: Politics and Army Administration in France, 1791–1799*, Oxford: Clarendon Press, 1995, ch. 3.

43. An excellent summary of the origins and outbreak of the insurrection is Roger Dupuy, *La République jacobine. Terreur, guerre et gouvernement révolutionnaire*. Paris: Éditions du Seuil, 2005, chs 3–4.

44. *Oeuvres*, vol. IX, pp. 487–94. See, too, vol. IX, pp. 513–15.

45. Marc Bouloiseau, *The Jacobin Republic 1792–1794*, translated by Jonathan Mandelbaum, Cambridge & Paris: Cambridge University Press and Éditions de la Maison des Sciences de l'Homme, 1983, p. 64.

46. Kennedy, *The Jacobin Clubs: The Middle Years*, pp. 378–81; Françoise Brunel, 'Les députés montagnards', in Soboul (ed.), *Girondins et Montagnards*, Appendix; Patrick, *Men of the First French Republic*.

47. *Oeuvres*, vol. V, pp. 360–63; vol. IX, pp. 455–56. See Thompson, *Robespierre*, pp. 351–66; Rapport, 'Robespierre and the Universal Rights of Man', pp. 321–22; Jean-Louis Matharan, 'Salut public et sentiment national', in Jessenne et al. (eds), *Robespierre*, pp. 337–47.

48. *Oeuvres*, vol. IX, pp. 459–62. See the excellent analysis by Jean-Pierre Gross, *Fair Shares for All: Jacobin Egalitarianism in Practice*, Cambridge & New York: Cambridge University Press, 1997; Françoise Theuriot, 'La Conception robespierriste du bonheur', *AHRF*, 192 (1968), pp. 207–26; Jean-Pierre Jessenne, 'The Land: Redefinition of the Rural Community', in Baker, *Terror*, ch. 13; Rosso, 'Réminiscences spartiates'; Mossé, *L'Antiquité dans la Révolution française*, ch. 4; Rose, 'The "Agrarian Law"'. The classic Marxist interpretation highlights more fundamental differences between the social programme of Robespierre and the *sans-culottes*: see, for example, Albert Soboul, 'Robespierre and the Popular Movement of 1793–4', *P&P*, 5 (1954), pp. 54–70.

49. Maslan, *Revolutionary Acts*, ch. 3; Friedland, *Political Actors*, pp. 283–84; *Oeuvres*, vol. IX, pp. 502–3. He made a similar point in December 1792: *Oeuvres*, vol. V, p. 129.

50. *Oeuvres*, vol. IX, pp. 495–510.

51. *Oeuvres*, vol. III, pp. 167–68. A banker and Jacobin, Aigoin gave his son the names Guillaume-August Maximilien Robespierre: Albert Mathiez, *The Fall of Robespierre, and Other Essays*, New York: A. M. Kelley, 1968, p. 44.

52. *Oeuvres*, vol. IX, pp. 416–21, 433–34. Robespierre decided against joining Desmoulins and fifty other Montagnards who openly expressed support for Marat, earning him a later rebuke that he was jealous of Marat's notoriety: Coquard, 'Marat et Robespierre', pp. 164–65.

53. *Oeuvres*, vol. V, pp. 169–70.

54. See the police reports in AN AF IV 1470. There is a lacuna 15 May–7 June.

55. *Oeuvres*, vol. IX, pp. 524–27; R. B. Rose, *The Enragés: Socialists of the French Revolution?*, Melbourne: Melbourne University Press, 1965, pp. 22–24.

56. *Oeuvres*, vol IX, pp. 370–71, 526, 541; Monnier, 'Robespierre et la Commune', pp. 134–37; Friedland, *Political Actors*, pp. 282–87; Morris Slavin, 'Robespierre and the Insurrection of 31 May–2 June 1793', in Haydon and Doyle (eds), *Robespierre*, pp. 141–43; *The Making of an Insurrection: Parisian Sections and the Gironde*, Cambridge, MA, & London: Harvard University Press, 1986, esp. pp. 21–22.

57. *Oeuvres*, vol. IX, pp. 539–41.

58. *Oeuvres*, vol. IX, pp. 544–47, 554–55.

59. See Hanson, *Jacobin Republic under Fire*, ch. 3; Bette W. Oliver, *Orphans on the Earth: Girondin Fugitives from the Terror, 1793–1794*, Lanham, MD: Lexington Books, 2009.

60. *Oeuvres*, vol. IX, p. 606.

61. *Oeuvres*, vol. IX, pp. 612–15. See Colin Lucas, 'Revolutionary Violence, the People and the Terror', in Baker, *Terror*, ch. 4; Hampson, *Will and Circumstance*, pp. 229–37; Jaume, *Discours jacobin*, Part 1, ch. 3.

62. *Oeuvres*, vol. IX, pp. 501–2, 566. See Anne Sa'adah, *The Shaping of Liberal Politics in Revolutionary France: A Comparative Perspective*, Princeton, N.J.: Princeton University Press, 1990, pp. 190–93; Pierangelo Catalano, ' "Peuple" et "citoyens" de Rousseau à Robespierre: racines romaines du concept démocratique de "République" ', in Michel Vovelle (ed.), *Révolution et République: l'exception française*, Paris: Éditions Kimé, 1994, pp. 27–36.

Chapter 10 'A complete regeneration': Paris, July–December 1793

1. *Oeuvres*, vol. IX, p. 553; Thompson, *Robespierre and the French Revolution*, pp. 78–80; *Papiers inédits trouvés chez Robespierre*, vol. 2, pp. 13–16.
2. *Oeuvres*, vol. X, p. 9.
3. *Oeuvres*, vol. X, p. 76.
4. Thompson, *Robespierre*, pp. 384–90; Palmer, *Twelve Who Ruled*, ch. 3; Bernard Gainot, *Dictionnaire des membres du Comité de salut public: dictionnaire analytique, biographique et comparé des 62 membres du Comité de salut public*, Paris: Tallandier, 1990. Hérault de Séchelles resigned on 29 December.
5. AN F7 4432, plaque 2; Raymonde Monnier, 'Les Sociétés populaires dans le département de Paris sous la Révolution', *AHRF*, 278 (1989), p. 371; Fleischmann, *Robespierre and the Women He Loved*, p. 101; Stéfane-Pol, *Autour de Robespierre*, p. 104; Jacob, *Robespierre vu par ses contemporains*, pp. 215–19; Yalom, *Blood Sisters*, pp. 115–25. The Duplays were later guarded about the nature of their conversations with Robespierre: AN W 79, liasse 23.
6. Gallo, *Robespierre*, pp. 62, 254.
7. Barras, *Memoirs*, vol. 1, p. 191; *Papiers inédits trouvés chez Robespierre*, vol. 1, pp. 247–49, 253–54, 333–34; vol. 2, p. 261; vol. 3, pp. 3–55, 237–41; *Oeuvres*, vol. III, passim.
8. Charlotte Robespierre, *Mémoires*, ch. IV. A generous view of Augustin's behaviour is presented by Sergio Luzzatto, *Bonbon Robespierre. La terreur à visage humain*, translated from the Italian by Simone Carpentari Messina, Paris: Arléa, 2010.
9. Nolibos, *Arras*, pp. 109–10; *Oeuvres*, vol. I, p. 27; vol. III, tome 2, pp. 83–85. In general on 1792–94, see Leuwers, Crépin and Rosselle, *Histoire des provinces françaises du nord*, ch. 4; Ivan Gobry, *Joseph Lebon: la Terreur dans le nord de la France*, Paris: Mercure de France, 1991, chs 1–3.
10. Serge Aberdam, 'Politiques agraires, questions agraires, Terreur et loi agraire', in Michel Biard (ed.), *Les Politiques de la Terreur, 1793–1794: actes du colloque international de Rouen, 11–13 janvier 2007*, Rennes: Presses Universitaires de Rennes; Paris: Société des études Robespierristes, 2008, pp. 291–306. Robespierre was of two minds in the heated debate about the desirability of draining fish ponds to increase crop production: Reynald Abad, *La Conjuration contre les carpes. Enquête sur les origines du décret de dessèchement des étangs du 14 frimaire an II*, Paris: Fayard, 2006, p. 164; *Papiers inédits trouvés chez Robespierre*, vol. 2, p. 19.
11. All secondary colleges in Paris had been closed with the exception of Louis-le-Grand (from September 1792 known as the College of Equality (Collège de l'Égalité)): Palmer, *School of the French Revolution*, pp. 7, 11, 22, 33–34.
12. *Oeuvres*, vol. X, pp. 10–12; R. R. Palmer, *The Improvement of Humanity: Education and the French Revolution*, Princeton, N.J.: Princeton University Press, 1985, pp. 137–42; Jean Bloch, *Rousseauism and Education in Eighteenth-Century France*, Oxford: Voltaire Foundation, 1995, ch. 8.
13. *Oeuvres*, vol. X, pp. 35–42. See Rosso, 'Réminiscences spartiates', pp. 69–76; Wilda Anderson, 'Régénérer la nation: les enfants terrorisés de la Révolution', *MLN*, 117 (2002), pp. 698–709.
14. *Oeuvres*, vol. X, pp. 69–70; *Moniteur Universel*, no. 91, 21 December 1793, vol. 19, 6; Dominique Julia, *Les Trois Couleurs du tableau noir. La Révolution*, Paris: Éditions Belin, 1981, pp. 122–23.
15. *Oeuvres*, vol. X, pp. 292–93; Jourdan, 'Robespierre and Revolutionary Heroism', pp. 63–67; Rosso, 'Réminiscences spartiates', pp. 63–64.

16. See the prospectus of the *Feuille du salut public*, the Committee's mouthpiece, cited by James A. Leith, 'The Terror: Adding the Cultural Dimension', *Canadian Journal of History/Annales canadiennes d'histoire*, 32 (1997), pp. 315–37.

17. Robespierre does not seem to have been enthusiastic about either the new calendar or the purge of Christian names.

18. Palmer, *Twelve Who Ruled*, p. 109. On the Committee's preoccupation with war, see the key archival series AN AF II 20–417, AF I* 1–305 and F7* 1–103: approximately 80 per cent of these vast collections directly concern the war. There are interesting comments about Robespierre's lack of expertise in Simon Duplay's interrogation in December 1794: W 79, liasse 23.

19. *Oeuvres*, vol. V, pp. 282, 295; vol. VII, p. 263. The evidence suggests that a critical dimension of the armies' successes was precisely this sense of patriotism: Alan Forrest, *Soldiers of the French Revolution*, Durham, N. C.; Duke University Press, 1990, pp. 132–40; idem, 'Robespierre, the War and its Organisation', pp. 127–40; Bertaud, *Army of the French Revolution*.

20. See *Oeuvres*, vol. III; AN F7 4433, plaque 2. The correspondence is well summarized in Thompson, *Robespierre*, pp. 414–24.

21. AN F7 4775/8–dossier Rouvet.

22. *Oeuvres*, vol. X, p. 88. See, for example, David A. Bell, *The First Total War: Napoleon's Europe and the Birth of Warfare as We Know It*, Boston: Houghton Mifflin; London: Bloomsbury, 2007; Jean-Yves Guiomar, *L'Invention de la guerre totale: XVIIIe–XXe siècle*, Paris: Le Félin, 2004. Robespierre's use of 'extermination'—a common term on all sides during these years—enables Reynald Secher to accuse him of 'genocide': *A French Genocide: The Vendée*, translated by George Holoch, Notre Dame, IN: University of Notre Dame Press, 2003, pp. 249–50. Cf. Sutherland, *French Revolution and Empire*, pp. 223–25.

23. On the structure and nature of the Terror, one may compare Martin, *Violence et Révolution*, with, for example, the contributions to the special issue edited by Antoine de Baecque of *Annales*, July 2002; Sutherland, *French Revolution and Empire*, chs 6–7; and Gueniffey, *Politique de la Terreur*.

24. See Jacques Guilhaumou, 'Fragments of a Discourse of Denunciation (1789–1794)', in Baker, *Terror*, p. 147; Martin, *Violence et Révolution*; Dupuy, *République jacobine*, ch. 6; Michel Biard and Christine Peyrard, 'Les Rouages de la Terreur', in Biard (ed.), *Politiques de la Terreur*, pp. 23–37. Jean-Clément Martin has argued compellingly that the term 'the Terror' should no longer be applied to the period, for example, in 'Violences et justice', in Biard (ed.), *Politiques de la Terreur*, pp. 129–40. On Jacobin ideology in general, see Patrice L. R. Higonnet, *Goodness beyond Virtue: Jacobins during the French Revolution*, Cambridge, MA: Harvard University Press, 1998, chs 4, 5, 7; Gross, *Fair Shares for All*.

25. G. A. Kelly, 'Conceptual Sources of the Terror', *Eighteenth-Century Studies*, 14 (1980), pp. 18–36.

26. Diane Ladjouzi, 'Les Journées des 4 et 5 septembre à Paris. Un movement d'union entre le peuple, la Commune de Paris et la Convention pour un exécutif révolutionnaire', *AHRF*, 321 (2000), pp. 27–44; Richard Cobb, *The People's Armies. The 'armées révolutionnaires': Instrument of the Terror in the Departments, April 1793 to Floréal Year II*, translated by Marianne Elliott, New Haven, CT, & London: Yale University Press, 1987.

27. The will to control excesses of popular vengeance is discussed in contrasting ways in Martin, *Violence et Révolution*; Haim Burstin, 'Pour une phénoménologie de la violence révolution-naire', *Historical Reflections*, 29 (2003), pp. 389–407; Sophie Wahnich, *La Liberté ou la mort: essai sur la Terreur et le terrorisme*, Paris: La Fabrique, 2003.

28. *Oeuvres*, vol. X, pp. 109–13.

29. *Oeuvres*, vol. X, pp. 82–83; Scott H. Lytle, 'The Second Sex (September, 1793)', *JMH*, 27 (1955), pp. 14–26; Dominique Godineau, *Citoyennes tricoteuses: les femmes du peuple à Paris pendant la Révolution française*, Aix-en-Provence: Alinéa, 1988, pp. 129–77; Blum, *Rousseau and the Republic of Virtue*, ch. 11; Suzanne Desan, 'Jacobin Women's Clubs', in Bryant T. Ragan and Elizabeth A. Williams (eds), *Re-creating Authority in Revolutionary France*, New Brunswick, N.J.: Rutgers University Press, 1992, ch. 1; Marie Cerati, *Le Club des citoyennes républicaines*

révolutionnaires, Paris: Éditions sociales, 1966; Rose, *Enragés*, chs 5–6; Sepinwall, 'Robespierre, Old Regime Feminist?'

30. David P. Jordan, 'The Robespierre Problem', in Haydon and Doyle (eds), *Robespierre*, p. 23; 'Robespierre and the Politics of Virtue', in Jourdan (ed.), *Robespierre–figure–réputation*, pp. 61–62.

31. *Papiers inédits trouvés chez Robespierre*, vol. 3, pp. 3–55; Hamel, *Histoire de Robespierre*, vol. 1, pp. 29–30; Stéfane-Pol, *Autour de Robespierre*, pp. 69–71; M. Favone, *Dans le sillage de Maximilien Robespierre: Joachim Vilate*, Paris: M. Rivière, 1938; Palmer (ed.), *Marc-Antoine Jullien*, ch. 2; Pierre Gascar, *L'Ombre de Robespierre*, Paris: Gallimard, 1979; Marisa Linton, 'Fatal Friendships: The Politics of Jacobin Friendship', *FHS*, 31 (2008), pp. 51–76.

32. *Papiers inédits trouvés chez Robespierre*, vol. 2, pp. 7–13; G. Lenôtre, *Le Tribunal révolutionnaire (1793–1795)*, Paris: Perrin, 1908, p. 243.

33. Charles Walton, *Policing Public Opinion in the French Revolution: The Culture of Calumny and the Problem of Free Speech*. Oxford & New York: Oxford University Press, 2009, pp. 109–12, 133–34, 207–10. The Revolutionary Committee of Robespierre's own Section des Piques seems a model of thoroughness in its investigation of civic virtue: AN F7 4778.

34. Jeremy Popkin, 'The Royalist Press in the Reign of Terror', in T. C. W. Blanning, *The Rise and Fall of the French Revolution*, Chicago: University of Chicago Press, 1996, pp. 417–32; Gough, 'Robespierre and the Press', pp. 124–26.

35. *Oeuvres*, vol. X, pp. 116–21; Hamel, *Histoire de Robespierre*, vol. 3, p. 139.

36. *Oeuvres*, vol. X, pp. 132–43. Note the incisive comments of Hunt, 'The World We Have Gained', p. 18; Carla Hesse, 'La Logique culturelle de la loi révolutionnaire', *Annales*, 57 (2002), pp. 915–33.

37. *Oeuvres*, vol. X, pp. 133–34; Linton, 'Conspiracies Real and Imagined', pp. 132–36; Hanson, *Jacobin Republic under Fire*, pp. 20–21. The deputies expressed their gratitude, collectively and individually: *Oeuvres*, vol. III, p. 197; Jacob, *Robespierre vu par ses contemporains*, pp. 130–31.

38. Kaiser, 'Catilina's Revenge', pp. 191–92, 200.

39. Fleischmann, *Robespierre and the Women He Loved*, pp. 179–82; Jeanne-Marie Roland de la Platière, *An Appeal to Impartial Posterity*, Oxford & New York: Woodstock Books, 1990, pp. 181–88. She did not send the letter.

40. See *Oeuvres*, vol. IX, p. 275; vol. X, pp. 71, 73, 110, 155, 166, 193, 278–79, 446; Thompson, *Robespierre*, pp. 326–27; Cubitt, 'Robespierre and Conspiracy Theories', p. 80; Jourdan, 'Robespierre and Revolutionary Heroism', pp. 60–63; Linton, 'Robespierre's Political Principles', pp. 46–48.

41. *Oeuvres*, vol. X, pp. 43–45, 143–45, 278. On the tension between the Revolution's 'universalism' and national military interests, see Albert Mathiez, *La Révolution et les étrangers: cosmopolitisme et défense nationale*, Paris: La Renaissance du Livre, 1918; Burgess, *Refuge in the Land of Liberty*, pp. 22–30; Sophie Wahnich, *L'Impossible citoyen. L'Étranger dans le discours de la Révolution française*, Paris: Albin Michel, 1997; Michael Rapport, *Nationality and Citizenship in Revolutionary France: The Treatment of Foreigners 1789–1799*, Oxford: Clarendon Press, 2000, pp. 202–3, 224–39; Peter Sahlins, *Unnaturally French: Foreign Citizens in the Old Regime and After*, Ithaca, N. Y., & London: Cornell University Press, 2004; Philippe Raxhon, 'Robespierre et la Belgique: histoire et mémoire', in Jessenne et al. (eds), *Robespierre*, pp. 381–87.

42. *Oeuvres*, vol. X, pp. 167–84; Bénot, 'Robespierre, les colonies et l'esclavage', pp. 418–19. When Robespierre asked Deforgues, Minister of External Relations, to identify who could best come to brief him for the speech, the official in question, Jean-Victor Colchen, retorted that Robespierre was the object of his 'loathing' and that he would have to arrange to see him if he wanted a briefing. Robespierre apparently did so with studied politeness: Georges Lefebvre, 'Robespierre et Colchen', *AHRF*, 27 (1955), pp. 1–4.

43. Robespierre had earlier been urged to ensure this, for example, by Jacobins in Strasbourg in February 1792: AN F7 4433, plaque 2.

44. *Oeuvres*, vol. X, pp. 226–32; Rapport, 'Robespierre and the Universal Rights of Man', pp. 323–24; Laurent Petit, 'Robespierre et le discours sur l'étranger: buts et limites d'une modélisation des nationalités', in Jessenne et al. (eds), *Robespierre*, pp. 315–36.
45. *Oeuvres*, vol. XI, pp. 397–415; Thompson, *Robespierre*, pp. 387–402.
46. On de-Christianization in general, see Michel Vovelle, *The Revolution against the Church: From Reason to the Supreme Being*, translated by Alan José, Cambridge: Polity Press, 1991; Suzanne Desan, 'The Family as Cultural Battleground: Religion vs Republic under the Terror', in Baker, *Terror*, ch. 10; Michael Kennedy, *The Jacobin Clubs in the French Revolution, 1793–1795*, New York: Berghahn Books, 2000, ch. 10.
47. *Oeuvres*, vol. III, pp. 213–14.
48. *Oeuvres*, vol. X, pp. 193–201.
49. *Oeuvres*, vol. X, pp. 238–40; Martine Braconnier, 'Robespierre et Couthon: de la Raison à l'Être Suprême: deux itinéraires', in Jessenne et al. (eds), *Robespierre*, pp. 185–86; Alain Corbin, *Les Cloches de la terre*, Paris: Albin Michel, 1994, p. 33 and ch. 1.
50. *Oeuvres*, vol. X, pp. 246–51, 257–62; William Doyle, *Aristocracy and its Enemies in the Age of Revolution*, Oxford: Oxford University Press, 2009, pp. 290–91; Wahnich, *L'Impossible citoyen*, pp. 185–200.
51. Cobb, *The People's Armies*, pp. 520–23; Françoise Brunel, *Thermidor, la chute de Robespierre*, Brussels: Éditions Complexe, 1999, pp. 16–17.
52. Gross, *Fair Shares for All*; McPhee, *Living the French Revolution*, ch. 7. Cf. David Andress, *The French Revolution and the People*, London & New York: Hambledon and London, 2004, for example, pp. 213, 216.
53. Kennedy, *Jacobin Clubs, 1793–1795*, pp. 54–55. Lists of deputies on mission are in AN F7 4444, plaque 2.
54. *Papiers inédits trouvés chez Robespierre*, vol. 2, pp. 199–217.
55. Barras, *Memoirs*, vol. 1, pp. 181–87; Henri Buisson, *Fouché, duc d'Otrante*, Bienne: Panorama, 1968, pp. 52, 573–74. For Paul Mansfield, the entire Committee shares responsibility for sanctioning excesses, and the Convention and Jacobin Club said nothing: 'The Repression of Lyon, 1793–4: Origins, Responsibility and Significance', *FH*, 2 (1988), pp. 74–101. Cf. Hanson, *Jacobin Republic under Fire*, p. 194.
56. See Norman Hampson, 'François Chabot and his Plot', *Transactions of the Royal Historical Society*, 5th series, 26 (1976), pp. 1–14; Andress, *Terror*, pp. 251–53, 261–62.
57. *Oeuvres*, vol. IX, pp. 617–19; vol. X, pp. 46, 52–53.
58. *Oeuvres*, vol. X, pp. 219–25.
59. Camille Desmoulins, *Le Vieux Cordelier*, Paris: Belin, 1977.
60. *Oeuvres*, vol. X, pp. 253–55.
61. *Oeuvres*, vol. X, pp. 262–65, 283–92; Blanc, *Histoire de la Révolution française*, vol. 2, p. 676.
62. Peter McPhee, *Collioure et la Révolution française, 1789–1815*, Perpignan: Le Publicateur, 1989, chs 2–3. Cf. Hardman, *Robespierre*, p. 93, who asserts that 'there were no foreign armies on French soil' by the end of 1793.

Chapter 11 'Men with changing tongues': Paris, January–June 1794

1. *Oeuvres*, vol. X, pp. 300–11. It was dated 5 Nivôse (25 December), but did not appear until 16 Nivôse (5 January).
2. From Rousseau's *Discourse on the Sciences and Arts*, awarded the prize by the Academy of Dijon in 1750. See Mossé, *L'Antiquité dans la Révolution française*, pp. 120–21.
3. *Oeuvres*, vol. X, pp. 311–15.
4. *Oeuvres*, vol. X, pp. 326–42. No. 6 was dated 10 Nivôse (30 December), but did not appear until 6 Pluviôse (25 January).
5. Linton, 'Conspiracies Real and Imagined', pp. 136–43; Thomas E. Kaiser, 'From the Austrian Committee to the Foreign Plot: Marie-Antoinette, Austrophobia, and the Terror', *FHS*, 26 (2003), pp. 579–617; Claretie, *Camille Desmoulins and his Wife*, ch. 5.

6. Kaiser, 'From the Austrian Committee to the Foreign Plot'; Jean Bouchary, *Les Manieurs d'argent à Paris à la fin du XVIIIe siècle*, 3 vols, Paris: Marcel Rivière, vol. 1, 1939.
7. *Oeuvres*, vol. IX, pp. 460–61. It is likely that he took the imagery of the coffin from Mirabeau: Luttrell, *Mirabeau*, p. 290.
8. Jean-Daniel Piquet, 'Robespierre et la liberté des noirs en l'an II', *AHRF*, 323 (2001), pp. 69–91; Piquet, *L'Émancipation des noirs dans la Révolution française (1789–1795)*, Paris: Karthala, 2002; Marcel Dorigny (ed.), *The Abolitions of Slavery: From Léger Félicité Sonthonax to Victor Schoelcher, 1793, 1794, 1848*, New York & Oxford: Berghahn Books; Paris: Éditions UNESCO, 2003, p. 169.
9. *Oeuvres*, vol. X, pp. 350–66; Rosso, 'Réminiscences spartiates', p. 62; Parker, *Cult of Antiquity*, ch. 13.
10. Jean-Clément Martin, 'La Révolution française: généalogie de l'ennemi', *Raisons politiques*, 5 (2002), pp. 69–79; Dupuy, *République jacobine*, ch. 11.
11. Fleischmann, *Robespierre and the Women He Loved*, pp. 112–15; Jacob, *Robespierre vu par ses contemporains*, pp. 132–33; Morris Slavin, *The Hébertistes to the Guillotine: Anatomy of a 'Conspiracy' in Revolutionary France*, Baton Rouge & London: Louisiana State University Press, 1994, pp. 46–47.
12. See the remarkable list in Walter, *Robespierre*, vol. 2, pp. 191–322.
13. Jacob, *Robespierre vu par ses contemporains*, pp. 146–47; Gallo, *Robespierre*, pp. 179–80, 222–24, 271–72; André Cadet de Gassecourt, *Une curieuse figure du passé: Joseph Souberbielle, neveu du Frère Côme*, Paris: Les Presses Modernes, 1934, p. 95; Bibliothèque de l'Institut national de médecine, Paris, Non-classés–dossier Joseph Souberbielle; Nabonne, *Vie privée de Robespierre*, pp. 124, 186–88. Victorien Sardou, who met Élisabeth Lebas in the 1840s, also claimed that Robespierre had varicose ulcers: Sardou, Preface to Stéfane-Pol, *Autour de Robespierre*, p. xii; Hamel, *Histoire de Robespierre*, vol. 3, pp. 286, 374–75, 412–14.
14. Linton, 'Conspiracies Real and Imagined'; Marcel Gauchet, 'Le Démon du soupçon', *Histoire*, 84 (1985), pp. 49–56; Kaiser, 'From the Austrian Committee to the Foreign Plot'; Blanc, *Corruption sous la Terreur*.
15. *Oeuvres*, vol. X, pp. 373–74; Slavin, *Hébertistes to the Guillotine*, p. 132. Jullien reported to Robespierre that he had found Carrier's conduct and protection of crimes 'revolting': *Oeuvres*, vol. III, p. 239. Robespierre's response to Carrier's atrocities did not protect him from later assumptions that Carrier had acted under his orders: see Jean-Clément Martin, 'Vendée: les criminels de guerre en procès', *Histoire*, 25 (2004), pp. 82–87. In general, see Louis Jacob, *Hébert, le Père Duchesne: chef des sans-culottes*, Paris: Gallimard, 1960, chs 12–15.
16. *Oeuvres*, vol. X, pp. 388–90.
17. Rapport, 'Robespierre and the Universal Rights of Man', pp. 327–29; Mathiez, *Études sur Robespierre*, p. 75. The argument for the guilt of those charged is put by Mathiez, *Un procès de corruption sous la Terreur: l'affaire de la Compagnie des Indes*, Paris: Félix Alcan, 1920.
18. Dated 15 Pluviôse (3 February), but not written until at least 15 Ventôse (5 March) and not printed until after Thermidor.
19. Jacob, *Robespierre vu par ses contemporains*, pp. 136–37.
20. *Oeuvres*, vol. X, pp. 421–22. Robespierre's 'petit-bourgeois' class interests are identified as fatal in the 'classic' Marxist analysis of Robespierre and the French Revolution by Albert Soboul, *The French Revolution, 1787–1799: From the Storming of the Bastille to Napoleon*, translated by Alan Forrest and Colin Jones, London: Unwin Hyman, 1989, esp. pp. 412–15; and, more specifically his 'Robespierre and the Popular Movement of 1793–4'; idem, 'Robespierre ou les contradictions du jacobinisme', *AHRF*, 50 (1978), pp. 1–19.
21. *Oeuvres*, vol. X, pp. 412–19; Hampson, *Danton*, pp. 157–64. At the end of March, Desmoulins claimed to a friend that he had tried to see Robespierre but had been refused entry: Bertaud, *Camille et Lucile Desmoulins*, p. 276 and ch. 9.
22. *Oeuvres*, vol. XI, p. 441; Thompson, *Robespierre*, pp. 463–70; Albert Mathiez, *Robespierre, terroriste*, Paris: Renaissance du livre, 1921; Hampson, *Danton*, ch. 4. Popkin, *You Are All Free*, pp. 366, 376, 384, sees Robespierre's concern to keep the colonies as contradicting earlier support for abolition, but cf. Piquet, 'Robespierre et la liberté des noirs'.

23. Linton, 'Conspiracies Real and Imagined', p. 143; Poumiès de la Siboutie, *Recollections of a Parisian Doctor under Six Sovereigns, Two Revolutions and a Republic (1789–1863)*, translated by Theodora Davidson, London: John Murray, 1911, ch. 2.

24. *Oeuvres*, vol. III, p. 160; vol. XI, p. 433; Marisa Linton, ' "The Tartuffes of Patriotism": Fears of Conspiracy in the Political Language of Revolutionary Government, France 1793–94', in Coward and Swann (eds), *Conspiracy in Early Modern Europe*, pp. 248–49; Hampson, *Danton*, pp. 162–63; Scurr, *Fatal Purity*, pp. 180, 184, 234; Thompson, *Robespierre*, pp. 463–70.

25. *Oeuvres*, vol. III, pp. 100, 274; Claretie, *Camille Desmoulins and his Wife*, pp. 137–40; Bertaud, *Camille et Lucile Desmoulins*, pp. 11, 173, 295. The witnesses to the civil declaration of Horace's birth were Laurent Lecointre and Antoine Merlin de Thionville, now estranged from Robespierre. Scurr, *Fatal Purity*, pp. 280–87, is excellent on the trial.

26. Wahnich, *Liberté ou la mort*, pp. 65–70. Olivier Blanc, *Last Letters: Prisons and Prisoners of the French Revolution 1793–1794*, translated by Alan Sheridan, New York: Farrar, Straus & Giroux, 1987, pp. 32–35, argues that Robespierre's enemies deliberately held up its operation.

27. Dupuy, *République jacobine*, p. 257; Arne Ording, *Le Bureau de police du Comité de salut public. Étude sur la Terreur.* Academi i Oslo: Skrifter utgitt av det Norske Videnskaps, no. 6, 1931; Thompson, *Robespierre*, pp. 511–18.

28. AN F7 4437.

29. Robespierre's notes on many of his acquaintances are in AN F7 4436/1, plaques 3–4. See, too, W 501.

30. Hardman, *Robespierre*, pp. 115–18.

31. Georges Lefebvre, *Questions agraires au temps de la Terreur. Documents publiés et annotés*, Strasbourg: Imprimeries F. Lenig, 1932, pp. 1–132; Jean-Pierre Hirsch, 'Terror and Property', in Baker, *Terror*, ch. 12.

32. *Oeuvres*, vol. X, 387, 503; Gough, 'Robespierre and the Press', p. 123; Jean-Paul Bertaud, 'An Open File: The Press under the Terror', in Baker, *Terror*, ch. 16; Edelstein, 'La Feuille villageoise', pp. 53, 62.

33. See the remarkable police reports in AN F7 3821–2; Bouloiseau, *Jacobin Republic*, p. 195.

34. Charlotte Robespierre, *Mémoires*, pp. 74–75; Thompson, *Robespierre and the French Revolution*, pp. 159–60.

35. Jacob, *Robespierre vu par ses contemporains*, pp. 157–60. Barras' memoirs were published in the 1820s.

36. Nolibos, *Arras*, p. 110; Jacob, *Robespierre vu par ses contemporains*, p. 197.

37. *Oeuvres*, vol. III, pp. 284–86; Fleischmann, *Robespierre and the Women He Loved*, pp. 170–71; *Papiers inédits trouvés chez Robespierre*, vol. 1, pp. 253–54; Gobry, *Joseph Le Bon*, ch. 13; Paris, *La Terreur dans le Pas-de-Calais*, pp. 513–17, livre XIII; AD Pas-de-Calais, 2L Arras 45. Certainly there seems to have been an abrupt change towards suspects being released after Lebon's recall.

38. *Oeuvres*, vol. X, pp. 442–65. On the Cult of the Supreme Being and Robespierre's repudiation of the 'materialism' of the *philosophes*, see Michel Vovelle, 'The Adventures of Reason, or From Reason to the Supreme Being', in Lucas (ed.), *Rewriting the French Revolution*, pp. 132–50; Blum, *Rousseau and the Republic of Virtue*, ch. 13.

39. Thompson, *Robespierre and the French Revolution*, pp. 123–24: this was 'the last testament of a republican idealist'. See the round-table discussion in Jessenne et al. (eds), *Robespierre*, pp. 427–39; Tallett, 'Robespierre and Religion', pp. 100–8; Guillemin, *Robespierre*, ch. 5; Carr, *Robespierre*, ch. 19; Barny, 'Robespierre et les Lumières', pp. 45–59. Rousseau was interred in the Panthéon on 14 April 1794, and the children Bara and Viala were interred there shortly afterwards.

40. Françoise Brunel, 'Le Jacobinisme, un "rigorisme de la vertu"? "Puritanisme" et révolution', in *Mélanges Michel Vovelle. Sur la Révolution, approches plurielles*, Paris: Société des études Robespierristes, 1997, p. 278; Ansart-Dourlen, *Action politique des personnalités*, pp. 58–90.

41. *Oeuvres*, vol. X, p. 445.

42. *Oeuvres*, vol. X, pp. 479–83; AN D XXXVIII 3. See Ozouf, *Festivals*, pp. 106–18; Favone, *Joachim Vilate*, ch. 6.

43. Dupuy, *République jacobine*, pp. 261–62; Hamel, *Histoire de Robespierre*, vol. 3, p. 543; Doyle, *The Oxford History of the French Revolution*, p. 277.

44. Claudine le Vaulchier, 'Iconographie des décors révolutionnaires', in *Les Architectes de la liberté, 1789–1800*, Paris: École nationale supérieure des Beaux-Arts, 1989, p. 265.

45. AN D XXXVIII 5; Scurr, *Fatal Purity*, pp. 292–93; Crane Brinton, *The Jacobins: An Essay in the New History*, New York: Russell & Russell, 1961, pp. 211, 225–26; Vovelle, *Revolution against the Church*, pp. 8, 26. Isaac Rodrigues' letter was communicated to me by Helen Davies.

46. *Oeuvres*, vol. X, p. 461.

47. That at least was the recollection of Louis-Philippe in 1850, but he was only eighteen when the incident may have taken place: *The Correspondence and Diaries of the Late Right Honourable John Wilson Croker*, 3 vols, London, 1885, vol. 3, p. 209.

48. Poumiès de la Siboutie, *Recollections*, ch. 2. Éléonore would have had to pass through her parents' bedroom to visit Maximilien at night: Nabonne, *Vie privée de Robespierre*, Part II, ch. 8.

49. Fleischmann, *Robespierre and the Women He Loved*, pp. 215–18, 224–26. The teacher may have been from a branch of the family unrelated to Mirabeau: Luttrell, *Mirabeau*, p. 292.

50. Burstin, *Faubourg Saint-Marcel*, pp. 796–98; Lenôtre, *Robespierre's Rise and Fall*, ch. 2.

51. Burstin, *Faubourg Saint-Marcel*, p. 785.

52. *Oeuvres*, vol. X, pp. 469–71.

53. Antoine de Baecque, 'The Trajectory of a Wound: From Corruption to Regeneration', in Baker, *Terror*, ch.9.

54. *Archives Parlementaires*, vol. 91, pp. 41–43; Joachim Vilate, *Causes secrètes de la révolution du 9 au 10 thermidor*, Paris, an III, pp. 33–38; AN W 37; Scurr, *Fatal Purity*, pp. 294–95; Antoine de Baecque, *The Body Politic: Corporeal Metaphor in Revolutionary France, 1770–1800*, translated by Charlotte Mandell, Stanford, CA: Stanford University Press, 1997, pp. 304–7. For police reports of threats to Robespierre, see AN F7 4437.

55. Thompson, *Robespierre*, pp. 531–37; *Oeuvres*, vol. III, p. 297, vol. III, part 2, pp. 115–17: undated (Floréal-Prairial) note found among Robespierre's papers.

56. Even Albert Mathiez, Robespierre's most fervent defender, while comparing the law with those passed during the First World War, believed that the assassination attempts of Admirat and Renault had provoked in Robespierre, still recovering from illness, 'a sort of *exaltation fébrile*': Mathiez, 'Robespierre terroriste', in *Études sur Robespierre*, pp. 79–80. For an interpretation of the Law of 22 Prairial as fair and 'efficient', see Liliane Abdoul-Melek, 'D'un choix politique de Robespierre: la Terreur', in Jessenne et al. (eds), *Robespierre*, pp. 191–203. Cf. the argument of Edelstein, *The Terror of Natural Right*, pp. 249–56, 268–69, for whom the Law is the 'natural' outcome of the Revolution.

57. *Oeuvres*, vol. X, pp. 484–90; Thompson, *Robespierre*, pp. 505–11, 548.

58. Hamel, *Histoire de Robespierre*, vol. 3, pp. 547–54.

59. Martin, *Violence et Révolution*, pp. 221–26.

Chapter 12 'The unhappiest man alive': Paris, July 1794

1. *Oeuvres*, vol. X, pp. 491–98.

2. AN F7 4436/1, plaque 3; *Papiers inédits trouvés chez Robespierre*, vol. 2, pp. 16–21. Robespierre had had François Bourdon expelled from the Jacobin Club.

3. Michel Eude, 'Points de vue sur l'affaire Catherine Théot', *AHRF*, 198 (1969), pp. 606–29; idem, 'Le Comité de sûreté générale en 1793–1794', *AHRF*, 261 (1985), pp. 295–306; Lenôtre, *Robespierre's Rise and Fall*, pp. 184–95, 272; Martyn Lyons, 'The 9 Thermidor: Motives and Effects', *European Studies Review*, 5 (1975), pp. 137–38; Burstin, *Faubourg Saint-Marcel*, pp. 796–98; Auricchio, *Adélaide Labille-Guiard*, pp. 96–97. Théot died in prison on 14 Fructidor (31 August).

4. Palmer, *Twelve Who Ruled*, p. 402.

5. *Correspondence of William Augustus Miles*, vol. I, pp. 175–78.

6. See AN F7 4436/1, plaque 1; Ording, *Le Bureau de police du Comité de salut public*, pp. 37–43; Mathiez, *Robespierre, terroriste*, pp. 88–89; Thompson, *Robespierre*, pp. 540–44; Guillemin, *Robespierre*, pp. 10–11. Cf. Hardman, *Robespierre*, pp. 151–56, who accuses Robespierre of having both a 'filthy temper' and of being obsessed with asking for more detail about the denunciations flooding across his desk, as if he should have been less fastidious.

7. See David Owen, *In Sickness and in Power: Illness in Heads of Government During the Last 100 years*, London: Methuen, 2008.

8. *Oeuvres*, vol. III, p. 293. This undated letter was among the papers found at Robespierre's lodgings after his death. See Charlotte Robespierre, *Mémoires*, ch. IV and pp. 76–77; Thompson, *Robespierre*, pp. 416–18.

9. Fleischmann, *Robespierre and the Women He Loved*, pp. 119–22; Charlotte Robespierre, *Mémoires*, pp. 95–96.

10. *Papiers inédits trouvés chez Robespierre*, vol. 1, pp. 247–52; Thompson, *Robespierre*, p. 544; Jacob, 'Buissart', p. 286; Luzzatto, *Bonbon Robespierre*, pp. 131–40.

11. *Papiers inédits trouvés chez Robespierre*, vol. 2, pp. 133–34, 151–55; Alphonse Esquiros, *Histoire des Montagnards*, Paris: Librairie rue Visconti, 1851, p. 111; Mathiez, *Fall of Robespierre*, ch. 2.

12. AN F7 3321.

13. See the remarkable police reports in AN F7 3821–2; Bouloiseau, *Jacobin Republic*, p. 195.

14. Mathiez, *Fall of Robespierre*, chs 8–9.

15. *Oeuvres*, vol. X, pp. 511–18.

16. *Oeuvres*, vol. X, pp. 518–24.

17. *Oeuvres*, vol. X, pp. 530–35; Hardman, *Robespierre*, pp. 138–41.

18. Jacques Bernet, 'Terreur et religion en l'an II. L'Affaire des Carmélites de Compiègne', in Biard (ed.), *Les Politiques de la Terreur*, pp. 435–46; Bluche, *Septembre 1792*, p. 243.

19. Jacob, *Robespierre vu par ses contemporains*, p. 131; Brunel, *Thermidor*, p. 71.

20. AN F7 4436/1.

21. Jeff Horn, 'The Terror in the Département of the Aube and the Fall of Robespierre', Paper presented at the Society for French Historical Studies, Wilmington, DE, 26 March 1994. Rousselin was briefly imprisoned.

22. Brunel, *Thermidor*, p. 77.

23. Bluche, *Septembre 1792*, p. 243; Brunel, *Thermidor*, p. 71. Cf. Scurr, *Fatal Purity*, on 'Robespierre's red summer'.

24. *Oeuvres*, vol. X, pp. 430–31; P. Raxhon, 'Les Réfugiés Liégeois à Paris: un état de la question', in M. Vovelle (ed.), *Paris et la Révolution* (1989), pp. 212–24; Rapport, 'Robespierre and the Universal Rights of Man', pp. 329–30; Marvin A. Carlson, 'The Citizen in the Theater', in Renée Waldinger, Philip Dawson and Isser Woloch (eds), *The French Revolution and the Meaning of Citizenship*, Westport, CT: Greenwood Press, 1993, pp. 84–85.

25. *Oeuvres*, vol. X, pp. 537–41; Aulard, *Société des Jacobins*, vol. 4, p. 231.

26. Thompson, *Robespierre*, pp. 554–58; Brown, *War, Revolution, and the Bureaucratic State*, pp. 120–21; AN F7 4433.

27. *Oeuvres*, vol. X, pp. 543–76. Two detailed documentary accounts are Gérard Walter, *La Conjuration du Neuf Thermidor, 27 July 1794*, Paris: Gallimard, 1974, and Richard Bienvenu, *The Ninth of Thermidor: The Fall of Robespierre*, Oxford and New York: Oxford University Press, 1968. Published in the year of his death, Walter's elderly reflection is far harsher on Robespierre than his biography written forty years earlier, but includes precious original documents, such as Part III on the responses of the sections.

28. Linton, 'Robespierre's Political Principles', pp. 51–52.

29. François Hincker, 'L'Affrontement Cambon–Robespierre le huit thermidor', in Jessenne et al. (eds), *Robespierre*, pp. 299–307; Bienvenu, *Ninth of Thermidor*, p. 179.

30. Mathiez, *Robespierre, terroriste*, pp. 84–87; Barras, *Memoirs*, vol. 1, pp. 205–11; Hampson, 'Robespierre and the Terror', p. 172.

31. Quoted in Bienvenu, *Ninth of Thermidor*, p. 184.

32. Aulard, *Société des Jacobins*, vol. 6, pp. 246, 282–83; Walter, *Conjuration du Neuf Thermidor*, p. 121; Jean Guilaine, *Billaud-Varenne: l'ascète de la Révolution (1756–1819)*, Paris: Fayard,

1969, ch. 9. The psychoanalyst Jacques André has argued that the speech verged on clinical paranoia: 'L'Incorruptible: considérations psychanalytiques', in Jourdan (ed.), *Robespierre—figure-réputation*, pp. 147–48.

33. AN W 79, liasses 1, 18.
34. Thompson, *Robespierre and the French Revolution*, p. 137.
35. Brunel, *Thermidor*, p. 7.
36. *Oeuvres*, vol. X, pp. 588–95; Jacob, *Robespierre vu par ses contemporains*, pp. 141–45; Linton, 'The Man of Virtue', pp. 417–18. Excellent descriptions of the day of 9 Thermidor are Andress, *Terror*, pp. 332–44; Thompson, *Robespierre*, pp. 565–82; Barras, *Memoirs*, vol. 1, ch. XIX.
37. See the comments of Jean d'Yzèz in Jacob, *Robespierre vu par ses contemporains*, p. 182. Another Jacobin made similar observations about the balance of forces: Joseph Cassanyes, *Un Catalan dans la Révolution française*, Perpignan: Fédération des Oeuvres Laïques, 1989, pp. 114–20.
38. AN F7 4432, plaque 1; 4433; 4778.
39. Huet, *Mourning Glory*, pp. 105–19; Mathiez, *Fall of Robespierre*, ch. 10; Stéfane-Pol, *Autour de Robespierre*, p. 292. Cf. Lenôtre, *Robespierre's Rise and Fall*, pp. 243, 313–14; Barras, *Memoirs*, p. 246; Walter, *Robespierre*, vol. 1, pp. 477–78.
40. Rapport des officiers de santé sur le pansement des blessures de Robespierre aîné: Notes et Archives. URL:http://www.royet.org/nea1789-1794) Accessed 15 October 2010; Autograph manuscript by J. Nicolas Jomard, 'Notes on the day of 9 thermidor Year II', in Christian Albertan and Anne-Marie Chouillet, 'Autographes et documents', *Recherches sur Diderot et sur l'Encyclopédie*, numéro 37 *Cyclopaedia*. URL: http://rde.revues.org/index4529. html. Accessed 15 October 2010.
41. Barras, *Memoirs*, p. 247; Lyons, '9 Thermidor', p. 126.
42. Antoine de Baecque, 'Le Tableau d'un cadavre. Les Récits d'agonie de Robespierre: du cadavre hideux au dernier héros', in Jourdan (ed.), *Robespierre—figure-réputation*, pp. 169–202. The death sentences are in AN W 434.
43. Jacob, *Robespierre vu par ses contemporains*, pp. 179–80.

Epilogue: 'That modern Procrustes'

1. Aulard, *Société des Jacobins*, vol. 6, pp. 295–96; Artarit, *Robespierre*, pp. 50–51; Paris, *Jeunesse*, Appendix, pp. 3–5; Forrest, *Soldiers of the French Revolution*, p. 115. Robespierre's former secretary went so far as to liken him simultaneously to Tiberius, Nero and Caligula: Villiers, *Souvenirs d'un déporté*, pp. 6, 128.
2. These reactions are from Jacob, *Robespierre vu par ses contemporains*, pp. 125, 136–37, 181–87.
3. There are 191 names on the *Liste des noms et domiciles des individus convaincus ou prévenus d'avoir pris part à la conjuration de l'infâme Robespierre*, Paris: n.p., Year II; Vilate, *Causes secrètes*, pp. 16, 23; Favone, *Joachim Vilate*. On Deschamps, see Dupuy, 'Du parrainage d'un enfant du peuple', pp. 122–23; AN W 439, dossier 34.
4. AN F 7, 4432; 4444, plaques 1 and 4; W 79, liasse 18; W 500–01.
5. AN F7 4694/1; W 499; Ording, *Le Bureau de police du Comité de salut public*, pp. 39–40; Yalom, *Blood Sisters*, pp. 125–30. The interrogations of the Duplays and the women's appeals are in W 79, liasse 23.
6. Jacob, *Robespierre vu par ses contemporains*, pp. 63, 101; Fleischmann, *Robespierre and the Women He Loved*, pp. 212–13; Berthe, *Dictionnaire*, pp. 55–56; Stéfane-Pol, *Autour de Robespierre*, p. 295; Jacob, 'Buissart', pp. 287–93; H. Piers, *Biographie de la ville de Saint-Omer*, St-Omer: J.-B. Lemaire, 1835, pp. 164–65. Buissart could also call on significant support from Arras: AN F7 4432, plaque 2. He subsequently retired from public life, until becoming a municipal councillor under the Restoration and a founder of the restored Academy in 1817. He died aged eighty-three in 1820.
7. AN F7 7904/4561; W 79, liasse 1; Jacques Bernet, 'La perception de Robespierre dans les clubs de Jacobins de Champagne et de Picardie (1791–1795)', in Jessenne et al. (eds),

Robespierre; Kennedy, *Jacobin Clubs, 1793–1795*, ch. 17; McPhee, *Living the French Revolution*, pp. 163–68; Ozouf, *Festivals*, p. 96.

8. In general, see Albert Mathiez, *After Robespierre: The Thermidorian Reaction*, translated by Catherine Alison Phillips, New York: Grosset & Dunlap, 1965; Bronislaw Baczko, *Ending the Terror: The French Revolution after Robespierre*, translated by Michael Petheram, Cambridge & New York: Cambridge University Press; Paris: Éditions de la maison des sciences de l'homme, 1994; Martin, *Violence et Révolution*, ch. 7; Françoise Brunel, 'Bridging the Gulf of the Terror', in Baker, *Terror*, ch. 18; Sergio Luzzatto, 'Un futur au passé; la Révolution dans les mémoires des conventionnels', *AHRF*, 61 (1989), pp. 455–75; François Furet and Mona Ozouf (eds), *The French Revolution and the Creation of Modern Political Culture*. vol. 3, *The Transformation of Political Culture 1789–1848*, Oxford: Pergamon Press, 1989, Part II. Letters of denunciation and interrogations are to be found, for example, in AN F7 4432, plaque 2; 4433, plaques 3 and 4, and in the Committee of General Security files in AN F7 4577–4775.

9. Antoine de Baecque, *Glory and Terror: Seven Deaths under the French Revolution*, translated by Charlotte Mandell, New York & London: Routledge, 2001, pp. 160–65. Felhémési (anagram for Méhée fils), *La Vérité toute entière, sur les vrais auteurs de la journée du 2 septembre 1792*, was used extensively by Carlyle, *French Revolution*, vol. 3, book 1, chs 4–6.

10. Hampson, *Danton*, pp. 51, 57–59, 145–46. Courtois and Danton had attended the same school in Troyes, but there were several years between them: cf. Claudine Wolikow, 'Danton', in Soboul et al. (eds), *Dictionnaire historique*, pp. 321–22.

11. Edme-Bonaventure Courtois, *Rapport fait au nom de la commission chargée de l'examen des papiers trouvés chez Robespierre et ses complices*, Paris: Imprimerie nationale des lois, Nivôse Year III [1795]; *Papiers inédits trouvés chez Robespierre*, vol. 1, pp. 1–111. See *Oeuvres*, vol. III, Introduction, p. 17; Fabienne Ratineau, 'Les Livres de Robespierre au 9 thermidor,' *AHRF*, 287 (1992), pp. 131–35; Thompson, *Robespierre*, pp. 598–99.

12. Courtois, *Rapport*, pp. 154–57; *Papiers inédits trouvés chez Robespierre*, vol. 1, pp. 154–59. Carr, *Robespierre*, p. 72, claims that Robespierre's taste for oranges was because of constipation causing constant irritability.

13. Watkin Tench, *Letters Written in France, to a Friend in London, Between the Month of November 1794, and the Month of May 1795*, Whitefish, MT: Kessinger Publishing, 2009, pp. 67, 191–92, 194–95, 198; Gavin Edwards (ed.), *Watkin Tench: Letters from Revolutionary France*, Cardiff: University of Wales Press, 2001, Introduction.

14. Jules Michelet, *La Révolution française*, 2 vols, Paris: Gallimard, 1952, vol. 2, p. 61; Antoine-Christophe Merlin de Thionville, *Portrait de Robespierre*, Paris: n.p., n.d. [c. 1794]; Jacob, *Robespierre vu par ses contemporains*, pp. 187–88. See, too, Gérard Minart, *Pierre Claude François Daunou, l'anti-Robespierre: de la Révolution à l'Empire, l'itinéraire d'un juste (1761–1840)*, Toulouse: Privat, 2001, pp. 97–98; Dominique Vivant Denon, *Lettres à Bettine*, Arles: Actes Sud, 1999, pp. 316, 328–29; Pierre-Louis Roederer, *Mémoires sur la Révolution, le Consulat et l'Empire*, Paris: Plon, 1942, pp. 75–83; Antoine de Baecque, 'Robespierre, monstre-cadavre du discours thermidorien', *Eighteenth-Century Life*, 21 (1997), pp. 203–21.

15. Proyart, *Vie et crimes de Robespierre*; Palmer, *School of the French Revolution*, pp. 181–84. See, too, Galart de Montjoie [pseud. Christophe Ventre], *Histoire de la conjuration de Maximilien Robespierre*, Paris: n.p., 1795, pp. 143–45.

16. Hamel, *Histoire de Robespierre*, vol. 3, pp. 547, 807. Another positive view of the Jacobins was published in 1847 by Alphonse Esquiros, *Histoire des Montagnards*. In general on nineteenth-century historiography, see Walter, *Robespierre*, vol. 2, pp. 159–89, 370–89.

17. Albert Soboul, *Understanding the French Revolution*, translated by April A. Knutson, New York: International Publishers, 1988, ch. 15; Mathiez, *Études sur Robespierre (1758–1794)*, pp. 32, 63–64; Georges Lefebvre, 'Remarks on Robespierre', translated by Beatrice F. Hyslop, *FHS*, 1 (1958), pp. 7–10; Ralph Korngold, *Robespierre, First Modern Dictator*, London: Macmillan, 1937; James Friguglietti, 'Rehabilitating Robespierre: Albert Mathiez and Georges Lefebvre as Defenders of the Incorruptible', in Haydon and Doyle (eds), *Robespierre*, pp. 212–23. Walter's exhaustive biography in its 'definitive edition' was first published in

1936–39. But National Socialists were also intrigued by Robespierre, for example, Friedrich Sieburg, *Robespierre*, translated by John Dilke, New York: Robert McBride, 1938.

18. Palmer, *Twelve Who Ruled*, p. 279.

19. Lecesne, *Arras*; Deramecourt, *Clergé du diocèse d'Arras*; Paris, *Jeunesse de Robespierre*. See Nolibos, *Arras*, pp. 111–13; François Wartelle, 'Destinées du Jacobinisme dans le Pas-de-Calais entre la chute de Robespierre et le coup d'État du 18 fructidor an V', Université de Paris-I, unpublished dissertation, 1987; Anne Gillion, 'La Mémoire de Robespierre à Arras', *Revue du Nord*, 71 (1989), pp. 1,037–50.

20. The mayor's speech is in ARBR, *Bulletin*, 2. On the stormy history of this episode see Kaplan, *Disputed Legacies*, pp. 450–56. A later president of the Société des études Robespierristes, Marc Bouloiseau, would insert a death notice every 28 July in *Le Monde* to commemorate the deaths of the Robespierres, Couthon and St-Just.

21. See ARBR, *Bulletins*, 4, 9, 19, 31, 59.

22. See ARBR, *Bulletin*, 1. With issue 24 in 1996 the newsletter became *L'Incorruptible* rather than a *Bulletin départemental*.

23. http://www.robespierre-europe.com/; http://teamrobespierre.blogspot.com/ accessed 1 October 2010.

24. Doyle and Haydon, 'Robespierre: After Two Hundred Years', p. 3; ARBR, *Bulletin*, 62, 63.

25. 'Robespierre indésirable à Paris', *Libération*, 1 October 2009, p. 12; 'Une rue Robespierre à Paris!', *Humanité*, 29 October 2009; Walter, *Robespierre*, vol. 2, pp. 380–87. In 1946, after the Liberation, the city council gave the name Robespierre to the Place Marché-Saint-Honoré, but its decision was repealed in 1950.

26. See, for example, Albert Parry, *Terrorism from Robespierre to Arafat*, New York: Vanguard Press, 1976; Andrew Sinclair, *An Anatomy of Terror: A History of Terrorism*, Basingstoke: Macmillan, 2003. The latter adds unsubstantiated claims about links to freemasonry.

27. The words were those of J.-B. Coffinhal of the Revolutionary Tribunal. Cf. Gillian Tindall's superb *Footprints in Paris: A Few Streets, a Few Lives*, London: Pimlico, 2010, p. 76.

28. Secher, *A French Genocide*, pp. 249–50; David A. Bell, *The Cult of the Nation in France: Inventing Nationalism, 1680–1800*, Cambridge, MA: Harvard University Press, 2001, p. 101.

29. Scurr, *Fatal Purity*, pp. 5, 7, 173, 207. A similar sketch is by Jordan, 'The Robespierre Problem', p. 17.

30. Bruce Mazlish, *The Revolutionary Ascetic: Evolution of a Political Type*, New York: Basic Books, 1976; Jacques André, *La Révolution fratricide. Essai de psychanalyse du lien social*, Paris: Presses universitaires de France, 1993; Carr, *Robespierre*; Huet, *Mourning Glory*, ch. 7; Saint-Paulien, *Robespierre*, pp. 49, 259. Saint-Paulien is the pseudonym of Maurice Yvan-Picard, a collaborator and anti-Semitic activist under Vichy; his biography of Robespierre is the most tendentious of the genre.

31. Dingli, *Robespierre*, pp. 23, 35, 435, Epilogue.

32. Artarit, *Robespierre*, for example pp. 55, 66, 68, 79, 81, 106–7, 112–14, 170, 366–67. Lantillette was the name used by Delmotte, an illiterate cobbler who became close to Robespierre during the drawing up of his corporation's *cahier* in 1789.

33. These themes are central to the views of Gueniffey, *Politique de la Terreur*; idem, 'Robespierre, itinéraire d'un tyran', *Histoire*, 177 (1994), pp. 36–47; Keith Michael Baker, *Inventing the French Revolution: Essays on French Political Culture in the Eighteenth Century*, Cambridge: Cambridge University Press, 1990, esp. pp. 304–5; Schama, *Citizens*, p. 447; Furet, *French Revolution*, pp. 146 and 142–58; and *Interpreting the French Revolution*, translated by Elborg Forster, Cambridge & Paris: Cambridge University Press and Éditions de la Maison des Sciences de l'Homme, 1981, pp. 56 and 55–72. Furet's charge that 'the Revolution is over', first published in 1971, was central to an angry interchange with Claude Mazauric: see *Interpreting*, especially pp. 81–131; Claude Mazauric, *Sur la Révolution française et l'homme moderne*, Paris: Éditions Messidor.

34. Jacob, *Robespierre vu par ses contemporains*, pp. 200–1; see, too, pp. 155–57, 202–3.

35. Peter Gay, 'Rhetoric and Politics in the French Revolution', *AHR*, 66 (1961), p. 674; *Freud for Historians*, New York & Oxford: Oxford University Press, 1985, p. 12. See, too, Gueniffey,

Politique de la Terreur, for example, pp. 337–40; Jordan, 'The Robespierre Problem', p. 31; Hampson, *Will and Circumstance*, p. 144.

36. Gay, 'Rhetoric and Politics'. In general, see the incisive discussions in Gay, *Freud for Historians*; Judith Brett, 'The Tasks of Political Biography', in Joy Damousi and Robert Reynolds (eds), *History on the Couch: Essays in History and Psychoanalysis*, Melbourne: Melbourne University Press, 2003, pp. 73–83.

37. See Desan, *Family on Trial*.

38. *Oeuvres*, vol. XI, pp. 281–97.

39. Poumiès de la Siboutie, *Recollections of a Parisian Doctor*, ch. 2; Blanc, *Révolution française*, vol. 2, p. 206. Poumiès claimed that Souberbielle had 'preserved all his faculties to the ripe age of ninety. I take no responsibility for his opinions.' Blanc noted that he had sanitized Souberbielle's expression. On Blanc's view of Robespierre, see Jean-François Jacouty, 'Robespierre selon Louis Blanc: le prophète christique de la Révolution française', *AHRF*, 331 (2003), pp. 103–27. Souberbielle's devotion did not impinge upon an insatiable and unsuccessful desire to receive the Légion d'Honneur and entry into the Royal Academy of Medicine under the restored monarchy, carefully omitting his association with Robespierre: see Bibliothèque de l'Institut national de médecine, Paris, Mss. 34 (34); 86 (58), papiers du docteur Joseph Souberbielle (1754–1846); Non-classés, dossier Joseph Souberbielle.

40. *Oeuvres*, vol. III, tome II, pp. 170–72; Charlotte Robespierre, *Mémoires*, Introduction, pp. 42–43; Yalom, *Blood Sisters*, pp. 109–12. On Charlotte's pension, see Stéfane-Pol, *Autour de Robespierre*, p. 86. She was encouraged to draft her memoirs by Albert Laponneraye, a militant republican fifty years her junior, then planning an edition of Robespierre's works. He published her memoirs after her death.

41. Peter McPhee, *Les Semailles de la République dans les Pyrénées-Orientales, 1846–1852: classes sociales, culture et politique*, Perpignan : L'Olivier, 1995, pp. 338–40. There were fifteen clandestine political clubs in this town of 2,300 people.

42. See the incisive discussion by James Livesey, 'The Limits of Terror: The French Revolution, Rights and Democratic Transition', *Thesis 11*, 97 (2009), pp. 63–79.

Bibliography

Primary Sources

Archives nationales, Paris

Série AF: Archives du pouvoir exécutif
    II: Conseil exécutif provisoire et Convention. Comité de Sûreté Public
        36–40: Correspondence du comité avec les représentants en mission, 1793: an IV
        47–8: Affaire du 9 thermidor
    IV: Secrétairerie d'État impériale an VIII: 1815
        1470: Rapports et déclarations faits au bureau de surveillance de la police, mars–juin 1793
Série D: Missions des représentants du peuple et comités des assemblées
    XXXVIII: Comité de l'instruction publique
        3: Fête de l'Être suprême
        5: Adresses, hommages et pièces en vers
    XLII: Comité de Salut public
        5: Massacres de septembre à Paris (1792)
Série F: Versements des ministères et des administrations qui en dépendent
    7: Police générale
        3821–2: Rapports de police de Paris et des départements (an II)
        4432: Comité de Sécurité Générale. Conspiration du 9 au 10 thermidor an II
        4433: Comité de Sécurité Générale. Documents rélatifs au 9 thermidor an II
        4436/1: Papiers saisis chez Robespierre
        4436/2: Rapport de Courtois sur les papiers saisis chez Robespierre
        4437: Comité de Sûreté Public. Rapport du Bureau de surveillance administrative et de la police générale
        4443–4: Pièces rélatives à divers députés
        4694/1: Duplay et sa famille
        4758: dossier Lagarde, Millau
        4772–4: Papiers de Joseph Le Bon, député
        4774/94: dossier Maximilien Robespierre
        4775/8: dossier Rouvet
        4778: Section des Piques. Comité révolutionnaire. Procès-verbal des séances, 28 mars 1793–29 fructidor an II
        7904/4561: Réunion tenue à la mémoire de Robespierre à Auxerre, an X

11: Subsistances
   267–8: Arrêtés du Comité de salut public, circulaires et instructions, an II–an V
13: Bâtiments civils
   281A: Tuileries et Louvre 1792, an IV
Série W: Juridictions extraordinaires. Tribunal révolutionnaire.
   37/2409: Arrestation de Crachet
   52/3363: Beauvoisin, complice de Robespierre
   60/3547: Crayssac, complice de Robespierre
   79–80: Affaire du 9 Thermidor
   389: Affaires Admiral, Renault
   434: Procès de Robespierre et associés
   439/34: Affaire Deschamps
   499: Procès des juges et jurés du tribunal révolutionnaire
   500–1: Affaire Fouquier-Tinville
   534–5: Registres des trois tribunaux révolutionnaires

Archives départementales du Pas-de-Calais, Arras

État Civil, Arras, 5M1 41; R8, 16, 17
Série L: Administration et tribunaux de la période révolutionnaire
   2L Arras 45: Lettres écrites et rapports décadaires de l'agent national, 5 pluviôse–3 sans-culottides an II
   2L Arras 67: Municipalité. Nominations 1790–an III

Bibliothèque de l'Institut national de médecine, Paris

Mss 34 (34); 86–88 (58–60); 103; 126: papiers du docteur Joseph Souberbielle (1754–1846)
Non-classés: dossier Joseph Souberbielle

Published works

Archives Parlementaires

Aulard, F. A. *La Société des Jacobins. Recueil des documents pour l'histoire du Club des Jacobins de Paris*, 6 vols, Paris: Librairies Jouaust, Noblet et Quantin, 1889–97.
Barras, Paul. *Memoirs*, translated by Charles E. Roche, 4 vols, London: Osgood, McIlvaine, 1895.
Berthe, Léon-Noël et al. *Villes et villages du Pas-de-Calais en 1790: 60 questions et leurs réponses*, vol. 1, *Districts d'Arras et de Bapaume*, Commission départementale d'histoire et d'archéologie du Pas-de-Calais, Arras, 1990.
Biré, Edmond. *The Diary of a Citizen of Paris during 'the Terror'*, translated by John de Villiers, London: Chatto & Windus, 1896.
Charavay, Étienne (ed.). *Assemblée électorale de Paris*, 3 vols, Paris: D. Jouaust, Charles Noblet, Maison Quantin, 1890–1905.
Courtois, Edme-Bonaventure. *Rapport fait au nom de la commission chargée de l'examen des papiers trouvés chez Robespierre et ses complices (. . .) dans la séance du 16 Nivôse, An IIIe de la République française, une et indivisible. Imprimé par ordre de la Convention nationale*, Paris: Imprimerie nationale des lois, an III [1795].
Croker, J. W. 'Robespierre', in *Essays on the Early Period of the French Revolution*, London: John Murray, 1857 (reprinted from the *Quarterly Review*, September 1835).
—. *The Correspondence and Diaries of the Late Right Honourable John Wilson Croker*, 3 vols, London: John Murray, 1885.
Desmoulins, Camille. *Le Vieux Cordelier*, Paris: Belin, 1977.
Dumont, Étienne. *Souvenirs sur Mirabeau et sur les deux premières assemblées législatives*, Paris: Librairie de Charles Gosselin, et chez Hector Bossange, 1832.

Felhémési [Jean-Claude-Hippolyte Méhée de la Touche]. *La Queue de Robespierre: ou les dangers de la liberté de la presse*, Paris: Imprimerie de Rougyff, 1795.

Felkay, Nicole and Hervé Favier (eds). *En prison sous la Terreur. Souvenirs de J.-B. Billecocq (1765–1829)*, Paris: Société des études Robespierristes, 1981.

Galart de Montjoie [pseud. Christophe Ventre]. *Histoire de la conjuration de Maximilien Robespierre*, Paris: n.p., 1795.

Gouges, Olympe de. *Écrits politiques 1792–1793*, Paris: Côté femmes, 1993.

Jacob, Louis. *Robespierre vu par ses contemporains*, Paris: A. Colin, 1938.

Jomard, J. Nicolas. 'Notes on the day of 9 thermidor Year II', in Christian Albertan and Anne-Marie Chouillet, 'Autographes et documents', *Recherches sur Diderot et sur l'Encyclopédie*, numéro 37 *Cyclopaedia*. http://rde.revues.org/index4529.html.

Liste des noms et domiciles des individus convaincus ou prévenus d'avoir pris part à la conjuration de l'infâme Robespierre, Paris: n.p., Year II.

Louvet de Couvray, Jean-Baptiste. *Accusation contre M. Robespierre*, Paris: Imprimerie nationale, 1792.

—. *À M. Robespierre et à ses royalistes, etc.*, Paris: Imprimerie du Cercle social, 1792.

—. *Mémoires*, Paris: Baudouin Frères, 1823.

Ménétra, Jacques-Louis. *Journal of My Life*, translated by Arthur Goldhammer, New York: Columbia University Press, 1986.

Merlin, Antoine-Christophe de Thionville. *Portrait de Robespierre*, Paris: n.p., n.d. [c. 1794].

Miles, William Augustus. *The Correspondence of William Augustus Miles 1789–1817*, London: Longmans, Green, 1890.

Le *Moniteur universel*, November 1789–July 1794.

Montesquiou-Fezensac, Abbé François-Xavier de. *Adresse aux provinces, ou examen des opérations de l'Assemblée Nationale*, n.p., n.l, 1790.

Moore, John. *The Works of John Moore, M. D. with Memoirs of his Life and Writings*, 7 vols, Edinburgh: Stirling and Slade, 1820.

Papiers inédits trouvés chez Robespierre, Saint-Just, Payan, etc. supprimés ou omis par Courtois, précédés du rapport de ce député à la Convention nationale, 3 vols, Geneva: Mégariotis Reprints, 1978.

Proyart, Abbé Lievin Bonaventure. *L'Écolier vertueux, ou vie édifiante d'un écolier de l'Université de Paris*, Tours: Alfred Mame, 1866.

—. *La Vie et les crimes de Robespierre, surnommé le Tyran, depuis sa naissance jusqu'à sa mort: ouvrage dédié à ceux qui commandent, et à ceux qui obéissent*, Augsbourg: n.p., 1795.

'Rapport des officiers de santé sur le pansement des blessures de Robespierre aîné', *Notes et Archives*. http://www.royet.org/nea1789–1794.

Reinhard Marcel, (ed.). *Correspondance de Babeuf avec l'Académie d'Arras (1785–1788)*, Paris: Institut d'histoire de la Révolution française, 1961.

Robespierre, Charlotte. *Mémoires de Charlotte Robespierre sur ses deux frères, précédés d'une introduction de Laponneraye*, Paris: Présence de la Révolution, 1987.

Robespierre, Maximilien. *Oeuvres de Maximilien Robespierre*, 11 vols, Paris: Société des études Robespierristes, 1912–2007.

Roland de la Platière, Jeanne-Marie, *An Appeal to Impartial Posterity*, Oxford & New York: Woodstock Books, 1990.

—. *Lettres de Madame Roland*, 2 vols, Paris: C. Perroud, 1900–2.

—. *Private Memoirs of Madame Roland*, translated by Edward Gilpin Johnson, London: Grant Richards, 1901.

Tench, Watkin. *Letters Written in France, to a Friend in London, Between the Month of November 1794, and the Month of May 1795*, Whitefish, MT: Kessinger Publishing, 2009.

Théroigne et Populus, ou, Le triomphe de la démocratie, drame national, en vers civiques. Corrigé et augmenté de deux actes, servant de suite aux deux premiers qui ont paru dans les actes des apôtres . . . London: n.p., 1790.

Thompson, J. M. (ed.), *English Witnesses of the French Revolution*, Oxford: Oxford University Press, 1938.

Vilate, Joachim. *Causes secrètes de la révolution du 9 au 10 thermidor*, Paris: n.p., an III [c.1795].

—. *Continuation des causes secrètes de la révolution du 9 au 10 thermidor*, Paris, an III [*c.* 1795].

—. *Les mystères de la mère de Dieu dévoilés: troisième volume des Causes secrètes de la Révolution du 9 au 10 thermidor*, Paris, an III [1795].

Villiers, Pierre. *Souvenirs d'un déporté*, Paris: chez l'Auteur, an X [1802].

Secondary Sources

Ado, Anatoli. *Paysans en Révolution. Terre, pouvoir et jacquerie 1789–1794*, translated by Serge Aberdam and Marcel Dorigny, Paris: Société des études Robespierristes, 1996.

Allen, Robert. *Les Tribunaux criminels sous la Révolution et l'Empire, 1792–1811*, translated by James Steven Bryant, Rennes: Presses universitaires de Rennes, 2005.

Alpaugh, Micah. 'The Politics of Escalation in French Revolutionary Protest: Political Demonstrations, Non-violence and Violence in the *grandes journées* of 1789', *FH*, 23 (2009), pp. 336 59.

Anderson, Wilda. 'Régénérer la nation: les enfants terrorisés de la Révolution', *MLN*, 117 (2002), pp. 698–709.

André, Jacques. *La Révolution fratricide. Essai de psychanalyse du lien social*, Paris: Presses universitaires de France, 1993.

Andress, David. *The French Revolution and the People*, London & New York: Hambledon & London, 2004.

—. *The Terror: Civil War in the French Revolution*, London: Little, Brown, 2005.

Andrews, Richard Mowery. *Law, Magistracy and Crime in Old Regime Paris, 1735–1789*, vol. 1, *The System of Criminal Justice*, Cambridge: Cambridge University Press, 1994.

—. 'Paris of the Great Revolution: 1789–1796', in Gene Brucker (ed.), *People and Communities in the Western World*, vol. 2, Homewood, IL: Dorsey Press, 1979, pp. 56–112.

Ansart-Dourlen, Michèle. *L'Action politique des personnalités et l'idéologie jacobine. Rationalisme et passions révolutionnaires*, Paris & Montreal: Harmattan, 1998.

Arasse, Daniel. *The Guillotine and the Terror*, translated by Christopher Miller, London: Penguin, 1989.

Arras à la veille de la Révolution, *Mémoires de l'Académie des Sciences, Lettres et Arts d'Arras*, 6e série, 1 (1990).

Artarit, Jean. *Robespierre, ou, l'impossible filiation*, Paris: Table Ronde, 2003.

Aston, Nigel. *The End of an Elite: The French Bishops and the Coming of the French Revolution*, Oxford: Clarendon Press, 1992.

—. *Religion and Revolution in France, 1780–1804*, Basingstoke: Macmillan, 2000.

Aulard, F. A. *Les Grands orateurs de la Révolution*, Paris: Rieder, 1914.

Auricchio, Laura. *Adélaïde Labille-Guiard: Artist in the Age of Revolution*, Los Angeles: J. Paul Getty Museum, 2009.

Baczko, Bronislaw. *Ending the Terror: The French Revolution after Robespierre*, translated by Michael Petheram, Cambridge & New York: Cambridge University Press; Paris: Éditions de la Maison des sciences de l'homme, 1994.

—. *Politiques de la Révolution française*, Paris: Gallimard, 2008.

Badinter, Élisabeth and Robert. *Condorcet: un intellectuel en politique*, Paris: Fayard, 1988.

Baecque, Antoine de. *Glory and Terror: Seven Deaths under the French Revolution*, translated by Charlotte Mandell, New York & London: Routledge, 2001.

—. 'Robespierre, monstre-cadavre du discours thermidorien', *Eighteenth-Century Life*, 21 (1997), pp. 203–21.

—. *The Body Politic: Corporeal Metaphor in Revolutionary France, 1770–1800*, translated by Charlotte Mandell, Stanford, CA: Stanford University Press, 1997.

Bailey, Charles R. 'French Secondary Education, 1763–1790: The Secularization of Ex-Jesuit Colleges', *Transactions of the American Philosophical Society*, 68 (1978), pp. 3–124.

Baker, Keith Michael. *Inventing the French Revolution: Essays on French Political Culture in the Eighteenth Century*, Cambridge: Cambridge University Press, 1990.

—. (ed.) *The French Revolution and the Creation of Modern Political Culture*, vol. 4, *The Terror*, Oxford: Pergamon Press, 1994.

Beik, Paul H. 'The French Revolution Seen from the Right: Social Theories in Motion, 1789–1799', *Transactions of the American Philosophical Society*, 46 (1956), pp. 1–122.

Bell, David A. *Lawyers and Citizens: The Making of a Political Elite in Old Regime France*, New York & Oxford: Oxford University Press, 1994.

—. *The Cult of the Nation in France: Inventing Nationalism, 1680–1800*, Cambridge, MA: Harvard University Press, 2001.

—. *The First Total War: Napoleon's Europe and the Birth of Warfare as We Know It*, Boston: Houghton Mifflin; London: Bloomsbury, 2007.

Ben-Israel, Hedva. *English Historians on the French Revolution*, Cambridge: Cambridge University Press, 1968.

Bernardin, Édith. *Jean-Marie Roland et le Ministère de l'Intérieur (1792–1793)*, Paris: Société des études Robespierristes, 1964.

Bertaud, Jean-Paul. *Camille et Lucile Desmoulins. Un couple dans la tourmente*, Paris: Presses de la Renaissance, 1986.

—. *The Army of the French Revolution: From Citizen-Soldiers to Instrument of Power*, translated by R. R. Palmer, Princeton, N.J.: Princeton University Press, 1988.

Berthe, Léon-Noël. *Dictionnaire des correspondents à l'Académie d'Arras au temps de Robespierre*, Arras: Chez l'auteur, 1969.

—. *Dubois de Fosseux, secrétaire de l'Académie d'Arras, 1785–1792 et son bureau de correspondance*, Arras: CNRS, 1969.

—. 'Robespierre et le fonds de Fosseux', *AHRF*, 172 (1963), pp. 185–94.

—. 'Un inédit de Robespierre: sa réponse au discours de réception de Mademoiselle de Kéralio—18 avril 1787', *AHRF*, 46 (1974), pp. 261–83.

Biard, Michel (ed.). *La Révolution française: une histoire toujours vivante*, Paris: Éditions Tallandier, 2010.

— (ed.). *Les Politiques de la Terreur, 1793–1794: actes du colloque international de Rouen, 11–13 janvier 2007*, Rennes: Presses Universitaires de Rennes; Paris: Société des études Robespierristes, 2008.

— and Pascal Dupuy (eds). *La Révolution française: dynamique et ruptures, 1787–1804*, Paris: A. Colin, 2008.

Bienvenu, Richard. *The Ninth of Thermidor: The Fall of Robespierre*, Oxford and New York: Oxford University Press, 1968.

Binkley, Susan Carpenter. *The Concept of the Individual in Eighteenth-Century French Thought from the Enlightenment to the French Revolution*, Lewiston, N.Y., Queenstown, Ontario, & Lampeter, Wales: Edwin Mellen Press, 2007.

Birembaut, Arthur. 'Quelques précisions sur l'affaire du paratonnerre', *AHRF*, 30 (1958), pp. 82–95.

Blanc, Louis. *Histoire de la Révolution française*, 3 vols, Paris: Librairie Internationale, 1869.

Blanc, Olivier. 'Cercles politiques et "salons" de début de la Révolution (1789–1793)', *AHRF*, 344 (2006), pp. 63–92.

—. *La Corruption sous la Terreur (1792–1794)*, Paris: Robert Laffont, 1992.

—. *Last Letters: Prisons and Prisoners of the French Revolution 1793–1794*, translated by Alan Sheridan, New York: Farrar, Straus & Giroux, 1987.

Blanning, T. C. W. (ed.). *The Rise and Fall of the French Revolution*, Chicago: University of Chicago Press, 1996.

Bloch, Jean. *Rousseauism and Education in Eighteenth-Century France*, Oxford: Voltaire Foundation, 1995.

Bluche, Frédéric. *Septembre 1792: logiques d'un massacre*, Paris: Robert Laffont, 1986.

Blum, André. *La Caricature révolutionnaire*, Paris: Jouve, 1916.

Blum, Carol. *Rousseau and the Republic of Virtue: The Language of Politics in the French Revolution*, Ithaca, N.Y., & London: Cornell University Press, 1986.

Bosc, Yannick, Florence Gauthier and Sophie Wahnich (eds). *Pour le Bonheur et pour la liberté*, Paris: Éditions La Fabrique, 2000.

Bouchary, Jean. *Les Faux-monnayeurs sous la Révolution française*, Paris: M. Rivière et Cie, 1946.

—. *Les Manieurs d'argent à Paris à la fin du XVIIIe siècle*, 3 vols, Paris: Marcel Rivière, 1939.

Bouloiseau, Marc. 'Aux origines des légendes contre-révolutionnaires. Robespierre vu par les journaux satiriques (1789–1791)', *Bulletin de la Société d'histoire moderne*, 57 (1958), pp. 6–8.

—. *Robespierre*, 5th edn, Paris: Presses universitaires de France, 1976.

—. *The Jacobin Republic 1792–1794*, translated by Jonathan Mandelbaum, Cambridge & Paris: Cambridge University Press and Éditions de la Maison des Sciences de l'Homme, Paris, 1983.

—. 'Une anecdote satirique sur Robespierre', *AHRF*, 29 (1957), pp. 1–5.

Brett, Judith. 'The Tasks of Political Biography', in Joy Damousi and Robert Reynolds (eds), *History on the Couch: Essays in History and Psychoanalysis*, Melbourne: Melbourne University Press, 2003, pp. 73–83.

Brinton, Crane. *The Jacobins: An Essay in the New History*, New York: Russell & Russell, 1961.

Brown, Howard. *War, Revolution, and the Bureaucratic State: Politics and Army Administration in France, 1791–1799*, Oxford: Clarendon Press, 1995.

Brunel, Françoise. 'Le Jacobinisme, un "rigorisme de la vertu"? "Puritanisme" et révolution', in *Mélanges Michel Vovelle. Sur la Révolution, approches plurielles*, Paris: Société des études Robespierristes, 1997.

—. *Thermidor, la chute de Robespierre*, Brussels: Éditions Complexe, 1999.

Buffenoir, Hippolyte. *Les Portraits de Robespierre: étude iconographique et historique, souvenirs, documents, témoignages*, Paris: Ernest Leroux, 1910.

Buisson, Henri. *Fouché, duc d'Otrante*, Bienne: Panorama, 1968.

Burgess, Greg. *Refuge in the Land of Liberty: France and its Refugees, from the Revolution to the End of Asylum, 1789–1939*, Basingstoke: Palgrave Macmillan, 2008.

Burrage, Michael. *Revolution and the Making of the Contemporary Legal Profession: England, France and the United States*, Oxford: Oxford University Press, 2006.

Burstin, Haim. 'Pour une phénoménologie de la violence révolutionnaire', *Historical Reflections*, 29 (2003), pp. 389–407.

—. *Une Révolution à l'oeuvre: le Faubourg Saint-Marcel (1789–1794)*, Seyssel: Champ Vallon, 2005.

Cadet de Gassecourt, André. *Une curieuse figure du passé: Joseph Souberbielle, neveu du Frère Côme*, Paris: Les Presses Modernes, 1934.

Campbell, Peter R. (ed.). *The Origins of the French Revolution*, Basingstoke: Palgrave Macmillan, 2006.

—, Thomas E. Kaiser and Marisa Linton (eds). *Conspiracy in the French Revolution*, Manchester: Manchester University Press, 2007.

Caron, Pierre. *Les Massacres de septembre*, Paris: Maison du livre français, 1935.

Carr, John Laurence. *Robespierre: The Force of Circumstance*, London: Constable, 1972.

Censer, Jack R. *Prelude to Power: The Parisian Radical Press, 1789–1791*, Baltimore, MD, & London: Johns Hopkins University Press, 1976.

—. 'Robespierre the Journalist', in Harvey Chisick (ed.), *The Press in the French Revolution*, Oxford: Voltaire Foundation, 1990, pp. 189–96.

Chisick, Harvey. 'Bourses d'études et mobilité sociale en France à la veille de la Révolution: bourses et boursiers du Collège Louis-le-Grand (1762–1789)', *Annales*, 30 (1975), pp. 1,562–84.

—. *The Production, Distribution and Readership of a Conservative Journal of the Early French Revolution: The Ami du Roi of the Abbé Royou*, Philadelphia: American Philosophical Society, 1992.

Claretie, Jules. *Camille Desmoulins and his Wife; Passages from the History of the Dantonists founded upon New and Hitherto Unpublished Documents*, translated by Cashel Hoey, London: Smith, Elder, 1876.

Clay, Stephen. 'Vengeance, Justice and the Reactions in the Revolutionary Midi', *FH*, 23 (2009), pp. 22–46.

Cobb, Richard. *Paris and its Provinces 1792–1802*, London: Oxford University Press, 1975.

—. *The People's Armies. The 'armées révolutionnaires': Instrument of the Terror in the Departments, April 1793 to Floréal Year II*, translated by Marianne Elliott, New Haven, CT, & London: Yale University Press, 1987.

Cobban, Alfred. *Aspects of the French Revolution*, London: Jonathan Cape, 1968.

Compère, Marie-Madeleine and Dominique Julia. *Les Collèges français: 16e–18e siècles*, vol. 2, Paris: INRP-CNRS, 1988.

Coward, Barry and Julian Swann (eds). *Conspiracy in Early Modern Europe*, Aldershot, Hants, & Burlington, VT: Ashgate, 2004.

Crook, Malcolm, William Doyle and Alan Forrest (eds). *Enlightenment and Revolution: Essays in Honour of Norman Hampson*, Burlington, VT, & Aldershot: Ashgate, 2004.

Cross, Máire F. and David Williams (eds). *The French Experience from Republic to Monarchy, 1792–1824*, Basingstoke: Palgrave Macmillan, 2000.

Crouzet, François. *Historians and the French Revolution: The Case of Maximilien Robespierre*, Swansea: University College of Swansea, 1989.

Daline, V. M. 'Robespierre et Danton vus par Babeuf', *AHRF*, 32 (1960), pp. 388–410.

Darnton, Robert. *The Kiss of Lamourette: Reflections in Cultural History*, New York: W.W. Norton, 1990.

Delbeke, Francis. *L'Action politique et sociale des avocats au XVIIIe siècle. Leur part dans la préparation de la Révolution française*, Louvain: Librairie universitaire, & Paris: Recueil Sirey, 1927.

Deramecourt, Augustin. *Le Clergé du diocèse d'Arras, Boulogne et Saint-Omer pendant la Révolution (1789–1802)*, 4 vols, Paris: Bray et Retaux, & Arras: Imprimerie du Pas-de-Calais, 1884–86.

Desan, Suzanne. *The Family on Trial in Revolutionary France*, Berkeley, CA, & London: University of California Press, 2004.

Dingli, Laurent. *Robespierre*, Paris: Flammarion, 2004.

Domecq, Jean-Philippe. *Robespierre, derniers temps: biographie. Suivi de La Fête de l'Être suprême et son interprétation*, Paris: Pocket, 2002.

Dommanget, Maurice. *1793, Les Enragés contre la vie chère–les curés rouges, Jacques Roux–Pierre Dolivier*, Paris: Spartacus, 1976.

Dorigny, Marcel (ed.). *The Abolitions of Slavery: From Léger Félicité Sonthonax to Victor Schoelcher, 1793, 1794, 1848*, New York & Oxford: Berghahn Books; Paris: Éditions UNESCO, 2003.

— and Bernard Gainot, *La Société des amis des noirs, 1788–1799: contribution à l'histoire de l'abolition de l'esclavage*, Paris: Éditions UNESCO, 1998.

Doyle, William. *Aristocracy and its Enemies in the Age of Revolution*, Oxford: Oxford University Press, 2009.

—. 'Dupaty (1746–1788): A Career in the Late Enlightenment', *Studies on Voltaire and the Eighteenth Century*, 230 (1985), pp. 82–106.

—. *Jansenism: Catholic Resistance to Authority from the Reformation to the French Revolution*, Basingstoke: Macmillan, 2000.

—. *The Oxford History of the French Revolution*, Oxford: Clarendon Press, 1989.

Dupont-Ferrier, Gustave. *Du Collège de Clermont au lycée Louis-le-Grand: la vie quotidienne d'un collège parisien pendant plus de 350 ans*, 3 vols, Paris: E. de Boccard, 1921–25.

Dupuy, Roger. *La République jacobine. Terreur, guerre et gouvernement révolutionnaire*, Paris: Éditions du Seuil, 2005.

Edelstein, Dan. *The Terror of Natural Right: Republicanism, the Cult of Nature, and the French Revolution*, Chicago: University of Chicago Press, 2009.

Ehrard, Jean, Antoinette Ehrard and Florence Devillez. *Images de Robespierre: actes du colloque international de Naples, 27–29 septembre 1993*, Napoli: Vivarium, 1996.

Esquiros, Alphonse. *Histoire des Montagnards*, Paris: Librairie rue Visconti, 1851.

Eude, Michel. 'La loi de prairial', *AHRF*, 254 (1983), pp. 544–59.

—. 'La politique de Robespierre en 1792, d'après le *Défenseur de la constitution*', *AHRF*, 28 (1956), pp. 1–28.

—. 'Le Comité de sûreté générale en 1793–1794', *AHRF*, 261 (1985), pp. 295–306.

—. 'Points de vue sur l'affaire Catherine Théot', *AHRF*, 198 (1969), pp. 606–29.

—. 'Robespierre a-t-il voulu faire destituer Fouquier-Tinville?', *AHRF*, 179 (1965), pp. 66–72.

Favone, M. *Dans le sillage de Maximilien Robespierre: Joachim Vilate*, Paris: M. Rivière, 1938.

Feher, Ferenc. *The Frozen Revolution: An Essay on Jacobinism*, Cambridge & Paris: Cambridge University Press and Éditions de la Maison des sciences de l'homme, 1987.

Fitzsimmons, Michael P. *The Night the Old Regime Ended: August 4, 1789 and the French Revolution*, University Park, PA: Pennsylvania State University Press, 2003.

—. *The Parisian Order of Barristers and the French Revolution*, Cambridge, MA: Harvard University Press, 1987.

—. *The Remaking of France: The National Assembly and the Constitution of 1791*, Cambridge & New York: Cambridge University Press, 1994.

Fleischmann, Hector. *Robespierre and the Women He Loved*, translated by Angelo S. Rappoport, London: John Long, 1913.

Forrest, Alan. *Conscripts and Deserters: The Army and French Society during the Revolution and Empire*, Oxford & New York: Oxford University Press, 1989.

—. *Paris, the Provinces and the French Revolution*, London: Arnold, 2004.

—. *Soldiers of the French Revolution*, Durham, N.C.: Duke University Press, 1990.

—and Peter Jones (eds). *Reshaping France: Town, Country and Region during the French Revolution*, Manchester & New York: Manchester University Press, 1991.

Friedland, Paul. *Political Actors: Representative Bodies and Theatricality in the Age of the French Revolution*, Ithaca, N.Y.: Cornell University Press, 2002.

Furet, François. *Interpreting the French Revolution*, translated by Elborg Forster, Cambridge & Paris: Cambridge University Press and Éditions de la Maison des Sciences de l'Homme, 1981.

—. *The French Revolution 1770–1814*, translated by Antonia Nevill, Oxford: Blackwell, 1992.

—and Mona Ozouf (eds). *Critical Dictionary of the French Revolution*, translated by Arthur Goldhammer, Cambridge, MA: Harvard University Press, 1989.

—and Mona Ozouf (eds). *La Gironde et les Girondins*, Paris: Éditions Payot, 1991.

—and Mona Ozouf (eds). *The French Revolution and the Creation of Modern Political Culture*. vol. 3, *The Transformation of Political Culture 1789–1848*, Oxford: Pergamon Press, 1989.

Gainot, Bernard. *Dictionnaire des membres du Comité de salut public: dictionnaire analytique, biographique et comparé des 62 membres du Comité de salut public*, Paris: Tallandier, 1990.

Gallo, Max. *Robespierre the Incorruptible: A Psycho-Biography*, translated by Raymond Rudorff, New York: Herder & Herder, 1971.

Garrioch, David. *Neighbourhood and Community in Paris, 1740–1790*, Cambridge: Cambridge University Press, 1986.

—. *The Making of Revolutionary Paris*, Berkeley, CA: University of California Press, 2002.

Gascar, Pierre. *L'Ombre de Robespierre*, Paris: Gallimard, 1979.

Gauthier, Florence. *L'Aristocratie de l'épiderme. Le Combat de la Société des citoyens de couleur, 1789–1791*, Paris: CNRS, 2007.

—. *Triomphe et mort du droit naturel en Révolution, 1789–1795–1802*, Paris: Presses universitaires de France, 1992.

— (ed.). *Périssent les colonies plutôt qu'un principe! Contributions à l'histoire de l'abolition de l'esclavage, 1789–1804*, Paris: Société des études Robespierristes, 2002.

Gay, Peter. *Freud for Historians*, New York & Oxford: Oxford University Press, 1985.

—. 'Rhetoric and Politics in the French Revolution', *AHR*, 66 (1961), pp. 664–76.

Germani, Ian. 'Robespierre's Heroes: The Politics of Heroization during the Year Two', *Consortium on Revolutionary Europe 1750–1850, Proceedings 1988*, pp. 133–56.

Gilchrist, J. and W. J. Murray (eds). *The Press in the French Revolution*, Melbourne & London: F.W. Cheshire & Ginn, 1971.

Gillion, Anne. 'La Mémoire de Robespierre à Arras', *Revue du Nord*, 71 (1989), pp. 1,037–50.

Gobry, Ivan. *Joseph Le Bon: la Terreur dans le nord de la France*, Paris: Mercure de France, 1991.

Godineau, Dominique. *Citoyennes tricoteuses: les femmes du peuple à Paris pendant la Révolution française*, Aix-en-Provence: Alinéa, 1988.

Goldhammer, Jesse. *The Headless Republic: Sacrificial Violence in Modern French Thought*, Ithaca, N.Y., & London: Cornell University Press, 2005.

Gough, Hugh. *The Newspaper Press in the French Revolution*, Chicago: Dorsey Press, 1988.

—. *The Terror in the French Revolution*, 2nd edn, Basingstoke: Palgrave, 2010.

Goulet, Jacques. *Robespierre, la peine de mort et la Terreur*, Pantin: Castor Astral, 1983.

Greer, Donald. *The Incidence of the Terror during the French Revolution: A Statistical Interpretation*, Cambridge, MA: Harvard University Press, 1935.

Gross, Jean-Pierre. *Fair Shares for All: Jacobin Egalitarianism in Practice*, Cambridge & New York: Cambridge University Press, 1997.

Gruder, Vivian R. *The Notables and the Nation: The Political Schooling of the French, 1787–1788*, Cambridge, MA: Harvard University Press, 2007.

Gueniffey, Patrice. *La Politique de la Terreur: essai sur la violence révolutionnaire*, Paris: Fayard, 2000.

—. 'Robespierre, itinéraire d'un tyran', *Histoire*, 177 (1994), pp. 36–47.

Guilhaumou, Jacques. *La Langue politique et la Révolution française: de l'événement à la raison linguistique*, Paris: Méridiens Klincksieck, 1989.

Guillemin, Henri. *Robespierre: politique et mystique*, Paris: Éditions du Seuil, 1987.

Guiomar, Jean-Yves. *L'Invention de la guerre totale: XVIIIe–XXe siècle*, Paris: Le Félin, 2004.

Hamel, Ernest. *Histoire de Robespierre, d'après des papiers de famille, les sources originales et des documents entièrement inédits*, 3 vols, Paris: Lacroix, 1865–67.

Hamersley, Rachel. *The English Republican Tradition and Eighteenth-Century France: Between the Ancients and Moderns*, Manchester: Manchester University Press, 2010.

Hampson, Norman. *Danton*, Oxford: Blackwell, 1978.

—. 'François Chabot and his Plot', *Transactions of the Royal Historical Society*, 5th series, 26 (1976), pp. 1–14.

—. *Saint-Just*, Oxford: Blackwell, 1991.

—. 'The Enlightenment and the Language of the French Nobility in 1789: the Case of Arras', in D. J. Mossop, G. E. Rodmell and D. B. Wilson (eds), *Studies in the French Eighteenth Century Presented to John Lough*, Durham: University of Durham, 1978, pp. 81–91.

—. *The Life and Opinions of Maximilien Robespierre*, London: Duckworth, 1974.

—. *Will and Circumstance: Montesquieu, Rousseau and the French Revolution*, London: Duckworth, 1983.

Hanson, Paul R. *Contesting the French Revolution*, Oxford: Wiley-Blackwell, 2009.

—. *The Jacobin Republic under Fire: The Federalist Revolt in the French Revolution*, University Park, PA: Pennsylvania State University Press, 2003.

Hardman, John. *Robespierre*, London & New York: Longman, 1999.

Hayakawa, Riho. 'L'Assassinat du boulanger Denis François le 21 octobre 1789', *AHRF*, 333 (2003), pp. 1–19.

Haydon, Colin and William Doyle (eds). *Robespierre*, Cambridge & New York: Cambridge University Press, 1999.

Hembree, Fred. 'Robespierre in the early Revolution, 1789–1792', *Consortium on Revolutionary Europe 1750–1850, Proceedings 1989*, Part 2, pp. 85–94.

Hesse, Carla. 'La Logique culturelle de la loi révolutionnaire', *Annales*, 57 (2002), pp. 915–33.

Heywood, Colin. *Growing up in France: From the Ancien Régime to the Third Republic*, Cambridge: Cambridge University Press, 2007.

Higonnet, Patrice L. R. *Goodness beyond Virtue: Jacobins during the French Revolution*, Cambridge, MA: Harvard University Press, 1998.

—. 'Terror, Trauma and the Young Marx Explanation of Jacobin Politics', *P&P*, 191 (2006), pp. 121–64.

Horn, Jeff. 'The Terror in the Département of the Aube and the Fall of Robespierre', Paper presented at the Society for French Historical Studies, Wilmington, DE, 26 March 1994.

Huet, Marie-Hélène. *Mourning Glory: The Will of the French Revolution*, University Park, PA: University of Pennsylvania Press, 1997.

Hunt, David. 'The People and Pierre Dolivier: Popular Uprisings in the Seine-et-Oise Department, 1791–1792', *FHS*, 11 (1979), pp. 184–214.

Hunt, Lynn. 'For Reasons of State', *The Nation*, 29 May 2006, pp. 24–28.

—. *Politics, Culture, and Class in the French Revolution*, Berkeley, CA: University of California Press, 1984.

—. *The Family Romance of the French Revolution*, Berkeley, CA: University of California Press, 1992.

—. 'The World We Have Gained: The Future of the French Revolution,' *AHR*, 108 (2003), pp. 1–19.

Jacob, Louis. *Hébert, le Père Duchesne: chef des sans-culottes*, Paris: Gallimard, 1960.

—. 'Un ami de Robespierre: Buissart (d'Arras)', *Revue du Nord*, 20 (1934), pp. 277–94.

Jacouty, Jean-François. 'Robespierre selon Louis Blanc: le prophète christique de la Révolution française', *AHRF*, 331 (2003), pp. 105–27.

Jaume, Lucien. *Le Discours jacobin et la démocratie*, Paris: Fayard, 1989.

Jean-Marie et Manon Roland. Actes du colloque national de Villefranche-sur-Saône 1989, Lyon: Union des sociétés historiques du Rhône, 1990.

Jessenne, Jean-Pierre. *Pouvoir au village et révolution: Artois, 1760–1848*, Lille: Presses universitaires de Lille, 1987.

—, Gilles Derégnaucourt, Jean-Pierre Hirsch and Hervé Leuwers (eds). *Robespierre: de la nation artésienne à la République et aux nations. Actes du colloque, Arras, 1–2–3 Avril 1993*, Villeneuve d'Asq: Centre d'histoire de la région du nord et de l'Europe du nord-ouest, Université Charles de Gaulle-Lille III, 1994.

Jones, Peter. *The Peasantry in the French Revolution*, Cambridge: Cambridge University Press, 1988.

Jordan, David P. *The King's Trial: The French Revolution vs. Louis XVI*, Berkeley, CA: University of California Press, 1979.

—. *The Revolutionary Career of Maximilien Robespierre*, New York: Free Press, 1985.

Jourdan, Annie. *La Révolution, une exception française?* Paris: Flammarion, 2004.

— (ed.). *Robespierre—figure-réputation*, Amsterdam & Atlanta, GA: Rodopi, 1996.

Julia, Dominique. *Les Trois Couleurs du tableau noir. La Révolution*, Paris: Éditions Belin, 1981.

Kagan, Richard L. 'Law Students and Legal Careers in Eighteenth-Century France', *P&P*, 68 (1975), pp. 38–72.

Kaiser, Thomas E. 'From the Austrian Committee to the Foreign Plot: Marie-Antoinette, Austrophobia, and the Terror', *FHS*, 26 (2003), pp. 579–617.

Kaplan, Steven L. *Farewell, Revolution: Disputed Legacies, France 1789/1989*, Ithaca, N.Y.: Cornell University Press, 1995.

—. *Farewell, Revolution: The Historians' Feud, France 1789/1989*, Ithaca, N.Y.: Cornell University Press, 1995.

Kelly, G. A. 'Conceptual Sources of the Terror', *Eighteenth-Century Studies*, 14 (1980), pp. 18–36.

Kennedy, Michael. *The Jacobin Clubs in the French Revolution: The First Years*, Princeton, N.J.: Princeton University Press, 1982.

—. *The Jacobin Clubs in the French Revolution: The Middle Years*, Princeton, N.J.: Princeton University Press, 1988.

—. *The Jacobin Clubs in the French Revolution, 1793–1795*, New York: Berghahn Books, 2000.

Korngold, Ralph. *Robespierre, First Modern Dictator*, London: Macmillan, 1937.

Krauss, Werner. 'Le Cousin Jacques: Robespierre et la Révolution française', *AHRF*, 32 (1960), pp. 305–8.

Ladjouzi, Diane. 'Les Journées des 4 et 5 septembre à Paris. Un movement d'union entre le people, la Commune de Paris et la Convention pour un exécutif révolutionnaire', *AHRF*, 321 (2000), pp. 27–44.

Lamartine, Alphonse de. *Histoire des Girondins*, 6 vols, Paris: Pagnerre, Hachette & Furne, 1860.

Lavoine, A. *La Famille de Robespierre, ses origines, le séjour des Robespierre à Vaudricourt, Béthune, Lens, Harnes, Hénin-Liétard, Carvin et Arras, 1452–1764*, Arras: Archives d'Arras, 1914.

Lebrun, François, Marc Venard and Jean Quéniart, *Histoire de l'enseignement et de l'éducation en France*, vol. 2, *De Gutenberg aux Lumières (1480–1789)*, Paris: Perrin, 2003.

Le Cour Grandmaison, Olivier. *Les Citoyennetés en Révolution (1789–1794)*, Paris: Presses universitaires de France, 1992.

Lecesne, E. *Arras sous la Révolution*, 3 vols, Arras: Sueur-Charruey, 1882–83.

Lefebvre, Georges. 'Remarks on Robespierre', translated by Beatrice F. Hyslop, *FHS*, 1 (1958), pp. 7–10.
—. 'Robespierre et Colchen', *AHRF*, 27 (1955), pp. 1–4.
—. 'Sur la loi du 22 prairial an II', *AHRF*, 23 (1951), pp. 225–56.
—. *The French Revolution*, translated by John Hall Stewart and James Friguglietti, 2 vols, London: Routledge & Kegan Paul, 1964–65.
Legay, Marie-Laure. *Les États provinciaux dans la construction de l'état moderne aux XVIIe et XVIIIe siècles*, Geneva: Librairie Droz, 2001.
—. *Robespierre et le pouvoir provincial: dénonciation et émancipation politique*, Arras: Commission départementale d'histoire et d'archéologie du Pas-de-Calais, 2002.
Leith, James A. 'The Terror: Adding the Cultural Dimension', *Canadian Journal of History/Annales canadiennes d'histoire*, 32 (1997), pp. 315–37.
Lemay, Edna Hindie. *Dictionnaire des constituants 1789–1791*, 2 vols, Oxford: Voltaire Foundation, 1991.
—. *La Vie quotidienne des députés aux Etats Généraux, 1789*, Paris: Hachette, 1987.
—. 'Une voix dissonante à l'Assemblée constituante: le prosélytisme de Robespierre', *AHRF*, 244 (1981), pp. 390–404.
— and Alison Patrick. *Revolutionaries at Work: The Constituent Assembly 1789–1791*, Oxford: Voltaire Foundation, 1996.
Lenoël, Pierre, and Marie-Françoise Lévy (eds). *L'Enfant, la famille et la Révolution française*, Paris: Olivier Orban, 1990.
Lenôtre, G. *Le Tribunal révolutionnaire (1793–1795)*, Paris: Perrin, 1908.
—. *Robespierre's Rise and Fall*, translation by R. Stawell of *Le mysticisme révolutionnaire. Robespierre et la 'Mère de Dieu'*, London: Hutchinson, 1927.
Leuwers, Hervé. *L'Invention du barreau français. La Construction nationale d'un groupe professionnel*, Paris: Éditions de l'École des hautes études en sciences sociales, 2006.
—. 'Révolution constituante et société judiciaire. L'Exemple septentrional', *AHRF*, 350 (2007), pp. 27–47.
—, Annie Crépin and Dominique Rosselle. *Histoire des provinces françaises du nord. La Révolution et l'Empire. Le Nord—Pas-de-Calais entre Révolution et contre-révolution*, Arras: Artois Presses Université, 2008.
Lewis, Gwynne. *The French Revolution: Rethinking the Debate*, London & New York: Routledge, 1993.
Linton, Marisa. 'Fatal Friendships: The Politics of Jacobin Friendship', *FHS*, 31 (2008), pp. 51–76.
—. 'Robespierre and the Terror', *History Today*, 56 (2006), pp. 23–30.
—. 'The Man of Virtue: The Role of Antiquity in the Political Trajectory of L. A. Saint-Just', *FH*, 24 (2010), pp. 393–419.
—. *The Politics of Virtue in Enlightenment France*, Basingstoke: Palgrave Macmillan, 2001.
Livesey, James. 'The Limits of Terror: The French Revolution, Rights and Democratic Transition', *Thesis 11*, 97 (2009), pp. 63–79.
Lizerand, Georges. *Robespierre*, Paris: Fustier, 1937.
Lucas, Colin (ed.). *Rewriting the French Revolution*, Oxford: Clarendon Press, 1991.
— (ed.). *The Political Culture of the French Revolution*, vol. 2, *The French Revolution and the Creation of Modern Political Culture*, Oxford & New York: Pergamon Press, 1988.
—. 'The Theory and Practice of Denunciation in the French Revolution', *JMH*, 68 (1996), pp. 768–85.
Luttrell, Barbara. *Mirabeau*, Carbondale & Edwardsville: Southern Illinois University Press, 1990.
Luzzatto, Sergio. *Bonbon Robespierre. La terreur à visage humain*, translated from the Italian by Simone Carpentari Messina, Paris: Arléa, 2010.
—. 'Un futur au passé: la Révolution dans les mémoires des conventionnels', *AHRF*, 61 (1989), pp. 455–75.
Lyons, Martyn. 'The 9 Thermidor: Motives and Effects', *European Studies Review*, 5 (1975), pp. 123–46.
Lytle, Scott H. 'The Second Sex (September, 1793)', *JMH*, 27 (1955), pp. 14–26.

McManners, John. *Church and Society in Eighteenth-Century France*, 2 vols, Oxford: Clarendon Press, 1998.

McNeil, Gordon H. 'Robespierre, Rousseau, and Representation', in Richard Herr and Harold T. Parker (eds), *Ideas in History: Essays Presented to Louis Gottschalk by his Former Students*, Durham, N.C.: Duke University Press, 1965, pp. 135–56.

McPhee, Peter. *Collioure et la Révolution française, 1789–1815*, Perpignan: Le Publicateur, 1989.

—. *Living the French Revolution, 1789–99*, London & New York: Palgrave Macmillan, 2006.

Manceron, Claude. *The Men of Liberty: Europe on the Eve of the French Revolution 1774–1778*, translated by Patricia Wolf, London: Eyre Methuen, 1977.

Mansfield, Paul. 'The Repression of Lyon, 1793–4: Origins, Responsibility and Significance', *FH*, 2 (1988), pp. 74–101.

Mantel, Hilary. *A Place of Greater Safety*, London: Viking, 1992.

—. 'If you'd seen his green eyes', *London Review of Books*, 20 April 2006, pp. 3, 8.

—. 'What a man this is, with his crowd of women around him!' *London Review of Books*, vol. 22, no. 7 (2000), pp. 3–8.

Markoff, John. *The Abolition of Feudalism: Peasants, Lords, and Legislators in the French Revolution*, University Park, PA: Pennsylvania State University Press, 1996.

Martin, Jean-Clément. *La France en Révolution 1789–1799*, Paris: Belin, 1990.

— (ed.). *La Révolution à l'oeuvre. Perspectives actuelles dans l'histoire de la Révolution française*, Rennes: Presses universitaires de Rennes, 2005.

—. 'La Révolution française: généalogie de l'ennemi', *Raisons politiques*, 5 (2002), pp. 69–79.

—. 'Vendée: les criminels de guerre en procès', *Histoire*, 25 (2004), pp. 82–87.

—. *Violence et Révolution: Essai sur la naissance d'un mythe national*, Paris: Éditions du Seuil, 2006.

Maslan, Susan. *Revolutionary Acts: Theater, Democracy, and the French Revolution*, Baltimore, MD: Johns Hopkins University Press, 2005.

Massin, Jean. *Robespierre*, Paris: Club français du livre, 1957.

Mathiez, Albert. *After Robespierre: The Thermidorian Reaction*, translated by Catherine Alison Phillips, New York: Grosset & Dunlap, 1965.

—. *Études sur Robespierre (1758–1794)*, Paris: Éditions sociales, 1958.

—. *Girondins et Montagnards*, Paris: Firmin-Didot, 1930.

—. *La Révolution et les étrangers: cosmopolitisme et défense nationale*, Paris: La Renaissance du Livre, 1918.

—. *La Vie chère et le mouvement social sous la Terreur*, Paris: Payot, 1927.

—. *Robespierre, terroriste*, Paris: Renaissance du livre, 1921.

—. *The Fall of Robespierre, and Other Essays*, New York: A. M. Kelley, 1968.

—. *Un procès de corruption sous la Terreur: l'affaire de la Compagnie des Indes*, Paris: Félix Alcan, 1920.

Matrat, Jean. *Robespierre: or, the Tyranny of the Majority*, translated by Alan Kendall, London: Angus and Robertson, 1975.

Mayer, Arno J. *The Furies: Violence and Terror in the French and Russian Revolutions*, Princeton, N.J.: Princeton University Press, 2000.

Maza, Sarah. *Private Lives and Public Affairs: The Causes Célèbres of Pre-Revolutionary France*, Berkeley, CA: University of California Press, 1993.

Mazauric, Claude (ed.). *La Révolution française et l'homme moderne*, Paris: Éditions Messidor, 1989.

—. *Robespierre. Écrits présentés par Claude Mazauric*, Paris: Messidor/Éditions sociales, 1989.

Michelet, Jules. *La Révolution française*, 2 vols, Paris: Gallimard, 1952.

Michon, Georges. *Robespierre et la guerre révolutionnaire, 1791–1792*, Paris: M. Rivière, 1937.

Minart, Gérard. *Pierre Claude François Daunou, l'anti-Robespierre: de la Révolution à l'Empire, l'itinéraire d'un juste (1761–1840)*, Toulouse: Privat, 2001.

Mitchell, C. J. *The French Legislative Assembly of 1791*, Leiden: E. J. Brill, 1988.

Monnier, Raymonde. *L'Espace public démocratique: essai sur l'opinion à Paris de la Révolution au Directoire*, Paris: Éditions Kimé, 1994.

—. 'Républicanisme et Révolution française', *FHS*, 26 (2003), pp. 87–118.

—. *Républicanisme, patriotisme et Révolution française*, Paris: Harmattan, 2005.

Mossé, Claude. *L'Antiquité dans la Révolution française*, Paris: Albin Michel, 1989.

Murray, William J. *The Right-Wing Press in the French Revolution: 1789–1792*, London: Royal Historical Society, 1986.

Nabonne, Bernard. *La Vie privée de Robespierre*, Paris: Hachette, 1943.

Nadeau, Martin. 'La Politique culturelle de l'an II: les infortunes de la propagande révolutionnaire au théâtre', *AHRF*, 327 (2002), pp. 57–74.

Nolibos, Alain. *Arras: de Nemetucam à la communauté urbaine*, Lille: La Voix du Nord, 2003.

Ording, Arne. *Le Bureau de police du Comité de salut public. Étude sur la Terreur*, Academi i Oslo: Skrifter utgitt av det Norske Videnskaps, no. 6, 1931.

Owen, David. *In Sickness and in Health: Illness in Heads of Government during the Last 100 Years*, London: Methuen, 2008.

Ozouf, Mona. *Festivals and the French Revolution*, translated by Alan Sheridan, Cambridge, MA: Harvard University Press, 1988.

—. 'Massacres de septembre: qui est responsable?', *Histoire*, 342 (2009), pp. 52–55.

Palmer, R. R. (ed.). *From Jacobin to Liberal: Marc-Antoine Jullien, 1775–1848*, Princeton, N.J.: Princeton University Press, 1993.

—. *The Improvement of Humanity: Education and the French Revolution*, Princeton, N.J.: Princeton University Press, 1985.

—. *The School of the French Revolution: A Documentary History of the College of Louis-le-Grand and its Director, Jean-François Champagne 1762–1814*, Princeton, N.J.: Princeton University Press, 1975.

—. *Twelve Who Ruled: The Year of the Terror in the French Revolution*, Princeton, N.J.: Princeton University Press, 1969.

Paris, Auguste Joseph. *La Jeunesse de Robespierre et la convocation des États généraux en Artois*, Arras: Rousseau-Leroy, 1870.

—. *La Terreur dans le Pas-de-Calais et dans le Nord: histoire de Joseph Le Bon et des tribunaux révolutionnaires d'Arras et de Cambrai*, Arras: Rousseau-Leroy, 1864.

Parker, Harold T. *The Cult of Antiquity and the French Revolutionaries: A Study in the Development of the Revolutionary Spirit* (1937), New York: Octagon, 1965.

Patrick, Alison. *The Men of the First French Republic: Political Alignments in the National Convention of 1792*, Baltimore, MD: Johns Hopkins University Press, 1972.

Pioro, Gabriel and Pierre Labracherie. 'Charlotte Robespierre et "Ses Mémoires"', *La Pensée*, 88 (1959), pp. 99–108.

Piquet, Jean-Daniel. *L'Émancipation des noirs dans la Révolution française (1789–1795)*, Paris: Karthala, 2002.

—. 'Robespierre et la liberté des noirs en l'an II', *AHRF*, 323 (2001), pp. 69–91.

Popkin, Jeremy D. *Revolutionary News: The Press in France, 1789–1799*, Durham, N.C., & London: Duke University Press, 1990.

—. *You Are All Free: The Haitian Revolution and the Abolition of Slavery*, New York: Cambridge University Press, 2010.

Poumiès de la Siboutie, *Recollections of a Parisian Doctor under Six Sovereigns, Two Revolutions and a Republic (1789–1863)*, translated by Theodora Davidson, London: John Murray, 1911.

Price, Munro. 'Mirabeau and the Court: Some New Evidence', *FHS*, 29 (2006), pp. 37–75.

Ragan, Bryant T. and Elizabeth A. Williams (eds). *Re-creating Authority in Revolutionary France*, New Brunswick, N.J.: Rutgers University Press, 1992.

Rapport, Michael. *Nationality and Citizenship in Revolutionary France: The Treatment of Foreigners 1789–1799*, Oxford: Clarendon Press, 2000.

—. 'Robespierre and the Universal Rights of Man, 1789–1794', *FH*, 10 (1996), pp. 303–33.

Ratineau, Fabienne. 'Les Livres de Robespierre au 9 thermidor', *AHRF*, 287 (1992), pp. 131–35.

Reddy, William M. *The Navigation of Feeling: A Framework for the History of Emotions*, Cambridge: Cambridge University Press, 2001.

Régent, Frédéric. *La France et ses esclaves. De la colonisation aux abolitions (1620–1848)*, Paris: Grasset, 2007.

Reinhard, Marcel. *Le Grand Carnot*, 2 vols, Paris: Hachette, 1950–52.

Riskin, Jessica. *Science in the Age of Sensibility: The Sentimental Empiricists of the French Enlightenment*, Chicago & London: University of Chicago Press, 2002.

Roberts, Warren. *Jacques-Louis David and Jean-Louis Prieur, Revolutionary Artists: The Public, the Populace, and Images of the French Revolution*, Albany, N.Y.: State University of New York Press, 2000.

Roche, Daniel. *The People of Paris: An Essay in Popular Culture in the 18th Century*, translated by Marie Evans, Berkeley & Los Angeles: University of California Press, 1987.

Rosanvallon, Pierre. *Democracy Past and Future*, New York: Columbia University Press, 2006.

Rose, R. B. *Gracchus Babeuf: The First Revolutionary Communist*, London: Edward Arnold, 1978.

—. *The Enragés: Socialists of the French Revolution?*, Melbourne: Melbourne University Press, 1965.

—. *The Making of the 'sans-culottes': Democratic Ideas and Institutions in Paris, 1789–92*, Manchester: Manchester University Press, 1983.

—. 'The "Red Scare" of the 1790s and the "Agrarian Law"', *P&P*, 103 (1984), pp. 113–30.

—. *Tribunes and Amazons: Men and Women of Revolutionary France 1789–1871*, Sydney: Macleay Press, 1998.

Rosso, Maxime. 'Les Réminiscences spartiates dans les discours et la politique de Robespierre de 1789 à Thermidor', *AHRF*, 349 (2007), pp. 51–77.

Roudinesco, Élisabeth. *Madness and Revolution: The Lives and Legends of Théroigne de Méricourt*, translated by Martin Thom, London & New York: Verso, 1991.

Rudé, George (ed.). *Robespierre: Great Lives Observed*, Englewood Cliffs, N.J.: Prentice-Hall, 1967.

—. *Robespierre: Portrait of a Revolutionary Democrat*, London: Collins, 1975.

Sagan, Eli. *Citizens and Cannibals: The French Revolution, the Struggle for Modernity, and the Origins of Ideological Terror*, Lanham, MD & Oxford: Rowman & Littlefield, 2001.

Sangnier, Georges. *Les Émigrés du Pas-de-Calais pendant la Révolution*, Paris: Blangermont, 1959.

Sanyal, Sukla. 'The 1792 Food Riot at Étampes and the French Revolution', *Studies in History*, 18 (2002), pp. 23–50.

Schama, Simon. *Citizens: a Chronicle of the French Revolution*, New York: Knopf, 1989.

Scurr, Ruth. *Fatal Purity: Robespierre and the French Revolution*, London: Chatto & Windus, 2006.

Secher, Reynald. *A French Genocide: The Vendée*, translated by George Holoch, Notre Dame, IN: University of Notre Dame Press, 2003.

Sepinwall, Alyssa Goldstein. 'Robespierre, Old Regime Feminist? Gender, the Late Eighteenth Century, and the French Revolution Revisited', *JMH*, 82 (2010), pp. 1–29.

—. *The Abbé Grégoire and the French Revolution: The Making of Modern Universalism*, Berkeley & Los Angeles: University of California Press, 2005.

Shapiro, Barry M. *Revolutionary Justice in Paris, 1789–1790*, Cambridge & New York: Cambridge University Press, 1993.

—. 'Self-Sacrifice, Self-Interest, or Self-Defence? The Constituent Assembly and the "Self-Denying Ordinance" of May 1791', *FHS*, 25 (2002), pp. 625–56.

—. *Traumatic Politics: The Deputies and the King in the Early French Revolution*, University Park, PA: Pennsylvania State University Press, 2009.

Short, Jeffrey Larrabee. 'The Lantern and the Scaffold: The Debate on Violence in Revolutionary France, April–October 1789', unpublished Ph.D thesis, State University of New York at Binghamton, 1990.

Shulim, Joseph I. 'Robespierre and the French Revolution', *AHR*, 82 (1977), pp. 20–38.

—. 'The Youthful Robespierre and His Ambivalence toward the Ancien Regime', *Eighteenth-Century Studies*, 5 (1972), pp. 398–420.

Slavin, Morris. *The Hébertistes to the Guillotine: Anatomy of a 'Conspiracy' in Revolutionary France*, Baton Rouge & London: Louisiana State University Press, 1994.

—. *The Making of an Insurrection: Parisian Sections and the Gironde*, Cambridge, MA & London: Harvard University Press, 1986.

Soboul, Albert (ed.). *Actes du colloque Girondins et Montagnards (Sorbonne, 14 décembre 1975)*, Paris: Société des études Robespierristes, 1980.

—. (ed.). *Actes du colloque Robespierre. XIIe congrès international des sciences historiques (Vienne, 3 septembre 1965)*, Paris: Société des études Robespierristes, 1967.

—. *Paysans, sans-culottes et Jacobins*, Paris: Clavreuil, 1966.

—. *Problèmes paysans de la Révolution, 1789–1848*, Paris: François Maspero, 1976.

—. 'Robespierre and the Popular Movement of 1793–4', *P&P*, 5 (1954), pp. 54–70.

—. 'Robespierre et les sociétés populaires', *AHRF*, 30 (1958), pp. 50–64.

—. 'Robespierre ou les contradictions du jacobinisme', *AHRF*, 50 (1978), pp. 1–19.

—. *The French Revolution, 1787–1799: From the Storming of the Bastille to Napoleon*, translated by Alan Forrest and Colin Jones, London: Unwin Hyman, 1989.

—. *The Parisian Sans-Culottes and the French Revolution, 1793–4*, translated by Gwynne Lewis, Oxford: Oxford University Press, 1964.

—. *Understanding the French Revolution*, translated by April A. Knutson, New York: International Publishers, 1988.

— et al. (eds). *Dictionnaire historique de la Révolution française*, Paris: Presses universitaires de France, 1989.

Stéfane-Pol [Paul Coutant]. *Autour de Robespierre: le conventionnel Le Bas, d'après des documents inédits et les mémoires de sa veuve*, Paris: E. Flammarion, 1901.

Sueur, Philippe. *Le Conseil provincial d'Artois (1640–1790). Une cour provinciale à la recherche de sa souveraineté*, Arras: Commission départementale des monuments historiques du Pas-de-Calais, 1978.

Sutherland, D. M. G. *The French Revolution and Empire: The Quest for a Civic Order*, Oxford: Blackwell, 2003.

Sydenham, Michael. *The Girondins*, London: Athlone Press, 1961.

Tackett, Timothy. *Becoming a Revolutionary: The Deputies of the French National Assembly and the Emergence of a Revolutionary Culture (1789–1790)*, Princeton, N.J.: Princeton University Press, 1996.

—. 'Collective Panics in the Early French Revolution, 1789–1791: A Comparative Perspective', *FH*, 17 (2003), pp. 149–71.

—. 'Conspiracy Obsession in a Time of Revolution: French Elites and the Origins of the Terror', *AHR*, 105 (2000), pp. 691–713.

—. 'Interpreting the Terror', *FHS*, 24 (2001), pp. 569–78.

—. *The First Terrorists: The French Revolution and the Origins of a Political Culture of Violence*, Melbourne: University of Melbourne, 2009.

—. *When the King Took Flight*, Cambridge, MA: Harvard University Press, 2003.

Talmon, J. L. *The Origins of Totalitarian Democracy*, London: Martin Secker & Warburg, 1952.

Theuriot, Françoise. 'La Conception robespierriste du bonheur', *AHRF*, 192 (1968), pp. 207–26.

Thiers, Adolphe, *Histoire de la Révolution Française*, 10 vols, Paris: Furne, 1854.

Thompson, Eric. *Popular Sovereignty and the French Constituent Assembly 1789–1791*, Manchester: Manchester University Press, 1952.

Thompson, J. M. *Leaders of the French Revolution*, Oxford: Blackwell, 1932.

—. *Robespierre*, Oxford: Blackwell, 1935.

—. *Robespierre and the French Revolution*, London: English Universities Press, 1952.

Van Kley, Dale. *The French Idea of Freedom: The Old Regime and the Declaration of Rights of 1789*, Stanford, CA: Stanford University Press, 1994.

—. *The Jansenists and the Expulsion of the Jesuits from France*, New Haven, CT, & London: Yale University Press, 1975.

—. *The Religious Origins of the French Revolution: From Calvin to the Civil Constitution, 1560–1791*, New Haven, CT, & London: Yale University Press, 1996.

Varaut, Jean-Marc. *La Terreur judiciaire. La Révolution contre les droits de l'homme*, Paris: Perrin, 1993.

Verjus, Anne. *Le Bon Mari: une histoire politique des hommes et des femmes à l'époque révolutionnaire*, Paris: Fayard, 2010.

Vovelle, Michel. *Combats pour la Révolution française*, Paris: Éditions la Découverte/Société des études Robespierristes, 1993.

—. *La Mentalité révolutionnaire: société et mentalité sous la Révolution française*, Paris: Messidor/ Éditions sociales, 1985.

— (ed.). *Révolution et République: l'exception française*, Paris: Éditions Kimé, 1994.

—. *The Revolution against the Church: From Reason to the Supreme Being*, translated by Alan José, Cambridge: Polity Press, 1991.

— and Antoine de Baecque (eds). *Recherches sur la Révolution*, Paris: La Découverte, 1991.

Wahnich, Sophie. *La liberté ou la mort: essai sur la Terreur et le terrorisme*, Paris: La Fabrique, 2003.

—. *L'Impossible citoyen. L'Étranger dans le discours de la Révolution française*, Paris: Albin Michel, 1997.

Waldinger, Renée, Philip Dawson and Isser Woloch (eds). *The French Revolution and the Meaning of Citizenship*, Westport, CT: Greenwood Press, 1993.

Walter, Gérard. *La Conjuration du Neuf Thermidor, 27 July 1794*, Paris: Gallimard, 1974.

—. *Robespierre*, 2 vols, Paris: Gallimard, 1961.

Walton, Charles. *Policing Public Opinion in the French Revolution: The Culture of Calumny and the Problem of Free Speech*, Oxford & New York: Oxford University Press, 2009.

Walzer, Michael (ed). *Regicide and Revolution: Speeches at the Trial of Louis XVI*, New York: Columbia University Press, 1992.

Wartelle, François. 'Destinées du Jacobinisme dans le Pas-de-Calais entre la chute de Robespierre et le coup d'État du 18 fructidor an V', Université de Paris-I: unpublished dissertation, 1987.

—. 'Les Communautés rurales du Pas-de-Calais et le système fédodal en 1789–1790', *Cahiers d'histoire de l'Institut de recherches marxistes*, 32 (1988), pp. 100–21.

Weber, Eugen. 'About Thermidor: The Oblique Uses of a Scandal', *FHS*, 17 (1991), pp. 330–42.

Woloch, Isser. *The New Regime: Transformations of the French Civic Order, 1789–1820s*, New York & London: W. W. Norton, 1994.

Yalom, Marilyn. *Blood Sisters: The French Revolution in Women's Memory*, New York: Basic Books, 1993.

Zimbardo, Philip. *The Lucifer Effect: Understanding How Good People Turn Evil*, New York: Rider, 2005.

Žižek, Slavoj. *Slavoj Žižek Presents Robespierre: Virtue and Terror*, London: Verso, 2007.

Index